Beginning F#

Robert Pickering

Forewords by Don Syme and Chance Coble

Apress®

Beginning F#

ISBN-13 (pbk): 978-1-4302-2389-4

ISBN-13 (electronic): 978-1-4302-2390-0

Printed and bound in the United States of America 9 8 7 6 5 4 3 2 1

Trademarked names may appear in this book. Rather than use a trademark symbol with every occurrence of a trademarked name, we use the names only in an editorial fashion and to the benefit of the trademark owner, with no intention of infringement of the trademark.

Distributed to the book trade worldwide by Springer-Verlag New York, Inc., 233 Spring Street, 6th Floor, New York, NY 10013. Phone 1-800-SPRINGER, fax 201-348-4505, e-mail orders-ny@springer-sbm.com, or visit http://www.springeronline.com.

For information on translations, please e-mail info@apress.com, or visit http://www.apress.com.

Apress and friends of ED books may be purchased in bulk for academic, corporate, or promotional use. eBook versions and licenses are also available for most titles. For more information, reference our Special Bulk Sales–eBook Licensing web page at http://www.apress.com/info/bulksales.

The information in this book is distributed on an "as is" basis, without warranty. Although every precaution has been taken in the preparation of this work, neither the author(s) nor Apress shall have any liability to any person or entity with respect to any loss or damage caused or alleged to be caused directly or indirectly by the information contained in this work.

The source code for this book is available to readers at http://www.apress.com.

Patrick wishes to dedicate this book to his father – "Everyday I attempt to approach his level of logic and perfection. Rest in peace."

Jim dedicates this book to his dad – "I've learned a lot from you and enjoyed the company."

Contents at a Glance

Contents

Foreword

A new language needs a simple and clear introductory book that makes it accessible to a broad range of programmers. In *Foundations of F#*, Robert Pickering has captured the essential elements that the professional programmer needs to master in order to get started with F# and .NET. As the designer of F#, I am thrilled to see Robert take up the challenge of presenting F# in a way that is accessible to a wide audience.

F# combines the simplicity and elegance of typed functional programming with the strengths of the .NET platform. Although typed functional programming is relatively new to many programmers and thus requires some learning, in many ways it makes programming simpler. This is mainly because F# programs tend to be built from compositional, correct foundational elements, and type inference makes programs shorter and clearer. Robert first introduces the three foundational paradigms of F#: functional programming, imperative programming, and object-oriented programming, and he shows how F# lets you use them in concert. He then shows how this multiparadigm approach can be used in conjunction with the .NET libraries to perform practical programming tasks such as GUI implementation, data access, and distributed programming. He then introduces some of the particular strengths of F# in the area of "language-oriented" programming.

F# is a practical language, and Robert has ensured that the reader is well equipped with information needed to use the current generation of F# tools well. Many computer professionals first encounter functional programming through a short section of the undergraduate curriculum and often leave these courses uncertain about the real-world applicability of the techniques they have been taught. Similarly, some people encounter functional programming only in its purest forms and are uncertain whether it is possible to combine the elements of the paradigm with other approaches to programming and software engineering. Robert has helped remove this uncertainty: typed functional programming is practical, easy to learn, and a powerful addition to the .NET programming landscape.

F# is also a research language, used in part to deliver recent advances in language design, particularly those that work well with .NET. It combines a stable and dependable base language with more recent extensions. Robert's book describes F# 2.0, the latest release of the language at the time of writing. The rest of the F# team and I are very grateful to Robert's many suggestions, and the language has been greatly improved through this.

Don Syme
Designer of F#, Microsoft Research
Original foreword to Foundations of F# (2007)

When Microsoft introduced F#, the .NET community gained a new paradigm—functional programming. That was a welcome event for coders who'd avoided .NET because the existing languages were geared toward rapid line-of-business development. But whether or not you've stayed clear of .NET, if you'd like to know what functional programming can bring to your work, Beginning F# is an excellent place to start the adventure.

When the first edition was published in 2007, functional languages were just starting to break into the mainstream. As it turned out, Robert Pickering displayed some impressive intuition about the importance they'd take on. In the short time since, they've become hot in the world of software architecture, so I'm especially pleased to see a second edition now.

Pickering is one of the most experienced F# programmers outside Microsoft, with a tremendous amount to offer people who are curious about the language. I'm excited to see that in this book he shares his perspective on everything from basic F# program design to large-scale software architecture. You'll find topics as deep as domain-specific languages and concurrency with a functional language. *Beginning F#* is truly geared toward professionals looking for real-world returns from this programming language.

I value that real-world approach—it helps me, and I believe it will help others use functional programming for their day-to-day work. I also prize the book as a powerful ally when I make the case that functional programming isn't just for academics anymore—it's a skill that software developers in the trenches should master. I even used the original edition of *Beginning F#* to convince my boss of functional programming's legitimacy. Thanks to the examples inside this book, I've witnessed more than one person make the transition from functional-programming novice to daily F# programmer, and I sincerely believe you'll have that experience.

Chance Coble
Chief Architect
Blacklight Solutions, LLC

About the Author

Robert Pickering was born in Sheffield, in the north of England, but a fascination with computers and the "madchester" indie music scene led him to cross the Pennines and study computer science at the University of Manchester.

After finishing his degree, Robert moved to London to catch the tail end of the dot-com boom, then went on to specialize in creating enterprise applications using the .NET Framework. He has worked as both a consultant and an engineer for a software house. After working on projects in Denmark, Holland, Belgium, and Switzerland, he finally settled in Paris, France, where he lives with his wife and three cats. He has been writing about F# almost since its beginning, and the F# wiki on his strangelights.com web site is among the most popular F# web sites.

About the Technical Reviewer

Michael de la Maza solves hard problems, often by applying computational techniques. He holds a PhD in computer science from MIT and is a Certified ScrumMaster, Certified Scrum Practitioner, and an IEEE Senior Member. Previously, he was VP of Corporate Strategy at Softricity (acquired by Microsoft in 2006) and a co-founder of Inquira.

Acknowledgments

If there is one person who must be acknowledged, it is Jim Huddleston, the editor of the first edition of this book. Jim was there from the beginning. He helped me get it commissioned, he worked with me to figure out the contents, he gave me much-needed encouragement and constructive criticism, and his skillful editing helped me convey the information effectively. Sadly, Jim died on Sunday, 25th February 2007, just as the orginal book was entering its final stages of production.

I feel very lucky to have worked on this project with my technical reviewer, Michael de la Maza, and lucky as well to have worked with the technical reviewer of the first edition, Don Syme, who went above and beyond the cause by contributing many ideas to the original book; his influence can still be seen in this edition.

Don, of course, is the creator and developer of F#, and I'd like to thank him and all the other members of the small but dedicated F# team. Specifically, I'd like to thank them for their hard work on the compiler, and to let them know that their quick responses to bugs and queries were very much appreciated.

I'm also indebted to the entire F# community, in particular, to Stephan Tolksdorf, who was a great help with the FParsec examples; André van Meulebrouck, who sent me many corrections; and Chance Coble for his encouragement and excellent foreword. And I'm grateful to Chris Barwick (a.k.a. optionsScalper) for his continued work on hubFS (http://cs.hubfs.net).

Finally, I'd like to thank everyone at Apress who took part in creating this book.

A number of people had to put up with me while I wrote this book, and they deserve special thanks. This includes my family: Mum, Dad, and sister, who got used to me sneaking off to write whenever I went to visit them; my work colleagues when writing the original book: Arnaud, Aurélie, Baptiste, Buuloc, Daniel, Dennis, Emmanuel, Fabrice, François, Frederik, Guillaume, Ibrahima, Jean-Marc, Laurent, Lionel, Oussama, Patrice, Philippe, Regis, Sebastien J., Sebastien P., Stefaan, Stefany, and Stephane; the people who helped keep me distracted in Geneva: Amy, Angela, Armand, Carmen, Emma, Erika, Francisco, Giovanna, Jordi, Laurent, Mattias, Peter, and Sameera; and the people I'm working with on my current project: Charels, Francois, Kyrylo, and Stefan. Last but by no means least, heartfelt thanks to my wife, Susan, for all the help and support she has given. Without her understanding, this book could never have happened.

Preface

In 2003 I was looking for a way to process IL—the intermediate language into which all .NET languages are compiled. At the time, .NET was fairly new and there weren't a lot of options for doing this. I quickly realized that the best option was an API called Abstract IL, AbsIL for short. AbsIL was written in a language called F#, and I decided to use this language to write a small wrapper around AbsIL so I could extract the information I needed from a DLL in a form more usable than with C#. But a funny thing happened while writing the wrapper: even though in those days writing F# was a little hard going as the compiler was far from polished, I found I actually enjoyed programming in F#, so much so that when I finished the wrapper, I didn't want to go back to C#. In short, I was hooked.

During this period, I was working as a consultant, so I needed to regularly check out new technologies and APIs, and I got to do all my experimenting with F#. At the same time, a new way to communicate on the Web was emerging, and a new word was about to enter the English language: *blog*. I decided I should have a blog because anyone who was any one in technology seemed to have one, so I created `strangelight.com,` where my blog can still be found today. I later created a wiki about F#, also at `strangelight.com,` which continues to be very popular.

My job meant I had to do a lot of traveling, so I spent quite a lot of time in hotel rooms or on trains and planes, and I came to view these occasions as time to try out stuff in F#. I ended up exchanging quite a lot e-mails with Don Syme, and eventually we met up. We went for a beer in the pub where Watson and Crick went after they first pieced together the structure of DNA. Will people talk about the pub were Syme and Pickering first met years from now? Errrm, perhaps not. Anyway, all this led me to wonder what I should do with my new-found knowledge of F# and functional programming. About this time, a guy named Jim Huddleston posted to the F# mailing list to ask if anyone would like to write a book about F#. Well, I just couldn't help myself—it sounded like the job for me and in May, 2007, "Foundations of F#" was published.

About half a year later, it was announced that F# would be productized and made available as part of Visual Studio 2010. This seemed too good an opportunity to miss so I signed up to write a new version of the book, with the ambition of documenting the language as it is in Visual Studio 2010. The result is the book you are holding in your hands.

It has been great fun watching F# evolve and turn from a rudimentary language into the fully fledged and highly usable tool you see today. I hope reading this book changes your life as much as writing it changed mine.

CHAPTER 1

■ ■ ■

Introduction

This introductory chapter will address some of the major questions you may have about F# and functional programming.

What Is Functional Programming?

Functional programming (FP) is the oldest of the three major programming paradigms. The first FP language, IPL, was invented in 1955, about a year before Fortran. The second, Lisp, was invented in 1958, a year before Cobol. Both Fortran and Cobol are imperative (or procedural) languages, and their immediate success in scientific and business computing made imperative programming the dominant paradigm for more than 30 years. The rise of the object-oriented (OO) paradigm in the 1970s and the gradual maturing of OO languages ever since have made OO programming the most popular paradigm today.

Despite the vigorous and continual development of powerful FP languages—SML, Objective Caml (OCaml), APL, and Clean, among others—and FP-like languages—Erlang, Lisp, and Haskell being the most successful for real-world applications—since the 1950s, FP remained a primarily academic pursuit until recently. The early commercial success of imperative languages made it the dominant paradigm for decades. Object-oriented languages gained broad acceptance only when enterprises recognized the need for more sophisticated computing solutions. Today, the promise of FP is finally being realized to solve even more complex problems—as well as the simpler ones.

Pure functional programming views all programs as collections of functions that accept arguments and return values. Unlike imperative and object-oriented programming, it allows no side effects and uses recursion instead of loops for iteration. The functions in a functional program are very much like mathematical functions because they do not change the state of the program. In the simplest terms, once a value is assigned to an identifier, it never changes, functions do not alter parameter values, and the results that functions return are completely new values. In typical underlying implementations, once a value is assigned to an area in memory, it does not change. To create results, functions copy values and then change the copies, leaving the original values free to be used by other functions and eventually be thrown away when no longer needed. (This is where the idea of garbage collection originated.)

The mathematical basis for pure functional programming is elegant, and FP therefore provides beautiful, succinct solutions for many computing problems. But its stateless and recursive nature makes the other paradigms convenient for handling many common programming tasks. However, one of F#'s great strengths is that you can use multiple paradigms and mix them to solve problems in the way you find most convenient.

Why Is Functional Programming Important?

When people think of functional programming, they often view its statelessness as a fatal flaw without considering its advantages. One could argue that since an imperative program is often 90 percent assignment and since a functional program has no assignment, a functional program could be 90 percent shorter. However, not many people are convinced by such arguments or attracted to the ascetic world of stateless recursive programming, as John Hughes pointed out in his classic paper "Why Functional Programming Matters."

> *The functional programmer sounds rather like a medieval monk, denying himself the pleasures of life in the hope that it will make him virtuous.*

John Hughes, Chalmers University of Technology
(http://www.math.chalmers.se/~rjmh/Papers/whyfp.html)

To see the advantages of functional programming, you must look at what FP permits rather than what it prohibits. For example, functional programming allows you to treat functions themselves as values and pass them to other functions. This might not seem all that important at first glance, but its implications are extraordinary. Eliminating the distinction between data and function means that many problems can be more naturally solved. Functional programs can be shorter and more modular than corresponding imperative and object-oriented programs.

In addition to treating functions as values, functional languages offer other features that borrow from mathematics and are not commonly found in imperative languages. For example, functional programming languages often offer *curried functions*, where arguments can be passed to a function one at a time and, if all arguments are not given, the result is a residual function waiting for the rest of its parameters. It's also common for functional languages to offer type systems with much better power-to-weight ratios, providing more performance and correctness for less effort.

Further, a function might return multiple values, and the calling function is free to consume them as it likes. I'll discuss these ideas, along with many more, in detail and with plenty of examples in Chapter 3.

What Is F#?

Functional programming is the best approach to solving many thorny computing problems, but pure FP isn't suitable for general-purpose programming. So FP languages have gradually embraced aspects of the imperative and OO paradigms, remaining true to the FP paradigm but incorporating features needed to easily write any kind of program. F# is a natural successor on this path. It is also much more than just an FP language.

Some of the most popular functional languages, including OCaml, Haskell, Lisp, and Scheme, have traditionally been implemented using custom runtimes, which leads to problems such as lack of interoperability. F# is a general-purpose programming language for .NET (a general-purpose runtime) that smoothly integrates all three major programming paradigms. With F#, you can choose whichever paradigm works best to solve problems in the most effective way. You can do pure FP if you're a purist, but you can easily combine functional, imperative, and object-oriented styles in the same program and exploit the strengths of each paradigm. Like other typed functional languages, F# is strongly typed but also uses inferred typing, so programmers don't need to spend time explicitly specifying types unless an ambiguity exists. Further, F# seamlessly integrates with the .NET Framework Base Class Library (BCL). Using the BCL in F# is as simple as using it in C# or Visual Basic (and maybe even simpler).

F# was modeled on OCaml, a successful object-oriented FP language, and then tweaked and extended to mesh well technically and philosophically with .NET. It fully embraces .NET and enables users to do everything that .NET allows. The F# compiler can compile for all implementations of the Common Language Infrastructure (CLI), it supports .NET generics without changing any code, and it even provides for inline Intermediate Language (IL) code. The F# compiler not only produces executables for any CLI but can also run on any environment that has a CLI, which means F# is not limited to Windows but can run on Linux, Apple Mac OS X, and OpenBSD. (Chapter 2 covers what it's like to run F# on Linux.)

The F# compiler is distributed with Visual Studio 2010 and is available as a plug-in for Visual Studio 2008. It supports IntelliSense expression completion and automatic expression checking. It also gives tool tips to show what types have been inferred for expressions. Programmers often comment that this really helps bring the language to life.

F# was first implemented by Dr. Don Syme at Microsoft Research (MSR) in Cambridge. The project has now been embraced by Microsoft Corporate in Redmond, and the implementation of the compiler and Visual Studio integration is now developed by a team located in both Cambridge and Redmond.

Although other FP languages run on .NET, F# has established itself as the de facto .NET functional programming language because of the quality of its implementation and its superb integration with .NET and Visual Studio.

No other .NET language is as easy to use and as flexible as F#!

Who Is Using F#?

F# has a strong presence inside Microsoft, both in MSR and throughout the company as a whole. Ralf Herbrich, coleader of MSR's Applied Games Group, which specializes in machine learning techniques, is typical of F#'s growing number of fans:

The first application was parsing 110GB of log data spread over 11,000 text files in over 300 directories and importing it into a SQL database. The whole application is 90 lines long (including comments!) and finished the task of parsing the source files and importing the data in under 18 hours; that works out to a staggering 10,000 log lines processed per second! Note that I have not optimized the code at all but written the application in the most obvious way. I was truly astonished as I had planned at least a week of work for both coding and running the application.

The second application was an analysis of millions of feedbacks. We had developed the model equations and I literally just typed them in as an F# program; together with the reading-data-from-SQL-database and writing-results-to-MATLAB-data-file the F# source code is 100 lines long (including comments). Again, I was astonished by the running time; the whole processing of the millions of data items takes 10 minutes on a standard desktop machine. My C# reference application (from some earlier tasks) is almost 1,000 lines long and is no faster. The whole job from developing the model equations to having first real world data results took 2 days.

Ralf Herbrich, Microsoft Research
(http://blogs.msdn.com/dsyme/archive/2006/04/01/566301.aspx)

F# usage outside Microsoft is also rapidly growing. I asked Chris Barwick, who runs hubFS (http://cs.hubFS.net), a popular web site dedicated to F#, about why F# was now his language of choice, and he said the following:

I've been in scientific and mathematics computing for more than 14 years. During that time, I have waited and hoped for a platform that would be robust in every manner. That platform has to provide effective tools that allow for the easy construction and usage of collateral and that makes a scientific computing environment effective. .NET represents a platform where IL gives rise to consistency across products. F# is the language that provides for competent scientific and mathematical computing on that platform. With these tools and other server products, I have a wide range of options with which to build complex systems at a very low cost of development and with very low ongoing costs to operate and to improve. F# is the cornerstone needed for advanced scientific computing.

Chris Barwick, JJB Research (private e-mail)

Finally, I talked to Chance Coble, a software architect, about what F# bought to his work.

F# has made its case to me over and over again. The first project I decided to try F# on was a machine vision endeavor, which would identify and extract fingerprints from submitted fingerprint cards and load them into a biometrics system. The project plan was to perform the fingerprint extraction manually, which was growing cumbersome, and the automation turned out to be a huge win (with very little code). Later we decided to include that F# work in a larger application that had been written in C#, and accomplished the integration with ease. Since then I have used F# in projects for machine learning, domain specific language design, 3D visualizations, symbolic analysis, and anywhere performance intensive data processing has been required. The ability to easily integrate functional modules into existing production scale applications makes F# not only fun to work with, but an important addition for project leads. Unifying functional programming with a mature and rich platform like .NET has opened up a great deal of opportunity.

Chance Coble, Chief Architect, Blacklight Solutions, LLC (private email)

Who Is This Book For?

This book is aimed primarily at IT professionals who want to get up to speed quickly on F#. A working knowledge of the .NET Framework and some knowledge of either C# or Visual Basic would be nice, but it's not necessary. All you really need is some experience programming in any language to be comfortable learning F#.

Even complete beginners who've never programmed before and are learning F# as their first computer language should find this book very readable. Though it doesn't attempt to teach introductory programming per se, it does carefully present all the important details of F#.

What's Next?

This book teaches F#, by example, as a compiled language rather than a scripting language. By this I mean most examples are designed to be compiled with the `fsc.exe` compiler, either in Visual Studio or on a command line, rather than executed interactively with `fsi.exe`, the F# interactive environment. In reality, most examples will run fine either way.

Chapter 2 gives you just enough knowledge about setting up an F# development environment to get you going.

Chapters 3, 4, 5, and 6 cover the core F# syntax. I deliberately keep the code simple, because this will give you a better introduction to how the syntax works.

Chapter 7 looks at the core libraries distributed with F# to introduce you to their flavor and power, rather than to describe each function in detail. The F# online documentation (`http://msdn.microsoft.com/fsharp`) is the place to get the details.

Then you'll dive into how to use F# for the bread-and-butter problems of the working programmer. Chapter 8 covers user interface programming, Chapter 9 covers data access, Chapter 10 covers concurrency and parallelism, and Chapter 11 covers how applications can take advantage of a network.

The final chapters take you through the topics you really need to know to master F#. Chapter 12 looks at support for creating little languages or domain-specific languages (DSLs), a powerful and very common programming pattern in F#. Chapter 13 covers parsing text, with an emphasis on using this as a front end for DSLs. Finally, Chapter 14 explores advanced interoperation issues.

■ ■ ■

CHAPTER 2

How to Obtain, Install, and Use F#

This chapter is designed to get you up and running with F# as quickly as possible. You'll look at how to obtain F#, how to install it on both Windows and Linux, and how to use the compiler in various ways. I'll also discuss what version of software was used to test the examples in this book.

Obtaining F#

F# is now included in Visual Studio 2010 by default, so if you have this installed on your machine you may already have F# installed. If you have Visual Studio 2010 installed but you can't see F#, then you need to ensure that you installed the package. This can be done through the Add/Remove Programs or Programs section of the control panel (see Figure 2-1).

If you're not a Visual Studio user or would prefer to use Visual Studio 2008 rather than 2010, then you'll have to download the F# distribution separately. The best place to look for all F#-related information is the MSDN F# resource center at http://msdn.microsoft.com /fsharp/. A link to the compiler distribution is included in the top, left-hand corner of the F# resource center page. There are two versions—an MSI version, which will automatically install F# Visual Studio integration if Visual Studio is installed, and a ZIP version of the distribution, which is primarily targeted at non-Windows users. The package includes the compiler fsc.exe, as well as fsi.exe (the F# interactive console), some F#-based parsing tools, the F# base class libraries, the F# documentation, and some F# samples.

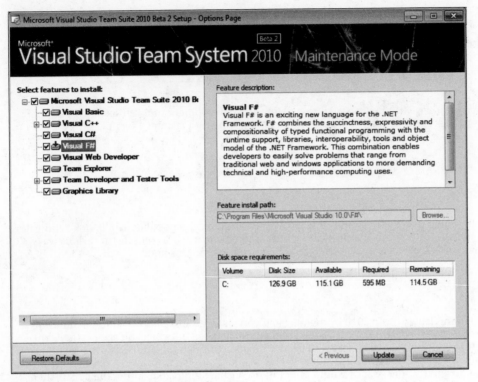

Figure 2-1. *Enabling F# in Visual Studio 2010*

Installing F# on Windows with Visual Studio 2008

This section is for people using an older version of Visual Studio. (As noted, Visual Studio 2010 users will already have F# installed.) Installing F# on Windows with Visual Studio 2008 is straightforward. You need to be running an account with system administrator privileges, then download the MSI version as described in the previous section, and execute it.

Please note that at the time of this writing the free Express Editions of Visual Studio do not support plug-ins, so you cannot use F# integration with them. However, you can install F#'s plug-in on top of the free Visual Studio 2008 Shell. See the MSDN Visual Studio Extensibility center for more details on Visual Studio 2008 Shell at http://msdn.microsoft.com/vsx2008/.

Installing F# on Linux

If you are unfamiliar with Linux and would like to try Mono, the simplest way is to download the SUSE Linux virtual machine (VM) image available on the Mono web site at http://www.go-mono.com/mono-downloads.

■**Note** Mono is a free, open-source, multi-platform implementation of the Common Language Runtime (CLR), which is compliant with the ECMA specifications of the Common Language Infrastructure (CLI) and compatible with Microsoft .NET. It is implemented by Novell with the aid of a number of community volunteers.

This VM image comes with the latest Mono runtime and development tools preinstalled, so there's no need to worry about setting up any of these. But the image does not currently include the F# compiler, so you will need to install it using the following instructions. I performed all of these steps as the root account.

- Still in the /usr/lib/fsharp directory, run the command sh install-mono.sh.

- Unpack the F# distribution and copy the resulting files to /usr/lib/fsharp.

- In the /usr/lib/fsharp directory, run chmod +x install-mono.sh.

- Run the dos2unix tool on the text file install-mono.sh.

- Still in the /usr/lib/fsharp directory, run the command sh install-mono.sh.

After performing those steps, I was able to use F# from the command line of any account by running mono/usr/lib/fsharp/bin/fsc.exe, followed by the command-line options. Obviously, this was inconvenient to run every time, so I created a shell script file in /usr/bin and as fsc.

```
#!/bin/sh
exec /usr/bin/mono $MONO_OPTIONS /usr/lib/fsharp/bin/fsc.exe "$@"
```

I then ran chmod +x fsc to give users permission to execute it. After this, running the F# compiler was as simple as typing fsc at the command line. The F# interactive compiler, fsi.exe, the shell script for this is as follows:

```
#!/bin/sh
exec /usr/bin/mono $MONO_OPTIONS /usr/lib/fsharp/bin/fsi.exe --no-gui "$@"
```

Figure 2-2 shows F# interactive running under Mono and Linux.

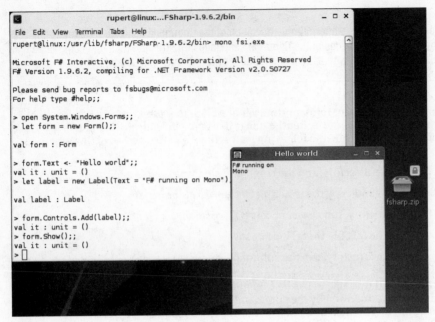

Figure 2-2. *F# interactive running under Mono and Linux*

Using F# in Different Ways

F# programs are just text files, so you can use any text editor to create them. Just save your program with the extension .fs, and use fsc.exe to compile them. For example, if you had the following program in the text file helloworld.fs:

```
printfn "Hello World"
```

you could just run fsc.exe helloworld.fs to compile your program into helloworld.exe, which would output the following to the console:

```
Hello World
```

Visual Studio

In my opinion, the easiest and quickest way to develop F# programs is in Visual Studio in conjunction with the F# interactive compiler (see Figure 2-3). You can type F# programs into the text editor, taking advantage of syntax highlighting and IntelliSense code completion; compile them into executables; and debug them interactively by setting breakpoints and pressing F5. Also, you can execute parts of your code interactively using F# interactive. Just highlight the code you want to execute and press Alt+Enter; F# interactive will execute the code and show the results. This is great for testing snippets individually.

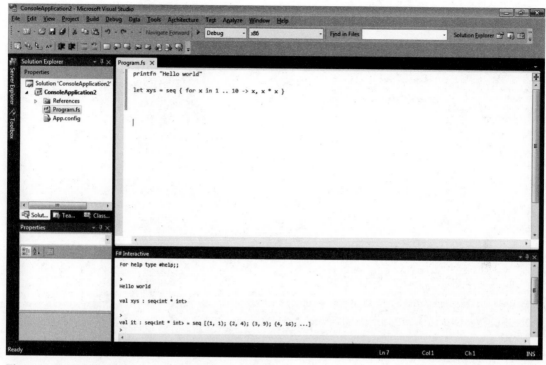

Figure 2-3. *Visual Studio 2010 hosting F# interactive*

SharpDevelop

SharpDevelop is an open-source IDE with F# bindings that can be used for .NET and Mono development. The F# bindings are packaged with SharpDevelop, so to use them all you need to do is ensure that F# is installed then install SharpDevelop. After that it's just a matter of creating a new F# project and off you go. The F# bindings for SharpDevelop do not offer as much functionality as Visual Studio does—only syntax highlighting and F# interactive are available. However, the development environment is still very useable, and the bindings are open source. So if you wish to extend them, you can help out with the project. Figure 2-4 shows SharpDevelop with an F# project open.

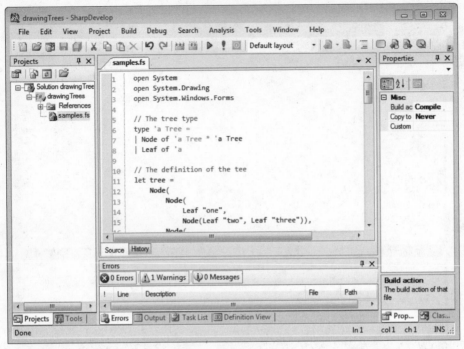

Figure 2-4. *SharpDevelop with an F# project open*

F# Interactive Command-Line

If you prefer, you can type your programs into the F# interactive console directly when it's running in stand-alone mode, as shown in Figure 2-5.

Figure 2-5. *The F# interactive console running in stand-alone mode*

When you use the interactive console, you type the code you want. When you've completed a section, you use two semicolons (;;) to indicate that the compiler should compile and run it.

F# interactive responds to commands in two ways: If you bind a value to an identifier, it prints the name of the identifier and its type. So, typing the following into F# interactive:

```
> let i = 1 + 2;;
```

gives the following:

```
val i : int
```

However, if you just type a value into F# interactive, it will respond slightly differently. Typing the following into F# interactive:

```
> 1 + 2;;
```

gives the following:

```
val it : int = 3
```

This means the value has been bound to a special identifier called it that is available to other code within the F# interactive session. When any expression is evaluated at the top level, its value is also printed after the equal sign (note the 3 in the previous example). As you get to know fsi.exe and F# in general, using F# interactive will become more and more useful for debugging programs and finding out how they work. (I discuss values, identifiers, and types in more detail in Chapter 3.)

You can get code completions by pressing Tab. I find this mode of working useful in testing short programs by copying and pasting them into the console or for checking properties on existing libraries. For example, in Figure 2-2 I checked the System.Environment.Version property. However, I find this mode inconvenient for creating longer programs since it's difficult to store the programs once they're coded; they have to be copied and pasted from the console. Using Visual Studio, even if you don't intend to just run them interactively, you can still easily execute snippets with Alt+Enter.

The Examples in This Book

The code in this book will focus on using fsc.exe rather than fsi.exe. Although fsi.exe is great for testing code, running simple scripts, and running experiments, I believe fsc.exe is more useful for producing finished software. Since there's little difference between the syntax and the commands, most examples will work with little or no adaptation in fsi.exe, and I'll warn you when any changes are necessary.

The samples can be downloaded from http://bfs.codeplex.com/. All the samples in this book were tested using .NET 4.0 running on Windows 7. A subset has also been tested running under Mono 2.4.2.3 on Linux.

Summary

This chapter described how to install and run F# and the different ways you can work with it. The following chapters will explain how to program with F#, starting in Chapter 3 with functional programming in F#.

CHAPTER 3

■ ■ ■

Functional Programming

You saw in Chapter 1 that pure functional programming treats everything as a value, including functions. Although F# is not a pure functional language, it does encourage you to program in the functional style; that is, it encourages you to use expressions and computations that return a result, rather than statements that result in some side effect. In this chapter, you'll survey the major language constructs of F# that support the functional programming paradigm and learn how they make it easier to program in the functional style.

Literals

Literals represent constant values and are useful building blocks for computations. F# has a rich set of literals, summarized in Table 3-1.

Table 3-1. *F# Literals*

Example	F# Type	.NET Type	Description
"Hello\t ", "World\n"	string	System.String	A string in which a backslash (\) is an escape character
@"c:\dir\fs", @""""	string	System.String	A verbatim string where a backslash (\) is a regular character
"bytesbytesbytes"B	byte array	System.Byte[]	A string that will be stored as a byte array
'c'	char	System.Char	A character
true, false	bool	System.Boolean	A Boolean
0x22	int/int32	System.Int32	An integer as a hexadecimal
0o42	int/int32	System.Int32	An integer as an octal
0b10010	int/ int32	System.Int32	An integer as a binary
34y	sbyte	System.SByte	A signed byte

Table 3-1. *Continued*

Example	F# Type	.NET Type	Description
34uy	byte	System.Byte	An unsigned byte
34s	int16	System.Int16	A 16-bit integer
34us	uint16	System.UInt16	An unsigned 16-bit integer
34l	int/int32	System.Int32	A 32-bit integer
34ul	uint32	System.UInt32	An unsigned 32-bit integer
34n	nativeint	System.IntPtr	A native-sized integer
34un	unativeint	System.UIntPtr	An unsigned native-sized integer
34L	int64	System.Int64	A 32-bit integer
34UL	uint64	System.Int64	An unsigned 32-bit integer
3.0F, 3.0f	float32	System.Single	A 32-bit IEEE floating-point number
3.0	float	System.Double	A 64-bit IEEE floating-point number
3474262622571I	bigint	Microsoft.FSharp.Math.BigInt	An arbitrary large integer
474262612536171N	bignum	Microsoft.FSharp.Math.BigNum	An arbitrary large number

In F#, string literals can contain newline characters, and regular string literals can contain standard escape codes. Verbatim string literals use a backslash (\) as a regular character, and two double quotes ("") are the escape for a quote. You can define all integer types using hexadecimal and octal by using the appropriate prefix and postfix indicator. The following example shows some of these literals in action, along with how to use the F# printf function with a %A pattern to output them to the console. The printf function interprets the %A format pattern using a combination of F#'s reflection (covered in Chapter 7) and the .NET ToString method, which is available for every type, to output values in a human-readable way.

```
// some strings
let message = "Hello
World\r\n\t!"
let dir = @"c:\projects"
```

```
// a byte array
let bytes = "bytesbytesbytes"B

// some numeric types
let xA = 0xFFy
let xB = 0o7777un
let xC = 0b10010UL

// print the results
let main() =
    printfn "%A" message
    printfn "%A" dir
    printfn "%A" bytes
    printfn "%A" xA
    printfn "%A" xB
    printfn "%A" xC

// call the main function
main()
```

The results of this example, when compiled and executed, are as follows:

```
"Hello
World
        !"
"c:\projects"
[|98uy; 121uy; 116uy; 101uy; 115uy; 98uy; 121uy; 116uy; 101uy; 115uy; 98uy;
  121uy; 116uy; 101uy; 115uy|]
-1y
4095un
18UL
```

Functions

In F#, functions are defined using the keyword fun. The function's arguments are separated by spaces, and the arguments are separated from the function body by a left ASCII arrow (->).

Here is an example of a function that takes two values and adds them together:

```
fun x y -> x + y
```

Notice that this function does not have a name; this is a sort of function literal. Functions defined in this way are referred to as *anonymous functions*, *lambda functions*, or just *lambdas*.

The idea that a function does not need a name may seem a little strange. However, if a function is to be passed as an argument to another function, it may not need a name, especially if the task it's performing is relatively simple.

If you need to give the function a name, you can bind it to an identifier, as described in the next section.

Identifiers and let Bindings

Identifiers are the way you give names to values in F# so you can refer to them later in a program. You define an identifier using the keyword let followed by the name of the identifier, an equal sign, and an expression that specifies the value to which the identifier refers. An expression is any piece of code that represents a computation that will return a value. The following expression shows a value being assigned to an identifier:

```
let x = 42
```

To most people coming from an imperative programming background, this will look like a variable assignment. There are a lot of similarities, but a key difference is that in pure functional programming, once a value is assigned to an identifier, it does not change. This is why I will refer to them throughout this book as *identifiers*, rather than as *variables*.

■**Note** Under some circumstances, you can redefine identifiers, which may look a little like an identifier changing value, but is subtly different. Also, in imperative programming in F#, in some circumstances, the value of an identifier can change. In this chapter, we focus on functional programming, where identifiers do not change their values.

An identifier can refer to either a value or a function, and since F# functions are really values in their own right, this is hardly surprising. This means F# has no real concept of a function name or parameter name; these are just identifiers. You can bind an anonymous function to an identifier the same way you can bind a string or integer literal to an identifier:

```
let myAdd = fun x y -> x + y
```

However, as it is very common to need to define a function with a name, F# provides a short syntax for this. You write a function definition the same way as a value identifier, except that a function has two or more identifiers between the let keyword and the equal sign, as follows:

```
let raisePowerTwo x = x ** 2.0
```

The first identifier is the name of the function, raisePowerTwo, and the identifier that follows it is the name of the function's parameter, x. If a function has a name, it is strongly recommended that you use this shorter syntax for defining it.

The syntax for declaring *values* and *functions* in F# is indistinguishable because functions *are* values, and F# syntax treats them both similarly. For example, consider the following code:

```
let n = 10
```

```
let add a b = a + b
```

```
let result = add n 4

printfn "result = %i" result
```

On the first line, the value 10 is assigned to the identifier n; then on the second line, a function, add, which takes two arguments and adds them together, is defined. Notice how similar the syntax is, with the only difference being that a function has parameters that are listed after the function name. Since everything is a value in F#, the literal 10 on the first line is a value, and the result of the expression a + b on the next line is also a value that automatically becomes the result of the add function. Note that there is no need to explicitly return a value from a function as you would in an imperative language.

The results of this code, when compiled and executed, are as follows:

```
result = 14
```

Identifier Names

There are some rules governing identifier names. Identifiers must start with an underscore (_) or a letter, and can then contain any alphanumeric character, underscore, or a single quotation mark ('). Keywords cannot be used as identifiers. As F# supports the use of a single quotation mark as part of an identifier name, you can use this to represent "prime" to create identifier names for different but similar values, as in this example:

```
let x = 42
let x' = 43
```

F# supports Unicode, so you can use accented characters and letters from non-Latin alphabets as identifier names:

```
let 标识符 = 42
```

If the rules governing identifier names are too restrictive, you can use double tick marks (``) to quote the identifier name. This allows you to use any sequence of characters—as long as it doesn't include tabs, newlines, or double ticks—as an identifier name. This means you could create an identifier that ends with a question mark, for example (some programmers believe it is useful to have names that represent Boolean values end with a question mark):

```
let ``more? `` = true
```

This can also be useful if you need to use a keyword as an identifier or type name:

```
let ``class`` = "style"
```

For example, you might need to use a member from a library that was not written in F# and has one of F#'s keywords as its name (you'll learn more about using non-F# libraries in Chapter 4). Generally, it's best to avoid overuse of this feature, as it could lead to libraries that are difficult to use from other .NET languages.

Scope

The *scope* of an identifier defines where you can use an identifier (or a type, as discussed in the "Defining Types" section later in this chapter) within a program. It is important to have a good understanding of scope, because if you try to use an identifier that's not in scope, you will get a compile error.

All identifiers—whether they relate to functions or values—are scoped from the end of their definitions until the end of the sections in which they appear. So, for identifiers that are at the top level (that is, identifiers that are not local to another function or other value), the scope of the identifier is from the place where it's defined to the end of the source file. Once an identifier at the top level has been assigned a value (or function), this value cannot be changed or redefined. An identifier is available only after its definition has ended, meaning that it is not usually possible to define an identifier in terms of itself.

You will have noticed that in F#, you never need to explicitly return a value; the result of the computation is automatically bound to its associated identifier. So, how do you compute intermediate values within a function? In F#, this is controlled by whitespace. An indentation creates a new scope, and the end of this scope is signaled by the end of the indentation. Indention means that the `let` binding is an intermediate value in the computation that is not visible outside this scope. When a scope closes (by the indentation ending), and an identifier is no longer available, it is said to *drop out of scope* or to be *out of scope*.

To demonstrate scope, the next example shows a function that computes the point halfway between two integers. The third and fourth lines show intermediate values being calculated.

```
// function to calculate a midpoint
let halfWay a b =
    let dif = b - a
    let mid = dif / 2
    mid + a

// call the function and print the results
printfn "(halfWay 5 11) = %i" (halfWay 5 11)
printfn "(halfWay 11 5) = %i" (halfWay 11 5)
```

First, the difference between the two numbers is calculated, and this is assigned to the identifier `dif` using the `let` keyword. To show that this is an intermediate value within the function, it is indented by four spaces. The choice of the number of spaces is left to the programmer, but the convention is four. After that, the example calculates the midpoint, assigning it to the identifier `mid` using the same indentation. Finally, the desired result of the function is the midpoint plus a, so the code can simply say `mid + a`, and this becomes the function's result.

■ **Note** You cannot use tabs instead of spaces for indenting, because these can look different in different text editors, which causes problems when whitespace is significant.

The results of this example are as follows:

```
(halfWay 5 11) = 8
(halfWay 11 5) = 8
```

THE F# LIGHTWEIGHT SYNTAX

By default, F# is whitespace-sensitive, with indentation controlling the scope of identifiers. The language F# was based on, Objective Caml (OCaml), is not whitespace-sensitive. In OCaml, scope is controlled though the use of the in keyword. For example the halfWay function from the previous example would look like the following (note the additional in keyword in the middle two lines):

```
let halfWay a b =
    let dif = b - a in
    let mid = dif / 2 in
    mid + a
```

The F# whitespace-sensitive syntax is said to be a *lightweight* syntax, because certain keywords and symbols–such as in, ;, begin, and end–are optional. This means the preceding function definition will be accepted by the F# compiler even with the additional in keywords. If you want to force the use of these keywords, add the declaration #light "off" to the top of each source file.

I believe that significant whitespace is a much more intuitive way of programming, because it helps the programmer decide how the code should be laid out. Therefore, in this book, I cover the F# lightweight syntax.

Identifiers within functions are scoped to the end of the expression in which they appear. Ordinarily, this means they are scoped until the end of the function definition in which they appear. So, if an identifier is defined inside a function, it cannot be used outside it. Consider the next example:

```
let printMessage() =
    let message = "Help me"
    printfn "%s" message

printfn "%s" message
```

This attempts to use the identifier message outside the function printMessage, which is out of scope. When trying to compile this code, you'll get the following error message:

```
Prog.fs(34,17): error: FS0039: The value or constructor 'message' is not defined.
```

Identifiers within functions behave a little differently from identifiers at the top level, because they can be redefined using the let keyword. This is useful because it means that you do not need to keep inventing names to hold intermediate values. To demonstrate, the next example shows a mathematical puzzle implemented as an F# function. Here, you need to calculate a lot of intermediate values that you don't particularly care about; inventing names for each one these would be an unnecessary burden on the programmer.

```fsharp
open System

let readInt() = int (Console.ReadLine())

let mathsPuzzle() =
    printfn "Enter day of the month on which you were born: "
    let input = readInt()
    let x = input * 4 // multiply it by 4
    let x = x + 13 // add 13
    let x = x * 25 // multiply the result by 25
    let x = x - 200 // subtract 200
    printfn "Enter number of the month you were born: "
    let input = readInt()
    let x = x + input
    let x = x * 2 // multiply by 2
    let x = x - 40 // subtract 40
    let x = x * 50 // multiply the result by 50
    printfn "Enter last two digits of the year of your birth: "
    let input = readInt()
    let x = x + input
    let x = x - 10500 // finally, subtract 10,500
    printf "Date of birth (ddmmyy): %i" x

mathsPuzzle()
```

The results of this example, when compiled and executed, are as follows:

```
Enter day of the month on which you were born: 23
Enter number of the month you were born: 5
Enter last two digits of the year of your birth: 78
Date of birth (ddmmyy): 230578
```

Note that this is different from changing the value of an identifier. Because you're redefining the identifier, you're able to change the identifier's type, as shown in the next example, but you still retain type safety.

■**Note** *Type safety*, sometimes referred to as *strong typing*, basically means that F# will prevent you from performing an inappropriate operation on a value; for example, you can't treat an integer as if it were a floating-point number. I discuss types and how they lead to type safety in the "Types and Type Inference" section later in this chapter.

```
let changeType () =
    let x = 1              // bind x to an integer
    let x = "change me"    // rebind x to a string
    let x = x + 1          // attempt to rebind to itself plus an integer
    printfn "%s" x
```

This example will not compile, because on the third line, the value of x changes from an integer to the string "change me", and then on the fourth line, it tries to add a string and an integer, which is illegal in F#, so you get a compile error:

```
prog.fs(55,13): error: FS0001: This expression has type
    int
but is here used with type
    string
stopped due to error
```

If an identifier is redefined, its old value is available while the definition of the identifier is in progress. But after it is defined—that is, at the end of the expression—the old value is hidden. If the identifier is redefined inside a new scope, the identifier will revert to its old value when the new scope is finished.

The next example defines a message and prints it to the console. It then redefines this message inside an *inner function* called innerFun, which also prints the message. Then it calls the function innerFun, and finally prints the message a third time.

```
let printMessages() =
    // define message and print it
    let message = "Important"
    printfn "%s" message;
    // define an inner function that redefines value of message
    let innerFun () =
        let message = "Very Important"
        printfn "%s" message
    // call the inner function
    innerFun ()
    // finally print the first message again
    printfn "%s" message

printMessages()
```

The results of this example, when compiled and executed, are as follows:

```
Important
Very Important
Important
```

A programmer from the imperative world might have expected that message, when printed out for the final time, would be bound to the value Very Important, rather than Important. It holds the value Important because the identifier message is rebound, rather than assigned, to the value Very Important inside the function innerFun, and this binding is valid only inside the scope of the function innerFun. Therefore, once this function has finished, the identifier message reverts to holding its original value.

■**Note** Using inner functions is a common and excellent way of breaking up a lot of functionality into manageable portions, and you will see their usage throughout the book. They are sometimes referred to as *closures* or *lambdas*, although these two terms have more specific meanings. A *closure* means that the function uses a value that is not defined at the top level. A *lambda* is an anonymous function.

Capturing Identifiers

You have already seen that in F#, you can define functions within other functions. These functions can use any identifier in scope, including definitions that are also local to the function where they are defined. Because these inner functions are values, they could be returned as the result of the function or passed to another function as an argument. This means that although an identifier is defined within a function, so it is not visible to other functions, its actual lifetime may be much longer than the function in which it is defined. Let's look at an example to illustrate this point. Consider the following function, defined as calculatePrefixFunction:

```
// function that returns a function to
let calculatePrefixFunction prefix =
    // calculate prefix
    let prefix' = Printf.sprintf "[%s]: " prefix
    // define function to perform prefixing
    let prefixFunction appendee =
        Printf.sprintf "%s%s" prefix' appendee
    // return function
    prefixFunction

// create the prefix function
let prefixer = calculatePrefixFunction "DEBUG"

// use the prefix function
printfn "%s" (prefixer "My message")
```

This function returns the inner function it defines, prefixFunction. The identifier prefix' is defined as local to the scope of the function calculatePrefixFunction; it cannot be seen by other functions outside calculatePrefixFunction. The inner function prefixFunction uses prefix', so when prefixFunction is returned, the value prefix' must still be available. calculatePrefixFunction creates the function prefixer. When prefixer is called, you see that its result uses a value that was calculated and associated with prefix':

```
[DEBUG]: My message
```

Although you should have an understanding of this process, most of the time you don't need to think about it, because it doesn't involve any additional work by the programmer. The compiler will automatically generate a *closure* to handle extending the lifetime of the local value beyond the function in which it is defined. The .NET garbage collection will automatically handle clearing the value from memory. Understanding this process of identifiers being captured in closures is probably more important when programming in imperative style, where an identifier can represent a value that changes over time. When programming in the functional style, identifiers will always represent values that are constant, making it slightly easier to figure out what has been captured in a closure.

The use Binding

It can be useful to have some action performed on an identifier when it drops out of scope. For example, it's important to close file handles when you've finished reading or writing to the file, so you may want to close the file as soon as the identifier that represents it drops out of scope. More generally, anything that is an operation system resource—such as network socket—or is precious because it's expensive to create or a limited number is available—such as a database connection—should be closed or freed as quickly as possible.

In .NET, objects that fall into this category should implement the IDisposable interface (for more information about objects and interfaces, see Chapter 5). This interface contains one method, Dispose, which will clean up the resource; for example, in the case of a file, it will close the open file handle. So, in many cases, it's useful to call this method when the identifier drops out of scope. F# provides the use binding to do just that.

A use binding behaves the same as a let binding, except that when the variable drops out of scope, the compiler automatically generates code to ensure that the Dispose method will be called at the end of the scope. The code generated by the compiler will always be called, even if an exception occurs (see the "Exceptions and Exception Handling" section later in this chapter for more information about exceptions). To illustrate this, consider the following example:

```
open System.IO

// function to read first line from a file
let readFirstLine filename =
    // open file using a "use" binding
    use file = File.OpenText filename
    file.ReadLine()

// call function and print the result
printfn "First line was: %s" (readFirstLine "mytext.txt")
```

Here, the function readFirstLine uses the .NET Framework method File.OpenText to open a text file for reading. The StreamReader that is returned is bound to the identifier file using a use binding. The example then reads the first line from the file and returns this as a result. At this point, the identifier file drops out of scope, so its Dispose method will be called and close the underlying file handle.

Note the following important constraints on the use of use bindings:

- You can use use bindings only with objects that implement the IDisposable interface.

- use bindings cannot be used at the top level. They can be used only within functions, because identifiers at the top level never go out of scope.

Recursion

Recursion means defining a function in terms of itself; in other words, the function calls itself within its definition. Recursion is often used in functional programming where you would use a loop in imperative programming. Many believe that algorithms are much easier to understand when expressed in terms of recursion rather than loops.

To use recursion in F#, use the rec keyword after the let keyword to make the identifier available within the function definition. The following example shows recursion in action. Notice how on the fifth line, the function makes two calls to itself as part of its own definition.

```
// a function to generate the Fibonacci numbers
let rec fib x =
    match x with
    | 1 -> 1
    | 2 -> 1
    | x -> fib (x - 1) + fib (x - 2)

// call the function and print the results
printfn "(fib 2) = %i" (fib 2)
printfn "(fib 6) = %i" (fib 6)
printfn "(fib 11) = %i" (fib 11)
```

The results of this example, when compiled and executed, are as follows:

```
(fib 2) = 1
(fib 6) = 8
(fib 11) = 89
```

This function calculates the *n*th term in the Fibonacci sequence. The Fibonacci sequence is generated by adding the previous two numbers in the sequence, and it progresses as follows: 1, 1, 2, 3, 5, 8, 13, …. Recursion is most appropriate for calculating the Fibonacci sequence, because the definition of any number in the sequence, other than the first two, depends on being able to calculate the previous two numbers, so the Fibonacci sequence is defined in terms of itself.

Although recursion is a powerful tool, you should be careful when using it. It is easy to inadvertently write a recursive function that never terminates. Although intentionally writing a program that does not terminate is sometimes useful, it is rarely the goal when trying to perform calculations. To ensure that recursive functions terminate, it is often useful to think of recursion in terms of a base case and a recursive case:

- The *recursive case* is the value for which the function is defined in terms of itself. For the function fib, this is any value other than 1 and 2.

- The *base case* is the nonrecursive case; that is, there must be some value where the function is not defined in terms of itself. In the fib function, 1 and 2 are the base cases.

Having a base case is not enough in itself to ensure termination. The recursive case must tend toward the base case. In the fib example, if x is greater than or equal to 3, then the recursive case will tend toward the base case, because x will always become smaller and at some point reach 2. However, if x is less than 1, then x will grow continually more negative, and the function will recurse until the limits of the machine are reached, resulting in a stack overflow error (System.StackOverflowException).

The previous code also uses F# pattern matching, which is discussed in the "Pattern Matching" section later in this chapter.

Operators

In F#, you can think of *operators* as a more aesthetically pleasing way to call functions.
F# has two different kinds of operators:

- A *prefix* operator is an operator where the operands come after the operator.

- An *infix* operator comes in between the first and second operands.

F# provides a rich and diverse set of operators that you can use with numeric, Boolean, string, and collection types. The operators defined in F# and its libraries are too numerous to be covered in this section, so rather than looking at individual operators, we'll look at how to use and define operators in F#.

As in C#, F# operators are overloaded, meaning you can use more than one type with an operator; however, unlike in C#, both operands must be the same type, or the compiler will generate an error. F# also allows users to define and redefine operators.

Operators follow a set of rules similar to C#'s for operator overloading resolution; therefore, any class in the BCL, or any .NET library, that was written to support operator overloading in C# will support it in F#. For example, you can use the + operator to concatenate strings, as well as to add a System. TimeSpan to a System.DataTime, because these types support an overload of the + operator. The following example illustrates this:

```
let rhyme = "Jack " + "and " + "Jill"

open System
let oneYearLater =
    DateTime.Now + new TimeSpan(365, 0, 0, 0, 0)
```

Unlike functions, operators are not values, so they cannot be passed to other functions as parameters. However, if you need to use an operator as a value, you can do this by surrounding it with parentheses. The operator will then behave exactly like a function. Practically, this has two consequences:

- The operator is now a function, and its parameters will appear after the operator:

  ```
  let result = (+) 1 1
  ```

- As it is a value, it could be returned as the result of a function, passed to another function, or bound to an identifier. This provides a very concise way to define the add function:

```
let add = (+)
```

You'll see how using an operator as a value can be useful later in this chapter when we look at working with lists.

Users can define their own operators or redefine any of the existing ones if they want (although this is not always advisable, because the operators then no longer support overloading). Consider the following perverse example that redefines + to perform subtraction:

```
let (+) a b = a - b
printfn "%i" (1 + 1)
```

User-defined (*custom*) operators must be nonalphanumeric and can be a single character or a group of characters. You can use the following characters in custom operators:

```
!$%&*+-./<=>?@^|~
```

The syntax for defining an operator is the same as using the let keyword to define a function, except the operator replaces the function name and is surrounded by parentheses so the compiler knows that the symbols are used as a name of an operator, rather than as the operator itself. The following example shows defining a custom operator, +*, which adds its operands and then multiplies them:

```
let ( +* ) a b = (a + b) * a * b
printfn "(1 +* 2) = %i" (1 +* 2)
```

The results of this example, when compiled and executed, are as follows:

```
(1 +* 2) = 6
```

Unary operators always come before the operand. User-defined binary operators are prefix if they start with an exclamation mark (!), a question mark (?), or a tilde (~); they are infix, with operators coming between the operands, for everything else.

Function Application

Function application, also sometimes referred to as *function composition* or *composing functions*, simply means calling a function with some arguments. The following example shows the function add being defined and then applied to two arguments. Notice that the arguments are not separated with parentheses or commas; only whitespace is needed to separate them.

```
let add x y = x + y

let result = add 4 5

printfn "(add 4 5) = %i" result
```

The results of this example, when compiled and executed, are as follows:

```
(add 4 5) = 9
```

In F#, a function has a fixed number of arguments and is applied to the value that appears next in the source file. You do not necessarily need to use parentheses when calling functions, but F# programmers often use them to define which function should be applied to which arguments. Consider the simple case where you want to add four numbers using the add function. You could bind the result of each function call to new identifier, but for such a simple calculation, this would be very cumbersome:

```
let add x y = x + y

let result1 = add 4 5
let result2 = add 6 7

let finalResult = add result1 result2
```

Instead, it often better to pass the result of one function directly to the next function. To do this, you use parentheses to show which parameters are associated with which functions:

```
let add x y = x + y

let result =
    add (add 4 5) (add 6 7)
```

Here, the second and third occurrences of the add function are grouped with the parameters 4, 5 and 6, 7, respectively, and the first occurrence of the add function will act on the results of the other two functions.

F# also offers another way to compose functions, using the *pipe-forward* operator (|>). This operator has the following definition:

```
let (|>) x f = f x
```

This simply means it takes a parameter, x, and applies that to the given function, f, so that the parameter is now given before the function. The following example shows a parameter, 0.5, being applied to the function System.Math.Cos using the pipe-forward operator:

```
let result = 0.5 |> System.Math.Cos
```

This reversal can be useful in some circumstances, especially when you want to chain many functions together. Here is the previous add function example rewritten using the pipe-forward operator:

```
let add x y = x + y

let result = add 6 7 |> add 4 |> add 5
```

Some programmers think this style is more readable, as it has the effect of making the code read in a more right-to-left manner. The code should now be read as "add 6 to 7, then forward this result to the next function, which will add 4, and then forward this result to a function that will add 5." A more detailed explanation of where it's appropriate to use this style of function application can be found in Chapter 4.

This example also takes advantage of the capability to partially apply functions in F#, as discussed in the next section.

Partial Application of Functions

F# supports the partial application of functions (these are sometimes called *partial* or *curried* functions). This means you don't need to pass all the arguments to a function at once. Notice that the final example in the previous section passes a single argument to the add function, which takes two arguments. This is very much related to the idea that functions are values.

Because a function is just a value, if it doesn't receive all its arguments at once, it returns a value that is a new function waiting for the rest of the arguments. So, in the example, passing just the value 4 to the add function results in a new function, which I named addFour, because it takes one parameter and adds the value 4 to it. At first glance, this idea can look uninteresting and unhelpful, but it is a powerful part of functional programming that you'll see used throughout the book.

This behavior may not always be appropriate. For example, if the function takes two floating-point parameters that represent a point, it may not be desirable to have these numbers passed to the function separately, because they both make up the point they represent. You may alternatively surround a function's parameters with parentheses and separate them with commas, turning them into a *tuple*. You can see this in the following code:

```
let sub (a, b) = a - b

let subFour = sub 4
```

When attempting to compile this example, you will receive the following error message:

```
prog.fs(15,19): error: FS0001: This expression has type
    int
but is here used with type
    'a * 'b
```

This example will not compile because the sub function requires both parameters to be given at once. sub now has only one parameter, the tuple (a, b), instead of two, and although the call to sub in the second line provides only one argument, it's not a tuple. So, the program does not type check, as the code is trying to pass an integer to a function that takes a tuple. Tuples are discussed in more detail in the "Defining Types" section later in this chapter.

In general, functions that can be partially applied are preferred over functions that use tuples. This is because functions that can be partially applied are more flexible than tuples, giving users of the function more choices about how to use them. This is especially true when creating a library to be used by other programmers. You may not be able to anticipate all the ways your users will want to use your functions, so it is best to give them the flexibility of functions that can be partially applied.

Pattern Matching

Pattern matching allows you to look at the value of an identifier and then make different computations depending on its value. It might be compared to the switch statement in C++ and C#, but it is much more powerful and flexible. Programs that are written in the functional style tend to be written as series of transformations applied to the input data. Pattern matching allows you to analyze the input data and decided which transformation should be applied to it, so pattern matching fits in well with programming in the functional style.

The pattern-matching construct in F# allows you to pattern match over a variety of types and values. It also has several different forms and crops up in several places in the language, including its exception-handling syntax, which is discussed in the "Exceptions and Exception Handling" section later in this chapter.

The simplest form of pattern matching is matching over a value. You have already seen this earlier in this chapter, in the "Recursion" section, where it was used to implement a function that generated numbers in the Fibonacci sequence. To illustrate the syntax, the next example shows an implementation of a function that will produce the Lucas numbers, a sequence of numbers as follows: 1, 3, 4, 7, 11, 18, 29, 47, 76, …. The Lucas sequence has the same definition as the Fibonacci sequence; only the starting points are different.

```
// definition of Lucas numbers using pattern matching
let rec luc x =
    match x with
    | x when x <= 0 -> failwith "value must be greater than 0"
    | 1 -> 1
    | 2 -> 3
    | x -> luc (x - 1) + luc (x - 2)

// call the function and print the results
printfn "(luc 2) = %i" (luc 2)
printfn "(luc 6) = %i" (luc 6)
printfn "(luc 11) = %i" (luc 11)
printfn "(luc 12) = %i" (luc 12)
```

The results of this example, when compiled and executed, are as follows:

```
(luc 2) = 3
(luc 6) = 18
(luc 11) = 199
(luc 12) = 322
```

The syntax for pattern matching uses the keyword match, followed by the identifier that will be matched, then the keyword with, then all the possible matching rules separated by vertical bars (|). In the simplest case, a rule consists of either a constant or an identifier, followed by an arrow (->), and then by the expression to be used when the value matches the rule. In this definition of the function luc, the second two cases are literals—the values 1 and 2—and these will be replaced with the values 1 and 3, respectively. The fourth case will match any value of x greater than 2, and this will cause two further calls to the luc function.

The rules are matched in the order in which they are defined, and the compiler will issue an error if pattern matching is incomplete; that is, if there is some possible input value that will not match any rule. This would be the case in the luc function if you had omitted the final rule, because any values of x greater than 2 would not match any rule. The compiler will also issue a warning if there are any rules that will never be matched, typically because there is another rule in front of them that is more general. This would be the case in the luc function if the fourth rule were moved ahead of the first rule. In this case, none of the other rules would ever be matched, because the first rule would match any value of x.

You can add a when guard (as in the first rule in the example) to give precise control about when a rule fires. A when guard is composed of the keyword when followed by a Boolean expression. Once the rule is matched, the when clause is evaluated, and the rule will fire only if the expression evaluates to true. If the expression evaluates to false, the remaining rules will be searched for another match. The first rule is designed to be the function's error handler. The first part of the rule is an identifier that will match any integer, but the when guard means the rule will match only those integers that are less than or equal to zero.

If you want, you can omit the first |. This can be useful when the pattern match is small and you want to fit it on one line. You can see this in the next example, which also demonstrates the use of the underscore (_) as a *wildcard*.

```
let booleanToString x =
    match x with false -> "False" | _ -> "True"
```

The _ will match any value and is a way of telling the compiler that you're not interested in using this value. For example, in this booleanToString function, you do not need to use the constant true in the second rule, because if the first rule is matched, you know that the value of x will be true. Moreover, you do not need to use x to derive the string "True", so you can ignore the value and just use _ as a wildcard.

Another useful feature of pattern matching is that you can combine two patterns into one rule through the use of the vertical bar (|). The next example, stringToBoolean, demonstrates this.

```
// function for converting a boolean to a string
let booleanToString x =
    match x with false -> "False" | _ -> "True"

// function for converting a string to a boolean
let stringToBoolean x =
    match x with
    | "True" | "true" -> true
    | "False" | "false" -> false
    | _ -> failwith "unexpected input"

// call the functions and print the results
printfn "(booleanToString true) = %s"
    (booleanToString true)
printfn "(booleanToString false) = %s"
    (booleanToString false)
printfn "(stringToBoolean \"True\") = %b"
    (stringToBoolean "True")
```

```
printfn "(stringToBoolean \"false\") = %b"
    (stringToBoolean "false")
printfn "(stringToBoolean \"Hello\") = %b"
    (stringToBoolean "Hello")
```

The first two rules have two strings that should evaluate to the same value, so rather than having two separate rules, you can just use | between the two patterns. The results of this examples, when compiled and executed, are as follows:

```
(booleanToString true) = True
(booleanToString false) = False
(stringToBoolean "True") = true
(stringToBoolean "false") = false
Microsoft.FSharp.Core.FailureException: unexpected input
    at FSI_0005.stringToBoolean(String x)
    at <StartupCode$FSI_0005>.$FSI_0005.main@()
```

It is also possible to pattern match over most of the types defined by F#. The next two examples demonstrate pattern matching over tuples, with two functions that implement a Boolean And and Or using pattern matching. Each takes a slightly different approach.

```
let myOr b1 b2 =
    match b1, b2 with
    | true, _ -> true
    | _, true -> true
    | _ -> false

let myAnd p =
    match p with
    | true, true -> true
    | _ -> false

printfn "(myOr true false) = %b" (myOr true false)
printfn "(myOr false false) = %b" (myOr false false)
printfn "(myAnd (true, false)) = %b" (myAnd (true, false))
printfn "(myAnd (true, true)) = %b" (myAnd (true, true))
```

The results of these examples, when compiled and executed, are as follows:

```
(myOr true false) = true
(myOr false false) = false
(myAnd (true, false)) = false
(myAnd (true, true)) = true
```

The myOr function has two Boolean parameters, which are placed between the match and with keywords and separated by commas to form a tuple. The myAnd function has one parameter, which is itself a tuple. Either way, the syntax for creating pattern matches for tuples is the same and similar to the syntax for creating tuples.

If it's necessary to match values within the tuple, the constants or identifiers are separated by commas, and the position of the identifier or constant defines what it matches within the tuple. This is shown in the first and second rules of the myOr function and in the first rule of the myAnd function. These rules match parts of the tuples with constants, but you could use identifiers if you want to work with the separate parts of the tuple later in the rule definition. Just because you're working with tuples doesn't mean you always need to look at the various parts that make up the tuple.

The third rule of myOr and the second rule of myAnd show the whole tuple matched with a single _ wildcard character. This, too, could be replaced with an identifier if you want to work with the value in the second half of the rule definition.

Because pattern matching is such a common task in F#, the language provides alternative shorthand syntax. If the sole purpose of a function is to pattern match over something, then it may be worth using this syntax. In this version of the pattern-matching syntax, you use the keyword function, place the pattern where the function's parameters would usually go, and then separate all the alternative rules with |. The next example shows this syntax in action in a simple function that recursively processes a list of strings and concatenates them into a single string.

```
// concatenate a list of strings into single string
let rec conactStringList =
    function head :: tail -> head + conactStringList tail
           | [] -> ""

// test data
let jabber = ["'Twas "; "brillig, "; "and "; "the "; "slithy "; "toves "; "..."]
// call the function
let completJabber = conactStringList jabber
// print the result
printfn "%s" completJabber
```

The results of this example, when compiled and executed, are as follows:

```
'Twas brillig, and the slithy toves ...
```

Pattern matching is one of the fundamental building blocks of F#, and we'll return to it several times in this chapter. We'll look at pattern matching over lists, with record types and union types, and with exception handling. The most advanced use of pattern matching is discussed in the "Active Patterns" section toward the end of the chapter. You can find details of how to pattern match over types from non-F# libraries in Chapters 4.

Control Flow

F# has a strong notion of *control flow*. In this way. it differs from many pure functional languages, where the notion of control flow is very loose, because expressions can be evaluated in essentially any order. The strong notion of control flow is apparent in the if … then … else … expression.

In F#, the if … then … else … construct is an expression, meaning it returns a value. One of two different values will be returned, depending on the value of the Boolean expression between the if and then keywords. The next example illustrates this. The if … then … else … expression is evaluated to return either "heads" or "tails", depending on whether the program is run on an even second or an odd second.

```
let result =
    if System.DateTime.Now.Second % 2 = 0 then
        "heads"
    else
        "tails"

printfn "%A" result
```

It's interesting to note that the if … then … else … expression is just a convenient shorthand for pattern matching over a Boolean value. So the previous example could be rewritten as follows:

```
let result =
    match System.DateTime.Now.Second % 2 = 0 with
    | true -> "heads"
    | false ->  "tails"
```

The if … then … else … expression has some implications that you might not expect if you are more familiar with imperative-style programming. F#'s type system requires that the values being returned by the if … then … else … expression must be the same type, or the compiler will generate an error. So, if in the previous example, you replaced the string "tails" with an integer or Boolean value, you would get a compile error. If you really require the values to be of different types, you can create an if … then … else … expression of type obj (F#'s version of System.Object), as shown in the next example, which prints either "heads" or false to the console.

```
let result =
    if System.DateTime.Now.Second % 2 = 0 then
        box "heads"
    else
        box false

printfn "%A" result
```

Imperative programmers may be surprised that an if … then … else … expression must have an else if the expression returns a value. This is pretty logical when you think about it and considering the examples you've just seen. If the else were removed from the code, the identifier result could not be assigned a value when the if evaluated to false, and having uninitialized identifiers is something that F# (and functional programming in general) aims to avoid. There is a way for a program to contain an if …

then expression without the else, but this is very much in the style of imperative programming, so I discuss it in Chapter 4.

Lists

F# *lists* are simple collection types that are built into F#. An F# list can be an *empty list*, represented by square brackets ([ ]), or it can be another list with a value concatenated to it. You concatenate values to the front of an F# list using a built-in operator that consists of two colons (::), pronounced "cons." The next example shows some lists being defined, starting with an empty list on the first line, followed by two lists where strings are placed at the front by concatenation:

```
let emptyList = []
let oneItem = "one " :: []
let twoItem = "one " :: "two " :: []
```

The syntax to add items to a list by concatenation is a little verbose, so if you just want to define a list, you can use shorthand. In this shorthand notation, you place the list items between square brackets and separate them with a semicolon (;), as follows:

```
let shortHand = ["apples "; "pears"]
```

Another F# operator that works on lists is the at symbol (@), which you can use to concatenate two lists together, as follows:

```
let twoLists = ["one, "; "two, "] @ ["buckle "; "my "; "shoe "]
```

All items in an F# list must be of the same type. If you try to place items of different types in a list— for example, you try to concatenate a string to a list of integers—you will get a compile error. If you need a list of mixed types, you can create a list of type obj (the F# equivalent of System.Object), as in the following code:

```
// the empty list
let emptyList = []

// list of one item
let oneItem = "one " :: []

// list of two items
let twoItem = "one " :: "two " :: []

// list of two items
let shortHand = ["apples "; "pairs "]

// concatenation of two lists
let twoLists = ["one, "; "two, "] @ ["buckle "; "my "; "shoe "]
// list of objects
let objList = [box 1; box 2.0; box "three"]
```

```
// print the lists
let main() =
    printfn "%A" emptyList
    printfn "%A" oneItem
    printfn "%A" twoItem
    printfn "%A" shortHand
    printfn "%A" twoLists
    printfn "%A" objList

// call the main function
main()
```

The results of this example, when compiled and executed, are as follows:

```
[]
["one "]
["one "; "two "]
["apples "; "pairs "]
["one, "; "two, "; "buckle "; "my "; "shoe "]
[1; 2.0; "three"]
```

I discuss types in F# in more detail in the "Types and Type Inference" section later in this chapter.

F# lists are *immutable*; in other words, once a list is created, it cannot be altered. The functions and operators that act on lists do not alter them, but they create a new, modified version of the list, leaving the old list available for later use if needed. The next example shows this.

```
// create a list of one item
let one = ["one "]
// create a list of two items
let two = "two " :: one
// create a list of three items
let three = "three " :: two

// reverse the list of three items
let rightWayRound = List.rev three

// function to print the results
let main() =
    printfn "%A" one
    printfn "%A" two
    printfn "%A" three
    printfn "%A" rightWayRound
// call the main function
main()
```

An F# list containing a single string is created, and then two more lists are created, each using the previous one as a base. Finally, the List.rev function is applied to the last list to create a new reversed list. When you print these lists, it is easy to see that all the original lists remain unaltered:

```
["one "]
["two "; "one "]
["three "; "two "; "one "]
["one "; "two "; "three "]
```

Pattern Matching Against Lists

The regular way to work with F# lists is to use pattern matching and recursion. The pattern-matching syntax for pulling the head item off a list is the same as the syntax for concatenating an item to a list. The pattern is formed by the identifier representing the head, followed by :: and then the identifier for the rest of the list. You can see this in the first rule of concatList in the next example. You can also pattern match against list constants; you can see this in the second rule of concatList, where there is an empty list.

```
// list to be concatenated
let listOfList = [[2; 3; 5]; [7; 11; 13]; [17; 19; 23; 29]]

// definition of a concatenation function
let rec concatList l =
    match l with
    | head :: tail -> head @ (concatList tail)
    | [] -> []

// call the function
let primes = concatList listOfList

// print the results
printfn "%A" primes
```

The results of this example, when compiled and executed, are as follows:

```
[2; 3; 5; 7; 11; 13; 17; 19; 23; 29]
```

Taking the head from a list, processing it, and then recursively processing the tail of the list is the most common way of dealing with lists via pattern matching, but it certainly isn't the only thing you can do with pattern matching and lists. The following example shows a few other uses of this combination of features.

```
// function that attempts to find various sequences
let rec findSequence l =
    match l with
```

```
    // match a list containing exactly 3 numbers
    | [x; y; z] ->
        printfn "Last 3 numbers in the list were %i %i %i"
            x y z
    // match a list of 1, 2, 3 in a row
    | 1 :: 2 :: 3 :: tail ->
        printfn "Found sequence 1, 2, 3 within the list"
        findSequence tail
    // if neither case matches and items remain
    // recursively call the function
    | head :: tail -> findSequence tail
    // if no items remain terminate
    | [] -> ()

// some test data
let testSequence = [1; 2; 3; 4; 5; 6; 7; 8; 9; 8; 7; 6; 5; 4; 3; 2; 1]

// call the function
findSequence testSequence
```

The first rule demonstrates how to match a list of a fixed length—in this case, a list of three items. Here, identifiers are used to grab the values of these items so they can be printed to the console. The second rule looks at the first three items in the list to see whether they are the sequence of integers 1, 2, 3; and if they are, it prints a message to the console. The final two rules are the standard head/tail treatment of a list, designed to work their way through the list, doing nothing if there is no match with the first two rules.

The results of this example, when compiled and executed, are as follows:

```
Found sequence 1, 2, 3 within the list
Last 3 numbers in the list were 3 2 1
```

Although pattern matching is a powerful tool for the analysis of data in lists, it's often not necessary to use it directly. The F# libraries provide a number of higher-order functions for working with lists that implement the pattern matching for you, so you don't need repeat the code. To illustrate this, imagine you need to write a function that adds one to every item in a list. You can easily write this using pattern matching:

```
let rec addOneAll list =
    match list with
    | head :: rest ->
        head + 1 :: addOneAll rest
    | [] -> []

printfn "(addOneAll [1; 2; 3]) = %A" (addOneAll [1; 2; 3])
```

The results of this example, when compiled and executed, are as follows:

```
(addOneAll [1; 2; 3]) = [2; 3; 4]
```

However, the code is perhaps a little more verbose than you would like for such a simple problem. The clue to solving this comes from noticing that adding one to every item in the list is just an example of a more general problem: the need to apply some transformation to every item in a list. The F# core library contains a function map, which is defined in the List module. It has the following definition:

```
let rec map func list =
    match list with
    | head :: rest ->
        func head :: map func rest
    | [] -> []
```

You can see that the map function has a very similar structure to the addOneAll function from the previous example. If the list is not empty, you take the head item of the list and apply the function, func, that you are given as a parameter. This is then appended to the results of recursively calling map on the rest of the list. If the list is empty, you simply return the empty list. The map function can then be used to implement adding one to all items in a list in a much more concise manner:

```
let result = List.map ((+) 1) [1; 2; 3]

printfn "List.map ((+) 1) [1; 2; 3] = %A" result
```

The results of this example, when compiled and executed, are as follows:

```
(List.map ((+) 1) [1; 2; 3]) = [2; 3; 4]
```

Also note that this example uses the add operator as a function by surrounding it with parentheses, as described earlier in this chapter in the "Operators" section. This function is then partially applied by passing its first parameter but not its second. This creates a function that takes an integer and returns an integer, which is passed to the map function.

The List module contains many other interesting functions for working with lists, such as List.filter and List.fold. These are explained in more detail in Chapter 7, which describes the libraries available with F#.

List Comprehensions

List comprehensions make creating and converting collections easy. You can create F# lists, sequences, and arrays directly using comprehension syntax. I cover arrays in more detail in the next chapter. *Sequences* are collections of type seq, which is F#'s name for the .NET BCL's IEnumerable type. I describe them in the "Lazy Evaluation" section later in this chapter.

The simplest comprehensions specify ranges, where you write the first item you want, either a number or a letter, followed by two periods (..), and then the last item you want, all within square brackets (to create a list) or braces (to create a sequence). The compiler then does the work of calculating all the items in the collection, taking the first number and incrementing it by 1, or similarly with characters, until it reaches the last item specified. The following example demonstrates how to create a list of numbers from 0 through 9 and a sequence of the characters from A through Z:

```
// create some list comprehensions
let numericList = [ 0 .. 9 ]
let alpherSeq = seq { 'A' .. 'Z' }

// print them
printfn "%A" numericList
printfn "%A" alpherSeq
```

The results of this example are as follows:

```
[0; 1; 2; 3; 4; 5; 6; 7; 8; 9]
seq ['A'; 'B'; 'C'; 'D'; ...]
```

To create more interesting collections, you can also specify a step size for incrementing numbers (note that characters do not support this type of list comprehension). You place the step size between the first and last items, separated by an extra pair of periods (..). The next example shows a list containing multiples of 3, followed by a list that counts backward from 9 to 0:

```
// create some list comprehensions
let multiplesOfThree = [ 0 .. 3 .. 30 ]
let revNumericSeq = [ 9 .. -1 .. 0 ]

// print them
printfn "%A" multiplesOfThree
printfn "%A" revNumericSeq
```

The results of this example are as follows:

```
[0; 3; 6; 9; 12; 15; 18; 21; 24; 27; 30]
[9; 8; 7; 6; 5; 4; 3; 2; 1; 0]
```

List comprehensions also allow loops to create a collection from another collection. The idea is that you enumerate the old collection, transform each of its items, and place any generated items in the new collection. To specify such a loop, use the keyword for, followed by an identifier, followed by the keyword in, at the beginning of the list comprehension. The next example creates a sequence of the squares of the first ten positive integers.

```
// a sequence of squares
let squares =
    seq { for x in 1 .. 10 -> x * x }
// print the sequence
printfn "%A" squares
```

The example uses for to enumerate the collection 1 .. 10, assigning each item in turn to the identifier x. It then uses the identifier x to calculate the new item, in this case multiplying x by itself to square it. The results of this example are as follows:

```
seq [1; 4; 9; 16; ...]
```

The use of the F# keyword yield gives you a lot of flexibility when defining list comprehensions. The yield keyword allows you to decide whether or not a particular item should be added to the collection. For example, consider the following example:

```
// a sequence of even numbers
let evens n =
    seq { for x in 1 .. n do
            if x % 2 = 0 then yield x }

// print the sequence
printfn "%A" (evens 10)
```

The goal is to create a collection of even numbers. So you test each number in the collection you are enumerating to see if it is a multiple of two. If it is, you return it using the yield keyword; otherwise, you perform no action. The results of this example are as follows:

```
seq [2; 4; 6; 8; ...]
```

It's also possible to use list comprehensions to iterate in two or more dimensions by using a separate loop for each dimension. The next example defines a function called squarePoints that creates a sequence of points forming a square grid, each point represented by a tuple of two integers.

```
// sequence of tuples representing points
let squarePoints n =
    seq { for x in 1 .. n do
            for y in 1 .. n do
                yield x, y }

// print the sequence
printfn "%A" (squarePoints 3)
```

The results of this example are as follows:

```
seq [(1, 1); (1, 2); (1, 3); (2, 1); ...]
```

You'll look at using comprehensions with arrays and collections from the .NET Framework BCL in Chapter 4.

Types and Type Inference

F# is a *strongly typed* language, which means you cannot use a function with a value that is inappropriate. You cannot call a function that has a string as a parameter with an integer argument; you must explicitly convert between the two. The way the language treats the type of its values is referred to as its *type system*. F# has a type system that does not get in the way of routine programming. In F#, all values have a type, and this includes values that are functions.

Ordinarily, you don't need to explicitly declare types; the compiler will work out the type of a value from the types of the literals in the function and the resulting types of other functions it calls. If everything is OK, the compiler will keep the types to itself; only if there is a type mismatch will the compiler inform you by reporting a compile error. This process is generally referred to as *type inference*. If you want to know more about the types in a program, you can make the compiler display all inferred types with the –i switch. Visual Studio users get tooltips that show types when they hover the mouse pointer over an identifier.

The way type inference works in F# is fairly easy to understand. The compiler works through the program, assigning types to identifiers as they are defined, starting with the top leftmost identifier and working its way down to the bottom rightmost. It assigns types based on the types it already knows—that is, the types of literals and (more commonly) the types of functions defined in other source files or assemblies.

The next example defines two F# identifiers and then shows their inferred types displayed on the console with the F# compiler's –i switch.

```
let aString = "Spring time in Paris"
let anInt = 42
```

```
val aString : string
val anInt : int
```

The types of these two identifiers are unsurprising—string and int, respectively. The syntax used by the compiler to describe them is fairly straightforward: the keyword val (meaning "value") and then the identifier, a colon, and finally the type.

The definition of the function makeMessage in the next example is a little more interesting.

```
let makeMessage x = (Printf.sprintf "%i" x) + " days to spring time"
let half x = x / 2
```

```
val makeMessage : int -> string
val half : int -> int
```

Note that the makeMessage function's definition is prefixed with the keyword val, just like the two values you saw before; even though it is a function, the F# compiler still considers it to be a value. Also, the type itself uses the notation int -> string, meaning a function that takes an integer and returns a string. The -> between the type names (an *ASCII arrow*, or just *arrow*) represents the transformation of the function being applied. The arrow represents a transformation of the value, but not necessarily the type, because it can represent a function that transforms a value into a value of the same type, as shown in the half function on the second line.

The types of functions that can be partially applied and functions that take tuples differ. The following functions, div1 and div2, illustrate this.

```
let div1 x y = x / y
let div2 (x, y) = x / y

let divRemainder x y = x / y, x % y
```

```
val div1 : int -> int -> int
val div2 : int * int -> int
val divRemainder : int -> int -> int * int
```

The function div1 can be partially applied, and its type is int -> int -> int, representing that the arguments can be passed in separately. Compare this with the function div2, which has the type int * int -> int, meaning a function that takes a pair of integers—a tuple of integers—and turns them into a single integer. You can see this in the function div_remainder, which performs integer division and also returns the remainder at the same time. Its type is int -> int -> int * int, meaning a curried function that returns an integer tuple.

The next function, doNothing, looks inconspicuous enough, but it is quite interesting from a typing point of view.

```
let doNothing x = x
```

```
val doNothing : 'a -> 'a
```

This function has the type 'a -> 'a, meaning it takes a value of one type and returns a value of the same type. Any type that begins with a single quotation mark (') means a *variable* type. F# has a type, obj, that maps to System.Object and represents a value of any type, a concept that you will probably be familiar with from other languages common language runtime (CLR)–based programming languages (and indeed, many languages that do not target the CLR). However, a variable type is not the same. Notice how the type has an 'a on both sides of the arrow. This means that, even though the compiler does not yet know the type, it knows that the type of the return value will be the same as the type of the argument. This feature of the type system, sometimes referred to as *type parameterization*, allows the compiler to find more type errors at compile time and can help avoid casting.

■**Note** The concept of a variable type, or type parameterization, is closely related to the concept of *generics* that were introduced in CLR version 2.0 and have now become part of the ECMA specification for CLI version 2.0. When F# targets a CLI that has generics enabled, it takes full advantage of them by using them anywhere it finds an undetermined type. Don Syme, the creator of F#, designed and implemented generics in the .NET CLR before he started working on F#. One might be tempted to infer that he did this so he could create F#!

The function doNothingToAnInt, shown next, is an example of a value being constrained—a *type constraint*. In this case, the function parameter x is constrained to be an int. It is possible to constrain any identifier, not just function parameters, to be of a certain type, though it is more typical to need to constrain parameters. The list stringList here shows how to constrain an identifier that is not a function parameter.

```
let doNothingToAnInt (x: int) = x
let intList = [1; 2; 3]

let (stringList: list<string>) = ["one"; "two"; "three"]
```

```
val doNothingToAnInt _int : int -> int
val intList : int list
val stringList : string list
```

The syntax for constraining a value to be of a certain type is straightforward. Within parentheses, the identifier name is followed by a colon (:), followed by the type name. This is also sometimes called a *type annotation*.

The intList value is a list of integers, and the identifier's type is int list. This indicates that the compiler has recognized that the list contains only integers, and in this case, the type of its items is not undetermined but is int. Any attempt to add anything other than values of type int to the list will result in a compile error.

The identifier stringList has a type annotation. Although this is unnecessary, since the compiler can resolve the type from the value, it is used to show an alternative syntax for working with undetermined types. You can place the type between angle brackets after the type that it is associated with instead of just writing it before the type name. Note that even though the type of stringList is constrained to be list<string> (a list of strings), the compiler still reports its type as string list when displaying the type, and they mean exactly the same thing. This syntax is supported to make F# types with a type parameter look like generic types from other .NET libraries.

Constraining values is not usually necessary when writing pure F#, though it can occasionally be useful. It's most useful when using .NET libraries written in languages other than F# and for interoperation with unmanaged libraries. In both these cases, the compiler has less type information, so it is often necessary to give it enough information to disambiguate things.

Defining Types

The type system in F# provides a number of features for defining custom types. All of F#'s type definitions fall into two categories:

- *Tuples* or *records*, which are a set of types composed to form a composite type (similar to structs in C or classes in C#)

- *Sum* types, sometimes referred to as *union* types

Tuple and Record Types

Tuples are a way of quickly and conveniently composing values into a group of values. Values are separated by commas and can then be referred to by one identifier, as shown in the first line of the next example. You can then retrieve the values by doing the reverse, as shown in the second and third lines, where identifiers separated by commas appear on the left side of the equal sign, with each identifier receiving a single value from the tuple. If you want to ignore a value in the tuple, you can use _ to tell the compiler you are not interested in the value, as in the second and third lines.

```
let pair = true, false
let b1, _ = pair
let _, b2 = pair
```

Tuples are different from most user-defined types in F# because you do not need to explicitly declare them using the type keyword. To define a type, you use the type keyword, followed by the type name, an equal sign, and then the type you are defining. In its simplest form, you can use this to give an alias to any existing type, including tuples. Giving aliases to single types is not often useful, but giving aliases to tuples can be very useful, especially when you want to use a tuple as a type constraint. The next example shows how to give an alias to a single type and a tuple, and also how to use an alias as a type constraint.

```
type Name = string
type Fullname = string * string

let fullNameToSting (x: Fullname) =
    let first, second = x in
    first + " " + second
```

Record types are similar to tuples in that they compose multiple types into a single type. The difference is that in record types, each *field* is named. The next example illustrates the syntax for defining record types.

```
// define an organization with unique fields
type Organization1 = { boss: string; lackeys: string list }
// create an instance of this organization
let rainbow =
    { boss = "Jeffrey";
      lackeys = ["Zippy"; "George"; "Bungle"] }

// define two organizations with overlapping fields
type Organization2 = { chief: string; underlings: string list }
type Organization3 = { chief: string; indians: string list }

// create an instance of Organization2
let (thePlayers: Organization2) =
    { chief = "Peter Quince";
      underlings = ["Francis Flute"; "Robin Starveling";
                    "Tom Snout"; "Snug"; "Nick Bottom"] }
// create an instance of Organization3
let (wayneManor: Organization3) =
    { chief = "Batman";
      indians = ["Robin"; "Alfred"] }
```

You place field definitions between braces and separate them with semicolons. A field definition is composed of the field name followed by a colon and the field's type. The type definition Organization1 is a record type where the field names are unique. This means you can use a simple syntax to create an instance of this type where there is no need to mention the type name when it is created. To create a record, you place the field names followed by equal signs and the field values between braces ({}), as shown in the Rainbow identifier.

F# does not force field names to be unique, so sometimes the compiler cannot infer the type of a field from the field names alone. In such a case, the compiler cannot infer the type of the record. To create records with nonunique fields, the compiler needs to statically know the type of the record being created. If the compiler cannot infer the type of the record, you need to use a type annotation, as described in the previous section. Using a type annotation is illustrated by the types Organization2 and Organization3, and their instances thePlayers and wayneManor. You can see the type of the identifier given explicitly just after its name.

Accessing the fields in a record is fairly straightforward. You simply use the syntax record identifier name, followed by a dot, followed by field name. The following example illustrates this, showing how to access the chief field of the Organization record.

```
// define an organization type
type Organization = { chief: string; indians: string list }

// create an instance of this type
let wayneManor =
    { chief = "Batman";
      indians = ["Robin"; "Alfred"] }

// access a field from this type
printfn "wayneManor.chief = %s" wayneManor.chief
```

Records are immutable by default. To an imperative programmer, this may sound like records are not very useful, since there will inevitably be situations where you need to change a value in a field. For this purpose, F# provides a simple syntax for creating a copy of a record with updated fields. To create a copy of a record, place the name of that record between braces, followed by the keyword with, followed by a list of fields to be changed, with their updated values. The advantage of this is that you don't need to retype the list of fields that have not changed. The following example demonstrates this approach. It creates an initial version of wayneManor and then creates wayneManor', in which "Robin" has been removed.

```
// define an organization type
type Organization = { chief: string; indians: string list }

// create an instance of this type
let wayneManor =
    { chief = "Batman";
      indians = ["Robin"; "Alfred"] }
// create a modified instance of this type
let wayneManor' =
    { wayneManor with indians = [ "Alfred" ] }

// print out the two organizations
printfn "wayneManor = %A" wayneManor
printfn "wayneManor' = %A" wayneManor'
```

The results of this example, when compiled and executed, are as follows:

```
wayneManor = {chief = "Batman";
 indians = ["Robin"; "Alfred"];}
wayneManor' = {chief = "Batman";
 indians = ["Alfred"];}
```

Another way to access the fields in a record is using pattern matching; that is, you can use pattern matching to match fields within the record type. As you would expect, the syntax for examining a record using pattern matching is similar to the syntax used to construct it. You can compare a field to a constant with *field = constant*. You can assign the values of fields with identifiers with *field = identifier*. You can ignore a field with *field = _*. The findDavid function in the next example illustrates using pattern matching to access the fields in a record.

```
// type representing a couple
type Couple = { him : string ; her : string }

// list of couples
let couples =
    [ { him = "Brad" ; her = "Angelina" };
      { him = "Becks" ; her = "Posh" };
      { him = "Chris" ; her = "Gwyneth" };
      { him = "Michael" ; her = "Catherine" } ]

// function to find "David" from a list of couples
let rec findDavid l =
    match l with
    | { him = x ; her = "Posh" } :: tail -> x
    | _ :: tail -> findDavid tail
    | [] -> failwith "Couldn't find David"

// print the results
printfn "%A" (findDavid couples)
```

The first rule in the findDavid function is the one that does the real work, checking the her field of the record to see whether it is "Posh", David's wife. The him field is associated with the identifier x so it can be used in the second half of the rule.

The results of this example, when compiled and executed, are as follows:

```
Becks
```

It's important to note that you can use only literal values when you pattern match over records like this. So, if you wanted to generalize the function to allow you to change the person you are searching for, you would need to use a when guard in your pattern matching:

```
let rec findPartner soughtHer l =
    match l with
    | { him = x ; her = her } :: tail when her = soughtHer -> x
    | _ :: tail -> findPartner soughtHer tail
    | [] -> failwith "Couldn't find him"
```

Field values can also be functions. Since this technique is mainly used in conjunction with a mutable state to form values similar to objects, I will cover that usage in Chapter 5.

Union or Sum Types

Union types, sometimes called *sum types* or *discriminated unions*, are a way of bringing together data that may have a different meaning or structure.

You define a union type using the type keyword, followed by the type name, followed by an equal sign, just as with all type definitions. Then comes the definition of the different *constructors*, separated by vertical bars. The first vertical bar is optional.

A constructor is composed of a name that must start with a capital letter, which is intended to avoid the common bug of getting constructor names mixed up with identifier names. The name can optionally be followed by the keyword of and then the types that make up that constructor. Multiple types that make up a constructor are separated by asterisks. The names of constructors within a type must be unique. If several union types are defined, then the names of their constructors can overlap; however, you should be careful when doing this, because it can be that further type annotations are required when constructing and consuming union types.

The next example defines a type Volume whose values can have three different meanings: liter, US pint, or imperial pint. Although the structure of the data is the same and is represented by a float, the meanings are quite different. Mixing up the meaning of data in an algorithm is a common cause of bugs in programs, and the Volume type is, in part, an attempt to avoid this.

```
type Volume =
    | Liter of float
    | UsPint of float
    | ImperialPint of float

let vol1 = Liter 2.5
let vol2 = UsPint 2.5
let vol3 = ImperialPint (2.5)
```

The syntax for constructing a new instance of a union type is the constructor name followed by the values for the types, with multiple values separated by commas. Optionally, you can place the values in parentheses. You use the three different Volume constructors to construct three different identifiers: vol1, vol2, and vol3.

To deconstruct the values of union types into their basic parts, you always use pattern matching. When pattern matching over a union type, the constructors make up the first half of the pattern-matching rules. You don't need a complete list of rules, but if the list is incomplete, there must be a default rule, using either an identifier or a wildcard to match all remaining rules. The first part of a rule for a constructor consists of the constructor name followed by identifiers or wildcards to match the various values within it. The following convertVolumeToLiter, convertVolumeUsPint, and convertVolumeImperialPint functions demonstrate this syntax:

```
// type representing volumes
type Volume =
    | Liter of float
    | UsPint of float
    | ImperialPint of float

// various kinds of volumes
let vol1 = Liter 2.5
let vol2 = UsPint 2.5
let vol3 = ImperialPint 2.5

// some functions to convert between volumes
let convertVolumeToLiter x =
    match x with
    | Liter x -> x
    | UsPint x -> x * 0.473
    | ImperialPint x -> x * 0.568
let convertVolumeUsPint x =
    match x with
    | Liter x -> x * 2.113
    | UsPint x -> x
    | ImperialPint x -> x * 1.201
let convertVolumeImperialPint x =
    match x with
    | Liter x -> x * 1.760
    | UsPint x -> x * 0.833
    | ImperialPint x -> x

// a function to print a volume
let printVolumes x =
    printfn "Volume in liters = %f,
in us pints = %f,
in imperial pints = %f"
        (convertVolumeToLiter x)
        (convertVolumeUsPint x)
        (convertVolumeImperialPint x)

// print the results
printVolumes vol1
printVolumes vol2
printVolumes vol3
```

The results of these examples, when compiled and executed, are as follows:

```
Volume in liters = 2.500000,
in us pints = 5.282500,
in imperial pints = 4.400000
Volume in liters = 1.182500,
in us pints = 2.500000,
in imperial pints = 2.082500
Volume in liters = 1.420000,
in us pints = 3.002500,
in imperial pints = 2.500000
```

An alternative solution to this problem is to use F#'s units of measure. This is discussed in the "Units of Measure" section later in the chapter.

Type Definitions with Type Parameters

Both union and record types can be parameterized. Parameterizing a type means leaving one or more of the types within the type being defined to be determined later by the consumer of the types. This is a similar concept to the variable types discussed earlier in this chapter. When defining types, you must be a little more explicit about which types are variable.

F# supports two syntaxes for type parameterization. In the first, you place the type being parameterized between the keyword type and the name of the type, as follows:

```
type 'a BinaryTree =
| BinaryNode of 'a BinaryTree * 'a BinaryTree
| BinaryValue of 'a

let tree1 =
    BinaryNode(
        BinaryNode ( BinaryValue 1, BinaryValue 2),
        BinaryNode ( BinaryValue 3, BinaryValue 4) )
```

In the second syntax, you place the types being parameterized in angle brackets after the type name, as follows:

```
type Tree<'a> =
| Node of Tree<'a> list
| Value of 'a

let tree2 =
    Node( [ Node( [Value "one"; Value "two"] ) ;
        Node( [Value "three"; Value "four"] ) ] )
```

Like variable types, the names of type parameters always start with a single quote (') followed by an alphanumeric name for the type. Typically, just a single letter is used. If multiple parameterized types are required, you separate them with commas. You can then use the type parameters throughout the type definition. The previous examples defined two parameterized types using the two different syntaxes that F# offers. The BinaryTree type used OCaml-style syntax, where the type parameters are placed before the name of the type. The tree type used .NET-style syntax, with the type parameters in angle brackets after the type name.

The syntax for creating and consuming an instance of a parameterized type does not change from that of creating and consuming a nonparameterized type. This is because the compiler will automatically infer the type parameters of the parameterized type. You can see this in the following construction of tree1 and tree2, and their consumption by the functions printBinaryTreeValues and printTreeValues:

```
// definition of a binary tree
type 'a BinaryTree =
    | BinaryNode of 'a BinaryTree * 'a BinaryTree
    | BinaryValue of 'a

// create an instance of a binary tree
let tree1 =
    BinaryNode(
        BinaryNode ( BinaryValue 1, BinaryValue 2),
        BinaryNode ( BinaryValue 3, BinaryValue 4) )

// definition of a tree
type Tree<'a> =
    | Node of Tree<'a> list
    | Value of 'a

// create an instance of a tree
let tree2 =
    Node( [ Node( [Value "one"; Value "two"] ) ;
        Node( [Value "three"; Value "four"] ) ] )

// function to print the binary tree
let rec printBinaryTreeValues x =
    match x with
    | BinaryNode (node1, node2) ->
        printBinaryTreeValues node1
        printBinaryTreeValues node2
    | BinaryValue x ->
        printf "%A, " x

// function to print the tree
let rec printTreeValues x =
    match x with
    | Node l -> List.iter printTreeValues l
    | Value x ->
        printf "%A, " x
```

```
// print the results
printBinaryTreeValues tree1
printfn ""
printTreeValues tree2
```

The results of this example, when compiled and executed, are as follows:

```
1, 2, 3, 4,
"one", "two", "three", "four",
```

You may have noticed that although I've discussed defining types, creating instances of them, and examining these instances, I haven't discussed updating them. It is not possible to update these kinds of types, because the idea of a value that changes over time goes against the idea of functional programming. However, F# does have some types that are updatable, and I discuss them in Chapter 4.

Recursive Type Definitions

Ordinarily, the scope of a type definition is from where it is declared forward to the end of the source file in which it is declared. If a type needs to reference a type declared later, it cannot typically do so. The only reason you'll need to do this is if types are *mutually recursive*.

F# provides a special syntax for defining types that are mutually recursive. The types must be declared together, in the same block. Types declared in the same block must be declared next to each other; that is, without any value definitions in between, and the keyword type is replaced by the keyword and for every type definition after the first one.

Types declared in this way are not any different from types declared the regular way. They can reference any other type in the block, and they can even be mutually referential.

The next example shows how you might represent an XML tree in F#, using union types and record types. Two types in this example are mutually recursive, XmlElement and XmlTree, declared in the same block. If they were declared separately, XmlElement would not be able to reference XmlTree because XmlElement is declared before XmlTree; because their declarations are joined with the keyword and, XmlElement can have a field of type XmlTree.

```
// represents an XML attribute
type XmlAttribute =
    { AttribName: string;
      AttribValue: string; }


// represents an XML element
type XmlElement =
    { ElementName: string;
      Attributes: list<XmlAttribute>;
      InnerXml: XmlTree }
```

```
// represents an XML tree
and XmlTree =
    | Element of XmlElement
    | ElementList of list<XmlTree>
    | Text of string
    | Comment of string
    | Empty
```

Active Patterns

Active patterns provide a flexible new way to use F#'s pattern-matching constructs. They allow you to execute a function to see whether a match has occurred or not, which is why they are called *active*. Their design goal is to permit you to make better reuse of pattern-matching logic in your application.

All active patterns take an input and then perform some computation with that input to determine whether a match has occurred. There are two sorts of active patterns:

- *Complete active patterns* allow you to break a match down into a finite number of cases.

- *Partial active patterns* can either match or fail.

First, we'll look at complete active patterns.

Complete Active Patterns

The syntax for defining an active pattern is similar to the syntax for defining a function. The key difference is that the identifier that represents an active pattern is surrounded by *banana brackets*, which are formed of parentheses and vertical bars ((| |)). The names of the different cases of the active pattern go between the banana brackets, separated by vertical bars. The body of the active pattern is just an F# function that must return each case of the active pattern given in the banana brackets. Each case may also return additional data, just like a union type. This can be seen in the first part of the following example, which shows an active pattern for parsing input string data.

```
open System

// definition of the active pattern
let (|Bool|Int|Float|String|) input =
    // attempt to parse a bool
    let success, res = Boolean.TryParse input
    if success then Bool(res)
    else
        // attempt to parse an int
        let success, res = Int32.TryParse input
        if success then Int(res)
```

```
        else
            // attempt to parse a float (Double)
            let success, res = Double.TryParse input
            if success then Float(res)
            else String(input)

// function to print the results by pattern
// matching over the active pattern
let printInputWithType input =
    match input with
    | Bool b -> printfn "Boolean: %b" b
    | Int i -> printfn "Integer: %i" i
    | Float f -> printfn "Floating point: %f" f
    | String s -> printfn "String: %s" s

// print the results
printInputWithType "true"
printInputWithType "12"
printInputWithType "-12.1"
```

The pattern is designed to decide if the input string is a Boolean, integer, floating-point, or string value. The case names are Bool, Int, Float, and String. The example uses the TryParse method provided by the base class library to decide, in turn, if the input value is a Boolean, integer, or floating-point value; if it is not one of these, then it is classified as a string. If parsing is successful, this is indicated by returning the case name along with the value parsed.

In the second half of the example, you see how the active pattern is used. The active pattern allows you to treat a string value as if it were a union type. You can match against each of the four cases and recover the data returned by the active pattern in a strongly typed manner.

The results of this example, when compiled and executed, are as follows:

```
Boolean: true
String: 12
Floating point: -12.100000
```

Incomplete Active Patterns

To define an incomplete active pattern, you use a syntax similar to that for a complete active pattern. An incomplete active pattern has only one case name, which is placed between banana brackets, as with the complete active pattern. The difference is that an incomplete active pattern must be followed by a vertical bar and an underscore to show it is incomplete (as opposed to a complete active pattern with just one case).

Remember that the key difference between complete and incomplete active patterns is that complete active patterns are guaranteed to return one of their cases; whereas active patterns either match or fail to match. So, an incomplete active pattern is the option type. The option type is simple union type that is already built into the F# base libraries. It has just two cases: Some and None. It has the following definition:

```
type option<'a> =
    | Some of 'a
    | None
```

This type, as it name suggests, is used to represent either the presence or absence of a value. So, an incomplete active pattern returns either Some, along with any data to be returned, to represent a match, or None to represent failure.

All active patterns can have additional parameters, as well as the input they act on. Additional parameters are listed before the active pattern's input.

The next example reimplements the problem from the previous example using an incomplete active pattern that represents the success or failure of a .NET regular expression. The regular expression pattern will be given as a parameter to the active pattern.

```
open System.Text.RegularExpressions

// the definition of the active pattern
let (|Regex|_|) regexPattern input =
    // create and attempt to match a regular expression
    let regex = new Regex(regexPattern)
    let regexMatch = regex.Match(input)
    // return either Some or None
    if regexMatch.Success then
        Some regexMatch.Value
    else
        None


// function to print the results by pattern
// matching over different instances of the
// active pattern
let printInputWithType input =
    match input with
    | Regex "$true|false^" s -> printfn "Boolean: %s" s
    | Regex @"$-?\d+^" s -> printfn "Integer: %s" s
    | Regex "$-?\d+\.\d*^" s -> printfn "Floating point: %s" s
    | _ -> printfn "String: %s" input

// print the results
printInputWithType "true"
printInputWithType "12"
printInputWithType "-12.1"
```

While complete active patterns behave in exactly the same way as a union type—meaning the compiler will raise a warning only if there are missing cases—an incomplete active pattern will always require a final catch-all case to avoid the compiler raising a warning. However incomplete active patterns do have the advantage that you can chain multiple active patterns together, and the first case that matches will be the one that is used. This can be seen in the preceding example, which chains three of the regular expression active patterns together. Each active pattern is parameterized with a different regular expression pattern: one to match Boolean input, another to match integer input, and the third to match floating-point input.

The results of this example, when compiled and executed, are as follows:

```
Boolean: true
String: 12
Floating point: -12.1
```

Units of Measure

Units of measure are an interesting addition to the F# type system. They allow you to classify numeric values into different units. The idea of this is to prevent you from accidentally using a numeric value incorrectly—for example, adding together a value that represents inches with a value that represents centimeters without first performing the proper conversion.

To define a unit of measure, you declare a type name and prefix it with the attribute Measure. Here is an example of creating a unit of type meters (abbreviated to m):

```
[<Measure>]type m
```

By default, units of measure work with floating-point values—that is, System.Double. To create a value with a unit, you simply postfix the value with the name of the unit in angled brackets. So, to create a value of the meter type, use the following syntax:

```
let meters = 1.0<m>
```

Now we are going to revisit the example from the "Defining Types" section, which used union types to prevent various units of volume from being mixed up. This example implements something similar using units of measure. It starts by defining a unit of measure for liters and another for pints. Then it defines two identifiers that represent different volumes: one with a pint unit and one with a liter. Finally, it tries to add these two values, an operation that should result in an error, since we can't add pints and liters without first converting them.

```
[<Measure>]type liter
[<Measure>]type pint

let vol1 = 2.5<liter>
let vol2 = 2.5<pint>

let newVol = vol1 + vol2
```

This program will not compile, resulting in the following error:

```
Program.fs(7,21): error FS0001: The unit of measure 'pint' does not match the unit of measure 'liter'
```

The addition or subtraction of different units of measure is not allowed, but the multiplication or division of different units of measure is allowed and will create a new unit of measure. For example, you know that to convert a pint to a liter, you need to multiply it by the ratio of liters to pints. One liter is made up of approximately 1.76 pints, so you can now calculate the correct conversion ratio in the program:

```
let ratio = 1.0<liter> / 1.76056338<pint>
```

The identifier ratio will have the type float<liter/pint>, which makes it clear that it is the ratio of liters to pints. Furthermore, when a value of type float<pint> is multiplied by a value of type float<liter/pint>, the resulting type will automatically be of type float<liter>, as you would expect. This means you can now write the following program, which ensures that pints are safely converted to liters before adding them:

```
// define some units of measure
[<Measure>]type liter
[<Measure>]type pint

// define some volumes
let vol1 = 2.5<liter>
let vol2 = 2.5<pint>

// define the ratio of pints to liters
let ratio = 1.0<liter> / 1.76056338<pint>

// a function to convert pints to liters
let convertPintToLiter pints =
    pints * ratio

// perform the conversion and add the values
let newVol = vol1 + (convertPintToLiter vol2)
```

Exceptions and Exception Handling

Defining exceptions in F# is similar to defining a constructor of a union type, and the syntax for handling exceptions is similar to pattern matching.

You define exceptions using the exception keyword, followed by the name of the exception, and then optionally the keyword of and the types of any values the exception should contain, with multiple types separated by asterisks. The next example shows the definition of an exception, WrongSecond, which contains one integer value.

```
exception WrongSecond of int
```

You can raise exceptions with the raise keyword, as shown in the else clause in the following testSecond function. F# also has an alternative to the raise keyword, the failwith function, as shown in the following if clause. If, as is commonly the case, you just want to raise an exception with a text description of what went wrong, you can use failwith to raise a generic exception that contains the text passed to the function.

```
// define an exception type
exception WrongSecond of int

// list of prime numbers
let primes =
    [ 2; 3; 5; 7; 11; 13; 17; 19; 23; 29; 31; 37; 41; 43; 47; 53; 59 ]

// function to test if current second is prime
let testSecond() =
    try
        let currentSecond = System.DateTime.Now.Second in
        // test if current second is in the list of primes
        if List.exists (fun x -> x = currentSecond) primes then
            // use the failwith function to raise an exception
            failwith "A prime second"
        else
            // raise the WrongSecond exception
            raise (WrongSecond currentSecond)
    with
    // catch the wrong second exception
    WrongSecond x ->
        printf "The current was %i, which is not prime" x

// call the function
testSecond()
```

As shown in testSecond, the try and with keywords handle exceptions. The expressions that are subject to error handling go between the try and with keywords, and one or more pattern-matching rules must follow the with keyword. When trying to match an F# exception, the syntax follows that of trying to match an F# constructor from a union type. The first half of the rule consists of the exception name, followed by identifiers or wildcards to match values that the exception contains. The second half of the rule is an expression that states how the exception should be handled. One major difference between this and the regular pattern-matching constructs is that no warning or error is issued if pattern matching is incomplete. This is because any exceptions that are unhandled will propagate until they reach the top level and stop execution. The example handles exception wrongSecond, while leaving the exception raised by failwith to propagate.

F# also supports a finally keyword, which is used with the try keyword. You can't use the finally keyword in conjunction with the with keyword. The finally expression will be executed whether or not an exception is thrown. The next example shows a finally block being used to ensure a file is closed and disposed of after it is written to:

```
// function to write to a file
let writeToFile() =
    // open a file
    let file = System.IO.File.CreateText("test.txt")
    try
        // write to it
        file.WriteLine("Hello F# users")
    finally
        // close the file, this will happen even if
        // an exception occurs writing to the file
        file.Dispose()

// call the function
writeToFile()
```

■**Caution** Programmers coming from an OCaml background should be careful when using exceptions in F#. Because of the architecture of the CLR, throwing an exception is pretty expensive—quite a bit more expensive than in OCaml. If you throw a lot of exceptions, profile your code carefully to decide whether the performance costs are worth it. If the costs are too high, revise the code appropriately.

Lazy Evaluation

Lazy evaluation goes hand in hand with functional programming. The theory is that if there are no side effects in the language, the compiler or runtime is free to choose the evaluation order of expressions.

As you know, F# allows functions to have side effects, so it's not possible for the compiler or runtime to have a free hand in function evaluation; therefore, F# is said to have a strict evaluation order, or to be a *strict language*. You can still take advantage of lazy evaluation, but you must be explicit about which computations can be delayed—that is, evaluated in a lazy manner.

You use the keyword lazy to delay a computation (invoke lazy evaluation). The computation within the lazy expression remains unevaluated until evaluation is explicitly forced with the force function from the Lazy module. When the force function is applied to a particular lazy expression, the value is computed, and the result is cached. Subsequent calls to the force function return the cached value–whatever it is—even if this means raising an exception.

The following code shows a simple use of lazy evaluation:

```
let lazyValue = lazy ( 2 + 2 )
let actualValue = Lazy.force lazyValue

printfn "%i" actualValue
```

The first line delays a simple expression for evaluation later. The next line forces evaluation. Finally, the value is printed.

The value has been cached, so any side effects that take place when the value is computed will occur only the first time the lazy value is forced. This is fairly easy to demonstrate, as shown by the next example.

```
let lazySideEffect =
    lazy
        ( let temp = 2 + 2
          printfn "%i" temp
          temp )

printfn "Force value the first time: "
let actualValue1 = Lazy.force lazySideEffect
printfn "Force value the second time: "
let actualValue2 = Lazy.force lazySideEffect
```

In this example, a lazy value has a side effect when it is calculated: it writes to the console. To show that this side effect takes place only once, it forces the value twice. As you can see from the result, writing to the console takes place only once:

```
Force value the first time:
4
Force value the second time:
```

Laziness can also be useful when working with collections. The idea of a lazy collection is that elements in the collection are calculated on demand. Some collection types also cache the results of these calculations, so there is no need to recalculate elements. The collection most commonly used for lazy programming in F# is the seq type, a shorthand for the BCL's IEnumerable type. seq values are created and manipulated using functions in the Seq module. Many other values are also compatible with the type seq; for example, all F# lists and arrays are compatible with this type, as are most other collection types in the F# libraries and the .NET BCL.

Possibly the most important function for creating lazy collections, and probably the most difficult to understand, is unfold. This function allows you to create a lazy list. What makes it complicated is that you must provide a function that will be repeatedly evaluated to provide the elements of the list. The function passed to Seq.unfold can take any type of parameter and must return an option type. An option type is a union type that can be either None or Some(x), where x is a value of any type. None is used to represent the end of a list. The Some constructor must contain a tuple. The first item in the tuple represents the value that will become the first value in the list. The second value in the tuple is the value that will be passed into the function the next time it is called. You can think of this value as an accumulator.

The next example shows how this works. The identifier lazyList will contain three values. If the value passed into the function is less than 13, it appends the list using this value to form the list element, and then adds 1 to the value passed to the list. This will be the value passed to the function the next time it is called. If the value is greater than or equal to 13, the example terminates the list by returning None.

```
// the lazy list definition
let lazyList =
    Seq.unfold
        (fun x ->
```

```
        if x < 13 then
            // if smaller than the limit return
            // the current and next value
            Some(x, x + 1)
        else
            // if great than the limit
            // terminate the sequence
            None)
    10

// print the results
printfn "%A" lazyList
```

The results of this example, when compiled and executed, are as follows:

```
10
11
12
```

Sequences are useful to represent lists that don't terminate. A nonterminating list can't be represented by a classic list, which is constrained by the amount of memory available. The next example demonstrates this by creating fibs, an infinite list of all the Fibonacci numbers. To display the results conveniently, the example uses the function Seq.take to turn the first 20 items into an F# list, but carries on calculating many more Fibonacci numbers, as it uses F# bigint integers, so it is not limited by the size of a 32-bit integer.

```
// create an infinite list of Fibonacci numbers
let fibs =
    Seq.unfold
        (fun (n0, n1) ->
            Some(n0, (n1, n0 + n1)))
        (1I,1I)

// take the first twenty items from the list
let first20 = Seq.take 20 fibs

// print the finite list
printfn "%A" first20
```

The results of this example are as follows:

```
[1I; 1I; 2I; 3I; 5I; 8I; 13I; 21I; 34I; 55I; 89I; 144I; 233I; 377I; 610I; 987I;
 1597I; 2584I; 4181I; 6765I]
```

Note that both of these sequences could also be created using the list comprehension discussed earlier in this chapter. If list comprehensions are based on sequences, they are automatically lazy.

Summary

In this chapter, you looked at the major functional programming constructs in F#. This is the core of the language, and I hope you've developed a good feel for how to approach writing algorithms and handling data in F#. The next chapter covers imperative programming, and you'll see how to mix functional and imperative programming techniques to handle tasks such as input and output.

CHAPTER 4

■ ■ ■

Imperative Programming

As you saw in Chapter 3, you can use F# for pure functional programming. However, some issues, most notably I/O, are almost impossible to address without some kind of state change. F# does not require that you program in a stateless fashion. It allows you to use *mutable* identifiers whose values can change over time. F# also has other constructs that support imperative programming. You've already seen some in Chapter 3. Any example that wrote to the console included a few lines of imperative code alongside functional code. In this chapter, you'll explore these constructs—and many others—in much more detail.

First, you'll look at F#'s unit type, a special type that means "no value," which enables some aspects of imperative programming. Second, you'll look at some of the ways F# can handle *mutable state*, or types whose values can change over time. These include mutable identifiers, the ref type, mutable record types, and arrays. Finally, you'll look at using .NET libraries. The topics will include calling static methods, creating objects and working with their members, using special members such as indexers and events, and using the F# |> operator, which is handy when dealing with .NET libraries.

The unit Type

Any function that does not accept or return values is of type unit, which is similar to the type void in C# and System.Void in the CLR. To a functional programmer, a function that doesn't accept or return a value might not seem interesting because a function that doesn't accept or return a value doesn't do anything. In the imperative paradigm, you know that side effects exist, so even if a function accepts or returns nothing, you know it can still have its uses. The unit type is represented as a *literal value*, or a pair of parentheses (()). This means that whenever you want a function that doesn't take or return a value, you put () in the code:

```
let aFunction() =
    ()
```

In this example, aFunction is a function because you placed parentheses after the identifier, where its parameters would go. If you hadn't done this, it would have meant aFunction was not a function, but a value that was not a function. You probably know that all functions are values, but here the difference between a function and a nonfunction value is important. If aFunction were a nonfunction value, the expressions within it would be evaluated only once. Because it is a function, the expressions will be evaluated each time it is called.

Similarly, placing () after the equals sign tells the compiler you will return nothing. Ordinarily, you need to put something between the equals sign and the empty parentheses, or the function is pointless. For the sake of keeping things simple, I'll leave this function pointless. Now you'll see the type of aFunction. The easiest way to see a function's type is to using the tool tips that are available in visual studio or by compiling it using F# interactive. Alternatively, you can compiler's fsc -i switch; the results of this are as follows:

```
val aFunction: unit -> unit
```

As you can see, the type of aFunction is a function that accepts unit and transforms it into a value of type unit. Because the compiler now knows the function doesn't return anything, you can now use it with some special imperative constructs. To call the function, you can use the let keyword followed by a pair of parentheses and the equals sign. This is a special use of the let keyword, which here means "call a function that does not return a value." Alternatively, you can use the keyword do, or you can simply call the function without any extra keywords at all, by placing the function at the top level:

```
let aFunction() =
    ()

let () = aFunction ()
// -- or --
do aFunction ()
// -- or --
aFunction ()
```

Similarly, you can chain functions that return unit together within a function—simply make sure they all share the same indentation. The next example shows several printfn functions chained together to print text to the console:

```
let poem() =
    printfn "I wandered lonely as a cloud"
    printfn "That floats on high o'er vales and hills,"
    printfn "When all at once I saw a crowd,"
    printfn "A host, of golden daffodils"

poem()
```

It's not quite true that the only functions that return a unit type can be used in this manner; however, using them with a type other than unit will generate a warning, which is something most programmers want to avoid. To avoid this, it's sometimes useful to turn a function that does return a value into a function of type unit, typically because the function has a side effect, as well as returning a value. The need to do this is fairly rare when you're using only F# libraries written in F# (although situations where it is useful do exist), but it is more common when using .NET libraries that were not written in F#.

The next example shows how to throw away the value of the result of a function, so that the resulting function that returns unit:

```
let getShorty() = "shorty"
let _ = getShorty()
// -- or --
ignore(getShorty())
// -- or --
getShorty() |> ignore
```

You begin by defining a function getShorty that returns a string. Now imagine, for whatever reason, you want to call this function and ignore its result. The next two lines demonstrate different ways to do this. First, you can use a let expression with an underscore (_) character in place of the identifier. The underscore tells the compiler this is a value in which you aren't interested. Second, this is such a common thing to do it has been wrapped into a function, ignore, that is available in the F# base libraries and is demonstrated on the third line. The final line shows an alternative way of calling ignore that uses the pass-forward operator to pass the result of getShorty() to the ignore function. See Chapter 3 for more information about the pass-forward operator.

The mutable Keyword

In Chapter 3, I talked about how you could bind identifiers to values using the keyword let and noted how, under some circumstances, you could redefine and rebound, but not modify, these identifiers. If you want to define an identifier whose value can change over time, you can do this using the mutable keyword. A special operator, the *left ASCII arrow* (or just *left arrow*), is composed of a less-than sign and a dash (<-), you use it to update these identifiers. An update operation using the left arrow has type unit, so you can chain these operations together as discussed in the previous section. The next example demonstrates how to define a mutable identifier of type string and then change the value that it holds:

```
// a mutable idendifier
let mutable phrase = "How can I be sure, "

// print the phrase
printfn "%s" phrase
// update the phrase
phrase <- "In a world that's constantly changing"
// reprint the phrase
printfn "%s" phrase
```

The results are as follows:

```
How can I be sure,
In a world that's constantly changing
```

At first glance this doesn't look too different from redefining an identifier, but it has a couple of key differences. When you use the left arrow to update a mutable identifier, you can change its value but not its type—when you redefine an identifier, you can do both. A compile error is produced if you try to change the type, as this example demonstrates:

```
let mutable number = "one"
phrase <- 1
```

If you attempt to compile this code, you get the following error message:

```
Prog.fs(9,10): error: FS0001: This expression has type
    int
but is here used with type
    string
```

The other major difference is where these changes are visible. When you redefine an identifier, the change is visible only within the scope of the new identifier. When it passes out of scope, it reverts to its old value. This is not the case with mutable identifiers. Any changes are permanent, whatever the scope, as this example demonstrates:

```
// demonstration of redefining X
let redefineX() =
    let x = "One"
    printfn "Redefining:\r\nx = %s" x
    if true then
        let x = "Two"
        printfn "x = %s" x
    printfn "x = %s" x

// demonstration of mutating X
let mutableX() =
    let mutable x = "One"
    printfn "Mutating:\r\nx = %s" x
    if true then
        x <- "Two"
        printfn "x = %s" x
    printfn "x = %s" x

// run the demos
redefineX()
mutableX()
```

Executing the preceding code produces the following results:

```
Redefining:
x = One
x = Two
x = One
Mutating:
x = One
x = Two
x = Two
```

Identifiers defined as mutable are somewhat limited because you can't use them within a subfunction, as this example illustrates:

```
let mutableY() =
    let mutable y = "One"
    printfn "Mutating:\r\nx = %s" y
```

```
let f() =
    // this causes an error as
    // mutables can't be captured
    y <- "Two"
    printfn "x = %s" y
f()
printfn "x = %s" y
```

If you attempt to compile this program, you get the following error message:

```
Prog.fs(35,16): error FS0191: The mutable variable 'y' is used in an invalid way. Mutable↵
 variables may not be captured by closures. Consider eliminating this use of mutation or↵
 using a heap-allocated mutable reference cell via 'ref' and '!'.
```

As the error messages says, this is why the ref type, a special type of mutable record, has been made available: to handle mutable variables that need to be shared among several functions. I discuss mutable records in the next section and the ref type in the section after that.

Defining Mutable Record Types

In Chapter 3, when you first met record types, I discussed how to update their fields. This is because record types are immutable by default. F# provides special syntax to allow you to update the fields in record types. You do this by using the keyword mutable before the field in a record type. I should emphasize that this operation changes the contents of the record's field, rather than changing the record itself:

```
// a record with a mutable field
type Couple = { Her: string; mutable Him: string }

// a create an instance of the record
let theCouple = { Her = "Elizabeth Taylor "; Him = "Nicky Hilton" }

// function to change the contents of
// the record over time
let changeCouple() =
    printfn "%A" theCouple
    theCouple.Him <- "Michael Wilding"
    printfn "%A" theCouple
    theCouple.Him <- "Michael Todd"
    printfn "%A" theCouple
    theCouple.Him <- "Eddie Fisher"
    printfn "%A" theCouple
    theCouple.Him <- "Richard Burton"
```

```
    printfn "%A" theCouple
    theCouple.Him <- "Richard Burton"
    printfn "%A" theCouple
    theCouple.Him <- "John Warner"
    printfn "%A" theCouple
    theCouple.Him <- "Larry Fortensky"
    printfn "%A" theCouple

// call the fucntion
changeCouple()
```

Executing the preceding code produces the following results:

```
{Her = "Elizabeth Taylor ";
 Him = "Nicky Hilton";}
{Her = "Elizabeth Taylor ";
 Him = "Michael Wilding";}
{Her = "Elizabeth Taylor ";
 Him = "Michael Todd";}
{Her = "Elizabeth Taylor ";
 Him = "Eddie Fisher";}
{Her = "Elizabeth Taylor ";
 Him = "Richard Burton";}
{Her = "Elizabeth Taylor ";
 Him = "Richard Burton";}
{Her = "Elizabeth Taylor ";
 Him = "John Warner";}
{Her = "Elizabeth Taylor ";
 Him = "Larry Fortensky";}
```

This example shows a mutable record in action. A type, couple, is defined where the field him is mutable, but the field her is not. Next, an instance of couple is initialized, after which you change the value of him many times, each time displaying the results. I should note that the mutable keyword applies per field, so any attempt to update a field that is not mutable will result in a compile error; for example, the next example will fail on the second line:

```
theCouple.Her <- "Sybil Williams"
printfn "%A" theCouple
```

If you attempt to compile this program, you get the following error message:

```
prog.fs(2,4): error: FS0005: This field is not mutable
```

The ref Type

The ref type is a simple way for a program to use mutable state, or values that change over time. The ref type is a record type with a single mutable field that is defined in the F# libraries. Some operators are defined to make accessing and updating the field as straightforward as possible. F#'s definition of the ref type uses *type parameterization*, a concept introduced in the previous chapter. Thus, although the value of the ref type can be of any type, you cannot change the type of the value once you create an instance of the value.

Creating a new instance of the ref type is easy; you use the keyword ref, followed by whatever item represents the value of ref. The next example shows the compiler's output (using the -i option, which shows that the type of phrase is string ref, or a reference type that can only contain strings):

```
let phrase = ref "Inconsistency"
```

```
val phrase : string ref
```

This syntax is similar to defining a union type's constructors, also shown in the previous chapter. The ref type has two built-in operators to access it; the exclamation point (!) provides access to the value of the reference type, and an operator composed of a colon followed by an equals sign (:=) enables you to update it. The ! operator always returns a value of the type that matches the ref type's contents, known to the compiler thanks to type parameterization. The := operator has the type unit because it doesn't return anything.

The next example shows how to use a ref type to total the contents of an array. On the third line of totalArray, you see the creation of the ref type. In this case, it is initialized to hold the value 0. On the seventh line, the let binding after the array definition, you see the ref type being both accessed and updated. First, ! is used to access the value with the ref type; second, after it has been added to the current value held in the array, the value of the ref type is updated through the use of the := operator. Now the code will correctly print 6 to the console:

```
let totalArray () =
    // define an array literal
    let array = [| 1; 2; 3 |]
    // define a counter
    let total = ref 0
    // loop over the array
    for x in array do
        // kep a running total
        total := !total + x
    // print the total
    printfn "total: %i" !total

totalArray()
```

Executing the preceding code produces the following result:

```
total: 6
```

■**Caution** If you are used to programming in one of the C family of programming languages, you should be careful here. When reading F# code, it is quite easy to misinterpret the ref type's ! operator as a Boolean "not" operator. F# uses a function called not for Boolean "not" operations.

The ref type is a useful way to share mutable values between several functions. An identifier can be bound to a ref type defined in scope that is common to all functions that want to use the value; then the functions can use the value of the identifier as they like, changing it or merely reading it. Because you can pass around functions in F# as if they were values, the value follows the function everywhere it goes. This process is known as *capturing a local* or *creating a closure*.

The next example demonstrates this by defining three functions: inc, dec, and show, which all share a common ref type holding an integer. The functions inc, dec, and show are all defined in their own private scopes and then returned to the top level as a *tuple*, so they are visible everywhere. Note how n is not returned; it remains private, but inc, dec, and show are all still able to access n. This is a useful technique for controlling what operations can take place on mutable data:

```
// capute the inc, dec and show funtions
let inc, dec, show =
    // define the shared state
    let n = ref 0
    // a function to increment
    let inc () =
        n := !n + 1
    // a function to decrement
    let dec () =
        n := !n - 1
    // a function to show the current state
    let show () =
        printfn "%i" !n

    // return the functions to the top level
    inc, dec, show

// test the functions
inc()
inc()
dec()
show()
```

Executing the preceding code produces the following result:

1

Arrays

Arrays are a concept that most programmers are familiar with, as almost all programming languages have some sort of array type. The F# array type is based on the BCL System.Array type, so anyone who has used arrays in C# or Visual Basic will find that the underlying concepts the same.

Arrays are a mutable collection type in F#; it's useful to compare them to the immutable list type explained in Chapter 3. Arrays and lists are both collections, but arrays have a couple a couple of properties that make them quite different from lists. The values within arrays are updatable, whereas lists are not, and lists can grow dynamically, whereas arrays cannot. One-dimensional arrays are sometimes referred to as *vectors*, and multidimensional arrays are sometimes called *matrices*. Arrays are defined by a sequence of items separated by semicolons (;) and delimited by an opening square bracket and a vertical bar ([|) and a closing bar and square bracket (|]). The syntax for referencing an array element is the name of the identifier of the array followed by a period (.) and then the index of the element in square brackets ([ ]). The syntax for retrieving the value of an element stops there. The syntax for setting the value of an element is the left arrow (<-) followed by the value to be assigned to the element.

The next example shows you how to read from and write to an array. First, you define an array, rhymeArray, and then you read all the members from it. Next, you insert new values into the array, and finally, you print out all the values you have:

```
// define an array literal
let rhymeArray =
    [| "Went to market";
       "Stayed home";
       "Had roast beef";
       "Had none" |]

// unpack the array into identifiers
let firstPiggy = rhymeArray.[0]
let secondPiggy = rhymeArray.[1]
let thirdPiggy = rhymeArray.[2]
let fourthPiggy = rhymeArray.[3]

// update elements of the array
rhymeArray.[0] <- "Wee,"
rhymeArray.[1] <- "wee,"
rhymeArray.[2] <- "wee,"
rhymeArray.[3] <- "all the way home"

// give a short name to the new line characters
let nl = System.Environment.NewLine
```

```
// print out the identifiers & array
printfn "%s%s%s%s%s%s%s"
    firstPiggy nl
    secondPiggy nl
    thirdPiggy nl
    fourthPiggy
printfn "%A" rhymeArray
```

When you compile this code, you see the following results:

```
Went to market
Stayed home
Had roast beef
Had none
[|"Wee,"; "wee,"; "wee,"; "all the way home"|]
```

Arrays, like lists, use type parameterization, so the type of the array's contents makes up part of the array's type. This is written as content type, followed by the array's type. Thus, rhymeArray has the type string array, which you might also write like this: string[].

Multidimensional arrays in F# come in two, slightly different flavors: jagged and rectangular. As the name suggests, jagged arrays are arrays where the second dimension is not a regular shape; rather they are arrays whose contents happen to be other arrays, and the length of the inner arrays is not forced to be the same. In *rectangular* arrays, all inner arrays are of the same length; in fact, there is no concept of an inner array because the whole array is the same object. The method of getting and setting items in the two different types of arrays differs slightly.

For jagged arrays, you use the period followed by the index in parentheses, but you have to use this twice (one time for each dimension) because the first time you get back the inner array, and the second time you get the element within it.

The next example demonstrates a simple jagged array, called jagged. You can access the array members in two different ways. The first inner array (at index 0) is assigned to the identifier singleDim, and then its first element is assigned to itemOne. On the fourth line, the first element of the second inner array is assigned to itemTwo, using one line of code:

```
// define a jagged array literal
let jagged = [| [| "one" |] ; [| "two" ; "three" |] |]

// unpack elements from the arrays
let singleDim = jagged.[0]
let itemOne = singleDim.[0]
let itemTwo = jagged.[1].[0]

// print some of the unpacked elements
printfn "%s %s" itemOne itemTwo
```

When you compile and execute the results of this example, you get the following result:

```
one two
```

To reference elements in rectangular arrays, use a period (.) followed by all the indexes in square brackets, separated by commas. Unlike jagged arrays, which are multidimensional but use the same ([| |]) syntax as single-dimensional arrays, you must create rectangular arrays with the create function of the Array2 and Array3 modules, which support two- and three-dimensional arrays, respectively. This doesn't mean rectangular arrays are limited to three dimensions because it's possible to use the System.Array class to create rectangular arrays with more than three dimensions; however, you should consider such an approach carefully because adding extra dimensions can quickly lead to extremely large objects.

In the next example, you create a rectangular array, square, and then populate its elements with the integers 1, 2, 3, and 4:

```
// create a square array,
// initally populated with zeros
let square = Array2D.create 2 2 0

// populate the array
square.[0,0] <- 1
square.[0,1] <- 2
square.[1,0] <- 3
square.[1,1] <- 4

// print the array
printfn "%A" square
```

Now let's look at the differences between jagged and rectangular arrays. First, you create a jagged array to represent Pascal's Triangle. Next, you create a rectangular array that contains various number sequences that are hidden within pascalsTriangle:

```
// define Pascal's Triangle as an
// array literal
let pascalsTriangle =
    [| [|1|];
       [|1; 1|];
       [|1; 2; 1|];
       [|1; 3; 3; 1|];
       [|1; 4; 6; 4; 1|];
       [|1; 5; 10; 10; 5; 1|];
       [|1; 6; 15; 20; 15; 6; 1|];
       [|1; 7; 21; 35; 35; 21; 7; 1|];
       [|1; 8; 28; 56; 70; 56; 28; 8; 1|]; |]
```

```
// collect elements from the jagged array
// assigning them to a square array
let numbers =
    let length = (Array.length pascalsTriangle) in
    let temp = Array2D.create 3 length 0 in
    for index = 0 to length - 1 do
        let naturelIndex = index - 1 in
        if naturelIndex >= 0 then
            temp.[0, index] <- pascalsTriangle.[index].[naturelIndex]
        let triangularIndex = index - 2 in
        if triangularIndex >= 0 then
            temp.[1, index] <- pascalsTriangle.[index].[triangularIndex]
        let tetrahedralIndex = index - 3 in
        if tetrahedralIndex >= 0 then
            temp.[2, index] <- pascalsTriangle.[index].[tetrahedralIndex]
    done
    temp

// print the array
printfn "%A" numbers
```

When you compile and execute this code, you get the following results:

```
[|[|0; 1; 2; 3; 4; 5; 6; 7; 8|]; [|0; 0; 1; 3; 6; 10; 15; 21; 28|];
  [|0; 0; 0; 1; 4; 10; 20; 35; 56|]|]
```

The following results show the types displayed when you use the compiler's –i switch:

```
val pascalsTriangle: int array array
val numbers: int [,]
```

As you might expect, jagged and rectangular arrays have different types. The type of a jagged array is the same as a single-dimensional array, except that it has an array per dimension, so the type of pascalsTriangle is int array array. Rectangular arrays use a notation more similar to C#. It begins with the name of the type of the array's elements, and then includes square brackets ([ ]) with one comma for every dimension greater than 1, so the type of our two-dimensional numbers array is int[,].

Array Comprehensions

I introduced comprehension syntax for lists and sequences in Chapter 3. You can use a corresponding syntax to create arrays. The only difference between this and the functional-style syntax is the characters that delimit the array. You use vertical bars surrounded by square brackets for arrays:

```
// an array of characters
let chars = [| '1' .. '9' |]

// an array of tuples of number, square
let squares =
    [| for x in 1 .. 9 -> x, x*x |]

// print out both arrays
printfn "%A" chars
printfn "%A" squares
```

Executing the preceding code produces the following results:

```
[|'1'; '2'; '3'; '4'; '5'; '6'; '7'; '8'; '9'|]
[|(1, 1); (2, 4); (3, 9); (4, 16); (5, 25); (6, 36); (7, 49); (8, 64); (9, 81)|]
```

Control Flow

Unlike the pseudo-control-flow syntax described in Chapter 3, F# does have some imperative control-flow constructs. In addition to the imperative use of if, there are also while and for loops.

The major difference from using the if expression in the imperative style—that is, using it with a function that returns the type unit—is that you aren't forced to use an else, as the next example demonstrates:

```
if System.DateTime.Now.DayOfWeek = System.DayOfWeek.Sunday then
    printfn "Sunday Playlist: Lazy On A Sunday Afternoon - Queen"
```

Although it isn't necessary to have an else expression if the if expression has the type unit, you can add one, if necessary. This too must have the type unit, or the compiler will issue an error:

```
if System.DateTime.Now.DayOfWeek = System.DayOfWeek.Monday then
        printfn "Monday Playlist: Blue Monday - New Order"
    else
        printfn "Alt Playlist: Fell In Love With A Girl - White Stripes"
```

You can use whitespace to detect where an if expression ends. You indent the code that belongs to the if expression, and the if expression ends when it goes back to its original indentation. In the next example, the string "Tuesday Playlist: Ruby Tuesday - Rolling Stones" will be printed on a Tuesday, while "Everyday Playlist: Eight Days A Week - Beatles" will be printed every day of the week:

```
if System.DateTime.Now.DayOfWeek = System.DayOfWeek.Tuesday then
    printfn "Tuesday Playlist: Ruby Tuesday - Rolling Stones"
printfn "Everyday Playlist: Eight Days A Week - Beatles"
```

If you want multiple statements to be part of the if statement, then you can give them the same indention, as shown in the next example, where both strings will be printed only on a Friday:

```
if System.DateTime.Now.DayOfWeek = System.DayOfWeek.Friday then
    printfn "Friday Playlist: Friday I'm In Love - The Cure"
    printfn "Friday Playlist: View From The Afternoon - Arctic Monkeys"
```

Most programmers are familiar with for loops because they are commonly found in imperative-programming languages. In F#, for loops are overloaded, so a for loop can either enumerate a collection, behaving in a similar way to the foreach loop available in many programming languages; or it can specify an identifier that will be incremented by one for each iteration of the loop.

First, let's look at using for to enumerate collections. In this case, the for loop performs an imperative action, one that returns the unit on each element in the collection. This is probably the most common imperative usage of for loops in F#. The syntax begins with the for keyword, followed by the identifier that will be bound to each item in the collection. Next comes the keyword in, followed by the collection, and then the keyword do. The code for processing each item in the collection comes next; you indented this to show that it belongs to the for loop. The following example demonstrates this syntax, enumerating an array of strings and printing each one:

```
// an array for words
let words = [| "Red"; "Lorry"; "Yellow"; "Lorry" |]

// use a for loop to print each element
for word in words do
    printfn "%s" word
```

Executing the preceding code produces the following results:

```
Red
Lorry
Yellow
Lorry
```

As you'll see later in this chapter, and in many examples throughout the book, this can be a convenient way to work with typed or untyped collections returned by .NET BCL methods.

The other usage of a for loop is to declare an identifier, whose scope is the for loop, that increases or decreases its value by 1 after each iteration of the loop. The identifier is given a starting value and an end value, and the end value provides the condition for loop termination. F# follows this syntax. It starts with the keyword for, followed by the identifier that will hold the counter value; next comes an equals sign, followed by an expression for the initial counter value, the keyword to, and then an expression for the terminal value. The code that forms the body of the for loop comes after this, sandwiched between the keywords do and done. The for loop has the type unit, so the code that forms the body of the loop should have the type unit; otherwise, the compiler will issue a warning.

The next example demonstrates a common usage of a for loop: to enumerate all the values in an array. The identifier index will take on values starting at 0 and ending at 1 less than the length of the array. You can use this identifier as the index for the array:

```
// a Ryunosuke Akutagawa haiku array
let ryunosukeAkutagawa = [| "Green "; "frog,";
    "Is"; "your"; "body"; "also";
    "freshly"; "painted?" |]

// for loop over the array printing each element
for index = 0 to Array.length ryunosukeAkutagawa - 1 do
    printf "%s " ryunosukeAkutagawa.[index]
```

When you compile and execute this code, you get the following results:

```
Green frog, Is your body also freshly painted?
```

In a regular for loop, the initial value of the counter must always be *less* than the final value, and the value of the counter will increase as the loop continues. There is a variation on this, where you replace to with downto. In this case, the initial counter value must always be *greater* than the final value, and the counter will decrease as the loop continues. You can see how to use downto in this example:

```
// a Shuson Kato hiaku array (backwards)
let shusonKato = [| "watching."; "been"; "have";
    "children"; "three"; "my"; "realize"; "and";
    "ant"; "an"; "kill"; "I";
    |]

// loop over the array backwards printing each word
for index = Array.length shusonKato - 1 downto 0 do
    printf "%s " shusonKato.[index]
```

When you compile and execute this code, you get the following results:

```
I kill an ant and realize my three children have been watching.
```

The while loop is another familiar imperative language construct. It is an expression that creates a loop over a section of code until a Boolean expression changes to false. To create a while loop in F#, you use the keyword while followed by a Boolean expression that determines whether the loop should continue. As with for loops, you place the body of the loop between the keywords do and done, and the body should have the type unit; otherwise, the compiler will issue a warning. This code illustrates how to create a while loop:

```
// a Matsuo Basho hiaku in a list reference
let matsuoBasho = ref [ "An"; "old"; "pond!";
    "A"; "frog"; "jumps"; "in-";
    "The"; "sound"; "of"; "water" ]
```

```
while (List.length !matsuoBasho > 0) do
    printf "%s " (List.head !matsuoBasho)
    matsuoBasho := List.tail !matsuoBasho
```

This program enumerates list, and the Boolean expression to terminate the loop is based on whether the list is empty. Within the body of the loop, you print the head of the list and then remove it, shortening the list on each iteration.

When you compile and execute this code, you get the following results:

```
An old pond! A frog jumps in- The sound of water
```

Calling Static Methods and Properties from .NET Libraries

One extremely useful feature of imperative programming in F# is the ability to use just about any library written in a .NET programming language, including the many methods and classes available as part of the BCL itself. I consider this to be imperative programming because libraries written in other languages make no guarantees about how state works inside them, so you can't know whether a method you call has side effects.

A distinction should be made between calling libraries written in F# and libraries written in any other language. This is because libraries written in F# have metadata that describes extra details about the library, such as whether a method takes a tuple or whether its parameters can be curried. This metadata is specific to F#, and it is stored in a binary format as a resource to the generated assembly. This is largely why the Microsoft.FSharp.Reflection API is provided: to bridge the gap between F# and .NET metadata.

You use the same basic syntax when calling static or instance properties or methods. Method calls to a non-F# library must have their arguments separated by commas and surrounded by parentheses. (Remember, F# function calls usually use whitespace to separate arguments, and you need to use parentheses only to impose precedence.) Method calls to a non-F# library cannot be curried; in fact, methods from non F# libraries behave as though they take a tuple of arguments. Despite this difference, calling a method from a non-F# library is straightforward. You start off by using static properties and methods:

```
open System.IO
// test whether a file "test.txt" exist
if File.Exists("test.txt") then
    printfn "Text file \"test.txt\" is present"
else
    printfn "Text file \"test.txt\" does not exist"
```

This example calls a static method from the .NET Framework BCL. Calling a static method is almost identical to calling an F# function. You begin with the class name followed by a period (.) and then the name of the method; the only real difference is in the syntax for passing the arguments, which are surrounded by parentheses and separated by commas. You make a call to the System.IO.File class's Exists method to test whether a file exists and print an appropriate message, depending on the result.

You can treat static methods from other .NET libraries as values in the same way that you can treat F# functions as values and pass them to other function as parameters. In the next example, you see how you can pass the File.Exist method to the F# library function List.map:

```
open System.IO

// list of files to test
let files1 = [ "test1.txt"; "test2.txt"; "test3.txt" ]

// test if each file exists
let results1 =  List.map File.Exists files1

// print the results
printfn "%A" results1
```

Because .NET methods behave as if they take tuples as arguments, you can also treat a method that has more than one argument as a value. Here you see how to apply the File.WriteAllBytes to a list of tuples; the tuples contain the file path (a string) and the desired file contents (an array of bytes):

```
open System.IO

// list of files names and desired contents
let files2 = [ "test1.bin", [| 0uy |];
               "test2.bin", [| 1uy |];
               "test3.bin", [| 1uy; 2uy |]]

// iterator over the list of files creating each one
List.iter File.WriteAllBytes files2
```

Often, you want to use the functionality of an existing .NET method, but you also want the ability to curry it. A common pattern in F# to achieve this is to *import* the .NET method function by writing a thin F# wrapper, as in the following example:

```
open System.IO

// import the File.Create function
let create size name =
    File.Create(name, size, FileOptions.Encrypted)

// list of files to be created
let names = [ "test1.bin"; "test2.bin"; "test3.bin" ]

// open the files create a list of streams
let streams = List.map (create 1024) names
```

Here you see how to import the File.Create; in this case, you use the overload that takes three parameters, but you expose only two of them as parameters: the buffer size (size) and the file name (name). Notice how you specify that the size parameter comes first. You do it this way because it's more likely that you'll want to create several files with the same buffer size than with the same name. In the final line of the listing, you apply the create function to a list of files names to create a list of files streams. You want each stream to be created with a buffer size of 1024 bytes, so pass the literal 1024 to the create function, like so: (create 1024). This returns a new function, which is then used with the List.map function.

When using .NET methods with lots of arguments, it can sometimes be helpful to know the names of the arguments to help you keep track of what each argument is doing. F# lets you use named arguments, where you give the name of the argument, an equals sign, and then the value of the argument. The following example demonstrates this with an overload of File.Open() that takes four arguments:

```
open System.IO

// open a file using named arguments
let file = File.Open(path = "test.txt",
                     mode = FileMode.Append,
                     access = FileAccess.Write,
                     share = FileShare.None)

// close it!
file.Close()
```

Using Objects and Instance Members from .NET Libraries

Using classes from non-F# libraries is also straightforward. The syntax for instantiating an object consists of the keyword new, name of the class you want to instantiate, and then constructor arguments separated by commas within parentheses. You can use the let keyword to bind an instance of a class to an identifier. Once associated with an identifier, the object behaves a lot like a record type; the object referred to cannot be changed, but its contents can. Also, if the identifier is not at the top level, then it can be redefined or hidden by an identifier of the same name in another scope. C# and Visual Basic programmers should find accessing fields, properties, events, and methods should be intuitive because the syntax is similar. To access any member, you use the identifier of the object followed by a period (.) and then the name of the member. Arguments to instance methods follow the same convention as for static methods, and they must be within parentheses and separated by commas. To retrieve the value of a property or field, you need only the name of member, and you set it using the left arrow (<-).

The next example demonstrates how to create a System.IO.FileInfo object and then use various members of the class to manipulate it in different ways. On the first line, you make the System.IO namespace available to F#. On the second, you create the FileInfo object, passing it the name of the file in which you're interested. Next, you check whether the file exists using the Exists instance property. If it doesn't exist, you create a new file using the CreateText() instance method and then set it to read-only using the Attributes instance property. Here, you use the use binding to clean up resources, by calling their Dispose method when they drop out of scope:

```
open System.IO
// create a FileInfo object
let file = new FileInfo("test.txt")

// test if the file exists,
// if not create a file
if not file.Exists then
    use stream = file.CreateText()
```

```
    stream.WriteLine("hello world")
    file.Attributes <- FileAttributes.ReadOnly

// print the full file name
printfn "%s" file.FullName
```

I explain this fully in Chapter 3. F# also allows you to set properties when constructing an object. It's quite common to set object properties as part of the process of initially configuring the object, especially in WinForms programming (see Chapter 8 for more information about WinForms). To set a property at construction time, you place the property name inside the constructor, followed by an equals sign and then by the value for the property. Separate multiple properties with commas. The following is a variation on the previous example; it sets the ReadOnly attribute when the object is the constructor:

```
open System.IO
// file name to test
let filename = "test.txt"

// bind file to an option type, depending on whether
// the file exist or not
let file =
    if File.Exists(filename) then
        Some(new FileInfo(filename, Attributes = FileAttributes.ReadOnly))
    else
        None
```

Note that you need to test for the file's existence to avoid a runtime exception when trying to set the Attributes property. F# allows you to set type parameters when calling a constructor because it is not always possible to infer the type parameter when making a constructor call. The type parameters are surrounded by angle brackets (<>) and separated by commas. The next example demonstrates how to set a type parameter when calling a constructor. You can create an instance of System.Collections.Generic.List, which can you use with integers only by setting its type parameter when you create it. In F#, System.Collections.Generic.List is called ResizeArray to avoid confusion with F# lists:

```
open System

// an integer list
let intList =
    let temp = new ResizeArray<int>() in
    temp.AddRange([| 1; 2; 3 |]);
    temp

// print each int using the ForEach member method
intList.ForEach( fun i -> Console.WriteLine(i) )
```

Executing the preceding code produces the following results:

```
1
2
3
```

The previous example also demonstrates another nice feature of F# when interoperating with non-F# libraries. .NET APIs often use a .NET construct called *delegates*, which are conceptually a kind of function value. F# functions will automatically be converted to .NET delegate objects if their signatures match. You can see this on the last line, where an F# function is passed directly to a method that takes a .NET delegate type.

To keep methods as flexible as possible, you might prefer not to specify a type parameter when you import methods that take generic delegates or when you create a wrapper F# function around constructors for a non-F# library. You achieve this by using the underscore (_) in place of the type parameter, as in the first line of the next example (the following example uses the forward operator, |>, which I explain in the "The |> Operator" section):

```
open System
// how to wrap a method that take a delegate with an F# function
let findIndex f arr = Array.FindIndex(arr, new Predicate<_>(f))

// define an array literal
let rhyme = [| "The"; "cat"; "sat"; "on"; "the"; "mat" |]

// print index of the first word ending in 'at'
printfn "First word ending in 'at' in the array: %i"
    (rhyme |> findIndex (fun w -> w.EndsWith("at")))
```

When you compile and execute this example, you get the following result:

```
First word ending in 'at' in the array: 1
```

Here you import the FindIndex method from the System.Array class, so you can use it in a curried style. If you had not explicitly created a delegate, the identifier f would have represented a predicate delegate rather than a function. This means all calls to findIndex would need to create a delegate object explicitly, which is not ideal. However, if you had specified a type when creating the Predicate delegate in the definition of findIndex, then you would have limited the use of the findIndex function to arrays of a specific type. Occasionally, this might be what you want to do, but that's not usually the case. By using the underscore, you avoid having to specify a type for the findIndex function, while keeping it nice and flexible.

Using Indexers from .NET Libraries

Indexers are a .NET concept that is designed to make a collection class look more like an array. Under the hood, an indexer is a special property that is always called Item and has one or more parameters. It is important you have easy access to an indexer property because many classes within the BCL have indexers.

F# offers two different syntaxes for accessing properties. You can explicitly use the Item property, or you can use an array-like syntax, with brackets instead of parentheses around the index:

```
open System.Collections.Generic

// create a ResizeArray
let stringList =
    let temp = new ResizeArray<string>() in
    temp.AddRange([| "one"; "two"; "three" |]);
    temp

// unpack items from the resize array
let itemOne = stringList.Item(0)
let itemTwo = stringList.[1]

// print the unpacked items
printfn "%s %s" itemOne itemTwo
```

This example associates the strings "one" and "two" with the identifiers itemOne and itemTwo, respectively. The association of "one" with itemOne demonstrates how to use the Item property explicitly. The association of "two" with itemTwo uses the bracket syntax.

■**Note** This example also demonstrates a common pattern in F#. Note how you want to create the identifier stringList as an object from a non-F# library, yet at the same time initialize it to a certain state. To do this, you assign the object to a temporary identifier and then call an instance member on the object to manipulate its state. Finally, you return the temporary identifier, so it becomes the value of stringList. In this way, you keep the object creation and initialization logic close together.

Working with Events from .NET Libraries

Events are special properties of objects that allow you to attach functions to them. The functions you attach to events are sometimes referred to as *handlers*. When the event occurs, it executes all the functions that have been attached to it. For example, you might create a Button object that exposes a Click event, which occurs when a user clicks the button. This would mean that any functions that have been attached to the button's Click event would execute when the button is clicked. This is extremely useful because it's common to need notifications of what the user has done when creating user interfaces.

Adding a hander to an event is fairly straightforward. Each event exposes a method called Add, and the handling event is passed to this method. Events come from non-F# libraries, so the Add method follows the convention that its arguments must be surrounded by parentheses. In F# it is common to place the handler function inside the Add method itself, using F#'s anonymous function feature. The type of the handler function must match the type of the Add method's parameter, and this parameter has the type 'a -> unit. This means that for events exposed by objects in the BCL, the parameter of the Add method will have a type similar to EventArgs -> Unit.

The next example shows the creation of a Timer object and a function being added to the timer's Elapsed event. A Timer object is an object that fires its Elapsed event at regular intervals. In this case, the handler shows a message box displaying a notice to the user. Notice how you do not care about the argument that will be passed to the handler function, so you ignore it using the underscore:

```
open System.Windows.Forms
open System.Timers

let timer =
    // define the timer
    let temp = new Timer(Interval = 3000.0,
                         Enabled = true)

    // a counter to hold the current message
    let messageNo = ref 0

    // the messages to be shown
    let messages = [ "bet"; "this"; "gets";
                     "really"; "annoying";
                     "very"; "quickly" ]

    // add an event to the timer
    temp.Elapsed.Add(fun _ ->
        // show the message box
        MessageBox.Show(List.nth messages !messageNo) |> ignore
        // update the message counter
        messageNo := (!messageNo + 1) % (List.length messages))

    // return the timer to the top level
    temp

// print a message then wait for a user action
printfn "Whack the return to finish!"
System.Console.ReadLine() |> ignore
timer.Enabled <- false
```

■**Note** If you want to compile this program, you need to add a reference to the System.Windows.Forms.dll assemblies. This gives you access to the System.Windows.Forms namespace.

It is also possible to remove handlers from events. To do this, you must keep the function you will add to the event in scope; you can pass it to the event's RemoveHandler method. The RemoveHandler method accepts a delegate, which is an object that wraps a regular .NET method to allow it to be passed around like a value. This means the handler function must be given to the event already wrapped in a delegate and must therefore use the event's AddHandler (or Removehandler) method instead of its Add (or Remove) method. Creating a delegate in F# is straightforward. You simply call the delegate's constructor, the same way you call any constructor for an object from any non-F# library, passing it the function that delegate should wrap:

```
open System
open System.Windows.Forms

// define a form
let form =
    // the temporary form defintion
    let temp = new Form(Text = "Events example")

    // define an event handler
    let stuff _ _ = MessageBox.Show("This is \"Doing Stuff\"") |> ignore
    let stuffHandler = new EventHandler(stuff)

    // define a button and the event handler
    let event = new Button(Text = "Do Stuff", Left = 8, Top = 40, Width = 80)
    event.Click.AddHandler(stuffHandler)


    // label to show the event status
    let label = new Label(Top = 8, Left = 96)

    // bool to hold the event status and function
    // to print the event status to the label
    let eventAdded = ref true
    let setText b = label.Text <- (Printf.sprintf "Event is on: %b" !b)
    setText eventAdded

    // define a second button and it's click event handler
    let toggle = new Button(Text = "Toggle Event",
                            Left = 8, Top = 8, Width = 80)
    toggle.Click.Add(fun _ ->
        if !eventAdded then
            event.Click.RemoveHandler(stuffHandler)
        else
            event.Click.AddHandler(stuffHandler)
        eventAdded := not !eventAdded
        setText eventAdded)

    // add the controls to the form
    let dc c = (c :> Control)
    temp.Controls.AddRange([| dc toggle; dc event; dc label; |])
```

```
    // return the form to the top level
    temp

// start the event loop and show the form
do Application.Run(form)
```

This example shows you how to create a simple WinForm in F#. Events are synonymous with user-interface programming, so I thought it would be good to show an example event of events being used in this context. Near the beginning of the example, you create a delegate, stuffHandler, which is then added to the Click event on the button event. Later you add a handler directly to the toggle button's Click event, which adds or removes the handler from the button's event.

■**Caution** The previous sample will not work in the F# interactive console, fsi, because of the call to Application.Run. Users of fsi should replace this with form.Visible <- true;;.

Pattern Matching over .NET Types

As you saw in Chapter 3, pattern matching is a powerful feature of F#. Pattern matching allows a programmer to specify that different computations are executed depending on the value being matched against. F# has a construct that allows pattern matching over .NET types. The rule to match a .NET type is formed with a colon and question mark operator (:?) followed by the name of the .NET type you want to match. Because it is impossible to have an exhaustive list of .NET types, you must always provide a default rule when pattern matching over .NET types:

```
// a list of objects
let simpleList = [ box 1; box 2.0; box "three" ]

// a function that pattern matches over the
// type of the object it is passed
let recognizeType (item : obj) =
    match item with
    | :? System.Int32 -> printfn "An integer"
    | :? System.Double -> printfn "A double"
    | :? System.String -> printfn "A string"
    | _ -> printfn "Unknown type"

// iterate over the list of objects
List.iter recognizeType simpleList
```

Executing the preceding code produces the following results:

```
An integer
A double
```

A string

This example shows a function, recognizeType, that is designed to recognize three of the .NET basic types via pattern matching. This function is then applied to a list. This function has a couple of noteworthy details. First, the function takes an argument of the type obj, and you need to use a type annotation to make sure it does. If you didn't use the type annotation, the compiler would infer that the function can take any type and would use type 'a. This would be a problem because you cannot use pattern matching of this kind over F#'s types, but only over .NET types. Second, the function's default case uses the underscore to ignore the value.

Once you recognize that a value is of a certain type, it's common to want to do something with that value. To use the value on the right side of a rule, you can use the as keyword followed by an identifier. You can see this in the next example, where you rewrite recognizeType to include the value in the message that is printed when a type is recognized:

```
// list of objects
let anotherList = [ box "one"; box 2; box 3.0 ]

// pattern match and print value
let recognizeAndPrintType (item : obj) =
    match item with
    | :? System.Int32 as x -> printfn "An integer: %i" x
    | :? System.Double as x -> printfn "A double: %f" x
    | :? System.String as x -> printfn "A string: %s" x
    | x -> printfn "An object: %A" x

// interate over the list pattern matching each item
List.iter recognizeAndPrintType anotherList
```

When you compile and execute this example, you get the following results:

```
A string: one
An integer: 2
A double: 3.000000
```

Notice how you use an identifier for a final default rule. You don't need to match it to a type because you already know it will be of the type obj, as the value being matched over is already of the type obj.

Pattern matching over .NET types is also useful for handling exceptions thrown by .NET methods. You form the pattern match rules in the same way, except you use them with the try … with construct instead of the try … match construct. The next example shows you how to match and catch two .NET exceptions. You match over the exceptions thrown and then print a different message to the console depending on the type of exception thrown:

```
try
    // look at current time and raise an exception
    // based on whether the second is a multiple of 3
    if System.DateTime.Now.Second % 3 = 0 then
```

```
        raise (new System.Exception())
    else
        raise (new System.ApplicationException())
with
| :? System.ApplicationException ->
    // this will handle "ApplicationException" case
    printfn "A second that was not a multiple of 3"
| _ ->
    // this will handle all other exceptions
    printfn "A second that was a multiple of 3"
```

The |> Operator

You have already met the *pipe-forward* operator (|>) in the composing functions sections in Chapter 3. This operator allows you to pass a value to a function, reversing the order that the function and parameter would normally appear in the source file. As a quick reminder, the example that follows shows the operator's definition and usage:

```
// the definition of the pipe-forward operator
let (|>) x f = f x

// pipe the parameter 0.5 to the sin function
let result = 0.5 |> System.Math.Sin
```

This technique proves especially useful when working with .NET libraries because it helps the compiler infer the correct types for a function's parameters, without the need for explicit type annotations.

To understand why this operator is useful, it is helpful to probe a little deeper into how right-to-left type inference works. Consider the following simple example, where you define a list of integers, called intList, of the type int list, and then pass this list as the second argument to the library function List.iter. The first argument to List.iter is a function of the type int -> unit:

```
let intList = [ 1; 2; 3 ]
    // val printInt: int list

let printInt = printf "%i"
    // val printInt: int -> unit

List.iter printInt intList
```

Now you need to understand how these expressions in the program were assigned their types. The compiler started at the top of the input file, found the identifier intList, and inferred its type from the literal that is bound to it. Then it found the identifier printInt and inferred its type to be int -> unit because this is the type of the function returned from the call to the printfn function. Next, it found the function List.iter and knew that its type is ('a -> unit) -> 'a list -> unit. Because it has a generic or undetermined type 'a within it, the compiler examines the next identifier to the right, in this case the function printInt. This function has the type int -> unit, so the compiler infers that the type of the generic parameter 'a is int, which means the list passed to the function must be of the type int list.

So it is the type of the function that determines that what the type of the list must be. However, it is often useful to have the type of the function inferred from the type of the list that it will be applied to. This is especially true when working with .NET type, as it allows you to access their members without a type annotation. The pipe forward operator lets you do this by allowing you to place the list before the function that operates on it. Consider the following example:

```
open System

// a date list
let importantDates = [ new DateTime(1066,10,14);
                       new DateTime(1999,01,01);
                       new DateTime(2999,12,31) ]

// printing function
let printInt = printf "%i "

// case 1: type annotation required
List.iter (fun (d: DateTime) -> printInt d.Year) importantDates

// case 2: no type annotation required
importantDates |> List.iter (fun d -> printInt d.Year)
```

Here you have two ways of printing the year from a list of dates. In the first case, you need to add a type annotation to access the methods and properties on the DateTime structure. The type annotation is required because the compiler has not yet encountered the importantDates, so it has no information it can use to infer what the type of the parameter d of the anonymous function is. In the second case, the compiler infers automatically that d is of the type DateTime because it has encountered the importantDates list already, which means it has enough information to infer the type of d.

The pipe-forward operator also proves useful when trying to chain functions together; that is, when one function operates on the result of another. Consider the next example, where you obtain a list of all the .NET assemblies in memory and then process this list until you end up with a list of all the .NET methods in memory. As each function operates on the result of the previous function, the forward operator is used to show the results being piped or passed forward to the next function. You don't need to declare intermediate variables to hold the results of a function:

```
// grab a list of all methods in memory
let methods = System.AppDomain.CurrentDomain.GetAssemblies()
                |> List.ofArray
                |> List.map ( fun assm -> assm.GetTypes() )
                |> Array.concat
                |> List.ofArray
                |> List.map ( fun t -> t.GetMethods() )
                |> Array.concat

// print the list
printfn "%A" methods
```

You'll find this a useful technique, and it will crop up now and again throughout the rest of the book.

Summary

In this chapter, you learned about the imperative features of F#. Combining this information with the functional features covered in Chapter 3 gives you a full range of techniques to attack any computing problem. F# allows you to choose techniques from the appropriate paradigm and combine them whenever necessary. In the next chapter, you'll see how F# supports the third major programming paradigm, *object-oriented programming*.

CHAPTER 5

■ ■ ■

Object-Oriented Programming

Object-oriented programming is the third major programming paradigm. There has been a tendency to try and show that the function paradigm and the object-oriented paradigm as competing, but I believe them to be complementary techniques that work well together, which I will try to demonstrate in this chapter. At its heart, object-oriented programming has a few simple ideas, sometimes referred to as the tenets of object-oriented programming: encapsulation, polymorphism, and inheritance.

Possibly the most important tenet is *encapsulation*, the idea that the implementations and state should be *encapsulated*, or hidden behind well-defined boundaries. This makes the structure of a program easier to manage. In F#, you hide things by using signatures for modules and type definitions, as well as by simply defining them locally to an expression or class construction (you'll see examples of both in this chapter).

The second tenet, *polymorphism*, is the idea that you can implement abstract entities in multiple ways. You've met a number of simple abstract entities already, such as function types. A function type is abstract because you can implement a function with a specific type in many different ways; for example, you can implement the function type int -> int as a function that increments the given parameter, a function that decrements the parameter, or any one of millions of mathematical sequences. You can also build other abstract entities out of existing abstract components, such as the interface types defined in the .NET BCL. You can also model more sophisticated abstract entities using user-defined interface types. Interface types have the advantage that you can arrange them hierarchically; this is called *interface inheritance*. For example, the .NET BCL includes a hierarchical classification of collection types, available in the System.Collections and System.Collections.Generic namespaces.

In OOP, you can sometimes arrange implementation fragments hierarchically. This is called *implementation inheritance*, and it tends to be less important in F# programming because of the flexibility that functional programming provides for defining and sharing implementation fragments. However, it is significant for domains such as graphical user interface (GUI) programming.

While the tenets of object-oriented programming are import, object-oriented programming has also become synonymous with organizing your code around the values of the system *nouns* and then providing operations on those values as members, functions, or methods that operate on this value. This is often as simple as taking a function written in the style where the function is applied to a value (such as String.length s) and rewriting it using the dot notation (such as s.Length). This simple act can often make your code a good deal clearer. You'll see in this chapter how F# allows you to attach members to any of its types, not just its classes, enabling you to organize all your code in an object-oriented style if you wish.

F# provides a rich object-oriented programming model that allows you to create classes, interfaces, and objects that behave similarly to those created by C# and VB.NET. Perhaps more importantly, the classes you create in F# are indistinguishable from those that are created in other languages when packaged in a library and viewed by a user of that library. However, object-oriented programming is more than simply defining objects, as you'll see when you start looking at how you can program in an object-oriented style using F# native types.

Records As Objects

It is possible to use the record types you met in Chapter 3 to simulate object-like behavior. This is because records can have fields that are functions, which you can use to simulate an object's methods. While this technique does have some limitations compared to using F# classes, it also has some advantages. Only the function's type (or as some prefer, its *signature*) is given in the record definition, so you can easily swap the implementation without having to define a derived class, as you would in object-oriented programming. I discuss defining new implementations of objects in greater detail in the "Object Expressions" and "Inheritance" section later in this chapter.

Let's take a look at a simple example of using records as objects. The next example defines a type, Shape, that has two members. The first member, Reposition, is a function type that moves the shape; and the second member, Draw, draws the shape. You use the function makeShape to create a new instance of the shape type. The makeShape function implements the reposition functionality for you; it does this by accepting the initPos parameter, which is then stored in a mutable ref cell and updated when the reposition function is called. This means the position of the shape is encapsulated, accessible only through the reposition member. Hiding values in this way is a common technique in F# programming:

```
open System.Drawing

// a Shape record that will act as our object
type Shape =
    { Reposition: Point -> unit;
      Draw: unit -> unit }

// create a new instance of Shape
let makeShape initPos draw =
    // currPos is the internal state of the object
    let currPos = ref initPos
    { Reposition =
        // the Reposition member updates the internal state
        (fun newPos -> currPos := newPos);
      Draw =
        // draw the shape passing the current position
        // to given draw function
        (fun () -> draw !currPos); }

// "draws" a shape, prints out the shapes name and position
let draw shape (pos: Point) =
    printfn "%s, with x = %i and y = %i"
        shape pos.X pos.Y

// creates a new circle shape
let circle initPos =
    makeShape initPos (draw "Circle")
```

```
// creates a new square shape
let square initPos =
    makeShape initPos (draw "Square")

// list of shapes in their inital positions
let shapes =
    [ circle (new Point (10,10));
      square (new Point (30,30)) ]

// draw all the shapes
let drawShapes() =
    shapes |> List.iter (fun s -> s.Draw())

let main() =
    drawShapes() // draw the shapes
    // move all the shapes
    shapes |> List.iter (fun s -> s.Reposition (new Point (40,40)))
    drawShapes() // draw the shapes

// start the program
do main()
```

```
Circle, with x = 10 and y = 10
Square, with x = 30 and y = 30
Circle, with x = 40 and y = 40
Square, with x = 40 and y = 40
```

This example might seem trivial, but you can go quite a long way with this technique. The next example takes things to their natural conclusion, drawing the shapes on a form:

```
open System
open System.Drawing
open System.Windows.Forms

// a Shape record that will act as our object
type Shape =
    { Reposition: Point -> unit;
      Draw : Graphics -> unit }

// create a new instance of Shape
let movingShape initPos draw =
    // currPos is the internal state of the object
    let currPos = ref initPos in
```

```
    { Reposition =
        // the Reposition member updates the internal state
        (fun newPos -> currPos := newPos);
      Draw =
        // draw the shape passing the current position
        // and graphics object to given draw function
        (fun g -> draw !currPos g); }

// create a new circle Shape
let movingCircle initPos diam =
    movingShape initPos (fun pos g ->
        g.DrawEllipse(Pens.Blue,pos.X,pos.Y,diam,diam))

// create a new square Shape
let movingSquare initPos size =
    movingShape initPos (fun pos g ->
    g.DrawRectangle(Pens.Blue,pos.X,pos.Y,size,size) )

// list of shapes in their inital positions
let shapes =
    [ movingCircle (new Point (10,10)) 20;
      movingSquare (new Point (30,30)) 20;
      movingCircle (new Point (20,20)) 20;
      movingCircle (new Point (40,40)) 20; ]

// create the form to show the items
let mainForm =
    let form = new Form()
    let rand = new Random()
    // add an event handler to draw the shapes
    form.Paint.Add(fun e ->
        shapes |> List.iter (fun s ->
        s.Draw e.Graphics))
    // add an event handler to move the shapes
    // when the user clicks the form
    form.Click.Add(fun e ->
        shapes |> List.iter (fun s ->
        s.Reposition(new Point(rand.Next(form.Width),
                               rand.Next(form.Height)))
        form.Invalidate()))
    form

// Show the form and start the event loop
[<STAThread>]
do Application.Run(mainForm)
```

This application produces a GUI, as shown in Figure 5-1.

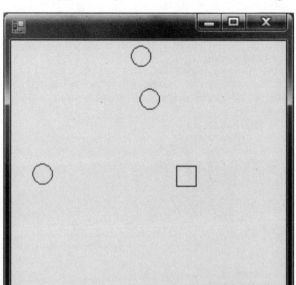

Figure 5-1. *Drawing shapes using records to simulate objects*

Again, you define a Shape record type that has the members Reposition and Draw. Next, you define the functions makeCircle and makeSquare to create different kinds of shapes, using them to define a list of Shape records. Finally, you define the form that will hold your records. Here you must do a bit more work than perhaps you would like. Because you don't use inheritance, the BCL's System.Winows.Forms.Form doesn't know anything about your shape *objects*, and you must iterate though the list, explicitly drawing each shape. This is quite simple to do, and it takes only three lines of code to you add an event handler to mainForm's Paint event:

```
temp.Paint.Add(
    fun e ->
        List.iter (fun s -> s.draw e.Graphics) shapes);
```

This example shows how you can quickly create multifunctional records without having to worry about any unwanted features you might also be inheriting. In the next section, you'll look at how you can represent operations on these objects in a more natural way: by adding members to F# types.

F# Types with Members

It is possible to add functions to both F#'s record and union types. You can call a function added to a record or union type using dot notation, just as you can a member of a class from a library not written in F#. It is also proves useful when you want to expose types you define in F# to other .NET languages. (I discuss this in more detail in Chapter 13.) Many programmers prefer to see function calls made on an instance value, and this technique provides a nice way of doing this for all F# types.

The syntax for defining an F# record or union type with members is the same as the syntax you learned in Chapter 3, except here it includes member definitions that always come at the end, after the with keyword. The definition of the members themselves start with the keyword member, followed by an identifier that represents the parameter of the type the member is being attached to, followed by a dot, the function name, and then any other parameters the function takes. After this comes an equals sign followed by the function definition, which can be any F# expression.

The following example defines a record type, Point. It has two fields, Left and Top; and a member function, Swap. The function Swap is a simple function that creates a new point with the values of Left and Top swapped over. Note how you use the x parameter, given before the function name Swap, within the function definition to access the record's other members:

```
// A point type
type Point =
    { Top: int;
      Left: int }
    with
        // the swap member creates a new point
        // with the left/top coords reveresed
        member x.Swap() =
            { Top = x.Left;
              Left = x.Top }

// create a new point
let myPoint =
    { Top = 3;
      Left = 7 }

let main() =
    // print the inital point
    printfn "%A" myPoint
    // create a new point with the coords swapped
    let nextPoint = myPoint.Swap()
    // print the new point
    printfn "%A" nextPoint

// start the app
do main()
```

When you compile and execute this example, you get the following results:

```
{Top = 3;
 Left = 7;}
{Top = 7;
 Left = 3;}
```

You might have noticed the x parameter in the definition of the function Swap:

```
member x.Swap() =
    { Top = x.Left;
      Left = x.Top }
```

This is the parameter that represents the object on which the function is being called. Now look at the case where you call a function on a value:

```
let nextPoint = myPoint.Swap()
```

The value you call the function on is passed to the function as an argument. This is logical when you think about it because the function needs to be able to access the fields and methods of the value on which you call it. Some OO languages use a specific keyword for this, such as this or Me, but F# lets you choose the name of this parameter by specifying a name for it after the keyword member—x, in this case.

Union types can have member functions, too. You define them in the same way that you define record types. The next example shows a union type, DrinkAmount, that has a function added to it:

```
// a type representing the amount of a specific drink
type DrinkAmount =
    | Coffee of int
    | Tea of int
    | Water of int
    with
        // get a string representation of the value
        override x.ToString() =
            match x with
            | Coffee x -> Printf.sprintf "Coffee: %i" x
            | Tea x -> Printf.sprintf "Tea: %i" x
            | Water x -> Printf.sprintf "Water: %i" x

// create a new instance of DrinkAmount
let t = Tea 2

// print out the string
printfn "%s" (t.ToString())
```

When you compile and execute this code, you get the following results:

```
Tea: 2
```

Note how this uses the keyword override in place of the keyword member. This has the effect of replacing, or *overriding*, an existing function of the base type. This is not that common a practice with function members associated with F# types because only four methods are available to be overridden:

ToString, Equals, GetHashCode, and Finalize. Every .NET type inherits these from System.Object. Because of the way some of these methods interact with the CLR, the only one I recommend overriding is ToString. Only four methods are available for overriding because record and union types can't act as base or derived classes, so you cannot inherit methods to override (except from System.Object).

Object Expressions

Object expressions are at the heart of succinct object-oriented programming in F#. They provide a concise syntax to create an object that inherits from an existing type. This is useful if you want to provide a short implementation of an abstract class or interface, or if you want to tweak an existing class definition. An object expression allows you to provide an implementation of a class or interface while at the same time creating a new instance of it.

You surround the definition of an object expression with braces. You put the name of the class or interfaces at the beginning. You must follow the name of a class with a pair of parentheses that can have any values passed to the constructor between them. Interface names need nothing after them, though both class names and interface names can have a type parameter following them; you need to surround this type parameter with angled brackets. Next, you include the keyword with and the definition of the methods of the class or interfaces you want to implement. You declare these methods just as you declare members on records and union types (see the previous section for more information on this). You declare each new method using the keywords member or override, followed by the instance parameter, a dot, and the method name. The name of the method must be the same as the name of a virtual or abstract method in the class or interface definition, and its parameters must be surrounded by parentheses and separated by commas, just as .NET methods must be (unless the method has one parameter, in which case you can get away with excluding the parentheses). Ordinarily you don't need to give type annotations; however, if the base class contains several overloads for a method, then you might have to give type annotations. You include an equals sign after the name of a method and its parameters, followed by the implementation of the method's body, which is an F# expression that must match the return value of the method:

```
open System
open System.Collections.Generic

// a comparer that will compare string in there reversed order
let comparer =
    { new IComparer<string>
        with
            member x.Compare(s1, s2) =
                // function to reverse a string
                let rev (s: String) =
                    new String(Array.rev (s.ToCharArray()))
                // reverse 1st string
                let reversed = rev s1
                // compare reversed string to 2nd strings reversed
                reversed.CompareTo(rev s2) }

// Eurovision winners in a random order
let winners =
    [| "Sandie Shaw"; "Bucks Fizz"; "Dana International" ;
```

```
        "Abba"; "Lordi" |]

// print the winners
printfn "%A" winners
// sort the winners
Array.Sort(winners, comparer)
// print the winners again
printfn "%A" winners
```

When you compile and execute the previous example, you get the following results:

```
[|"Sandie Shaw"; "Bucks Fizz"; "Dana International"; "Abba"; "Lordi"|]
[|"Abba"; "Lordi"; "Dana International"; "Sandie Shaw"; "Bucks Fizz"|]
```

This short snippet shows how to implement the IComparer interface. This is an interface with one method, Compare, that takes two parameters and returns an integer that represents the result of the parameter comparison. It accepts one type parameter; in this case, you pass it a string. You can see this on the second line of the definition of the identifier comparer. Next, you include the definition of the method body, which in this case compares reversed versions of the string parameters. Finally, you use the comparer by defining an array and then sorting, displaying the before and after results in the console.

It is possible to implement multiple interfaces or a class and several other interfaces within one object expression. It's also possible to attach an interface to a pre-existing class without altering any of the class methods. However, it is not possible to implement more than one class within an object expression, basically because neither F# nor the CLR allow multiple inheritance of classes. When you implement a class and an interface, the class must always come first in the expression. Regardless, the implementation of any other interfaces after the first interface or class must come after the definitions of all the methods of the first interface or class. You prefix the name of the interface with the keyword interface and follow that with the keyword with. The definition of the methods is the same as for the first interface or class. If you don't change any methods on the class, then you don't use the keyword with:

```
open System
open System.Drawing
open System.Windows.Forms

// create a new instance of a number control
let makeNumberControl (n: int) =
    { new TextBox(Tag = n, Width = 32, Height = 16, Text = n.ToString())
        // implement the IComparable interface so the controls
        // can be compared
```

```
        interface IComparable with
            member x.CompareTo(other) =
                let otherControl = other :?> Control in
                let n1 = otherControl.Tag :?> int in
                n.CompareTo(n1) }

// a sorted array of the numbered controls
let numbers =
    // initalize the collection
    let temp = new ResizeArray<Control>()
    // initalize the random number generator
    let rand = new Random()
    // add the controls collection
    for index = 1 to 10 do
        temp.Add(makeNumberControl (rand.Next(100)))
    // sort the collection
    temp.Sort()
    // layout the controls correctly
    let height = ref 0
    temp |> Seq.iter
        (fun c ->
            c.Top <- !height
            height := c.Height + !height)
    // return collection as an array
    temp.ToArray()

// create a form to show the number controls
let numbersForm =
    let temp = new Form() in
    temp.Controls.AddRange(numbers);
    temp

// show the form
[<STAThread>]
do Application.Run(numbersForm)
```

The previous example shows the definition of the object expression that implements the interface IComparable for the TextBox class. IComparable allows objects that implement this interface to be compared, primarily so they can be sorted. In this case, the implementation of IComparable's CompareTo method sorts the controls according to which number is displayed as the text of the TextBox. After you implement the makeNumberControl function, you create an array of controls, numbers. The definition of numbers is a little complicated. Begin by initializing it so it's full of controls in a random order, then you sort the array. Finally, ensure that each control is displayed at the appropriate height. You can see the resulting user interface in Figure 5-2.

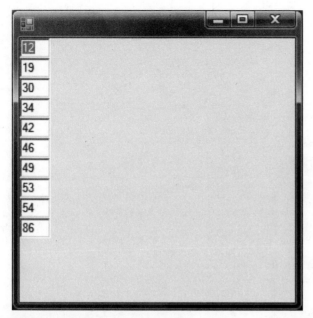

Figure 5-2. *Sorted text box controls*

You might also want to override methods from the object in the object expression. To do that in this case, you would use the same syntax, except you would follow the object name with the keyword with. Imagine that, instead of displaying the numbers in a text box, you want to custom draw them by overriding an object's OnPaint method:

```
open System
open System.Drawing
open System.Windows.Forms

// create a new instance of a number control
let makeNumberControl (n: int) =
    { new Control(Tag = n, Width = 32, Height = 16) with
        // override the controls paint method to draw the number
        override x.OnPaint(e) =
            let font = new Font(FontFamily.Families.[2], 12.0F)
            e.Graphics.DrawString(n.ToString(),
                                  font,
                                  Brushes.Black,
                                  new PointF(0.0F, 0.0F))
```

```
// implement the IComparable interface so the controls
// can be compared
interface IComparable with
    member x.CompareTo(other) =
        let otherControl = other :?> Control in
        let n1 = otherControl.Tag :?> int in
        n.CompareTo(n1) }
```

You can see the resulting user interface in Figure 5-3.

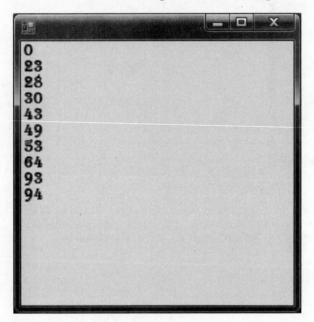

Figure 5-3. *Sorted, custom-drawn controls*

Object expressions are a powerful mechanism to quickly and concisely introduce object-oriented functionality from objects from non-F# libraries into your F# code. They have the drawback that they do not allow you to add extra properties or methods to these objects. For example, in the previous example, notice how it was necessary to place the number associated with control in the control's Tag property. This is more of a workaround than a proper solution. However, sometimes you don't need extra properties or methods on a type, and this syntax can be useful for those cases.

Defining Classes

You have already seen quite a few examples of using classes defined in the .NET BCL library; next, you'll learn how to define your own classes. In object-oriented programming, a class should model some concept used within the program or library you are creating. For example, the String class models a collection of characters, and the Process class models an operating-system process.

A class is a type, so a class definition starts with the type keyword, followed by the name of the class and the parameters of the class's constructor between parentheses. Next comes an equals sign, followed by a class's member definitions. The most basic member of a class is called a *method*, which is a function that has access to the parameters of the class.

The next example shows a class that represents a user. The user class's constructor takes two parameters: the users name and a hash of the user's password. Your class provides two member methods: Authenticate, which checks whether the user's password is valid; and LogonMessage, which gets a user-specific logon message:

```
open Strangelights.Samples.Helpers

// a class that represents a user
// it's constructor takes two parameters, the user's
// name and a hash of their password
type User(name, passwordHash) =
    // hashs the users password and checks it against
    // the known hash
    member x.Authenticate(password) =
        let hashResult = hash (password, "sha1")
        passwordHash = hashResult

    // gets the users logon message
    member x.LogonMessage() =
        Printf.sprintf "Hello, %s" name

// create a new instance of our user class
let user = User("Robert", "AF73C586F66FDC99ABF1EADB2B71C5E46C80C24A")


let main() =
    // authenticate user and print appropriate message
    if user.Authenticate("badpass") then
        printfn "%s" (user.LogonMessage())
    else
        printfn "Logon failed"

do main()
```

The second half of the example demonstrates how to use the class. It behaves exactly as like other classes you've seen from the .NET BCL. You can create a new instance of User using the new keyword, then call its member methods.

It's often useful to define values that are internal to your classes. Perhaps you need to pre-calculate a value that you share between several member methods, or maybe you need to retrieve some data for the object from an external data source. To enable this, objects can have let bindings that are internal to the object, but shared between all members of the object. You place the let bindings at the beginning of the class definition, after the equals sign, but before the first member definition. These let bindings form an implicit construct that execute when the object is constructed; if the let bindings have any side effects, then these too will occur when the object is constructed. If you need to call a function that has the unit type, such as when logging the objects construction, you must prefix the function call with the do keyword.

The next example demonstrates private let bindings by taking your User class and modifying it slightly. Now the class constructor takes a firstName and lastName, which you use in the let binding to calculate the user's fullName. To see what happens when you call a function with a side effect, you can print the user's fullName to the console:

```
open Strangelights.Samples.Helpers

// a class that represents a user
// it's constructor takes three parameters, the user's
// first name, last name and a hash of their password
type User(firstName, lastName, passwordHash) =
    // calculate the user's full name and store of later use
    let fullName = Printf.sprintf "%s %s" firstName lastName
    // print users fullname as object is being constructed
    do printfn "User: %s" fullName

    // hashs the users password and checks it against
    // the known hash
    member x.Authenticate(password) =
        let hashResult = hash (password, "sha1")
        passwordHash = hashResult

    // retrieves the users full name
    member x.GetFullname() = fullName
```

Notice how the members also have access to class's let bindings, the member GetFullName returns the pre-calculated fullName value.

It's common to need to be able to change values within classes. For example, you might need to provide a ChangePassword method to reset the user's password in the User class. F# gives you two approaches to accomplish this. You can make the object immutable; in this case, you copy the object's parameters, changing the appropriate value as you go. This method is generally considered to fit better with functional-style programming, but it can be a little inconvenient if the object has a lot of parameters or is expensive to create. For example, doing this might be computationally expensive, or it might require a lot of I/O to construct it. The next example illustrates this approach. Notice how in the ChangePassword method you call the hash function on the password parameter, passing this to the User object's constructor along with the user's name:

```
open Strangelights.Samples.Helpers

// a class that represents a user
// it's constructor takes two parameters, the user's
// name and a hash of their password
type User(name, passwordHash) =
    // hashs the users password and checks it against
    // the known hash
    member x.Authenticate(password) =
        let hashResult = hash (password, "sha1")
        passwordHash = hashResult

    // gets the users logon message
    member x.LogonMessage() =
        Printf.sprintf "Hello, %s" name

    // creates a copy of the user with the password changed
    member x.ChangePassword(password) =
        new User(name, hash password)
```

The alternative to an immutable object is to make the value you want to change mutable. You do this by binding it to a mutable let binding. You can see this in the next example, where you bind the class's parameter passwordHash to a mutable let binding of the same name:

```
open Strangelights.Samples.Helpers

// a class that represents a user
// it's constructor takes two parameters, the user's
// name and a hash of their password
type User(name, passwordHash) =
    // store the password hash in a mutable let
    // binding, so it can be changed later
    let mutable passwordHash = passwordHash

    // hashs the users password and checks it against
    // the known hash
    member x.Authenticate(password) =
        let hashResult = hash (password, "sha1")
        passwordHash = hashResult

    // gets the users logon message
    member x.LogonMessage() =
        Printf.sprintf "Hello, %s" name
```

```
// changes the users password
member x.ChangePassword(password) =
    passwordHash <- hash password
```

This means you are free to update the passwordHash to a let binding, as you do in the ChangePassword method.

Optional Parameters

Member methods of classes (as well as member methods of other types) and class constructors can have optional parameters. These are useful because they allow you to set default input values. This means users of your class don't have to specify all its arguments, which can help make client code look cleaner and less cluttered.

You mark a parameter as optional by prefixing it with a question mark. You can have more than one optional parameter, but optional parameters must always appear at the end of the parameter list. Also, you must use *tuple* style in cases where you have a member method that contains more than one argument with one or more optional arguments. You do this by surrounding optional arguments with parentheses, separated by commas. An optional parameter might (or might not) have a type annotation. This type annotation appears after the parameter name, separated by a colon. Optional parameters are always of the option<'a> type, so you must not include them in the type annotation.

The following example shows some optional parameters in action. Here you define a class, AClass, that has an optional integer as a parameter of its constructor. This class has one member method, PrintState, and two parameters (the second parameter is optional). As you might expect, you use pattern matching over the option<'a> type to test whether the optional parameters were passed as an argument:

```
type AClass(?someState:int) =
    let state =
        match someState with
        | Some x -> string x
        | None -> "<no input>"
    member x.PrintState (prefix, ?postfix) =
        match postfix with
        | Some x -> printfn "%s %s %s" prefix state x
        | None -> printfn "%s %s" prefix state

let aClass = new AClass()
let aClass' = new AClass(109)

aClass.PrintState("There was ")
aClass'.PrintState("Input was:", ", which is nice.")
```

The second half of the example shows some of the class's client code. You create two instances of the class: you create the first class without any arguments being passed to the constructor; and you create the second with a value of 109 being passed to the constructor. Next, you call the PrintState member of the class, calling it initially without the optional argument, then calling it again with the optional argument. Compiling and executing this code produces the following results:

```
There was  <no input>
Input was: 109 , which is nice.
```

Currently functions defined by let bindings cannot have optional parameters. It is under investigation how optional parameters for functions might be added to the language in a future version.

Defining Interfaces

Interfaces can contain only abstract methods and properties, or members that you declare using the keyword abstract. Interfaces define a *contract* for all classes that implement them, exposing those components that clients can use while insulating clients from their actual implementation. A class can inherit from only one base class, but it can implement any number of interfaces. Because any class implementing an interface can be treated as being of the interface type, interfaces provide similar benefits to multiple-class inheritance, while avoiding the complexity of that approach.

You define interfaces by defining a type that has no constructor and where all the members are abstract. The following example defines an interface that declares two methods: Authenticate and LogonMessage. Notice how the interface name starts with a capital I; this is a naming convention that is strictly followed thought the .NET BCL, and you should follow it in your code too because it will help other programs distinguish between classes and interfaces when reading your code:

```
// an interface "IUser"
type IUser =
    // hashs the users password and checks it against
    // the known hash
    abstract Authenticate: evidence: string -> bool
    // gets the users logon message
    abstract LogonMessage: unit -> string

let logon (user: IUser) =
    // authenticate user and print appropriate message
    if user.Authenticate("badpass") then
        printfn "%s" (user.LogonMessage())
    else
        printfn "Logon failed"
```

The second half of the example illustrates the advantages of interfaces. You can define a function that uses the interface without knowing the implementation details. You define a logon function that takes an IUser parameter and uses it to perform a logon. This function will then work with any implementations of IUser. This is extremely useful in many situations; for example, it enables you to write one set of client code that you can reuse with several different implementations of the interface.

Implementing Interfaces

To implement an interface, use the keyword `interface`, followed by the interface name, the keyword `with`, and then the code to implement the interface members. You prefix member definitions with the keyword `member`, but they are otherwise the same as the definition of any method or property. You can implement interfaces by either classes or structs; you can learn how to create classes in some detail in the following sections, and you can learn more about structs in the "Structs" section later in this chapter.

The next example defines, implements, and uses an interface. The interface is the same IUser interface you implemented in the previous section; here you implement it in a class called User:

```
open Strangelights.Samples.Helpers

// an interface "IUser"
type IUser =
    // hashs the users password and checks it against
    // the known hash
    abstract Authenticate: evidence: string -> bool
    // gets the users logon message
    abstract LogonMessage: unit -> string

// a class that represents a user
// it's constructor takes two parameters, the user's
// name and a hash of their password
type User(name, passwordHash) =
    interface IUser with
        // Authenticate implementation
        member x.Authenticate(password) =
            let hashResult = hash (password, "sha1")
            passwordHash = hashResult

        // LogonMessage implementation
        member x.LogonMessage() =
            Printf.sprintf "Hello, %s" name

// create a new instance of the user
let user = User("Robert", "AF73C586F66FDC99ABF1EADB2B71C5E46C80C24A")
// cast to the IUser interface
let iuser = user :> IUser
// get the logon message
let logonMessage = iuser.LogonMessage()
```

```
let logon (iuser: IUser) =
    // authenticate user and print appropriate message
    if iuser.Authenticate("badpass") then
        printfn "%s" logonMessage
    else
        printfn "Logon failed"

do logon user
```

Notice how in the middle of example you see *casting* for the first time; you can find a more detailed explanation of casting at the end of the chapter in the "Casting" section. But for now here's a quick summary of what happens: the identifier user is cast to the interface IUser via the downcast operator, :?>:

```
// create a new instance of the user
let user = User("Robert", "AF73C586F66FDC99ABF1EADB2B71C5E46C80C24A")
// cast to the IUser interface
let iuser = user :?> IUser
```

This is necessary because interfaces are explicitly implemented in F#. Before you can use the method LogonMessage, you must have an identifier that is of the type IUser and not just of a class that implements IUser. Toward the end of the example, you will work around this in a different way. The function logon takes a parameter of the IUser type:

```
let logon (iuser: IUser) =
```

When you call logon with a class that implements IUser, the class is implicitly downcast to this type.

You can add the interface members to the definition of the class if you want the methods of the interface to be available directly on the class that implements it, instead of after forcing the users of your class to cast the object to the interface in some way. To revise the example, you simply add the methods Authenticate and LogonMessage as members of the class User. Now it is no longer necessary to cast the identifier user (you'll learn about adding members to methods in the "Classes and Methods" section later in the chapter):

```
open Strangelights.Samples.Helpers

// a class that represents a user
// it's constructor takes two parameters, the user's
// name and a hash of their password
type User(name, passwordHash) =
    interface IUser with
        // Authenticate implementation
        member x.Authenticate(password) =
            let hashResult = hash (password, "sha1")
            passwordHash = hashResult
```

```
        // LogonMessage implementation
        member x.LogonMessage() =
            Printf.sprintf "Hello, %s" name


    // Expose Authenticate implementation
    member x.Authenticate(password) = x.Authenticate(password)
    // Expose LogonMessage implementation
    member x.LogonMessage() = x.LogonMessage()
```

Classes and Inheritance

I have already covered inheritance in a limited way in the "Object Expressions" and "Implementing Interfaces" sections. Inheritance allows you to extend a class that is already defined, as well as to add new functionality or possibly to modify or replace the original functionality. Like most modern, object-oriented languages, F# allows single inheritance (from one base class), as well as the implementation of multiple interfaces (see the previous sections, "Defining interfaces" and "Implementing Interfaces"). This section will cover the basics of inheriting from a base class and adding new functionality. The next section, "Methods and Inheritance," will show you how to implement methods to make full use of inheritance.

You specify inheritance with the inherit keyword, which must come directly after the equals sign, which follows a class's constructor. After the keyword inheritance, you provide the name of the class you want to inherit from, followed by the arguments you intend to pass to its constructor. Let's kick things off by looking at a simple example of inheritance between two F# types. The following example shows an F# class, Sub, that derives from a base class, Base. The class Base has one method, GetState; and the class Sub also has one method, called GetOtherState. The example shows that how the Sub-derived class can use both methods because GetState is inherited from the base class:

```
type Base() =
    member x.GetState() = 0

type Sub() =
    inherit Base()
    member x.GetOtherState() = 0

let myObject = new Sub()

printfn
    "myObject.state = %i, myObject.otherState = %i"
    (myObject.GetState())
    (myObject.GetOtherState())
```

When you compile and execute this example, you get the following results:

```
myObject.state = 0, myObject.otherState = 0
```

Methods and Inheritance

The preceding sections gave you the basics of inheritance between classes. Now you'll take a look at getting the most out of object-oriented programming by learning how to override methods and give them new behaviors. A derived class can define new methods, as well as override methods inherited from its base class.

You define methods are defined using one of four keywords: member, override, abstract, or default. You've already seen the keywords member and abstract, which you use to define methods. The Member keyword defines a simple method that cannot be overridden with an implementation, while the abstract keyword defines a method with no implementation that must be overridden in a derived class. The override keyword defines a method that overrides an inherited method that has an implementation in a base class. Finally, the keyword default has a similar meaning to the override keyword, except it is used only to override an abstract method.

The next example illustrates how to use all four kinds of methods:

```
// a base class
type Base() =
    // some internal state for the class
    let mutable state = 0
    // an ordinary member method
    member x.JiggleState y = state <- y
    // an abstract method
    abstract WiggleState: int -> unit
    // a default implementation for the abstract method
    default x.WiggleState y = state <- y + state
    member x.GetState() = state

// a sub class
type Sub() =
    inherit Base()
    // override the abstract method
    default x.WiggleState y = x.JiggleState (x.GetState() &&& y)

// create instances of both methods
let myBase = new Base()
let mySub = new Sub()

// a small test for our classes
let testBehavior (c : #Base) =
    c.JiggleState 1
    printfn "%i" (c.GetState())
    c.WiggleState 3
    printfn "%i" (c.GetState())
```

```
// run the tests
let main() =
    printfn "base class: "
    testBehavior myBase
    printfn "sub class: "
    testBehavior mySub

do main()
```

When you compile and execute the results of this example, you get the following results:

```
base class:
1
4
sub class:
1
1
```

You first implement a method, JiggleState, in class Base. The method cannot be overridden, so all derived classes will inherit this implementation. You then define an abstract method, WiggleState, that can be overridden (and, in fact, must be) by derived classes. To define a new method that can be overridden, you always need to use a combination of the abstract and default keywords. This could mean that you use abstract on the base class, while you use default on the derived class; however, you will often use them together in the same class, as shown in the previous example. This requires you to give types explicitly to a method you provide to be overridden. Although the F# philosophy doesn't generally require the programmer to give explicit types, leaving it to the compiler work them out, the compiler has no way to infer these types, so you must give them explicitly.

As shown in the preceding results, the behavior remains the same in both the base class and the derived class when JiggleState is called; this is in contrast to the behavior of WiggleState, which changes because it is overridden.

Accessing the Base Class

When accessing a virtual method within a class, the version of the method in the most-derived class is called. This means that if you try to call a method on the base class that has been overridden by the derived class, then it will automatically call the version on the derived class. Ordinarily, you use this technique to call the base implementation of a method you want to override. This isn't always necessary, but it's generally required by library design-guidelines because it can lead to the base class malfunctioning if you do not do this.

To get access to methods on the base class, you use the base keyword that gives you access to the base class's methods. The following example shows an implementation of a class that derives from System.Windows.Form. The identifier base is assigned to base class Form, as shown at the top of the definition of the MySquareForm class. The example uses implicit class construction, indicated by the fact that the type MySquareForm takes a single parameter, color:

```
open System.Drawing
open System.Windows.Forms

// define a class that inherits from 'Form'
type MySquareForm(color) =
    inherit Form()
    // override the OnPaint method to draw on the form
    override x.OnPaint(e) =
        e.Graphics.DrawRectangle(color,
                                 10, 10,
                                 x.Width - 30,
                                 x.Height - 50)
        base.OnPaint(e)
    // override the OnResize method to respond to resizing
    override x.OnResize(e) =
        x.Invalidate()
        base.OnResize(e)

// create a new instance of the form
let form = new MySquareForm(Pens.Blue)

// show the form
do Application.Run(form)
```

In this form, you override two methods, OnPaint and OnResize; and in these methods, you use the keyword base, which grants access to the base class that you use to call the base class's implementation of this method.

Properties and Indexers

A property is a special type of method that looks like a value to the code that calls it. Indexers fulfill a similar purpose; they make a method look a bit like a collection to the calling code. Both properties and indexers have accessors, which include a get accessor for reading and a set accessor for writing.

A property definition starts the same way as a method definition, with the keyword member followed by the parameter that represents the object. Next, you include a dot and then the member name. Instead of using the method parameters after this, you use the keyword with, followed by either get or set. The parameters come next; a get method must take unit, and a set method must take a single parameter. An equals sign follows next, then an expression that forms the method body. If a second method is required, you use the keyword and to join them together.

The following sample shows the definition of a class that has a single property, MyProp, which returns a random number. Setting the property resets the seed of the random-number generator:

```
// a class with properties
type Properties() =
    let mutable rand = new System.Random()
```

```
    // a property definition
    member x.MyProp
        with get () = rand.Next()
        and set y = rand <- new System.Random(y)

// create a new instance of our class
let prop = new Properties()

// run some tests for the class
prop.MyProp <- 12
printfn "%d" prop.MyProp
printfn "%d" prop.MyProp
printfn "%d" prop.MyProp
```

When you compile and execute this example, you get the following results:

```
2137491492
726598452
334746691
```

You can also declare abstract properties. The syntax is similar, but you replace the keyword member with abstract, and you omit the parameter that represents the object, just as you do for a method. After the member name, you include the name of the type, separated from the member name by a colon. The keyword with comes next, followed by either get or set, which represents whether the inheritor must implement a get or set method, or both, separated by a comma. Properties look exactly like a field to the calling code.

The next example revises the previous one so now it uses an interface, IAbstractProperties. You will notice how the derived class ConcreteProperties must implement the get and set methods using the keywords with and and:

```
// an interface with an abstract property
type IAbstractProperties =
    abstract MyProp: int
        with get, set

// a class that implements our interface
type ConcreteProperties() =
    let mutable rand = new System.Random()
    interface IAbstractProperties with
        member x.MyProp
            with get() = rand.Next()
            and set(y) = rand <- new System.Random(y)
```

Indexers are properties that take two or more parameters, one to represent the element being placed in the pseudo-collection and others to represent the index in it. In C#, all indexers are called Item in the underlying implementation, but the programmer never uses this name because it is always implicit. In F#, the programmer can choose the name of the indexer property. If the programmer chooses the name Item, then F# provides special syntax for accessing the property.

The syntax for creating an indexer is the same as for a property, except that a get method has one or more parameters, and a set method has two or more parameters. The next step is to access an element in an indexer. If its name is Item, you can use a special syntax that looks like array access, except you use replace the parentheses replaced with square brackets:

```
// a class with indexers
type Indexers(vals:string[]) =
    // a normal indexer
    member x.Item
        with get y = vals.[y]
        and set y z = vals.[y] <- z
    // an indexer with an unusual name
    member x.MyString
        with get y = vals.[y]
        and set y z = vals.[y] <- z

// create a new instance of the indexer class
let index = new Indexers [|"One"; "Two"; "Three"; "Four"|]

// test the set indexers
index.[0] <- "Five";
index.Item(2) <- "Six";
index.MyString(3) <- "Seven";

// test the get indexers
printfn "%s" index.[0]
printfn "%s" (index.Item(1))
printfn "%s" (index.MyString(2))
printfn "%s" (index.MyString(3))
```

When you compile and execute the preceding example, you get the following results:

```
Five
Two
Six
Seven
```

■**Note** When working with indexers with a name other than Item, you should keep in mind that it will be difficult for other .NET languages to use your classes.

Overriding Methods from Non-F# Libraries

When overriding methods from non-F# libraries, you must implement the method definition in the tuple style; that is, you must surround the parameters with parentheses and separated them by commas.

The following sample shows a class that implements the interface, System.Net.ICredentials. Its single method, GetCredential, has two parameters. Just after the place where you implement the interface, you can see how to use the interface as a value in the method GetCredentialList:

```
type CredentialsFactory() = class
    interface System.Net.ICredentials with
        member x.GetCredential(uri, authType) =
            new System.Net.NetworkCredential("rob", "whatever", "F# credentials")
    member x.GetCredentialList uri authTypes =
        let y = (x :> System.Net.ICredentials)
        let getCredential s = y.GetCredential(uri, s)
        List.map getCredential authTypes
end
```

You can learn more about the relationship between F# signatures and C# signatures in Chapter 14.

Abstract Classes

The generally accepted way of defining a contract in F# is to use an interface, which works well for the most part. However, interfaces have one significant drawback: any change to an interface's definition is a breaking change to client code. This isn't a problem if you're creating the application, and you have complete control over the code base. Indeed, it can even be useful because the compiler will automatically notify you of all the code than needs changing. However, if you're shipping the interface as part of a library, then you are likely to run into problems if you change your interface's definition. This is where abstract classes prove useful. For example, assume you have an interface that an abstract class defines as a *contract*; the important difference here is that abstract bases classes can have concrete methods and properties. This makes versioning an abstract-base class easier than versioning an interface because you can add a concrete member without making breaking changes. Unlike interfaces, abstract class can have concrete members, which means a class can only inherit from one abstract class.

The abstract class syntax is exactly the same as the syntax for a class, except an abstract class can have abstract members. To ensure that you haven't made a mistake in adding an abstract member that you didn't provide an implementation for, you need to make the abstract class with the [<AbstactClass>] attribute. The next example shows what your User example might look like if you were to choose to use an abstract class:

```
// a abstract class that represents a user
// it's constructor takes one parameters,
// the user's name
[<AbstractClass>]
type User(name) =
    // the implmentation of this method should hashs the
    // users password and checks it against the known hash
    abstract Authenticate: evidence: string -> bool
```

```
// gets the users logon message
member x.LogonMessage() =
    Printf.sprintf "Hello, %s" name
```

Classes and Static Methods

Static methods are like instance methods, except they are not specific to any instance of a class, so have no access to a class's fields.

To create a static method, you use the keyword static, followed by the keyword member. Next, you include the method name, its parameters, an equals sign, and then the method definition. This is basically the same as declaring an instance method, but with the addition of the keyword static and the removal of the parameter that represents the object. Removing the parameter that represents the object is quite logical because the method has no access to the object's properties.

Static methods are useful for providing alternative ways of creating a new instance of an object. F# provides no way of overloading class constructors, so you provide a static method that calls the class's constructor. In the next example, you return to the User class example, this time adding a static method that allows you to create a user from its unique identifier in the database:

```
open Strangelights.Samples.Helpers

// a class that represents a user
// it's constructor takes two parameters, the user's
// name and a hash of their password
type User(name, passwordHash) =
    // hashs the users password and checks it against
    // the known hash
    member x.Authenticate(password) =
        let hashResult = hash (password, "sha1")
        passwordHash = hashResult

    // gets the users logon message
    member x.LogonMessage() =
        Printf.sprintf "Hello, %s" name

    // a static member that provides an alterative way
    // of creating the object
    static member FromDB id =
        let name, ph = getUserFromDB id
        new User(name, ph)

let user = User.FromDB 1
```

Notice that the static methods called use the name of the type they are associated with, rather than a value of the type the method is associated with.

Static methods can also be useful for providing operators for your classes to use. The basic syntax for declaring an operator is the same as for declaring any other static method, except that you replace the name of the method with the operator in brackets. You must provide the parameters of the operator as a tuple; typically, you need to use type annotations to indicate their types.

The following example assumes that you want to reimplement the int type in a class called MyInt. The MyInt class has a plus operator defined on it:

```
type MyInt(state:int) = class
    member x.State = state
    static member ( + ) (x:MyInt, y:MyInt) : MyInt = new MyInt(x.State + y.State)
    override x.ToString() = string state
end

let x = new MyInt(1)
let y = new MyInt(1)

printfn "(x + y) = %A" (x + y)
```

When you compile and execute the preceding example, you get the following results:

```
(x + y) = 2
```

Classes with Explicit Fields and Constructors

So far this chapter has concentrated on the *implicit* syntax for classes, but F# also has another type of syntax: the *explicit* syntax. The implicit syntax is generally preferable for a number of reasons. First, it's often a good deal shorter than the explicit syntax. Second, the F# compiler can optimize the class. The implicit syntax often means that let bindings and parameters to the class's constructor don't need to become fields in the class. With the implicit syntax, the compiler is free to remove them, if possible (making the object smaller in memory). However, these optimizations are occasionally unwelcome. Certain APIs that use reflection require classes and their instances to have certain fields; in this case, you as a programmer need the additional control that using the explicit syntax can give you.

In the explicit syntax, you don't provide the class constructor after the type name; instead, the type name is followed directly by the equals sign, the keyword class, and the definition (such as type User = class ...). When using the explicit syntax, you terminate the class with the keyword end.

You define fields using the keyword val, followed by the name of the field and the name of the type, which is separated from the property name by a colon. Fields in a class are immutable by default; once they have been bound to a value, the value can be rebound to another value. From time to time, it can be useful to rebind a field to another value. To allow this to happen, F# provides the keyword mutable; when a field is defined as mutable, it can be rebound whenever the programmer chooses.

To enable you to create an instance of the class, you must explicitly add a constructor. To do this, you need to add a member, which is always named new and is followed by the constructor within parentheses. Next, you include an equals sign, followed by a block (delimited by braces) that contains expressions to initialize every field in the class. It's possible to overload constructors, which you accomplish by adding a second constructor with a different number of parameters. If you want to overload with parameters of different types, then you must provide type annotations.

The next example rewrites the first class example you saw, a demonstration of a simple User class, in the explicit style. This makes the example several lines longer:

```
open System.Web.Security

// give shorte name to password hashing method
let hash = FormsAuthentication.HashPasswordForStoringInConfigFile

// a class that represents a user
// it's constructor takes two parameters, the user's
// name and a hash of their password
type User = class
    // the class' fields
    val name: string
    val passwordHash: string

    // the class' constructor
    new (name, passwordHash) =
        { name = name; passwordHash = passwordHash }

    // hashs the users password and checks it against
    // the known hash
    member x.Authenticate(password) =
        let hashResult = hash (password, "sha1")
        x.passwordHash = hashResult

    // gets the users logon message
    member x.LogonMessage() =
        Printf.sprintf "Hello, %s" x.name
end
```

Casting

You've already encountered casting, which was discussed briefly in the "Implementing Interfaces" section of this chapter. Casting is a way of explicitly altering the static type of a value by either throwing information away, which is known as *upcasting*, or rediscovering it, which is known as *downcasting*. In F#, upcasts and downcasts have their own operators. The type hierarchy starts with obj (or System.Object) at the top, with all its descendants below it. An upcast moves a type up the hierarchy, while a downcast moves a type down the hierarchy.

Upcasts change a value's static type to one of its ancestor types. This is a safe operation. The compiler can always tell whether this will work because the compiler always knows all the ancestors of a type, so it's able to work use static analysis to determine whether an upcast will be successful. An upcast is represented by a colon, followed by the greater-than sign (:>). The following code shows you how to use an upcast to convert a string to an obj:

```
let myObject = ("This is a string" :> obj)
```

Generally, you must use upcasts when defining collections that contain disparate types. If you don't use an upcast, the compiler will infer that the collection has the type of the first element and give a compile error if elements of other types are placed in the collection. The next example demonstrates how to create an array of controls, a common task when working with WinForms. Notice that you upcast all the individual controls to their common base class, Control:

```
open System.Windows.Forms

let myControls =
    [| (new Button() :> Control);
       (new TextBox() :> Control);
       (new Label() :> Control) |]
```

An upcast also has the effect of automatically boxing any value type. Value types are held in memory on the program stack, rather than on the managed heap. Boxing means that the value is pushed onto the managed heap, so it can be passed around by reference. The following example demonstrates how to box a value:

```
let boxedInt = (1 :> obj)
```

A downcast changes a value's static type to one of its descendant types; thus, it recovers information hidden by an upcast. Downcasting is dangerous because the compiler doesn't have any way to determine statically whether an instance of a type is compatible with one of its derived types. This means you can get it wrong, and this will cause an invalid cast exception (System.InvalidCastException) to be issued at runtime. Due to the inherent danger of downcasting, many developers prefer to replace it with pattern matching over .NET types, as demonstrated in Chapter 3. Nevertheless, a downcast can be useful in some places, so a downcast operator, which consists of a colon, question mark, and a greater-than sign (:?>), is available. The next example shows you how to use downcasting:

```
open System.Windows.Forms

let moreControls =
    [| (new Button() :> Control);
       (new TextBox() :> Control) |]

let control =
    let temp = moreControls.[0]
    temp.Text <- "Click Me!"
    temp

let button =
    let temp = (control :?> Button)
    temp.DoubleClick.Add(fun e -> MessageBox.Show("Hello") |> ignore)
    temp
```

The preceding example creates an array of two Windows control objects, upcasting them to their base class, `Control`. Next, it binds the first control to the `control` identifier; downcasts this to its specific type, `Button`; and adds a handler to its `DoubleClick` event, an event not available on the `Control` class.

Type Tests

Closely related to casting is the idea of type tests. You can bind an identifier to an object of a derived type, as you did earlier when you bound a `string` to an identifier of type `obj`:

```
let myObject = ("This is a string" :> obj)
```

You can bind an identifier to an object of a derived type, so it is often useful to be able to test what this type is. To do this, F# provides a type-test operator, which consists of a colon followed by a question mark (`:?`). To compile, the operator and its operands must be surrounded by parentheses. If the identifier in the type test is of the specified type or a type derived from it, the operator returns true; otherwise, it returns false. The next example shows two type tests, one that returns true and another that returns false:

```
let anotherObject = ("This is a string" :> obj)

if (anotherObject :? string) then
    printfn "This object is a string"
else
    printfn "This object is not a string"

if (anotherObject :? string[]) then
    printfn "This object is a string array"
else
    printfn "This object is not a string array"
```

First you create an identifier, `anotherObject`, of type `obj`, binding it to a `string`. Then you test whether the `anotherObject` is a `string`, which returns true. Next, you test whether it is a `string array`, which, of course, returns false.

Type Annotations for Subtyping

As shown in Chapter 3, type annotations provide a way of constraining an identifier, usually a parameter of a function, to a certain type. What might seem counterintuitive to an OO programmer is that the form of type annotation introduced in Chapter 3 is rigid; in other words, it does not take into account the inheritance hierarchy. This means that if you apply such a type annotation to an expression, then that expression must have precisely that type statically; a derived type will not fit in its place. To illustrate this point, consider the following example:

```
open System.Windows.Forms

let showForm (form : Form) =
    form.Show()
```

```
// PrintPreviewDialog is defined in the BCL and is
// derived directly the Form class
let myForm = new PrintPreviewDialog()

showForm myForm
```

When you try to compile the previous example, you receive the following error:

```
Prog.fs(11,10): error: FS0001: This expression has type
    PrintPreviewDialog
but is here used with type
    Form
```

One way to call a function with a rigid type annotation on a parameter is to use an explicit upcast at the place where you call the function to change the type so it's the same as the type of the function's parameter. The following line of code changes the type of myForm to match the type of the parameter of showForm:

```
showForm (myForm :> Form)
```

Upcasting the argument to showForm is a solution, but it's not a pretty one because it means littering client code with upcasts. So, F# provides another type annotation, the *derived type annotation*, in which the type name is prefixed with a hash sign. This has the effect of constraining an identifier to be of a certain type or any of its derived types. This means you can rewrite the preceding example to remove the need for explicit upcasts in the calling code, which is a huge benefit to anyone using the functions you define:

```
open System
open System.Windows.Forms

let showFormRevised (form : #Form) =
    form.Show()

// ThreadExceptionDialog is define in the BCL and is
// directly derived type of the Form class
let anotherForm = new ThreadExceptionDialog(new Exception())
showFormRevised anotherForm
```

You can use this kind of type annotation to tidy up code that uses a lot of casting. For example, you often need a lot of casting when creating a collection with a common base type, and this can leave code looking a little bulkier than it should (the "Casting" section earlier in this chapter illustrates this point nicely). A good way to remove this repeated casting—as with any commonly repeated section of code— is to define a function that does it for you:

```
open System.Windows.Forms

let myControls =
    [| (new Button() :> Control);
       (new TextBox() :> Control);
       (new Label() :> Control) |]

let uc (c : #Control) = c :> Control

let myConciseControls =
    [| uc (new Button()); uc (new TextBox()); uc (new Label()) |]
```

This example shows how to define two arrays of controls. The first, myControls, explicitly upcasts every control; the second, myConciseControls, delegates this job to a function. This is also a good technique to adopt given that the bigger the array, the more effort and code this technique saves you. It is quite common for these arrays to get quite big when working with WinForms.

Defining Delegates

Delegates are the mechanism that both C# and Visual Basic use to treat their methods as values. A delegate basically acts as a .NET object that wraps the method and provides an invoke method so the method can be called. You rarely need to define delegates in F# because it can treat a function as a value, without the need for any wrapper. However, sometimes delegates prove useful, such as when you need to define delegates to expose F# functionality to other .NET languages in a friendlier manner, or you need to define callbacks for directly calling C code from F#.

To define a delegate, you use the keyword delegate, followed directly by the keyword of, and the type of the delegate's signature, which follows the standard F# type annotation.

The next example shows the definition of a delegate, MyDelegate, which takes an int and returns unit. You then create a new instance of this delegate and apply it to a list of integers. As you've already seen in Chapter 3, you implement this functionality in F# in much shorter ways:

```
type MyDelegate = delegate of int -> unit

let inst = new MyDelegate (fun i -> printf "%i" i)
let ints = [1 ; 2 ; 3 ]

ints
|> List.iter (fun i -> inst.Invoke(i))
```

When you compile and execute the preceding example, you get the following results:

Structs

You define structs in a similar manner to classes. You replace the keyword class with struct. The main difference between a class and struct is the area of memory where the object will be allocated. When used as a local variable or parameter, a struct is allocated on the stack, while a class is allocated on the managed heap. Structs are allocated on the stack, so they are not garbage collected, but automatically deallocated when a function exits. Generally, it's slightly faster to access a struct's fields than a class's; however, it's slightly slower to pass them to methods. That said, these differences tend to be quite small. Because they are allocated on the stack, it is generally best to create structs with a small number of fields to avoid stack overflow. You can't use inheritance when implementing structs, which means structs can't define virtual methods or abstract methods.

The next example defines a struct that represents an IP address. Note the only difference from defining a class is that you use the keyword struct:

```
type IpAddress = struct
    val first : byte
    val second : byte
    val third : byte
    val fourth : byte
    new(first, second, third, fourth) =
        { first = first;
          second = second;
          third = third;
          fourth = fourth }
    override x.ToString() =
        Printf.sprintf "%O.%O.%O.%O" x.first x.second x.third x.fourth
    member x.GetBytes() = x.first, x.second, x.third, x.fourth
end
```

The question is this: when should you use a class, and when should you use a struct? A good rule of thumb is to avoid structs, using them only when absolutely necessary, such as when interoperating with unmanaged C/C++ code (see Chapter 13 for more details on this).

Enums

Enums allow you to define a type made up of a finite set of identifiers, with each identifier mapping to an integer. This defines a type that can then take the value associated with any one of the defined identifiers.

You define an enum by giving the names of the identifiers followed by the equals sign and the values of the constants associated with the identifiers. You separate the identifiers that are members of the enum with vertical bars. The following example shows you how to define an enum Scale:

```
type Scale =
| C = 1
| D = 2
| E = 3
| F = 4
| G = 5
| A = 6
| B = 7
```

It's quite common to define enums that you intend to combine logically. To do this, choose constants so that each number is represented by a single bit, or the numbers 0, 1, 2, 4, 8, and so on. F#'s binary literals are a great help here because it's easy to see how you might combine the constants:

```
[<System.Flags>]
type ChordScale =
| C = 0b0000000000000001
| D = 0b0000000000000010
| E = 0b0000000000000100
| F = 0b0000000000001000
| G = 0b0000000000010000
| A = 0b0000000000100000
| B = 0b0000000001000000
```

The module Enum provides functionality for dealing with enums in F# (you can learn more about this module in Chapter 7).

Summary

You've now seen how to use the three major programming paradigms in F# and how flexible F# is for coding in any mix of styles. In the next chapter, you'll look at how code is organized in F#, as well as how to annotate and "quote" it.

CHAPTER 6

■ ■ ■

Organizing, Annotating, and Quoting Code

An important part of any programming language is the ability to organize code into logical units. F# provides *modules* and *namespaces* for this; you can learn more about them in this chapter's "Modules," "Namespaces," and "Opening Namespaces and Modules" sections. To attain a good understanding of F#'s module system, it's also important that you understand the scope of a module, as well as how it will be initialized and executed. You can learn more about these two concepts in the in "Module Scope" and "Module Execution" sections.

For a module to be effective, it's important to able to make parts of the module private, so it cannot be seen by the outside world. F# provides two different ways to achieve this; you'll learn how to do this in the "Signature Files and Private" and "Internal let Bindings and Members" sections.

It's also important to be able to annotate code with notes about what it does for future users, maintainers, and even yourself; you will learn how to do this in the "Comments" section.

To support cross-compiling with O'Caml and other advanced scenarios, it's often useful to have optional compilation. F# provides two forms of this, one of which, "Comments for Cross Compilation," is specifically designed for cross-compiling with O'Caml. The other, more general form is described in the "Optional Compilation" section.

It has also become common to use attributes and data structures to annotate assemblies and the types and values within them. Other libraries or the CLR can then interpret these attributes. You will learn about this technique of marking functions and values with attributes in this chapter's "Attributes" Section. The technique of compiling code into data structures is known as *quoting*, which you will learn about in the "Quoted Code" section toward the end of the chapter.

Modules

F# code is organized into modules, which are basically a way of grouping values and types under a common name. This organization has an effect on the scope of identifiers. Inside a module, identifiers can reference each other freely. To reference identifiers outside a module, you must qualify the identifier with the module name unless the module is explicitly opened with the open directive (see the "Opening Namespaces and Modules" section later in this chapter).

By default, each module is contained in a single source file. The entire contents of the source file make up the module; if the module isn't explicitly named, it gets the name of its source file, with the first letter capitalized. (F# is case sensitive, so it's important to remember this.) It's recommended that you use such *anonymous* modules only for simple programs.

To name a module explicitly, use the keyword module. The keyword has two modes of operation: the first gives the same name to the whole of the source file, while the second gives a name to a section of a source file. This enables you to make several modules appear in a source file.

To include the entire contents of a source file in the same, explicitly named module, you must place the module keyword at the top of the source file. A module name can contain dots, and these separate the name into parts, as you can see in this snippet:

```
module Strangelights.Beginning.ModuleDemo
```

You can define nested modules within the same source file. Nested module names cannot contain dots. After the nested module's name, you include an equals sign followed by the indented module definition. You can also use the keywords begin and end. To wrap the module definition, you can nest submodules. The following code defines three submodules: FirstModule, SecondModule, and ThirdModule. ThirdModule is nested within SecondModule:

```
// create a top level module
module ModuleDemo

// create a first module
module FirstModule =
    let n = 1

// create a second module
module SecondModule =
    let n = 2
    // create a third module
    // nested inside the second
    module ThirdModule =
        let n = 3
```

■**Note** You cannot use the module keyword without an equals sign in F# interactive. When you use the module keyword without an equals sign, it affects the whole of the source file, and F# interactive does not have the concept of a source file; instead all code entered is treated as if it were in the same source file. This means that when you use the version of the module keyword without an equals sign in F# interactive, you get an error. You can still use module with an equals sign to create submodules in F# interactive.

Note that different submodules can contain the same identifiers without any problems. Modules affect the scope of an identifier. To access an identifier outside of its module, you need to qualify it with the module name, so there is no ambiguity between identifiers in different modules. In the previous example, you define the identifier n in all three modules. The following example shows how to access the identifier n specific to each of the modules:

```
// unpack the values defined in each module
let x = ModuleDemo.FirstModule.n
let y = ModuleDemo.SecondModule.n
let z = ModuleDemo.SecondModule.ThirdModule.n
```

This code compiles into a .NET class, with the values becoming methods and fields within that class. You can find more details about what an F# module looks like compared to other .NET programming languages in Chapter 14.

Namespaces

Namespaces help you organize your code hierarchically. To help keep modules names unique across assemblies, you qualify the module name with a namespace name, which is just a character string with parts separated by dots. For example, F# provides a module named List, and the .NET BCL provides a class named List. There is no name conflict, because the F# module is in the namespace Microsoft.FSharp.Collections, and the BCL class is in the namespace System.Collections.Generic. Namespaces keep the module names of compiled code separate, so they are not allowed in F# interactive because they serve no purpose.

It's important that namespace names be unique. The most popular convention is to start namespace names with the name of a company or organization, followed by a specific name that indicates a piece of functionality. You aren't obligated to do this, but the convention is so widely followed that if you intend to distribute your code, especially in the form of a class library, then you should adopt this practice, too.

■**Note** There is no real concept of namespaces at the IL level of F#. The name of a class or module is nothing more than a long identifier that might or might not contain dots. You implement namespaces at the compiler level. When you use an open directive, you tell the compiler to do some extra work; to qualify all your identifiers with the given name, if it needs to; and to see whether this results in a match with a value or type.

In the simplest case, you can place a module in a namespace by using a module name with dots in it. The module and namespace names will be the same. You can also explicitly define a namespace for a module with the namespace directive. For example, look at this code:

```
module Strangelights.Beginning.ModuleDemo
```

You could replace the preceding code with this to get the same result:

```
namespace Strangelights.Beginning
module ModuleDemo
```

This might not be too useful for modules, but as noted in the previous section, submodules names cannot contain dots, so you use the namespace directive to place submodules within a namespace, as in this example:

```
// put the file in a name space
namespace Strangelights.Beginning

// create a first module
module FirstModule =
    let n = 1
```

```
// create a second module
module SecondModule =
    let n = 2
    // create a third module
    // nested inside the second
    module ThirdModule =
        let n = 3
```

After you compile this code to the outside world, the first instance of n will be accessible using the identifier Strangelights.Beginning.FirstModule.n rather than just FirstModule.n. It's also possible to place several namespace declarations in the same source file, but you must declare them at the top level. In the previous example, this means you could have declared FirstModule and SecondModule in separate namespaces. You cannot declare SecondModule and ThirdModule in separate namespaces; because ThirdModule is nested inside SecondModule, you can't declare a separate namespace for ThirdModule.

It's possible to define a namespace without also using a module directive, but then the namespace can contain only type definitions, as in this example:

```
// a namespace definition
namespace Strangelights.Beginning

// a record defintion
type MyRecord = { Field: string }
```

The following example will not compile because you can't place a value definition directly into a namespace without explicitly defining a module or submodule within the namespace:

```
// a namespace definition
namespace Strangelights.Beginning

// a value defintion, which is illegal
// directly inside a namespace
let value = "val"
```

In fact, the namespace directive has some interesting and subtle effects on what your code looks like to other languages; you can learn more about this in Chapter 13.

Opening Namespaces and Modules

As you have seen in the previous two sections, you must use its qualified name to specify a value or type that is not defined in the current module. This can quickly become tedious because some qualified names can be quite long. Fortunately, F# provides the open directive, so you can use simple names for types and values.

You follow the open keyword by the name of the namespace or module you want to open. For example, consider this code:

```
System.Console.WriteLine("Hello world")
```

You could replace the preceding code with this:

```
open System

Console.WriteLine("Hello world")
```

Note that you don't need to specify the whole namespace name. You can specify the front part of it and use the remaining parts to qualify simple names. For example, you can specify `System.Collections` rather than the namespace, `System.Collections.Generic`, and then use `Generic.List` to create an instance of the generic `List` class, as follows:

```
open System.Collections
// create an instance of a dictionary
let wordCountDict =
    new Generic.Dictionary<string, int>()
```

■**Caution** The technique of using partially qualified names, such as `Generic.Dictionary`, can make programs difficult to maintain. You should use either the name and the full namespace or the name only.

You can open F# modules, but you cannot open classes from non-F# libraries. If you open a module, you can reference values and types within it by using their simple names. The following example opens two modules: `Microsoft.FSharp.Math.PhysicalConstants` and `Microsoft.FSharp.Math.SI`, both of which you can find in the FSharp.PowerPack assembly. These modules contain standard constants and standard units of measure, respectively. You use the constant c, the speed of light, to implement Einstein's famous equation $e = mc^2$:

```
open Microsoft.FSharp.Math.PhysicalConstants
open Microsoft.FSharp.Math.SI

// mass
let m = 1.<kg>
// energy
let e = m * (c * c)
```

Some argue that this ability to open modules directly should be used sparingly because it can make it difficult to figure out where identifiers originated. Note that many modules from the F# libraries cannot be opened directly. In fact, you can typically divide modules into two categories: those that are designed to be accessed using qualified names, and those that are designed to be opened directly. Most modules are designed to be accessed with qualified names; a few are designed to be directly opened. The typical reason to open a module directly is so that you can use operators within it directly. The next example defines a custom module that contains a *triple equals* operator and then opens this module to use the operator:

```
// module of operators
module MyOps =
    // check equality via hash code
    let (===) x y =
        x.GetHashCode() =
            y.GetHashCode()

// open the MyOps module
open MyOps

// use the triple equal operator
let equal = 1 === 1
let nEqual = 1 === 2
```

If you open two namespaces that contain modules or classes of the same name, it won't cause a compile error. You can even use values from the modules or classes with the same name, as long as the names of the values are not the same. You can see the open namespace System in Figure 6-1. You can see that contains the class Array; you can also see a module Array that's available in F#'s libraries. In the figure, you can see both static methods from BCL's Array class, which all start with a capital letter, and values from F#'s Array module, which start with a small letter:

Figure 6-1. *Visual Studio's IntelliSense*

Giving Modules Aliases

You might occasionally find it useful to give an alias to a module to avoid naming clashes. This is useful when two modules share the same name and a value with a common name, and it can also be a convenient way of switching some of your code to use two different implementations of similar modules. You can only give module aliases to modules that have been created in F#.

The syntax for this is the `module` keyword, followed by an identifier, an equals sign, and then the name of the namespace or module you want to alias. The following example defines `ArrayThreeD` as the alias for the namespace `Microsoft.FSharp.Collections.Array3`:

```
// give an alias to the Array3 module
module ArrayThreeD = Microsoft.FSharp.Collections.Array3D

// create an matrix using the module alias
let matrix =
    ArrayThreeD.create 3 3 3 1
```

Signature Files

Signature files give you a way of making function and value definitions private to a module. You've already seen the syntax for the definition of a signature file in Chapter 2. A signature file can be generated using the compiler's `-i` switch. Any definitions that appear in a signature file are public, and anyone can access them using the module. Any definitions that are not in the signature file are private and can be used only inside the module itself. The typical way to create a signature file is to generate it from the module source, and then go through and erase any values and functions that you want to be private.

The signature file name must be the same as the name of the module with which it is paired. It must have the extension `.fsi` or `.mli`, and you must specify the signature file to the compiler. On the command line, you must give it directly before the source file for its module. In Visual Studio, the signature file must appear before the source file in Solution Explorer.

For example, assume you have the following in the file `Lib.fs`:

```
// define a function to be exposed
let funkyFunction x =
    x + ": keep it funky!"

// define a function that will be hidden
let notSoFunkyFunction x = x + 1
```

Now assume you want to create a library that exposes `funkyFunction` but not `notSoFunkyFunction`. You would use the signature code like this and save it as `Lib.fsi`:

```
// expose a function
val funkyFunction: string -> string
```

Next, you would use the command line like this:

```
fsc -a Lib.fsi Lib.fs
```

This gives you an assembly named `Lib.dll` with one class named `Lib`, one public function named `funkyFunction`, and one private function named `notSoFunkyFunction`.

Private and Internal let Bindings and Members

F# supports another way of controlling the visibility of a value or type. You can use the `private` or `internal` keywords directly after the `let` of a let binding to make it private or internal, as the following example demonstrates:

```
let private aPrivateBinding = "Keep this private"
let internal aInternalBinding = "Keep this internal"
```

The private keyword makes the value or type visible only within the current module, and the internal keyword makes the value or type visible only within the current assembly. The `private` and `internal` keywords have roughly the same meaning as the `private` and `internal` keywords in C#. The internal keyword is particularly useful to make types that are specific to F# invisible outside the assembly, while allowing them to be shared between modules within the assembly. The following example shows how to hide a union type using the `internal` keyword:

```
// This type will not visible outside the current assembly
type internal MyUnion =
    | String of string
    | TwoStrings of string * string
```

You see this style of programming frequently when programming in the object-oriented style. To support this, you can also hide members of objects using the `private` or `internal` keywords. Doing this is as simple as placing the `private` or `internal` keywords directly after the member keyword, as shown in the following example:

```
namespace Strangelight.Beginning

type Thing() =
    member private x.PrivateThing() =
        ()
    member x.ExternalThing() =
        ()
```

The private and internal keywords offer similar functionality to interface files, so you might wonder which one you should use in real-world programming. The answer is not clear cut: interface files provide a nice overview of a module and excellent place to keep the documentation of the interface. They also help you to avoid littering the source code with extra keywords. However, interface files can get a little annoying because every external definition is repeated to some extent. This means that you must update the definitions in two places when you refactor code. Given the double update problem, I generally prefer to use the `private` and `internal` keywords; however, I think either choice is valid, and it's much more important to be consistent throughout your project.

Module Scope

The order that you pass modules to the compiler is important because it affects the scope of identifiers within the modules, as well as the order in which you execute the modules. I cover scope in this section, and execution order in the next.

Values and types within a module cannot be seen from another module unless the module they're in appears on the command line before the module that refers to them. This is probably easier to understand with an example. Suppose you have a source file, ModuleOne.fs, that contains the following:

```
module ModuleOne
// some text to be used by another module
let text = "some text"
```

And let's assume that you have another module, ModuleTwo.fs, that contains the following:

```
module ModuleTwo
// print out the text defined in ModuleOne
printfn "ModuleOne.text: %s" ModuleOne.text
```

You can compile these two modules successfully with the following code:

```
fsc ModuleOne.fs ModuleTwo.fs -o ModuleScope.exe
```

However, you would face a complication with the following command:

```
fsc ModuleTwo.fs ModuleOne.fs -o ModuleScope.exe
```

The preceding command would result in this error message:

```
ModuleTwo.fs(3,17): error: FS0039: The namespace or module 'ModuleOne' is not
 defined.
```

This error occurs because ModuleOne is used in the definition of ModuleTwo, so ModuleOne must appear before ModuleTwo in the command line, or else ModuleOne will not be in scope for ModuleTwo.

Visual Studio users should note that files are passed to the compiler in the same order that files appear in Solution Explorer. This means you must sometimes spend a few moments rearranging the order of the files when you add a new file to a project. Visual Studio allows you to change the file order using the context menu of the solution explorer (see Figure 6-2).

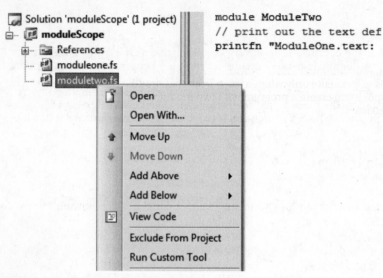

Figure 6-2. *Visual Studio's file reordering context menu*

Module Execution

Roughly speaking, execution in F# starts at the top of a module and works its way down to the bottom. Any values that are not functions are calculated, and any statements at the top-level or any top-level do statements are executed. Consider the following code:

```
module ModuleOne
// statements at the top-level
printfn "This is the first line"
printfn "This is the second"

// a value defined at the top-level
let file =
    let temp = new System.IO.FileInfo("test.txt") in
    printfn "File exists: %b" temp.Exists
    temp
```

Executing the preceding code gives the following result:

```
This is the first line
This is the second
File exists: false
```

This is all as you might expect. When a source file is compiled into an assembly, none of the code in it will execute until a value from it is used by a currently executing function. Then, when the first value in the file is touched, all the let expressions and do statements in the module will execute in their lexical order. When you split a program over more than one module, the last module passed to the compiler is special. All the items in this module will execute, and the other items will behave as they were in an assembly. Items in other modules will execute only when a value from that module is used by the module currently executing. Suppose you create a program with two modules.

This code is placed in ModuleOne.fs:

```
module ModuleOne
// then this one should be printed
printfn "This is the third and final"
```

This code is placed in ModuleTwo.fs:

```
module ModuleTwo
// these two lines should be printed first
printfn "This is the first line"
printfn "This is the second"
```

Now assume you compile the preceding code with the following command:

```
fsc ModuleOne.fs ModuleTwo.fs -o ModuleExecution.exe
```

Doing this gives you the following result:

```
This is the first line
This is the second
```

This might not be what you expected, but it is important to remember that ModuleOne was the not the last module passed to the compiler, so nothing in it will execute until a value from it is used by a function currently executing. In this case, no value from ModuleOne is ever used, so it never executes. Taking this into account, you can fix your program so it behaves more as you expect.

This code is placed in ModuleOne.fs:

```
module ModuleOne
// this will be printed when the module
// member n is first accessed
printfn "This is the third and final"

let n = 1
```

And this code is placed in ModuleTwo.fs:

```
module ModuleTwo
// these two lines should be printed first
printfn "This is the first line"
printfn "This is the second"

// function to access ModuleOne
let funct() =
    printfn "%i" ModuleOne.n

funct()
```

You can compile the preceding example with the following command:

```
fsc ModuleOne.fs ModuleTwo.fs -o ModuleExecution.exe
```

This gives the following result:

```
This is the first line
This is the second
This is the third and final
1
```

However, using this sort of trick to get the results you want is not recommended. It is generally best to use only statements at the top level in the last module passed to the compiler. In fact, the typical form of an F# program is to have one statement at the top level at the bottom of the last module that is passed to the compiler.

Optional Compilation

Optional compilation is a technique where the compiler can ignore various bits of text from a source file. Most programming languages support some kind of optional compilation. It can be handy, for example, if you want to build a library that supports both .NET 1.1 and 2.0, and you want to include extra values and types that take advantage of the new features of version 2.0. However, you should use the technique sparingly and with great caution because it can quickly make code difficult to understand and maintain.

In F#, optional compilation is supported by the compiler switch `--define FLAG` and the command `#if FLAG` in a source file. You can also define these using Visual Studio's Build configuration menu (see Figure 6-3).

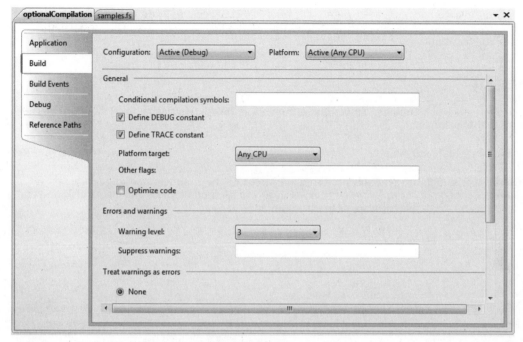

Figure 6-3. *Visual Studio's Build configuration menu*

Notice that Visual Studio lets you add two predefined switches: DEBUG and TRACE. These switches are special because they affect some framework methods; for example, assertions via a call to Assert.Debug only fire when the DEBUG symbol is defined.

The following example shows how to define two different versions of statements that execute at the top-level, one for when the code is compiled, and the other for when the code is running as a script F# interactive (if you wish to compile this code, you also need to add a reference to System.Windows. Forms.dll):

```
open System.Windows.Forms

// define a form
let form = new Form()

// do something different depending if we're runing
// as a compiled program of as a script
#if COMPILED
Application.Run form
#else
form.Show()
#endif
```

In this example, you do not have to define a symbol COMPILED because F# defines this for you if you compile a program. Similarly, F# interactive defines the symbol INTERACTIVE, so you can test whether you're in interactive mode.

Comments

F# provides two kinds of comments. *Single-line* comments start with two slashes and extend to the end of a line, as in this example:

```
// this is a single-line comment
```

Single-line comments are generally preferred in F# because the comment opening characters are quicker and easier to type. *Multiple-line* comments start with a left parenthesis and an asterisk, and end with an asterisk and a right parenthesis, as in this example:

```
(* this is a comment *)
```

Or this one:

```
(* this
   is a
   comment
*)
```

Typically, you use multiple-line comments only for temporarily commenting out large blocks of code. Unlike a lot of other languages, F# lets you can nest multiline comments; this is the same behavior you see in O'Caml comments. You get a compile error if you leave a multiple-line comment unclosed.

Doc Comments

Doc comments allow you to extract comments from the source file in the form of XML or HTML. This is useful because it allows programmers to browse code comments without having to browse the source. This is especially convenient for the vendors of APIs because it allows them to provide documentation about the code without having to provide the source itself. This approach also makes more convenient to browse the docs without having to open the source. In addition, the documentation is stored alongside the source where it has more chance of being updated when code changes.

Doc comments start with three slashes instead of two. They can be associated only with top-level values or type definitions and are associated with the value or type they appear immediately before. The following code associates the comment this is an explanation with the value myString:

```
/// this is an explanation
let myString = "this is a string"
```

To extract doc comments into an XML file, you use the –doc compiler switch. For example, assume you were to this command in a source file:

```
fsc -doc doc.xml Prog.fs
```

Doing this would produce the following XML:

```
<?xml version="1.0" encoding="utf-8"?>
<doc>
<assembly><name>Prog</name></assembly>
<members>
<member name="F:Prog.myString">
<summary>
 this is an explanation
</summary>

</member>
<member name="T:Prog">

</member>
</members>
</doc>
```

You can then process the XML using various tools, such as Sandcastle (http://www.codeplex.com/Sandcastle), to transform it into a number of more readable formats; I found that Sandcastle worked well when I used it with "Sandcastle Help File Builder" (http://www.codeplex.com/SHFB). The compiler also supports the direct generation of HTML from doc comments. This is less flexible than XML, but it can produce usable documentation with less effort. It can also produce better results under some circumstances because notations such as generics and union types are not always well supported by documentation-generation tools. You will learn about the compiler switches that generate HTML in Chapter 12.

In F#, you don't need to add any XML tags explicitly; for example, the <summary> and </summary> tags were added automatically. This is useful because it saves you a lot of typing and avoids wasted space in the source file; however, you can take control and write out the XML tags explicitly if you want. The following is a doc comment where the tags have been explicitly written out:

```
/// <summary>
/// divides the given parameter by 10
/// </summary>
/// <param name="x">the thing to be divided by 10</param>
let divTen x = x / 10
```

The preceding code produces the following XML:

```
<?xml version="1.0" encoding="utf-8"?>
<doc>
<assembly><name>AnotherProg</name></assembly>
<members>
<member name="M:AnotherProg.divTen (System.Int32)">
<summary>
divides the given parameter by 10
</summary>
<param name="x">the thing to be divided by 10</param>

</member>
<member name="T:AnotherProg">

</member>
</members>
</doc>
```

If no signature file exists for the module file, then the doc comments are taken directly from the module file itself. However, if a signature file exists, then doc comments come from the signature file. This means that even if doc comments exist in the module file, they will not be included in the resulting XML or HTML if the compiler is given a signature file for the module.

Comments for Cross Compilation

To enable easier cross-compilation between F# and O'Caml, F# supports some optional compilations flags disguised as comment tags. Any code you place between these comment tags (*F# F#*) will be compiled as if the comment tags were not there. This code would appear as a normal comment to the O'Caml compiler, so it would be ignored. Similarly, the F# compiler will ignore any code placed between the comments (*IF-OCAML*) (*ENDIF-OCAML*) as if it were a comment. However, the code between these two comment tags would be treated as normal code by the O'Caml compiler. This provides a simple but effective mechanism for working around small differences in the two languages to make cross-compilation easier. The following sample shows these comments in action. If you use the O'Caml-compatible version of the F# syntax, then you should save your file with the extension .ml instead of .fs:

```
(*F#
printfn "This will be printed by an F# program"
F#*)

(*IF-OCAML*)
Format.printf "This will be printed by an O'Caml program"
(*ENDIF-OCAML*)
```

You'll get the following results when F# compiles the preceding code:

This will be printed by an F# program

Custom Attributes

Custom attributes add information to your code that will be compiled into an assembly and stored alongside your values and types. This information can then be read programmatically via reflection or by the runtime itself.

Attributes can be associated with types, members of types, and top-level values. They can also be associated with do statements. You specify an attribute in brackets, with the attribute name in angle brackets, as in this example:

```
[<Obsolete>]
```

By convention, Attribute names end with the string Attribute, so the actual name of the Obsolete attribute is ObsoleteAttribute.

An attribute must immediately precede what it modifies. The following code marks the function, functionOne, as obsolete:

```
open System
[<Obsolete>]
let functionOne () = ()
```

An attribute is essentially a class; using an attribute basically makes a call to its constructor. In the previous example, Obsolete has a parameterless constructor, and you can call it with or without parentheses. In this case, you called it without parentheses. If you want to pass arguments to an attribute's constructor, then you must use parentheses and separate arguments with commas, as in this example:

```
open System
[<Obsolete("it is a pointless function anyway!")>]
let functionOne () = ()
```

Sometimes an attribute's constructor does not expose all the properties of the attribute. If you want to set such a property, you need to specify the property and a value for it. You specify the property name, an equals sign, and the value after the other arguments to the constructor. The next example sets the Unrestricted property of the PrintingPermission attribute to true:

```
open System.Drawing.Printing
open System.Security.Permissions

[<PrintingPermission(SecurityAction.Demand, Unrestricted = true)>]
let functionThree () = ()
```

You can use two or more attributes by separating the attributes with semicolons:

```
open System
open System.Drawing.Printing
open System.Security.Permissions

[<Obsolete; PrintingPermission(SecurityAction.Demand)>]
let functionFive () = ()
```

So far, you've used attributes only with values, but using them with type or type members is just as straightforward. The following example marks a type and all its members as obsolete:

```
open System

[<Obsolete>]
type OOThing = class
    [<Obsolete>]
    val stringThing : string
    [<Obsolete>]
    new() = {stringThing = ""}
    [<Obsolete>]
    member x.GetTheString () = x.stringThing
end
```

If you intend to use WinForms or Windows Presentation Foundation (WPF) graphics in your program, you must ensure that the program is a *single-thread apartment.* This is because the libraries that provide the graphical components use *unmanaged* code (not compiled by the CLR) under the covers. The easiest way to do this is by using the STAThread attribute. This must modify the first do statement in the last file passed to the compiler; that is, the first statement that will execute when the program runs:

```
open System
open System.Windows.Forms

let form = new Form()

[<STAThread>]
Application.Run(form)
```

Once you attach attributes to types and values, it's possible to use reflection to find which values and types are marked with which attributes. You usually do this with the IsDefined or GetCustomAttributes methods of the System.Reflection.MemberInfo class, which means these methods are available on most objects used for reflection, including System.Type. The next example shows you how to look for all types that are marked with the Obsolete attribute:

```
open System

// create a list of all obsolete types
let obsolete = AppDomain.CurrentDomain.GetAssemblies()
                    |> List.ofArray
                    |> List.map (fun assm -> assm.GetTypes())
                    |> Array.concat
                    |> List.ofArray
                    |> List.filter (fun m ->
                      m.IsDefined(typeof<ObsoleteAttribute>, true))

// print the lists
printfn "%A" obsolete
```

Executing the preceding code produces the following results:

```
[System.ContextMarshalException;( System.Collections.IHashCodeProvider;
 System.Collections.CaseInsensitiveHashCodeProvider;
 System.Runtime.InteropServices.IDispatchImplType;
 System.Runtime.InteropServices.IDispatchImplAttribute;
 System.Runtime.InteropServices.SetWin32ContextInIDispatchAttribute;
 System.Runtime.InteropServices.BIND_OPTS;
 System.Runtime.InteropServices.UCOMIBindCtx;
 System.Runtime.InteropServices.UCOMIConnectionPointContainer;
...
```

You've seen how you can use attributes and reflection to examine code; now let's look at a similar, but more powerful technique for analyzing compiled code, called *quotation*.

Quoted Code

Quotations give you a way to tell the compiler, "Don't generate code for this section of the source file; turn it into a data structure, or an *expression tree*, instead." You can then interpret this expression tree in a number of ways, transform or optimize it, compile it into another language, or even ignore it.

To quote an expression, place it between the <@ @> operators:

```
// quote the integer one
let quotedInt = <@ 1 @>

// print the quoted integer
printfn "%A" quotedInt
```

Executing the preceding code produces this result:

```
Value (1)
```

The following example defines an identifier and uses it in a quotation:

```
// define an identifier n
let n = 1
// quote the identifier
let quotedId = <@ n @>

// print the quoted identifier
printfn "%A" quotedId
```

Executing the preceding code produces the following result:

```
PropGet (None, Int32 n, [])
```

Next we can quote a function applied to a value. Notice that you are quoting two items, so the result of this quotation is split into two parts. The first part represents the function, and the second part represents the value to which it is applied:

```
// define a function
let inc x = x + 1
// quote the function applied to a value
let quotedFun = <@ inc 1 @>

// print the quotation
printfn "%A" quotedFun
```

Executing the preceding code produces the following result:

```
Call (None, Int32 inc(Int32), [Value (1)])
```

The next example shows how to apply an operator to two values. Notice how you return an expression that is similar to the function call; this is because operators are basically function calls:

```
open Microsoft.FSharp.Quotations

// quote an operator applied to two operands
let quotedOp = <@ 1 + 1 @>

// print the quotation
printfn "%A" quotedOp
```

Executing the preceding code produces this result:

```
Call (None, Int32 op_Addition[Int32,Int32,Int32](Int32, Int32),
      [Value (1), Value (1)])
```

The next example quotes an anonymous function. You should notice how now the resulting expression is a Lambda:

```
open Microsoft.FSharp.Quotations

// quote an anonymous function
let quotedAnonFun = <@ fun x -> x + 1 @>

// print the quotation
printfn "%A" quotedAnonFun
```

When you execute the preceding code, you get the following result:

```
Lambda (x,
        Call (None, Int32 op_Addition[Int32,Int32,Int32](Int32, Int32),
              [x, Value (1)]))
```

Quotations are simply a discriminating union of `Microsoft.FSharp.Quotations.Expr`; working with them is as simple as pattern matching over the quotation. The next example defines a function, `interpretInt`, that queries the expression passed to it to see whether it is an integer. If it is, it prints the value of that integer; otherwise, it prints the string, "not an int":

```
open Microsoft.FSharp.Quotations.Patterns

// a function to interpret very simple quotations
let interpretInt exp =
    match exp with
    | Value (x, typ) when typ = typeof<int> -> printfn "%d" (x :?> int)
    | _ -> printfn "not an int"

// test the function
interpretInt <@ 1 @>
interpretInt <@ 1 + 1 @>
```

Executing the preceding code produces the following result:

```
1
not an int
```

You printed two expressions with `interpretInt`. The first was an integer value, so it printed out the value of that integer. The second was not an integer, although it contained integers. Pattern matching over quotations like this can be a bit tedious, so the F# libraries define a number of active patterns to help you do this. You can find these active patterns defined in the `Microsoft.FSharp.Quotations.DerivedPatterns` namespace. The following example shows how to use the `SpecificCall` active pattern to recognize a call to the plus operator:

```
open Microsoft.FSharp.Quotations.Patterns
open Microsoft.FSharp.Quotations.DerivedPatterns

// a function to interpret very simple quotations
let rec interpret exp =
    match exp with
    | Value (x, typ) when typ = typeof<int> -> printfn "%d" (x :?> int)
    | SpecificCall <@ (+) @> (_, _, [l;r])  -> interpret l
                                               printfn "+"
                                               interpret r

    | _ -> printfn "not supported"

// test the function
interpret <@ 1 @>
interpret <@ 1 + 1 @>
```

Executing the preceding code produces the following result:

```
1
1
+
1
```

Note that you can use the `SpecificCall` active pattern to recognize function calls, as well as operators.

No library functions exist to compile a quotation back into F# and execute it, although this feature might appear in a future version of the language. Instead, you can mark any top-level function with the `ReflectedDefinition` attribute. This attribute tells the compiler to generate the function or value, as well as to generate an expression tree. You can then retrieve the quotation using the `<@@ @@>` operator, which is similar to the quotation operator (note the double ampersand). The following example demonstrates the use of the `ReflectedDefinition` attribute; notice how you have the quote for inc available, but you can also use the function inc directly:

```
// this defines a function and quotes it
[<ReflectedDefinition>]
let inc n = n + 1

// fetch the quoted defintion
let incQuote = <@@ inc @@>

// print the quotation
printfn "%A" incQuote
// use the function
printfn "inc 1: %i" (inc 1)
```

Executing this code produces the following result:

```
Lambda (n@5, Call (None, Int32 inc(Int32), [n@5]))
inc 1: 2
```

This example might seem limited, but I believe this technique has great potential for enabling runtime analysis of functions before you call them. It is also used extensively in the F# web toolkit developed by Tomas Petricek (http://www.codeplex.com/fswebtools).

Quotations are a huge topic, and it would be impossible to cover them completely in this section (or even in this book). You will, however, learn more about them in Chapter 11.

Summary

In this chapter, you saw how to organize code in F#. You also saw how to comment, annotate, and quote code, but you have only scratched the surface of both annotation and quoting.

This concludes the tour of the F# core language. The rest of the book will focus on how to use F#, from working with relational databases to creating user interfaces. You will begin this process with a look at the F# core libraries in the next chapter.

CHAPTER 7

■ ■ ■

The F# Libraries

Although F# can use all the classes available in the .NET BCL, it also ships with its own set of libraries.

The F# libraries are split into two, FSharp.Core.dll, which is also referred to as the F# core library or the native F# library, and FSharp.PowerPack.dll, sometimes just referred to as the power pack. The F# core library contains everything that the F# compiler really needs to work. For example, it contains the Tuple class that is used when you use a tuple. The power pack is designed to supplement the F# core library with other useful functions. There are two primary reasons for splitting the library in two: first, an effort was made to try and keep the core library as small as possible, so if application developers were making an effort to keep the footprint small the dependency on FSharp.Core.dll would not cause too much trouble. Secondly, and perhaps more importantly, to try and keep FSharp.Core.dll as stable as possible, so that it will only change with new releases of the compiler and allow the F# team to ship new versions of FSharp.PowerPack.dll, with interesting new features, more often.

The objective of this chapter is not to completely document every nuance of every F# library type and function. It is to give you an overview of what the modules can do, with a particular focus on features that aren't readily available in the BCL. The F# online documentation (http://msdn.microsoft.com/fsharp) is the place to find detailed documentation about each function.

The Native F# Library FSharp.Core.dll

The native F# library contains all the classes that you need to make the compiler work, such as the definition of the type into which F#'s list literal compiles. I'll cover the following modules:

Microsoft.FSharp.Core.Operators: A module containing functions that are mathematical operators.

Microsoft.FSharp.Reflection: A module containing functions that supplement the .NET Framework's reflection classes to give a more accurate view of F# types and values.

Microsoft.FSharp.Collections.Seq: A module containing functions for any type that supports the IEnumerable interface.

Microsoft.FSharp.Text.Printf: A module for formatting strings.

Microsoft.FSharp.Control.Event: A module for working with events in F#.

The Microsoft.FSharp.Core.Operators Module

In F#, operators are defined by libraries rather than built into the language. This module contains some of the language's operators. It also contains some useful operators such as functions, and it is these that I'll be covering here. The module is open by default, which means the user can use these functions with no prefix. Specifically, I will cover the following types of functions:

Arithmetic operators: Operators for basic arithmetic operations such as addition and subtraction.

Floating-point arithmetic functions: More advanced arithmetic functions including logarithms and trigonometry.

Mutable integer functions: Functions on mutable integers.

Tuple functions: Functions on tuples.

Conversion functions: Functions for converting between primitive types, such as strings, floats and integers.

Arithmetic Operators

As already covered in Chapter 2, F# operators can be defined by the programmer, so all the arithmetic operators are defined in the Operators module rather than built into the language. Therefore, the majority of operators that you will use in your day-to-day programming in F# are defined in the Operators module. I imagine that operators such as + and – need little explanation, since their usage is straightforward:

```
let x1 = 1 + 1
let x2 = 1 - 1
```

By default, F# operators are unchecked, which means that if a value is too big then it will wrap. Therefore, this is the value that will become the smallest possible value, rather than causing an error. If you would prefer to use checked operators that raise an exception when a value overflows you can do so by opening the Microsoft.FSharp.Core.Operators.Checked:

```
open Microsoft.FSharp.Core.Operators.Checked
let x = System.Int32.MaxValue + 1
```

The above example will now throw an error when executed, where as if the module Microsoft.FSharp.Core.Operators.Checked was not open the value in x would simply be wrapped to -2147483648.

The F# equality operator is a bit more subtle than most of the other arithmetic operators. This is because in F# equality is *structural* equality, meaning that the contents of the objects are compared to check whether the items that make up the object are the same. This is opposed to *referential* equality, which determines whether two identifiers are bound to the same object or the same physical area of memory. A referential equality check can be performed using the method obj.ReferenceEquals. The structural equality operator is =, and the structural inequality operator is <>. The next example demonstrates this. The records robert1 and robert2 are equal, because even though they are separate objects, their contents are the same. On the other hand, robert1 and robert3 are not equal because their contents are different.

```
type person = { name : string ; favoriteColor : string }

let robert1 = { name = "Robert" ; favoriteColor = "Red" }
let robert2 = { name = "Robert" ; favoriteColor = "Red" }
let robert3 = { name = "Robert" ; favoriteColor = "Green" }

printfn "(robert1 = robert2): %b" (robert1 = robert2)
printfn "(robert1 <> robert3): %b" (robert1 <> robert3)
```

The results of this code, when compiled and executed, are as follows:

```
(robert1 = robert2): true
(robert1 <> robert3): true
```

Structural comparison is also used to implement the > and < operators, which means they too can be used to compare F#'s record types. This is demonstrated here:

```
type person = { name : string ; favoriteColor : string }

let robert2 = { name = "Robert" ; favoriteColor = "Red" }
let robert3 = { name = "Robert" ; favoriteColor = "Green" }

printfn "(robert2 > robert3): %b" (robert2 > robert3)
```

The results of this code, when compiled and executed, are as follows:
```
(robert2 > robert3): true
```

If you need to determine whether two objects are physically equal, then you can use the PhysicalEquality function available in the LanguagePrimitives module, as in the following example:

```
type person = { name : string ; favoriteColor : string }

let robert1 = { name = "Robert" ; favoriteColor = "Red" }
let robert2 = { name = "Robert" ; favoriteColor = "Red" }

printfn "(LanguagePrimitives.PhysicalEquality robert1 robert2): %b"
    (LanguagePrimitives.PhysicalEquality robert1 robert2)
```

Floating-Point Arithmetic Functions

The Operators module also offers a number of functions (see Table 7-1) specifically for floating-point numbers, some of which are used in the following sample:

```
printfn "(sqrt 16.0): %f" (sqrt 16.0)
printfn "(log 160.0): %f" (log 160.0)
printfn "(cos 1.6): %f" (cos 1.6)
```

The results of this code, when compiled and executed, are as follows:

```
(sqrt 16.0): 4.000000
(log 160.0): 5.075174
(cos 1.6): -0.029200
```

Table 7-1. *Arithmetic Functions for Floating-Point Numbers*

Function	Description
abs	Returns the absolute value of the argument
acos	Returns the inverse cosine (arccosine) of the argument, which should be specified in radians
asin	Returns the inverse sine (arcsine) of the argument, which should be specified in radians
atan	Returns the inverse tangent (arctangent) of the argument, which should be specified in radians
atan2	Returns the inverse tangent (arctangent) of the two arguments, which should both be specified in radians
ceil	Returns the next highest integer value by rounding up the value if necessary; the value returned is still of type float
floor	Returns the next lowest integer value by rounding up the value if necessary; the value returned is still of type float
exp	Returns the exponential
infinity	Returns the floating-point number that represents infinity
log	Returns the natural log of the floating-point number
log10	Returns the base 10 log of the floating-point number
nan	Returns the floating-point number that represents "not a number"
sqrt	Returns the square root of the number
cos	Returns the cosine of the parameter, which should be specified in radians
cosh	Returns the hyperbolic cosine of the parameter, which should be specified in radians
sin	Returns the sine of the parameter, which should be specified in radians

sinh	Returns the hyperbolic sine of the parameter, which should be specified in radians
tan	Returns the tangent of the parameter, which should be specified in radians
tanh	Returns the hyperbolic tangent of the parameter, which should be specified in radians
truncate	Returns the parameter converted to an integer
float	Takes an integer and returns it as a `float`
float32	Takes an integer and returns it as a `float32`

Tuple Functions

The `Operators` module also offers two useful functions that operate on tuples. You can use the functions `fst` and `snd` to break up a tuple with two items in it. The following example demonstrates their use:

```
printfn "(fst (1, 2)): %i" (fst (1, 2))
printfn "(snd (1, 2)): %i" (snd (1, 2))
```

The results of this code are as follows:

```
(fst (1, 2)): 1
(snd (1, 2)): 2
```

The Conversion Functions

The operator module offers a number of overload functions for converting between the primitive types. For example, the function `float` is overload to convert from a string or integer type to a floating point number, a `System.Double`. The following example shows how to convert from an enumeration to an integer and then convert it back to an enumeration. Converting from an enumeration to an integer is straightforward. You just use the `int` function. Converting back is slightly more complicated; you use the `enum` function, but you must provide a type annotation so that the compile knows which type of enumeration to convert it to. You can see this in the following sample where you add the annotation `DayOfWeek` to the identifier `dayEnum`:

```
open System

let dayInt = int DateTime.Now.DayOfWeek
let (dayEnum : DayOfWeek) = enum dayInt

printfn "%i" dayInt
printfn "%A" dayEnum
```

The results of this code, when compiled and executed, are as follows:

```
0
Sunday
```

The Logical Or and And Operators

The other common tasks that you need to perform with enumerations is to combine them using a logical "or" and then test them using a logical "and." Enum types marked with the System.Flags attribute support the use of the &&& and ||| operators to perform these operations directly. For example, you can use ||| operator to combine several enum values. You can test to see if value is part of an enum using the &&& operators in the form v1 &&& v2 <> enum 0:

```
open System.Windows.Forms

let anchor = AnchorStyles.Left ||| AnchorStyles.Left

printfn "test AnchorStyles.Left: %b"
    (anchor &&& AnchorStyles.Left <> enum 0)
printfn "test AnchorStyles.Right: %b"
    (anchor &&& AnchorStyles.Right <> enum 0)
```

The Microsoft.FSharp.Reflection Module

This module contains F#'s own version of reflection. F# contains some types that are 100 percent compatible with the CLR type system, but aren't precisely understood with .NET reflection. For example, F# uses some sleight of hand to implement its union type, and this is transparent in 100 percent F# code. It can look a little strange when you use the BCL to reflect over it. The F# reflection system addresses this kind of problem. But, it blends with the BCL's System.Reflection namespace, so if you are reflecting over an F# type that uses BCL types, you will get the appropriate object from the System.Reflection namespace.

In F#, you can reflect over types or over values. The difference is a bit subtle and is best explained with an example. Those of you familiar with .NET reflection might like to think of reflection over types as using the Type, EventInfo, FieldInfo, MethodInfo, and PropertyInfo types and reflections over values as calling their members, such as GetProperty or InvokeMember to get values dynamically. Yet reflection over values offers a high-level, easy-to-use system.

- *Reflection over types:* Lets you examine the types that make up a particular value or type.

- *Reflection over values:* Let you examine the values that make up a particular composite value.

Reflection Over Types

The following example shows a function that will print the type of any tuple:

```
open Microsoft.FSharp.Reflection

let printTupleTypes (x: obj) =
    let t = x.GetType()
    if FSharpType.IsTuple t then
        let types = FSharpType.GetTupleElements t
        printf "("
        types
        |> Seq.iteri
            (fun i t ->
            if i <> Seq.length types - 1 then
                printf " %s * " t.Name
            else
                printf "%s" t.Name)
        printfn " )"
    else
        printfn "not a tuple"

printTupleTypes ("hello world", 1)
```

First, you use the objects GetType method to get the System.Type that represents the object. You can then use this value with the function FSharpType.IsTuple to get to test if it is a tuple. You then use function FSharpType.GetTupleElements to get an array of System.Type that describes the elements that make up the tuple. These could represent F# types, so you could recursively call the function to investigate what they are. In this case, you know they are types from the .NET BCL you simply print out the type names. This means when compiled and run, the sample outputs the following:

```
( String * Int32 )
```

Reflection Over Values

Imagine instead of displaying the types of a tuple that you wanted to display the values that make up the tuple. To do this, you would use reflection over values, and you would need to use the function FSharpValue.GetTupleFields to get an array of objects that are the values that make up the tuple. These objects could be tuples, or other F# types, so you could recursively call the function to print out the objects value. However, in this case, you know there are fundamental values from the BCL library, so you simply use the F# printfn function to print them out. The F# printf module is described later in the chapter. The following example implements such a function:

```
open Microsoft.FSharp.Reflection
let printTupleValues (x: obj) =
    if FSharpType.IsTuple(x.GetType()) then
        let vals = FSharpValue.GetTupleFields x
        printf "("
        vals
        |> Seq.iteri
            (fun i v ->
                if i <> Seq.length vals - 1 then
                    printf " %A, " v
                else
                    printf " %A" v)
        printfn " )"
    else
        printfn "not a tuple"

printTupleValues ("hello world", 1)
```

The result of this code, when compiled and executed, is as follows:

```
( "hello world", 1 )
```

Reflection is used both within the implementation of fsi, the interactive command-line tool that is part of the F# tool suite, and within the F# library the printf function family. If you want to learn more about the way you can use reflection, take a look at the source for printf, available in the distribution in the files \source\fsharp\printf.fs and \source\fsharp\layout.ml.

The Microsoft.FSharp.Collections.Seq Module

The Microsoft.FSharp.Collections.Seq module contains functions that work with any collection that supports the IEnumerable interface, which is most of the collections in the .NET Framework's BCL. The module is called Seq because F# gives the alias seq to the IEnumerable interface to shorten it and make it easier to type and read. This alias is used when type definitions are given.

■**Note** FSLib contains several modules designed to work with various types of collections. These include Array, Array2 (two-dimensional arrays), Array3 (three-dimensional arrays), Hashtbl (a hash table implementation), IEnumerable, LazyList, List, Map, and Set. I'll cover only Seq because it should generally be favored over these collections because of its ability to work with lots of different types of collections. Also, although each module has functions that are specific to it, many functions are common to them all.

Some of these functions can be replaced by the list comprehension syntax covered in Chapters 3 and 4. For simple tasks and working with untyped collections, it's generally easier to use list comprehension, but for more complicated tasks you will want to stick to these functions. You will take a look at the following functions:

map and iter: These two functions let you apply a given function to every item in the collection.

concat: This function lets you concatenate a collection of collections into one collection.

fold: This function lets you create a summary of a list by folding the items in the collection together.

exists and forall: These functions let you make assertions about the contents of a collection.

filter, find and tryFind: These functions let you pick elements in the list that meet certain conditions.

choose: This function lets you perform a filter and map at the same time.

init and initInfinite: These functions let you initialize collections.

unfold: This provides a more flexible way to initialize lists.

cast: This is a way to convert from the nongeneric version of IEnumerable, rather than IEnumerable<T>.

The map and iter Functions

You'll look at map and iter first. These apply a function to each element in a collection. The difference between them is that map is designed to create a new collection by transforming each element in the collection, while iter is designed to apply an operation that has a side effect to each item in the collection. A typical example of a side effect would be writing the element to the console. The following example shows both map and iter in action:

```
let myArray = [|1; 2; 3|]

let myNewCollection =
    myArray |>
    Seq.map (fun x -> x * 2)

printfn "%A" myArray

myNewCollection |> Seq.iter (fun x -> printf "%i ... " x)
```

The results of this code, when compiled and executed, are as follows:
```
[|1; 2; 3|]
2 ... 4 ... 6 ...
```

The concat Function

The previous example used an array, because it was convenient to initialize this type of collection, but you could use any of the collection types available in the BCL. The next example uses the List type provided in the System.Collections.Generic namespace and demonstrates how to use the concat function, which has type #seq< #seq<'a> > -> seq<'a> and which collects IEnumerable values into one IEnumerable value:

```
open System.Collections.Generic

let myList =
    let temp = new List<int[]>()
    temp.Add([|1; 2; 3|])
    temp.Add([|4; 5; 6|])
    temp.Add([|7; 8; 9|])
    temp

let myCompleteList = Seq.concat myList

myCompleteList |> Seq.iter (fun x -> printf "%i ... " x)
```

The results of this code, when compiled and executed, are as follows:

```
1 ... 2 ... 3 ... 4 ... 5 ... 6 ... 7 ... 8 ... 9 ...
```

The fold Function

The next example demonstrates the fold function, which has type ('b -> 'a -> 'b) -> 'b -> #seq<'a> -> 'b. This is a function for creating a summary of a collection by threading an accumulator value through each function call. The function takes two parameters. The first of these is an accumulator, which is the result of the previous function, and the second is an element from the collection. The function body should combine these two values to form a new value of the same type as the accumulator. In the next example, the elements of myPhrase are concatenated to the accumulator so that all the strings end up combined into one string.

```
let myPhrase = [|"How"; "do"; "you"; "do?"|]

let myCompletePhrase =
    myPhrase |>
    Seq.fold (fun acc x -> acc + " " + x) ""

printfn "%s" myCompletePhrase
```

The result of this code, when compiled and executed, is as follows:

```
How do you do?
```

The exists and forall Functions

The next example demonstrates two functions that you can use to determine facts about the contents of collections. These functions are exists and forall, which both have the type ('a -> bool) -> #seq<'a> -> bool. You can use the exists function to determine whether any element in the collection exists that meets certain conditions. The conditions that must be met are determined by the function passed to exists, and if any of the elements meet this condition, then exists will return true. The function forall is similar except that all the elements in the collection must meet the condition before it will return true. The following example first uses exists to determine whether there are any elements in the collections that are multiples of 2 and then uses forall to determine whether all items in the collection are multiples of 2:

```
let intArray = [|0; 1; 2; 3; 4; 5; 6; 7; 8; 9|]

let existsMultipleOfTwo =
    intArray |>
    Seq.exists (fun x -> x % 2 = 0)

let allMultipleOfTwo =
    intArray |>
    Seq.forall (fun x -> x % 2 = 0)

printfn "existsMultipleOfTwo: %b" existsMultipleOfTwo
printfn "allMultipleOfTwo: %b" allMultipleOfTwo
```

The results of this code, when compiled and executed, are as follows:

```
existsMultipleOfTwo: true
allMultipleOfTwo: false
```

The filter, find, and tryFind Functions

The next example looks at three functions that are similar to exists and forall. These functions are filter of type ('a -> bool) -> #seq<'a> -> seq<'a>, find of type ('a -> bool) -> #seq<'a> -> 'a and tryfind of type ('a -> bool) -> #seq<'a> -> 'a option. They are similar to exists and forall, because they use functions to examine the contents of a collection. Instead of returning a Boolean, these functions actually return the item or items found. The function filter uses the function passed to it to check every element in the collection. The filter function then returns a list that contains all the elements that have met the condition of the function. If no elements meet the condition, then an empty list is returned. The functions find and tryfind both return the first element in the collection to meet the condition specified by the function passed to them. Their behavior is altered when no element in the collection meets the condition. find throws an exception, whereas tryfind returns an option type that will be None if no element is found. Since exceptions are relatively expensive in .NET, you should prefer tryfind over find.

In the following example, you'll look through a list of words. First, you use filter to create a list containing only the words that end in *at*. Then you'll use find to find the first word that ends in *ot*. Finally, you'll use tryfind to check whether any of the words end in *tt*.

```fsharp
let shortWordList = [|"hat"; "hot"; "bat"; "lot"; "mat"; "dot"; "rat";|]

let atWords =
    shortWordList
    |> Seq.filter (fun x -> x.EndsWith("at"))

let otWord =
    shortWordList
    |> Seq.find (fun x -> x.EndsWith("ot"))

let ttWord =
    shortWordList
    |> Seq.tryFind (fun x -> x.EndsWith("tt"))

atWords |> Seq.iter (fun x -> printf "%s ... " x)
printfn ""
printfn "%s" otWord
printfn "%s" (match ttWord with | Some x -> x | None -> "Not found")
```

The results of this code, when compiled and executed, are as follows:

```
hat ... bat ... mat ... rat ...
hot
Not found
```

The choose Function

The next Seq function you'll look at is a clever function that allows you to do a filter and a map at the same time. This function is called choose and has the type ('a -> 'b option) -> #seq<'a> -> seq<'b>. To do this, the function that is passed to choose must return an option type. If the element in the list can be transformed into something useful, the function should return Some containing the new value. When the element is not wanted, the function returns None.

In the following example, you'll take a list of floating-point numbers and multiply them by 2. If the value is an integer, it is returned. Otherwise, it is filtered out. This leaves you with just a list of integers.

```
let floatArray = [|0.5; 0.75; 1.0; 1.25; 1.5; 1.75; 2.0 |]

let integers =
    floatArray |>
    Seq.choose
        (fun x ->
            let y = x * 2.0
            let z = floor y
            if y - z = 0.0 then
                Some (int z)
            else
                None)

integers |> Seq.iter (fun x -> printf "%i ... " x)
```

The results of this code, when compiled and executed, are as follows:

```
1 ... 2 ... 3 ... 4 ...
```

The init and initInfinite Functions

Next, you'll look at two functions for initializing collections, init of type int -> (int -> 'a) -> seq<'a> and initInfinite of type (int -> 'a) -> seq<'a>. You can use the function initFinite to make a collection of a finite size. It does this by calling the function passed to it the number of times specified by the number passed to it. You can use the function initInfinite to create a collection of an infinite size. It does this by calling the function passed to it each time it is asked for a new element this way. In theory, a list of unlimited size can be created, but in reality you are constrained by the limits of the machine performing the computation.

The following example shows init being used to create a list of ten integers, each with the value 1. It also shows a list being created that should contain all the possible 32-bit integers and demonstrates using the function take to create a list of the first ten.

```
let tenOnes = Seq.init 10 (fun _ -> 1)
let allIntegers = Seq.initInfinite (fun x -> System.Int32.MinValue + x)
let firstTenInts = Seq.take 10 allIntegers

tenOnes |> Seq.iter (fun x -> printf "%i ... " x)
printfn ""
printfn "%A" firstTenInts
```

The results of this code, when compiled and executed, are as follows:

```
1 ... 1 ... 1 ... 1 ... 1 ... 1 ... 1 ... 1 ... 1 ... 1 ...
[-2147483648; -2147483647; -2147483646; -2147483645; -2147483644; -2147483643;
 -2147483642; -2147483641; -2147483640; -2147483639]
```

The unfold Function

You already met unfold in Chapter 3. It is a more flexible version of the functions init and initInfinite. The first advantage of unfold is that it can be used to pass an accumulator through the computation, which means you can store some state between computations and do not simply have to rely on the current position in the list to calculate the value, like you do with init and initInfinite. The second advantage is that it can be used to produce a list that is either finite or infinite. Both of these advantages are achieved by using the return type of the function passed to unfold. The return type of the function is 'a * 'b option, meaning an option type that contains a tuple of values. The first value in the option type is the value that will be placed in the list, and the second is the accumulator. If you want to continue the list, you return Some with this tuple contained within it. If want to stop it, you return None.

The following example, repeated from Chapter 2, shows unfold being used to compute the Fibonacci numbers. You can see the accumulator being used to store a tuple of values representing the next two numbers in the Fibonacci sequence. Because the list of Fibonacci numbers is infinite, you never return None.

```
let fibs =
    (1,1) |> Seq.unfold
        (fun (n0, n1) ->
            Some(n0, (n1, n0 + n1)))

let first20 = Seq.take 20 fibs
printfn "%A" first20
```

The results of this code, when compiled and executed, are as follows:

```
[1; 1; 2; 3; 5; 8; 13; 21; 34; 55; 89; 144; 233; 377; 610; 987;
 1597; 2584; 4181; 6765]
```

The example demonstrates using unfold to produce a list that terminates. Imagine you want to calculate a sequence of numbers where the value decreases by half its current value, such as a nuclear source decaying. Imagine beyond a certain limit the number becomes so small that you are no longer interested in it. You can model such a sequence in the following example by returning None when the value has reached its limit:

```
let decayPattern =
    Seq.unfold
        (fun x ->
            let limit = 0.01
            let n = x - (x / 2.0)
```

```
        if n > limit then
            Some(x, n)
        else
            None)
    10.0

decayPattern |> Seq.iter (fun x -> printf "%f ... " x)
```

The results of this code, when compiled and executed, are as follows:

```
10.000000 ... 5.000000 ... 2.500000 ... 1.250000 ...
0.625000 ... 0.312500 ... 0.156250 ... 0.078125 ... 0.039063 ...
```

The generate Function

The generate function of type (unit -> 'b) -> ('b -> 'a option) -> ('b -> unit) -> seq<'a> is a useful function for creating IEnumerable collections. It allows you to generate collections from some kind of cursor, such as file stream or database record set. The cursor can be a file stream, as shown in these examples, or perhaps more commonly a database cursor. In fact, it can be any type that will generate a sequence of elements. The generate function takes three functions: one to open the cursor (the opener function in the following example), one to do the work of actually generating the collection (the generator function), and one to close the cursor (the closer function). The collection can then be treated as any other IEnumerable collection, but behind the scenes, the functions you have defined will be called to go to the data source and read the elements from it. The following example shows the function being used to read a comma-separated list of words from a file:

```
open System
open System.Text
open System.IO

// test.txt: the,cat,sat,on,the,mat
let opener() = File.OpenText("test.txt")
let generator (stream : StreamReader) =
    let endStream = ref false
    let rec generatorInner chars =
        match stream.Read() with
        | -1 ->
        endStream := true
        chars
        | x ->
            match Convert.ToChar(x) with
            | ',' -> chars
            | c -> generatorInner (c :: chars)
```

```
    let chars = generatorInner []
    if List.length chars = 0 && !endStream then
        None
    else
        Some(new string(List.toArray (List.rev chars)))

let closer (stream : StreamReader) =
    stream.Dispose()

let wordList =
    Seq.generate
        opener
        generator
        closer

wordList |> Seq.iter (fun s -> printfn "%s" s)
```

The results of this code, when compiled and executed, are as follows:

```
the
cat
sat
on
the
mat
```

The cast Function

The .NET Framework's BCL contains two versions of the IEnumerable interface, one defined in System. Collections.Generic and an older one defined in System.Collections. All the samples shown so far have been designed to work with the new generic version from System.Collections.Generic. However, sometimes it might be necessary to work with collections that are not generic, so the F# IEnumerable module also provides a function to work with that converts from nongeneric collections to a generic one.

Before using this function, I strongly recommend that you see whether you can use the list comprehension syntax covered in Chapters 3 and 4 instead. This is because the list comprehension syntax can infer the types of many untyped collections, usually by looking at the type of the Item indexer property, so there is less need for type annotations, which generally makes programming easier.

If for any reason you'd prefer not to use the list comprehension syntax you can convert a non generic collection to a generic one using the function cast, which is demonstrated in the following example:

```
open System.Collections
open System.Collections.Generic
```

```
let floatArrayList =
    let temp = new ArrayList()
    temp.AddRange([| 1.0; 2.0; 3.0 |])
    temp

let (typedFloatSeq: seq<float>) = Seq.cast floatArrayList
```

Using cast function always required using type annotations to tell the compiler what type of list you are producing. Here you have a list of floats, so you use the type annotation IEnumerable<float> to tell the compiler it will be an IEnumerable collection containing floating-point numbers.

The Microsoft.FSharp.Text.Printf Module

The Printf module provides functions for formatting strings in a type-safe way. The functions in the Printf module take a string with placeholders for values as their first argument. This returns another function that expects values for the placeholders. You form placeholders by using a percentage sign and a letter representing the type that they expect. Table 7-2 shows the full list.

Table 7-2. Printf *Placeholders and Flags*

Flag	Description
%b	bool, formatted as "true" or "false"
%s	string, formatted as its unescaped contents
%d, %i	Any basic integer type (that is, sbyte, byte, int16, uint16, int32, uint32, int64, uint64, nativeint, or unativeint) formatted as a decimal integer, signed if the basic integer type is signed
%u	Any basic integer type formatted as an unsigned decimal integer
%x, %X, %o	Any basic integer type formatted as an unsigned hexadecimal, (a-f)/Hexadecimal (A-F)/Octal integer
%e, %E	Any basic floating-point type (that is, float or float32), formatted using a C-style floating-point format specification, signed value having the form [-]d.dddde[sign]ddd where *d* is a single decimal digit, *dddd* is one or more decimal digits, *ddd* is exactly three decimal digits, and *sign* is + or –
%f	Any basic floating-point type, formatted using a C-style floating-point format specification, signed value having the form [-]dddd.dddd, where *dddd* is one or more decimal digits. The number of digits before the decimal point depends on the magnitude of the number, and the number of digits after the decimal point depends on the requested precision

Table 7-2. *Continued*

Flag	Description
%g, %G	Any basic floating-point type, formatted using a C-style floating-point format specification, signed value printed in f or e format, whichever is more compact for the given value and precision
%M	System.Decimal value
%O	Any value, printed by boxing the object and using its ToString method(s)
%A	Any value, values will be pretty printed allowing the user to see the values of properties and fields
%a	A general format specifier; requires two arguments: A function that accepts two arguments: a context parameter of the appropriate type for the given formatting function (such as a System.IO.TextWriter) and a value to print that either outputs or returns appropriate text. The particular value to print
%t	A general format specifier; requires one argument: a function that accepts a context parameter of the appropriate type for the given formatting function (such as a System.IO.TextWriter) and that either outputs or returns appropriate text
0	A flag that adds zeros instead of spaces to make up the required width
-	A flag that left justifies the result within the width specified
+	A flag that adds a + character if the number is positive (to match the – sign for negatives)
' '	Adds an extra space if the number is positive (to match the – sign for negatives)

The following example shows how to use the printf function. It creates a function that expects a string and then passes a string to this function.

```
Printf.printf "Hello %s" "Robert"
```

The results of this code are as follows:

```
Hello Robert
```

The significance of this might not be entirely obvious, but the following example will probably help explain it. If a parameter of the wrong type is passed to the printf function, then it will not compile:

```
Printf.printf "Hello %s" 1
```

The previous code will not compile, giving the following error:

```
Prog.fs(4,25): error: FS0001: This expression has type
    int
but is here used with type
    string
```

This also has an effect on type inference. If you create a function that uses printf, then any arguments that are passed to printf will have their types inferred from this. For example, the function myPrintInt, shown here, has the type int -> unit because of the printf function contained within it:

```
let myPrintInt x =
    Printf.printf "An integer: %i" x
```

The basic placeholders in a Printf module function are %b for a Boolean; %s for a string; %d or %i for an integer; %u for an unsigned integer; and %x, %X, or %o for an integer formatted as a hexadecimal. It is also possible to specify the number of decimal places that are displayed in numeric types. The following example demonstrates this:

```
let pi = System.Math.PI

Printf.printfn "%f" pi
Printf.printfn "%1.1f" pi
Printf.printfn "%2.2f" pi
Printf.printfn "%2.8f" pi
```

The results of this code are as follows:

```
3.141593
3.1
3.14
3.14159265
```

The Printf module also contains a number of other functions that allow a string to be formatted in the same ways as printf itself, but allow the result to be written to a different destination. The following example shows some of the different versions available:

```
// write to a string
let s = Printf.sprintf "Hello %s\r\n" "string"
printfn "%s" s
// prints the string to a .NET TextWriter
Printf.fprintf System.Console.Out "Hello %s\r\n" "TextWriter"
// create a string that will be placed
// in an exception message
Printf.failwithf "Hello %s" "exception"
```

The results of this code are as follows:

```
Hello string
Hello channel
Hello TextWriter
Microsoft.FSharp.FailureException: Hello exception
    at Microsoft.FSharp.Text.Printf.failwithf@60.Invoke(String s)
    at Microsoft.FSharp.Text.PrintfImpl.Make@188.Invoke(A inp))
    at <StartupCode>.FSI_0003._main()
stopped due to error
```

The Microsoft.FSharp.Control.Event Module

You can think of an event in F# as a collection of functions that can be triggered by a call to a function. The idea is that functions will register themselves with the event, the collection of functions, to await notification that the event has happened. The trigger function is then used to give notice that the event has occurred, causing all the functions that have added themselves to the event to be executed.

I will cover the following features of the Event module:

Creating and handling events: The basics of creating and handling events using the create and add functions.

The filter *function*: A function to filter the data coming into events.

The partition *function*: A function that splits the data coming into events into two.

The map *function*: A function that maps the data before it reaches the event handler.

Creating and Handling Events

The first example looks at a simple event being created using by call the constructor of the Event object, you should pass a type parameter to the construct representing the type of event you want. This object contains a Trigger function and a property that represents the event itself called Publish. You use the event's Publish property's Add function to add a handler method, and finally you trigger the event using the trigger function:

```
let event = new Event<string>()
event.Publish.Add(fun x -> printfn "%s" x)
event.Trigger "hello"
```

The result of this code is as follows:

```
hello
```

In addition to this basic event functionality, the F# Event module provides a number of functions that allow you to filter and partition events to give fine-grained control over which data is passed to which event handler.

The filter Function

The following example demonstrates how you can use the Event module's filter function so that data being passed to the event is filtered before it reaches the event handlers. In this example, you filter the data so that only strings beginning with H are sent to the event handler:

```
let event = new Event<string>()
let newEvent = event.Publish |> Event.filter (fun x -> x.StartsWith("H"))

newEvent.Add(fun x -> printfn "new event: %s" x)

event.Trigger "Harry"
event.Trigger "Jane"
event.Trigger "Hillary"
event.Trigger "John"
event.Trigger "Henry"
```

The results of this code, when compiled and executed, are as follows:

```
new event: Harry
new event: Hillary
new event: Henry
```

The partition Function

The Event module's partition function is similar to the filter function except two events are returned, one where data caused the partition function to return false and one where data caused the partition function to return true. The following example demonstrates this:

```
let event = new Event<string>()
let hData, nonHData = event.Publish |> Event.partition (fun x -> true)

let x  = Event.partition


hData.Add(fun x -> printfn "H data: %s" x)
nonHData.Add(fun x -> printfn "None H data: %s" x)
```

```
event.Trigger "Harry"
event.Trigger "Jane"
event.Trigger "Hillary"
event.Trigger "John"
event.Trigger "Henry"
```

The results of this code are as follows:

```
H data: Harry
None H data: Jane
H data: Hillary
None H data: John
H data: Henry
```

The map Function

It is also possible to transform the data before it reaches the event handlers. You do this using the map function provided in the Event module. The following example demonstrates how to use it:

```
let event = new Event<string>()
let newEvent = event.Publish |> Event.map (fun x -> "Mapped data: " + x)
newEvent.Add(fun x -> printfn "%s" x)

event.Trigger "Harry"
event.Trigger "Sally"
```

The results of this code are as follows:

```
Mapped data: Harry
Mapped data: Sally
```

This section has just provided a brief overview of events in F#. You will return to them in more detail in Chapter 8 when I discuss user interface programming, because that is where they are most useful.

The Power Pack Library FSharp.PowerPack.dll

The power pack contains a number of useful features that were not included in the FSharp.Core.dll either because of space issues or because they were considered experimental and likely to evolve more rapidly than the FSharp.Core.dll will. This includes modules that are suitable for cross compilation with OCaml, extra collections, extra mathematical function, asynchronous workflows (covered in Chapter 10) and functions for supporting text parsing via fslex and fsyacc. Next, I will cover Microsoft.FSharp.Math: A namespace that contains several modules related to mathematics. These include arbitrary precision integers and rationals, vectors, matrices, and complex numbers.

The Microsoft.FSharp.Math Namespace

The Microsoft.FSharp.Math namespace is designed to enable F# to ensure that the F# libraries include definitions of some of the foundational constructs used across a wide range of graphics, mathematical, scientific, and engineering applications. First, you will look briefly at the modules that make it up, and then you'll dive into a more detailed example.

It contains arbitrary precision numbers. These are numbers whose values have no upper limit and include the modules BigInt and BigNum. A typical use of these would be in a program that searches for large prime numbers, perhaps for use in cryptography.

The modules Matrix, Vector, RowVector, and Notations all contain operations related to matrices and vectors. *Matrices* are sets of numbers arranged in rows and columns to form a rectangular array. Vectors are a column of numbers and are like a matrix with one column but are a separate type. A *vector* is a quantity characterized by magnitude and direction, so a two-dimensional vector is specified by two coordinates, a three-dimensional vector by three coordinates, and so on. Therefore, vectors are represented as a matrix made up of one column with the number of rows depending on the dimension of the vector.

There is a module, Complex, for working with complex numbers. The complex numbers are the base for many types of fractal images, so I will demonstrate how you can use the F# complex number library to draw the most famous fractal of all, the Mandelbrot set. The Mandelbrot set is generated by repeated iteration of the following equation:

$$Cn+1 = Cn2 + c$$

The next number in the series is formed from the current number squared plus the original number. If repeated iteration of this equation stays between the complex number C(1, 1i) and C(–1, –1i), then the original complex number is a member of the Mandelbrot set. This can be implemented in F# with the following:

```
open Microsoft.FSharp.Math
open Microsoft.FSharp.Math.Notation

let cMax = complex 1.0 1.0
let cMin = complex -1.0 -1.0
let iterations = 18
let isInMandelbrotSet c0 =
    let rec check n c =
        (n = iterations)
        or (cMin < c) && (c < cMax) && check (n + 1) ((c * c) + c0)
    check 0 c0
```

The function isInMandelbrotSet tests whether a complex number is in the Mandelbrot set by recursively calling the check function with the new c value of ((c * c) + c0) until either the complex number passes one of the constants cMax or cMin or the number of iterations exceeds the constant iterations. If the number of iterations specified by iterations is reached, then number is a member of the set. Otherwise, it is not.

Because the complex numbers consist of two numbers, they can be represented in a two-dimensional plane. The Mandelbrot complex numbers exist between C(1, 1i) and C(–1, –1i), so the plane that you need to draw has the origin, which is the point 0, 0, in the center, and its axis extends out in either direction until reaching a maximum of 1.0 and a minimum of –1.0, such as the plane on the right of Figure 7-1. However, when it comes to pixels on a computer screen, you must deal with a plane where the origin is in the top-right corner and it extends rightward and downward. Because this type plane is made up of pixels, which are discrete values, it is represented by integers typically somewhere in the range 0 to 1600. Such a plane appears on the left of Figure 7-1.

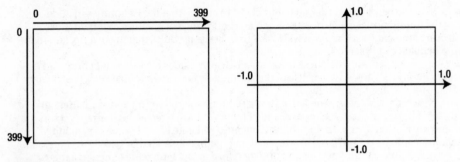

Figure 7-1. *A bitmap plane vs. a complex plane*

The application must map the points in the bitmap plane to points in the complex plane so that you can tell whether a pixel is part of the complex plane.

It is easy to perform this mapping in just a few lines of F# code:

```
open Microsoft.FSharp.Math
open Microsoft.FSharp.Math.Notation

let scalingFactor = 1.0 / 200.0
let offset = -1.0

let mapPlane (x, y) =
    let fx = ((float x) * scalingFactor) + offset
    let fy = ((float y) * scalingFactor) + offset
    complex fx fy
```

Once this is complete, you just need to cycle through all the points in your bitmap plane, mapping them to the complex plane using the mapPlane function. Then you need to test whether the complex number is in the Mandelbrot set using the function isInMandelbrotSet. Finally, you set the color of the pixel. The full program is as follows:

```
open System
open System.Drawing
open System.Windows.Forms
open Microsoft.FSharp.Math

let cMax = complex 1.0 1.0
let cMin = complex -1.0 -1.0
```

```
let iterations = 18

let isInMandelbrotSet c0 =
    let rec check n c =
        (n = iterations)
        || (cMin < c)
        && (c < cMax)
        && check (n + 1) ((c * c) + c0)
    check 0 c0

let scalingFactor = 1.0 / 200.0
let offset = -1.0

let mapPlane (x, y) =
    let fx = ((float x) * scalingFactor) + offset
    let fy = ((float y) * scalingFactor) + offset
    complex fx fy

let form =
    let image = new Bitmap(400, 400)
    for x = 0 to image.Width - 1 do
        for y = 0 to image.Height - 1 do
            let isMember = isInMandelbrotSet ( mapPlane (x, y) )
            if isMember then
                image.SetPixel(x,y, Color.Black)
    let temp = new Form() in
    temp.Paint.Add(fun e -> e.Graphics.DrawImage(image, 0, 0))
    temp

[<STAThread>]
do Application.Run(form)
```

This program produces the image of the Mandelbrot set in Figure 7-2.

Figure 7-2. *The Mandelbrot set*

Summary

I covered a lot of ground in this chapter, since the F# libraries have a diverse range of functionalities. First, you looked through the FSharp.Core.dll library with its useful Collections, Reflection, and Math modules. Then you looked at FSharp.PowerPack.dll, which provides functions that are excellent building blocks for all applications. Its Seq module is something that any nontrivial F# program will not be able to do without.

The next three chapters will look at how you can use F# with various .NET APIs for common programming tasks. You'll start with a look at implementing user interfaces in Chapter 8, then you'll move to data access in Chapter 9, and distributed applications in Chapter 10.

CHAPTER 8

■ ■ ■

User Interfaces

In this chapter, you will learn about one of the most common tasks a programmer needs to perform: the art of putting pixels on the screen. In F#, this is all about the libraries and APIs that you call, and you have a lot of choices in this area, with more emerging as the .NET platform involves. The first choice you need to make is whether you want to build a desktop application; an application that runs locally and uses a series of windows and controls to display information to the user; or a web application, where you define the application's interface in HTML, which is then rendered by a browser.

You have four GUI library choices when creating desktop applications in .NET: WinForms, Windows Presentation Foundation (WFP), GTK#, and DirectX. In this chapter, you'll learn about WinForms, WFP and GTK#, but not DirectX. WinForms, WFP, and GTK# have the same basic metaphors of windows and controls. WinForms is the oldest and simplest, and you've already met a few WinForms examples. WFP is a new library; it's slightly more complex than WinForms, but it's also more consistent and offers more features, including impressive 3D graphics. GTK# offers much better platform support than the other two libraries. WinForms now runs on all platforms, thanks to the Mono implementation, and GTK# is recommended by the Mono team for non-Windows platforms. DirectX is mainly targeted at game producers who want fast 3D graphics. WFP offers a simpler way to produce 3D graphics, so this book won't cover DirectX.

To create a web application, you can use the ASP.NET framework, which gives you a simple way to create server-based dynamic HTML applications. ASP.NET provides a flexible way for you to generate HTML in response to a HTTP request from a browser. Web applications have evolved greatly in recent years; not surprisingly, the ASP.NET platform has evolved greatly alongside it. ASP.NET has added ASP.NET AJAX, ASP.NET MVC, and Silverlight, and a rival platform called Mono Rail has also emerged. However, this book doesn't cover these things because the aim is to show off the basics of generating HTML using F#.

Whole books have been written on each of the topics you'll learn about in this chapter, so be aware that this chapter focuses mainly on the basics. Whichever technology you choose to create your UIs, you're probably going to have to invest some time learning how the library works before you can create great UIs.

Introducing WinForms

The WinForms classes are contained in the `System.Drawing.dll` and `System.Forms.Windows.dll`, and you will need to add references to these to compile all of the WinForms examples. The libraries are based on the `System.Windows.Forms.Form` class, which represents a window that you show to the user. You essentially create a new window when you create an instance of this class. You must then create an *event loop*, a way of ensuring that you respond to user interactions with the window. You do this by calling the `System.Windows.Forms.Application.Run` method and passing it the form object you created. You can control the look of the form by setting its properties and calling its methods. The following example demonstrates how to do this:

```
open System.Drawing
open System.Windows.Forms

// create a new form
let form = new Form(BackColor = Color.Purple, Text = "Introducing WinForms")

// show the form
Application.Run(form)
```

This example will not work with F# interactive, fsi, because you cannot start an event loop from within fsi. To work with forms in fsi, you call the form's Show method or set the form's Visible property to true. This example shows the second technique:

```
> open System.Drawing
open System.Windows.Forms

let form = new Form(BackColor=Color.Purple,
                    Text="Introducing WinForms",
                    Visible=true);;
```

Either way, you can dynamically interact with your form object:

```
> form.Text <- "Dynamic !!!";;
```

When working with WinForms, you can take one of two approaches: draw the forms yourself or use controls to build them. You'll begin by drawing your own forms, and then move on to using controls.

Drawing WinForms

Drawing your own forms means that you take responsibility for the pixels that appear on the screen. This low-level approach might appeal to those F# users who believe that many controls that come with the WinForms library are not perfectly suited to displaying data structures or the results of functions and algorithms. However, be warned that this approach can be time-consuming, and your time is usually better spent looking for a graphics library that abstracts away some of the presentation logic.

To draw a WinForm, you attach an event handler to the Paint event of the form or the control. This means that your function is called every time Windows requests the form to be drawn. The event argument that is passed into this function has a property called Graphics, which contains an instance of a class also called Graphics. This class has methods (such as DrawLine) that allow you to draw pixels on the form. The following example shows a simple form where you draw a pie on it:

```
open System.Drawing
open System.Windows.Forms

let form =
    // create a new form setting the minimum size
    let temp = new Form(MinimumSize = new Size(96, 96))
```

```
             he form when it is resize
             Add (fun _ -> temp.Invalidate())

             o provide the shapes color
let brush = new SolidBrush(Color.Red)
temp.Paint.Add (fun e ->
    // calculate the width and height of the shape
    let width, height = temp.Width - 64, temp.Height - 64
    // draw the required shape
    e.Graphics.FillPie (brush, 32, 32, width, height, 0, 290))

// return the form to the top level
temp

Application.Run(form)
```

You can see the form that results from executing this code in Figure 8-1.

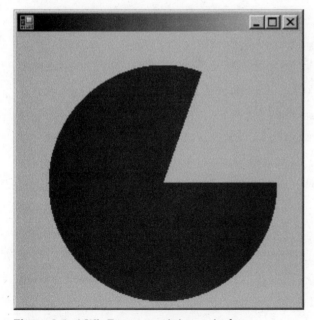

Figure 8-1. *A WinForm containing a pie shape*

This image is linked to the size of the form, so you must tell the form to redraw itself whenever the form is resized. You do this by attaching an event-handling function to the Resize event. In this function, you call the form's Invalidate method, which tells the form that it needs to redraw itself.

Now let's look at a more complete WinForms example. Imagine you want to create a form to display the Tree type defined in the next code example (see Figure 8-2):

```
// The tree type
type 'a Tree =
| Node of 'a Tree * 'a Tree
| Leaf of 'a

// The definition of the tree
let tree =
    Node(
        Node(
            Leaf "one",
            Node(Leaf "two", Leaf "three")),
        Node(
            Node(Leaf "four", Leaf "five"),
            Leaf "six"))
```

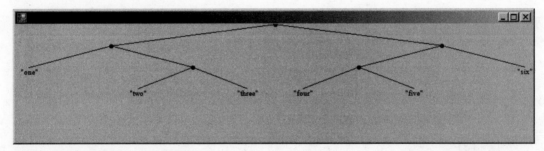

Figure 8-2. *A WinForm showing a tree structure*

You can draw this tree with the code shown in Listing 8-1.

Listing 8-1. *Drawing a Tree*

```
open System
open System.Drawing
open System.Windows.Forms

// The tree type
type 'a Tree =
| Node of 'a Tree * 'a Tree
| Leaf of 'a
```

```
// The definition of the tee
let tree =
    Node(
        Node(
            Leaf "one",
            Node(Leaf "two", Leaf "three")),
        Node(
            Node(Leaf "four", Leaf "five"),
            Leaf "six"))

// A function for finding the maximum depth of a tree
let getDepth t =
    let rec getDepthInner t d =
        match t with
        | Node (l, r) ->
            max
                (getDepthInner l d + 1.0F)
                (getDepthInner r d + 1.0F)
        | Leaf x -> d
    getDepthInner t 0.0F

// Constants required for drawing the form
let brush = new SolidBrush(Color.Black)
let pen = new Pen(Color.Black)
let font = new Font(FontFamily.GenericSerif, 8.0F)

// a useful function for calculating the maximum number
// of nodes at any given depth
let raise2ToPower (x : float32) =
    Convert.ToSingle(Math.Pow(2.0, Convert.ToDouble(x)))

let drawTree (g : Graphics) t =
    // constants that relate to the size and position
    // of the tree
    let center = g.ClipBounds.Width / 2.0F
    let maxWidth = 32.0F * raise2ToPower (getDepth t)
    // function for drawing a leaf node
    let drawLeaf (x : float32) (y : float32) v =
        let value = sprintf "%A" v
        let l = g.MeasureString(value, font)
        g.DrawString(value, font, brush, x - (l.Width / 2.0F), y)
```

```
    // draw a connector between the nodes when necessary
    let connectNodes (x : float32) y p =
        match p with
        | Some(px, py) -> g.DrawLine(pen, px, py, x, y)
        | None -> ()
    // the main function to walk the tree structure drawing the
    // nodes as we go
    let rec drawTreeInner t d w p =
        let x = center - (maxWidth * w)
        let y = d * 32.0F
        connectNodes x y p
        match t with
        | Node (l, r) ->
            g.FillPie(brush, x - 3.0F, y - 3.0F, 7.0F, 7.0F, 0.0F, 360.0F)
            let d = (d + 1.0F)
            drawTreeInner l d (w + (1.0F / d)) (Some(x, y))
            drawTreeInner r d (w - (1.0F / d)) (Some(x, y))
        | Leaf v -> drawLeaf x y v
    drawTreeInner t 0.0F 0.0F None

// create the form object
let form =
    let temp = new Form(WindowState = FormWindowState.Maximized)
    temp.Resize.Add(fun _ -> temp.Invalidate())
    temp.Paint.Add
        (fun e ->
            e.Graphics.Clip <-
                new Region(new Rectangle(0, 0, temp.Width, temp.Height))
            drawTree e.Graphics tree)
    temp

Application.Run(form)
```

Note how you define a function, drawTree. This function has two parameters, the Graphics object and the tree you want to draw:

```
let drawTree (g : Graphics) t =
```

This is a common pattern when drawing WinForms. Creating a function that takes the Graphics object and a data type to be drawn allows different forms and controls to reuse the function easily.

To implement drawTree, you first calculate a couple of constants the function will use: center and maxWidth. Functions outside drawTree can't see these constants, so you can use them in drawTree's inner functions without having to pass them around as parameters:

```
// constants that relate to the size and position
// of the tree
let center = g.ClipBounds.Width / 2.0F
let maxWidth = 32.0F * raise2ToPower (getDepth t)
```

You implement the rest of the function by breaking it down into inner functions. You define drawLeaf to take care of drawing leaf nodes:

```
// function for drawing a leaf node
let drawLeaf (x : float32) (y : float32) v =
    let value = sprintf "%A" v
    let l = g.MeasureString(value, font)
    g.DrawString(value, font, brush, x - (l.Width / 2.0F), y)
```

You use connectNodes to take care of drawing the connections between nodes, where appropriate:

```
// draw a connector between the nodes when necessary
let connectNodes (x : float32) y p =
    match p with
    | Some(px, py) -> g.DrawLine(pen, px, py, x, y)
    | None -> ()
```

Finally, you define drawTreeInner as a recursive function that does the real work of walking the Tree type and drawing it:

```
// the main function to walk the tree structure drawing the
// nodes as we go
let rec drawTreeInner t d w p =
    let x = center - (maxWidth * w)
    let y = d * 32.0F
    connectNodes x y p
    match t with
    | Node (l, r) ->
        g.FillPie(brush, x - 3.0F, y - 3.0F, 7.0F, 7.0F, 0.0F, 360.0F)
        let d = (d + 1.0F)
        drawTreeInner l d (w + (1.0F / d)) (Some(x, y))
        drawTreeInner r d (w - (1.0F / d)) (Some(x, y))
    | Leaf v -> drawLeaf x y v
```

This function uses parameters to store values between recursive calls. Because this is an inner function, you know that the outside world cannot misuse it by initializing it incorrectly; this is because the outside world cannot see it. Hiding parameters to store working values between recursive function calls is another common pattern in functional programming.

In some ways, this tree-drawing function is satisfactory: it gives a nice hierarchical overview of the tree in a fairly concise 86 lines of F# code. However, this approach scales only so far. As you draw more complicated images, the number of lines of code can grow rapidly, and working out all the geometry can become time-consuming. To help manage this complexity, F# lets you use controls, as you'll learn in the next section.

To make the most of drawing on WinForms, you should get to know the System.Drawing namespace contained in System.Drawing.dll. You should also concentrate on two areas. First, you need to learn how to use the Graphics object, particularly its overloads of methods prefixed with either Draw or Fill. Table 8-1 provides a helpful summary of the methods on the Graphics object.

Table 8-1. *Important Methods on the* System.Drawing.Graphics *Object*

Method Name	Description
DrawArc	Draws a portion of an ellipse
DrawBezier	Draws a Bézier spline, which is a curve represented by two endpoints and two free-floating points that controll the angle of the curve
DrawCurve	Draws a curved line defined by an array of points
DrawClosedCurve	Draws a closed curved line defined by an array of points
DrawEllipse	Draws the outline of an ellipse, which you represent with a rectangle or rectangular set of points
DrawPie	Draws a portion of the outline of an ellipse, which you represent with a rectangle and two radial lines that illustrate the start and finish angles
DrawLine	Draws a single line from two points
DrawLines	Draws a set of lines from an array of points
DrawPolygon	Draws the outline of a polygon, which is a closed set of lines from an array of points
DrawRectangle	Draws the outline of a rectangle, which you represent with a coordinate, as well as its width and height
DrawRectangles	Draws the outline of a set of rectangles from an array of rectangles
FillClosedCurve	Draws a solid closed curve defined by an array of points
FillEllipse	Draws a solid ellipse, which you represent with a rectangle or rectangular set of points
FillPie	Draws a portion of a solid ellipse, which you represent with a rectangle and two radial lines that show the start and finish angles
FillPolygon	Draws a solid polygon, which is a closed set of lines from an array of points
FillRectangle	Draws a solid rectangle, which you represent with a coordinate and its width and height

Method Name	Description
FillRectangles	Draws a solid set of rectangles from an array of rectangles.
DrawIcon	Draws an image specified by the System.Drawing.Icon type
DrawImage	Draws an image specified by the System.Drawing.Image type
DrawImageUnscaled	Draws an image specified by the System.Drawing.Image type with no scaling
DrawString	Draws a string of characters
MeasureString	Gives the dimensions of a string of characters, so you can calculate where you want to place it on the image
DrawPath	Draws an outline, which you represent with the System.Drawing.Drawing2D.GraphicsPath, a class that allows you to add geometric constructs such as the curves, rectangles, ellipses, and polygons described earlier to save you from recalculating them each time (this is useful if you want to draw something that is complicated but fairly static)
FillPath	Provides the same functionality as DrawPath, except that it draws an image that is solid, rather than an outline

The second area you need to concentrate on in the System.Drawing namespace is closely related to the System.Drawing.Graphics object; you need to learn how to create the Icon, Image, Pen, and Brush objects used by the methods of the Graphics object. Table 8-2 shows examples of how to create these objects via their constructors.

Table 8-2. *Creating Objects Used with the* System.Drawing.Graphics *Object*

Snippet	Description
Color.FromArgb(33, 44, 55)	Creates a color from its red, green, and blue components
Color.FromKnownColor(KnownColor.Crimson)	Creates a color from a member of the KnownColor enumeration
Color.FromName("HotPink")	Creates a color from its name in string form
new Font(FontFamily.GenericSerif, 8.0f)	Creates a new generic serif font that is eight points tall
Image.FromFile("myimage.jpg")	Creates a new image from a file
Image.FromStream(File.OpenRead("myimage.gif"))	Creates a new image from a stream

Table 8-2. *Continued*

Snippet	Description
new Icon("myicon.ico")	Creates a new icon from a file
new Icon(File.OpenRead("myicon.ico"))	Creates a new icon from a stream
new Pen(Color.FromArgb(33, 44, 55))	Creates a colored pen that you can use to draw lines
new Pen(SystemColors.Control, 2.0f)	Creates a pen, that you can use to draw lines, from a color and with a width of 2 pixels
new SolidBrush(Color.FromName("Black"))	Creates a solid brush that you can use to draw filled shapes
new TexturedBrush(Image.FromFile ("myimage.jpg"))	Creates a new textured brush from an image and draws a filled shape with an image mapped across it

If you prefer to use standard objects, you can use several classes in the System.Drawing namespace that contain predefined objects, including Brushes, Pens, SystemBrushes, SystemColors, SystemFonts, SystemIcons, and SystemPens. The following quick example illustrates how to use these predefined objects:

```
open System.Drawing

let myPen = Pens.Aquamarine
let myFont = SystemFonts.DefaultFont
```

Working with Controls in WinForms

A *control* is simply a class that derives from System.Windows.Forms.Control. You can display any class that derives from this class in a form by adding it to the Controls collection on the form object.

Next, you'll look at a way to draw the tree using controls. The WinForms library defines a TreeView class, which exists specifically for displaying tree-like structures; obviously you use this control to display the tree. To use TreeView, you create an instance of it and configure it by setting its properties and calling its methods. Most importantly, you add the nodes you want to display to its Nodes collection. Once the control is ready to be displayed, you add it to the form's Controls collection.

The TreeView class uses TreeNode objects to represent nodes, so you define the function mapTreeToTreeNode to walk the tree structure recursively and create a TreeNode graph. The program in Listing 8-2 produces the tree in Figure 8-3.

Listing 8-2. *Drawing a Tree via a* TreeView *Control*

```
open System.Windows.Forms

// The tree type
type 'a Tree =
| Node of 'a Tree * 'a Tree
| Leaf of 'a

// The definition of the tree
let tree =
    Node(
        Node(
            Leaf "one",
            Node(Leaf "two", Leaf "three")),
        Node(
            Node(Leaf "four", Leaf "five"),
            Leaf "six"))

// A function to transform our tree into a tree of controls
let mapTreeToTreeNode t =
    let rec mapTreeToTreeNodeInner t (node : TreeNode) =
        match t with
        | Node (l, r) ->
            let newNode = new TreeNode("Node")
            node.Nodes.Add(newNode) |> ignore
            mapTreeToTreeNodeInner l newNode
            mapTreeToTreeNodeInner r newNode
        | Leaf x ->
            node.Nodes.Add(new TreeNode(sprintf "%A" x)) |> ignore
    let root = new TreeNode("Root")
    mapTreeToTreeNodeInner t root
    root

// create the form object
let form =
    let temp = new Form()
    let treeView = new TreeView(Dock = DockStyle.Fill)
    treeView.Nodes.Add(mapTreeToTreeNode tree) |> ignore
    treeView.ExpandAll()
    temp.Controls.Add(treeView)
    temp

Application.Run(form)
```

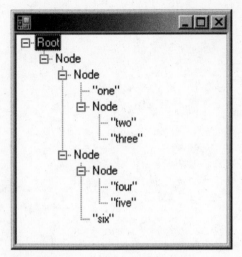

Figure 8-3. *A* TreeView *control used to view a tree*

This code is about half the length of Listing 8-1, where you drew the tree yourself. It is also more functional because it allows you to fold away parts of the tree that don't interest you. This greatly improves the size of tree that you display in a manageable way.

In this example, you use the *dock style* to control how the control looks. You do this by setting the control's Dock property with a member of the DockStyle enumeration. A *docked* control takes up as much space as is available in the portion of the form that contains it. For example, you can dock a control on the left side if you use DockStyle.Left, on the right side if you use DockStyle.Right, at the top if you use DockStyle.Top, on the bottom if you use DockStyle.Bottom, and on the whole form if you use DockStyle.Fill. This is great when you have only a few controls because it creates a nice, dynamic effect where the controls are resized when the user resizes the form. However, this approach doesn't work well with a lot of controls because it is difficult to get many controls to fit together nicely using this technique. For example, if you have two controls that are docked to the left, it can be confusing to determine which one is supposed to be the leftmost one and how much of the left side they should both take up. If you have a lot of controls, a better solution is to control their layout explicitly using the Top and Left properties. You can create a dynamic effect by using the Anchor property to anchor the control to the edge of the containing form. The following example creates a form with a single textbox on it; this form grows or shrinks as the user resizes the form:

```
open System
open System.Windows.Forms

let form =
    // create a form
    let temp = new Form()
```

```
// create a text box and set its anchors
let textBox = new TextBox(Top=8,Left=8, Width=temp.Width - 24,
                          Anchor = (AnchorStyles.Left |||
                                    AnchorStyles.Right |||
                                    AnchorStyles.Top))

// add the text box to the form and return the form
temp.Controls.Add(textBox)
temp

[<STAThread>]
do Application.Run(form)
```

Unfortunately, this method of working with controls is not always satisfactory. Here you displayed only one control, but often you want to display tens (or even hundreds) of controls on a form. Writing all the code to create and configure the controls can quickly become tedious and error-prone. To help you get around this, Visual Studio provides some form designers that allow you to create forms visually. However, no designer exists for F# at this time, so the next section will explain how to use F# to work with forms created with the C# designer.

One of the difficulties facing the WinForms programmer when working with controls is that there are many controls from which to choose. This chapter covers only one control. Unfortunately, there's no substitute for experience when it comes to learning what works. The MSDN library (http://msdn.microsoft.com) provides an excellent reference, but the volume of information in that library can be a little off-putting for those new to the subject. Table 8-3 flattens out this learning curve slightly by summarizing some of the most useful controls.

Table 8-3. *Common WinForm Controls and How to Use Them*

Control	Description
Label	This control to displays text information to the user; most other controls should be accompanied by a Label that explains their usage. Placing an & in the text of the Text property of the Label underlines the letter directly after it, enabling the keyboard user to hop to the control associated with the Label (the control next in the tab order) by pressing Alt+<letter>; this is a good technique for improving application usability.
TextBox	This control provides a box for entering text. The default is a single line of text, but you can change this to support multiple-line entry if you set the Multiline property to true. You should also check that the WordWrap and ScrollBar properties are to your liking. This control is also useful for displaying text to the user that you want them to be able to copy and paste; you do this by setting the ReadOnly property to true.
MaskedTextBox	This control is a textbox similar in a lot of respects to the previous control; it allows you limit the data a user can enter by setting the Mask property.
Button	This control provides a button for the user to click; as with the Label control, placing an & in the text of the Text property of the Button control underlines the letter directly after it and allows the keyboard user to hop to the Button by pressing Alt+<letter>. Again, this is great for usability.

Table 8-3. *Continued*

Control	Description
LinkLabel	This control's name is slightly misleading. You don't really use this as a label, but as a type of button that looks like an HTML link. This control works great for users used to a web environment; it also lets you indicate that clicking the button will open a web page.
CheckBox	This control displays a box for the users to check if you have a set of options that are not mutually exclusive.
RadioButton	This control behaves a lot like a CheckBox, but you use it to display options that are mutually exclusive. Placing several of these in the same container makes all the options mutually exclusive. The container is usually a Form.
DateTimePicker	This control allows the user to pick a date via a drop-down calendar.
MonthCalander	This control allows a user to pick a date from a calendar that is permanently on display.
ComboBox	This control allows a user to make a selection from a drop-down list; this is great for showing a dynamic set of data via data binding (see Chapter 9 for more details on this).
ListBox	This control is similar to a ComboBox, but the list of items is displayed within the form rather than as a drop-down list. You should favor this one if your form has a lot of free space.
DataGridView	This control provides an excellent way to display information from a database table, although you can use it to display any kind of tabular data. You should always choose this option over the older DataGrid (you'll learn more about this in Chapter 9).
TreeView	This control is also great for showing dynamic data; however, it is most useful for displaying data in a tree-like form.
ProgressBar	This control gives your users feedback about any long-running activity that is vital for a usable application.
RichTextBox	This control provides a way to display and edit rich text documents, which is useful if your users want a little more formatting than what the standard textbox offers.
WebBrowser	This control displays HTML documents; it's useful because a lot of information is available in HTML format.
Panel	This control breaks your form into different sections; this is highly effective when you combine the control with HScrollBar and VScrollBar.
HScrollBar	This control is a horizontal scroll bar; you can use it to fit more information on a Form or Panel.
VScrollBar	This control is a vertical scroll bar; you use it to fit more information on a Form or Panel.
TabControl	This control is a form that uses a series of tabs to display user controls.

Using the Visual Studio Form Designer's Forms in F#

F# does not yet have a form designer of its own; however, thanks to the great interoperability of .NET, it is easy to use forms created with the Visual Studio's form designer in F#. You have two approaches. First, you can create an F# library and call functions from this library in your Windows form. Second, you can create a library of forms and use them from your F# application. You learn both approaches in this chapter, as well as their comparative strengths and weaknesses. Both examples will rely on the same Fibonacci calculator (see Figure 8-4).

■**Caution** This book is about F#, and you don't need knowledge of any other programming language for the majority of its material. However, this topic requires that you understand a little of bit about another .NET programming language: C#. Specifically, you'll see two short C# listings in this section. You can easily replace the C# code with Visual Basic .NET code if you feel more comfortable with that language.

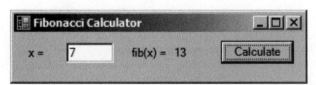

Figure 8-4. *A Fibonacci calculator form created with the Visual Studio designer*

Your main consideration in creating an F# library that you can use from a form: You want to make it easy to use that library from your form. In this case, you'll create a function to calculate the Fibonacci number, which takes and returns an integer. This makes things simple because a form has no problem using the .NET integer type. You want the library to be reasonably efficient, so you also want to create a lazy list of Fibonacci numbers and define a function that can get the *n*th number:

```
module Strangelights.Fibonacci

// an infinite sequence of Fibonacci numbers
let fibs =
    (1,1) |> Seq.unfold
        (fun (n0, n1) ->
            Some(n0, (n1, n0 + n1)))

// a function to get the nth fibonacci number
let get n =
    Seq.nth n fibs
```

It's easy to use this function from a form; you just need to reference your F# .dll from the Visual Studio form project. You can use the module Strangelights.Fibonacci by opening the Strangelights namespace and treating Fibonacci as if it were a class in C#. The following example shows you how to call the function in C# and place the result in a control. Note that this form was created with Visual Studio 2005, so the control definitions are in a separate source file:

```
using System;
using System.Windows.Forms;
using Strangelights;

namespace CSApp {
        public partial class FibForm : Form {
                public FibForm() {
                        InitializeComponent();
                }

                private void calculate_Click(object sender, EventArgs e) {
                        // convert input to an integer
                        int n = Convert.ToInt32(input.Text);
                        // caculate the apropreate fibonacci number
                        n = Fibonacci.get(n);
                        // display result to user
                        result.Text = n.ToString();
                }
        }
}
```

If you want to use the form created in C# from F#, you need to expose certain controls as properties. You don't need to expose all of the controls—just the ones that you want to interact with from F#. The following example shows how to do this in C#; again, any designer-generated code is hidden in a separate file:

```
using System;
using System.Windows.Forms;

namespace Strangelights.Forms {
        public partial class FibForm : Form {
                // public constructor for the form
                public FibForm() {
                        InitializeComponent();
                }

                // expose the calculate button
                public Button Calculate {
                        get { return calculate; }
                }

                // expose the results label
                public Label Result {
                        get { return result; }
                }
```

```
                    // expose the inputs text box
                    public TextBox Input {
                            get { return input; }
                    }
            }
}
```

It is then very straightforward to reference the C# .dll from F# and create an instance of the form and use it. The following example demonstrates the code you use to do this:

```
open System.Windows.Forms
open Strangelights.Forms

// an infinite sequence of Fibonacci numbers
let fibs =
    (1,1) |> Seq.unfold
        (fun (n0, n1) ->
        Some(n0, (n1, n0 + n1)))

// a function to get the nth fibonacci number
let getFib n =
    Seq.nth n fibs

let form =
    // create a new instance of the form
    let temp = new FibForm()
    // add an event handler to the form's click event
    temp.Calculate.Click.Add
        (fun _ ->
            // convert input to an integer
            let n = int temp.Input.Text
            // caculate the apropreate fibonacci number
            let n = getFib n
            // display result to user
            temp.Result.Text <- string n)
    temp

Application.Run(form)
```

You can use both techniques to produce similar results, so the question remains: which is best to use for which occasions? The problem with a C# form calling F# is that you will inevitably end up writing quite a bit of C# to glue everything together. It can also be difficult to use some F# types, such as union types, from C#. Given these two facts, I generally create a C# forms library and use this from F#. You can learn more about making F# libraries ready for use with other .NET languages in Chapter 14.

Working with WinForms Events and the Event Module

Chapter 7 introduced the Event module, which can be useful when working with events in WinForms. When working with events in a WinForm, you often encounter cases where no event exactly fits what you want. For example, the MouseButton event is raised when either the left or right mouse button is clicked, but you might want to respond only to the click of the left-mouse button. In this case, you might find it useful to use the Event.filter function to create a new event that responds only to a click of the leftmouse button. The next example demonstrates how to do this:

```
open System.Windows.Forms
let form =
    // create a new form
    let temp = new Form()

    // subscribe the mouse click event filtering so it only
    // reacts to the left button
    temp.MouseClick
    |> Event.filter (fun e -> e.Button = MouseButtons.Left)
    |> Event.add (fun _ -> MessageBox.Show("Left button") |> ignore)

    // return the form
    temp

Application.Run(form)
```

Here you use the filter function with a function that checks whether the left-mouse button is pressed; the resulting event is then piped forward to the listen function that adds an event handler to the event, exactly as if you had called the event's .Add method. You could have implemented this using an if expression within the event handler, but this technique has the advantage of separating the logic that controls the event firing from what happens during the event itself. Several event handlers can reuse the new event, depending on your needs.

Listing 8-3 demonstrates how to use more of Event's functions to create a simple drawing application (see Figure 8-5). Here you want to use the MouseDown event in different ways: first, you use it to monitor whether the mouse is pressed at all; second, you use it to split the event into left- or right-button presses using the Event.partition function. You can use this to control the drawing color, whether red or black:

Listing 8-3. *Using Events to Implement a Simple Drawing Application*

```
open System
open System.Drawing
open System.Windows.Forms

let form =
    // create the form
    let temp = new Form(Text = "Scribble !!")
```

```fsharp
// some refrence cells to hold the applications state
let pointsMasterList = ref []
let pointsTempList = ref []
let mouseDown = ref false
let pen = ref (new Pen(Color.Black))

// subscribe to the mouse down event
temp.MouseDown.Add(fun _ -> mouseDown := true)

// create a left mouse down and right mouse down events
let leftMouse, rightMouse =
    temp.MouseDown
    |> Event.partition (fun e -> e.Button = MouseButtons.Left)

// use the new left and right mouse events to choose the color
leftMouse.Add(fun _ -> pen := new Pen(Color.Black))
rightMouse.Add(fun _ -> pen := new Pen(Color.Red))

// the mouse up event handler
let mouseUp _ =
    mouseDown := false
    if List.length !pointsTempList > 1 then
        let points = List.toArray !pointsTempList
        pointsMasterList :=
            (!pen, points) :: !pointsMasterList
    pointsTempList := []
    temp.Invalidate()

// the mouse move event handler
let mouseMove (e: MouseEventArgs) =
    pointsTempList := e.Location :: !pointsTempList
    temp.Invalidate()

// the paint event handler
let paint (e: PaintEventArgs) =
    if List.length !pointsTempList > 1 then
        e.Graphics.DrawLines
            (!pen, List.toArray !pointsTempList)
    !pointsMasterList
    |> List.iter
        (fun (pen, points) ->
            e.Graphics.DrawLines(pen, points))
```

```
    // wire up the event handlers
    temp.MouseUp |> Event.add mouseUp

    temp.MouseMove
    |> Event.filter(fun _ -> !mouseDown)
    |> Event.add mouseMove

    temp.Paint |> Event.add paint

    // return the form object
    temp

[<STAThread>]
do Application.Run(form)
```

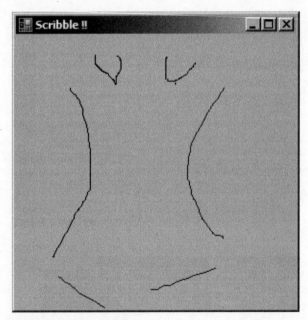

Figure 8-5. *Scribble: a simple drawing application implemented using events*

You can also publish events you create in this way on the form's interface, which means the code that consumes the form can also take advantage of these events.

Again, a big problem facing a programmer working with events in WinForms is the volume of events available, which can make choosing the right one difficult. Perhaps surprisingly, most events are defined on the class Control, with each specialization providing only a handful of extra events. This generally makes life a bit easier because, if you have used an event with a control, odds are it will also be available on another control. Table 8-4 provides a helpful summary of the most common events on the Control class:

Table 8-4. *A Summary of Events on the Control Class*

Event	Description
Click	This event is caused by the user clicking the control. It is a high-level event, and although it is ordinarily caused by the user clicking with the mouse, it might also be caused by the user pressing Enter or the spacebar when hovering over a control. A series of events—MouseDown, MouseClick, and MouseUp— provide more detailed information about the actions of the mouse. However, these events provide information only about the mouse actions, so you should usually handle the Click, instead of these events. Otherwise, this will lead to the control not responding in the way users expect, because it will not respond to keystrokes and only mouse clicks.
DoubleClick	This event is raised when a user clicks the mouse twice in quick succession. Note that the user's operating system settings determine the interval the two clicks must occur in. You need to be careful when handling this event because every time this event is raised, a Click event will have been raised immediately before it. This means you must handle either this event or the Click event.
Enter	This event is raised when the control becomes active—either because the user presses Tab to enter it, the programmer calls Select or SelectNextControl, or the user clicks it with the mouse. Typically, you use this control to draw attention to the fact that the control is active; for example, you might set the background to a different color. Note that this event is suppressed on the Form class, where you should use Activated instead.
Leave	This event is raised when the control is deactivated—either because the user presses Tab to leave it, the programmer calls Select or SelectNextControl, or the user clicks another control with the mouse. You might be tempted to use this event for validation, but you should use the Validating and Validated events, instead. This event is suppressed on the Form class, where you should use Activated instead.
KeyPress	This event is part of a sequence of events that you can use to get detailed information about the state of the keyboard. To get details about when a key is first pressed, use KeyDown; to find out when it is released, use KeyUp.
Move	This event is raised whenever a user moves the control.
MouseHover	This event is useful for finding out whether the mouse is hovering over a control; you can use it to give a user more information about the control. The events MouseEnter and MouseLeave are also useful for this.
Paint	This event occurs when the form will be repainted by Windows; you need to handle this event if you want to take care of drawing the control yourself. For more information about this, see the "Drawing WinForms" section earlier in this chapter.
Resize	This event occurs when the user resizes the form; you could handle this event to adjust the layout of the form to a new size.

Creating New Forms Classes

So far you've looked only at a script style of programming, where you use an existing form and controls to put forms together quickly. This style of programming is great for the rapid development of single-form applications, but it has some limitations in cases where you want to create applications composed of multiple forms quickly, or you want to create libraries of forms for use with other .NET languages. In these cases, you must take a more component-oriented approach.

Typically, you want to use some forms repeatedly when you create a large WinForms application; furthermore, you typically want these forms to be able to communicate with each other by adjusting each other's properties and calling each other's methods. You usually do this by defining a new form class that derives from System.Windows.Forms. Listing 8-4 shows a simple example of this, using the class syntax introduced in Chapter 5.

Listing 8-4. *A Demonstration of Creating a New Type of Form*

```
open System
open System.Windows.Forms

// a class that derives from "Form" and add some user controls
type MyForm() as x =
    inherit Form(Width=174, Height=64)

    // create some controls to add the form
    let label = new Label(Top=8, Left=8, Width=40, Text="Input:")
    let textbox = new TextBox(Top=8, Left=48, Width=40)
    let button = new Button(Top=8, Left=96, Width=60, Text="Push Me!")

    // add a event to the button
    do button.Click.Add(fun _ ->
        let form = new MyForm(Text=textbox.Text)
        form.Show())

    // add the controls to the form
    do x.Controls.Add(label)
    do x.Controls.Add(textbox)
    do x.Controls.Add(button)

    // expose the text box as a property
    member x.Textbox = textbox

// create an new instance of our form
let form =
    let temp = new MyForm(Text="My Form")
    temp.Textbox.Text <- "Next!"
    temp

[<STAThread>]
do Application.Run(form)
```

Executing the preceding code produces the forms shown in Figure 8-6.

Figure 8-6. *Creating a new type of form for easy reuse*

In the preceding example, you create a form with three fields: label, textbox, and button. You can then manipulate these fields using external code. At the end of the example, you create a new instance of this form and then set the Text property of the textbox field.

Events can be exposed on the interface of a form in much the same way that fields can. This takes a little more work because of some inherent restrictions. The idea is to create a new event, store this event in a field in the class, and finally, to make this event a subscriber to the filtered event. You can see this demonstrated in the next example, where you filter the MouseClick event to create a LeftMouseClick:

```
open System.Windows.Forms

// a form with addation LeftMouseClick event
type LeftClickForm() as x =
    inherit Form()
    // create the new event
    let event = new Event<MouseEventArgs>()

    // wire the new event up so it fires when the left
    // mouse button is clicked
    do x.MouseClick
        |> Event.filter (fun e -> e.Button = MouseButtons.Left)
        |> Event.add (fun e -> event.Trigger e)

    // expose the event as property
    [<CLIEvent>]
    member x.LeftMouseClick = event.Publish
```

Forms you create in this component-based manner will undoubtedly be easier to use than forms you create with a more scripted approach; however, you still face pitfalls when you create libraries for other .NET languages. Please refer to Chapter 13 for more information about making F# libraries usable by other .NET languages.

Introducing Windows Presentation Foundation

WPF is a library that offers a completely new programming model for user interfaces. It is aimed at creating desktop applications that have more pizzazz than the ones that are created with WinForms. WPF also comes with a new XML-based language called XAML, which you can use to code the bulk of this form's layout, leaving you free to use F# to code the interesting parts of your application.

■**Note** Several XAML designers now exist; these designers allow F# users to design their interface using a graphical WYSWIG tool and then add interactivity to it using F#. For example, Mobiform offers a designer called Aurora (www.mobiform.com/products/aurora/aurora.htm), and Microsoft offers a designer called Expression Blend (www.microsoft.com/expression/products/overview.aspx?key=blend).

WPF is part of .NET 3.0, and it installs by default if you use Windows Vista. Users of other versions of Windows need to install .NET 3.0 to get access to WPF; the easiest way to do this is to download the .NET *Windows SDK for Windows Server 2008 and .NET Framework 3.5* (*http://is.gd/521hd*). To make the examples in this section work, you need to add references to the following dlls: PresentationCore.dll, PresentationFramework.dll, and WindowsBase.dll.

The first example you'll look at shows you how to create a simple form in XAML and then display it to the user using F# (see Listing 8-5). This example shows the XAML definition of a form with four controls: two labels, a textbox, and a button.

Listing 8-5. *A Simple Form Created in XAML*

```
<Window
xmlns="http://schemas.microsoft.com/winfx/2006/xaml/presentation"
xmlns:sys="clr-namespace:System;assembly=mscorlib"
xmlns:x="http://schemas.microsoft.com/winfx/2006/xaml" >
<Grid>
<Grid.ColumnDefinitions>
<ColumnDefinition Width="64" />
<ColumnDefinition Width="128" />
<ColumnDefinition Width="128" />
<ColumnDefinition Width="128" />
</Grid.ColumnDefinitions>
<Grid.RowDefinitions>
<RowDefinition Height="24"/>
</Grid.RowDefinitions>
```

```
<Label Grid.Row="0" Grid.Column="0" >Input: </Label>
<TextBox Name="input" Grid.Column="1" Text="hello" />
<Label Name="output" Grid.Row="0" Grid.Column="2" ></Label>
<Button Name="press" Grid.Column="3" >Press Me</Button>
</Grid>
</Window>
```

To make this XAML definition of a form useful, you need to do two things. First, you must load the form's definition and show it to the user; however, doing only this will offer no interaction with the user. Thus, the second thing you need to do is make the form interactive. To do this, you use F# to add event handlers to the controls; in this case, you use it to add an event handler to the button that places the contents of the textbox into the second label. The function createWindow is a general-purpose function for loading a XAML form. You then use this function to create the value window, and you pass this value to the form's FindName method to find the controls within the form, so you can interact with them. Finally, you create an instance of the Application class in the main function and use this to show the form (see Listing 8-6).

Listing 8-6. *Displaying the XAML Form and Adding Event Handlers to It*

```
open System
open System.Collections.Generic
open System.Windows
open System.Windows.Controls
open System.Windows.Markup
open System.Xml

// creates the window and loads the given XAML file into it
let createWindow (file : string) =
    using (XmlReader.Create(file)) (fun stream ->
        (XamlReader.Load(stream) :?> Window))

// create the window object and add event handler
// to the button control
let window =
    let temp = createWindow "Window1.xaml"
    let press = temp.FindName("press") :?> Button
    let textbox = temp.FindName("input") :?> TextBox
    let label = temp.FindName("output") :?> Label
    press.Click.Add (fun _ -> label.Content <- textbox.Text )
    temp

// run the application
let main() =
    let app = new Application()
    app.Run(window) |> ignore

[<STAThread>]
do main()
```

To get this program to compile, you must add references to `PresentationCore.dll`, `PresentationFramework.dll`, and `WindowsBase.dll`, which you can usually find0 in the directory `C:\Program Files\Reference Assemblies\Microsoft\Framework\v3.0`. In the other examples in this chapter, you didn't need to add references because the compiler referenced the libraries automatically. You can see the form created by the preceding example as in Figure 8-17.

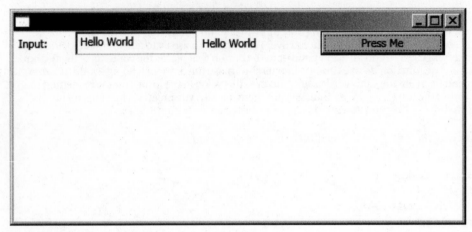

Figure 8-7. *A form created using XAML and F#*

Introducing Windows Presentation Foundation 3D

Another great advantage of WPF is the huge number of controls it offers. One control that you'll dig a little deeper into is `Viewport3D`, which offers the ability to create impressive 3D graphics, something not readily available with the WinForms library. You'll learn how you can use this control to display a 3D plane and then map an equation over it.

The example starts with the XAML script. Both XAML and 3D graphics are huge topics, and it would it exceed this book's ambitions to cover them fully. But you'll still learn enough about them to get an idea of what they involve, as well as how you might and branch off and explore these topics on your own. The following XAML script describes a window with one control, a `Viewport3D`, on it. The script is fairly lengthy because making a 3D scene requires that you include quite a few elements. You begin by defining a camera, so you know which direction you're looking at the scene from. You do this using the `<Viewport3D.Camera>` element:

```
<Viewport3D.Camera>
  <PerspectiveCamera Position="0,0,2" LookDirection="0,0,-1" FieldOfView="60" />
</Viewport3D.Camera>
```

The tags inside `<Model3DGroup>` describe what the scene will look like, while the `<AmbientLight Color="White" />` tag describes how you will light the scene , and the `<GeometryModel3D.Geometry>` tag describes the 3D shape in the scene:

```
<GeometryModel3D.Geometry>
  <MeshGeometry3D />
</GeometryModel3D.Geometry>
```

Here you *could* use the `<MeshGeometry3D />` tag to describe all the objects that make up the scene by providing the specific points that make up the objects; however, you don't use this tag to describe the points that make up the shape because it is a lot easier to do this in F# than in XAML. The `<GeometryModel3D.Material>` tag describes what the surface of the shape will look like:

```
<GeometryModel3D.Material>
  <DiffuseMaterial>
    <DiffuseMaterial.Brush>
      <ImageBrush ImageSource="venus.jpg" />
    </DiffuseMaterial.Brush>
  </DiffuseMaterial>
</GeometryModel3D.Material>
```

The `<GeometryModel3D.Transform>` tag describes a transformation that you want to apply to the shape; that is, it describes the angle you want to rotate the shape by:

```
<GeometryModel3D.Transform>
  <RotateTransform3D>
    <RotateTransform3D.Rotation>
      <AxisAngleRotation3D
        x:Name="MyRotation3D"
        Angle="45"
        Axis="0,1,0"/>
    </RotateTransform3D.Rotation>
  </RotateTransform3D>
</GeometryModel3D.Transform>
```

You do this mainly so you can use the `<Viewport3D.Triggers>` tag to define an animation that you use to alter the angle you display the shape at over time:

```
<Viewport3D.Triggers>
  <EventTrigger RoutedEvent="Viewport3D.Loaded">
    <EventTrigger.Actions>
      <BeginStoryboard>
        <Storyboard>
          <DoubleAnimation
            From="-80"
            To="80"
            Duration="0:0:12"
```

```
                Storyboard.TargetName="MyRotation3D"
                Storyboard.TargetProperty="Angle"
                RepeatBehavior="Forever"
                AutoReverse="True" />
        </Storyboard>
      </BeginStoryboard>
    </EventTrigger.Actions>
  </EventTrigger>
</Viewport3D.Triggers>
```

Listing 8-7 shows the complete example, so you can see how these various sections hang together.

Listing 8-7. *A XAML Definition of a 3D Scene*

```
<Window
xmlns="http://schemas.microsoft.com/winfx/2006/xaml/presentation"
xmlns:x="http://schemas.microsoft.com/winfx/2006/xaml">
<Viewport3D Name="ViewPort">
<Viewport3D.Camera>
<PerspectiveCamera Position="0,0,2" LookDirection="0,0,-1" FieldOfView="60" />
</Viewport3D.Camera>
<Viewport3D.Children>
<ModelVisual3D>
<ModelVisual3D.Content>
<Model3DGroup >
<Model3DGroup.Children>
<AmbientLight Color="White" />
<GeometryModel3D>
<GeometryModel3D.Geometry>
<MeshGeometry3D />
</GeometryModel3D.Geometry>
<GeometryModel3D.Transform>
<RotateTransform3D>
<RotateTransform3D.Rotation>
<AxisAngleRotation3D
x:Name="MyRotation3D"
Angle="45"
Axis="0,1,0"/>
</RotateTransform3D.Rotation>
</RotateTransform3D>
</GeometryModel3D.Transform>
```

```xml
<GeometryModel3D.Material>
<DiffuseMaterial>
<DiffuseMaterial.Brush>
<ImageBrush ImageSource="venus.jpg" />
</DiffuseMaterial.Brush>
</DiffuseMaterial>
</GeometryModel3D.Material>
</GeometryModel3D>
</Model3DGroup.Children>
</Model3DGroup>
</ModelVisual3D.Content>
</ModelVisual3D>
</Viewport3D.Children>
<Viewport3D.Triggers>
<EventTrigger RoutedEvent="Viewport3D.Loaded">
<EventTrigger.Actions>
<BeginStoryboard>
<Storyboard>
<DoubleAnimation
From="-80"
To="80"
Duration="0:0:12"
Storyboard.TargetName="MyRotation3D"
Storyboard.TargetProperty="Angle"
RepeatBehavior="Forever"
AutoReverse="True" />
</Storyboard>
</BeginStoryboard>
</EventTrigger.Actions>
</EventTrigger>
</Viewport3D.Triggers>
</Viewport3D>
</Window>
```

You will use F# to extend Listing 8-7 in Listing 8-8, borrowing a couple of functions from Listing 8-6; note that you save the code in Listing 8-7 to a file called Window2.xaml. You use the createWindow function to load the window and use a similar main function to display the window. You then use the findMeshes function to find any meshes in the picture (a *mesh* is a set of points used to describe the 3D plane). You find the meshes by walking the various objects in the Viewport3D and building up a list:

```fsharp
// finds all the MeshGeometry3D in a given 3D view port
let findMeshes ( viewport : Viewport3D ) =
    viewport.Children
    |> Seq.choose
        (function :? ModelVisual3D as c -> Some(c.Content) | _ -> None)
```

```
|> Seq.choose
    (function :? Model3DGroup as mg -> Some(mg.Children) | _ -> None)
|> Seq.concat
|> Seq.choose
    (function :? GeometryModel3D as mg -> Some(mg.Geometry) | _ -> None)
|> Seq.choose
    (function :? MeshGeometry3D as mv -> Some(mv) | _ -> None)
```

You should keep this function generic, so it can work with any Viewport3D. It is highly likely that you will want to grab a list of all the meshes in your 3D scene for any 3D work you do in XAML and F#. The reason: You will probably want to use F# to manipulate your meshes in some way. Then you use createPlaneItemList, createSquare, createPlanePoints, createIndicesPlane, and addPlaneToMesh to add a flat plane to the mesh object in the scene. The function mapPositionsCenter centers the plane, placing it in the middle of the scene. Finally, a clever little function called changePositions maps the function movingWaves repeatedly across the plane ten times a second. The core of changePositions creates a new Point3DCollection from the Point3D objects contained in the old collection using the function movingWaves to decide what the new Z position should be:

```
let changePositions () =
    let dispatcherTimer = new DispatcherTimer()
    dispatcherTimer.Tick.Add
        (fun e ->
            let t = (float DateTime.Now.Millisecond) / 2000.0
            let newPositions =
                mesh.Positions
                |> Seq.map
                    (fun position ->
                        let z = movingWaves t position.X position.Y
                        new Point3D(position.X, position.Y, z))
            mesh.Positions <- new Point3DCollection(newPositions))
    dispatcherTimer.Interval <- new TimeSpan(0,0,0,0,100)
    dispatcherTimer.Start()
```

You use the DispatcherTimer class to execute the code on the thread that created the form, which means you don't need to call back to this thread to update the form. You need to call this class at least ten times a second to create a smooth animation effect (see Listing 8-8 for the complete example).

Listing 8-8. *Displaying and Interacting with a 3D XAML Scene*

```
open System
open System.Collections.Generic
open System.IO
open System.Windows
open System.Windows.Controls
open System.Windows.Markup
open System.Windows.Media
```

```
open System.Windows.Media.Media3D
open System.Windows.Threading
open System.Xml

// creates the window and loads the given XAML file into it
let createWindow (file : string) =
    using (XmlReader.Create(file))
        (fun stream ->
            let temp = XamlReader.Load(stream) :?> Window
            temp.Height <- 400.0
            temp.Width <- 400.0
            temp.Title <- "F# meets Xaml"
            temp)
// finds all the MeshGeometry3D in a given 3D view port
let findMeshes ( viewport : Viewport3D ) =
    viewport.Children
    |> Seq.choose
        (function :? ModelVisual3D as c -> Some(c.Content) | _ -> None)
    |> Seq.choose
        (function :? Model3DGroup as mg -> Some(mg.Children) | _ -> None)
    |> Seq.concat
    |> Seq.choose
        (function :? GeometryModel3D as mg -> Some(mg.Geometry) | _ -> None)
    |> Seq.choose
        (function :? MeshGeometry3D as mv -> Some(mv) | _ -> None)

// loop function to create all items necessary for a plane
let createPlaneItemList f (xRes : int) (yRes : int) =
    let list = new List<_>()
    for x = 0 to xRes - 1 do
        for y = 0 to yRes - 1 do
            f list x y
    list

// function to initialize a point
let point x y = new Point(x, y)

// function to initialize a "d point
let point3D x y = new Point3D(x, y, 0.0)

// create all the points necessary for a square in the plane
let createSquare
    f (xStep : float) (yStep : float) (list : List<_>) (x : int) (y : int) =
    let x' = float x * xStep
    let y' = float y * yStep
```

```
        list.Add(f x' y')
        list.Add(f (x' + xStep) y')
        list.Add(f (x' + xStep) (y' + yStep))
        list.Add(f (x' + xStep) (y' + yStep))
        list.Add(f x' (y' + yStep))
        list.Add(f x' y')

// create all items in a plane
let createPlanePoints f xRes yRes =
    let xStep = 1.0 / float xRes
    let yStep = 1.0 / float yRes
    createPlaneItemList (createSquare f xStep yStep) xRes yRes

// create the 3D positions for a plane, i.e., the thing that says where
// the plane will be in 3D space
let createPlanePositions xRes yRes =
    let list = createPlanePoints point3D xRes yRes
    new Point3DCollection(list)

// create the texture mappings for a plane, i.e., the thing that
// maps the 2D image to the 3D plane
let createPlaneTextures xRes yRes =
    let list = createPlanePoints point xRes yRes
    new PointCollection(list)

// create indices list for all our triangles
let createIndicesPlane width height =
    let list = new System.Collections.Generic.List<int>()
    for index = 0 to width * height * 6 do
        list.Add(index)
    new Int32Collection(list)

// center the plane in the field of view
let mapPositionsCenter (positions : Point3DCollection) =
    let newPositions =
        positions
        |> Seq.map
            (fun position ->
                new Point3D(
                            (position.X - 0.5 ) * -1.0,
                            (position.Y - 0.5 ) * -1.0,
                            position.Z))
    new Point3DCollection(newPositions)
```

```fsharp
// create a plane and add it to the given mesh
let addPlaneToMesh (mesh : MeshGeometry3D) xRes yRes =
    mesh.Positions <- mapPositionsCenter
                        (createPlanePositions xRes yRes)
    mesh.TextureCoordinates <- createPlaneTextures xRes yRes
    mesh.TriangleIndices <- createIndicesPlane xRes yRes

let movingWaves (t : float) x y =
    (Math.Cos((x + t) * Math.PI * 4.0) / 3.0) *
    (Math.Cos(y * Math.PI * 2.0) / 3.0)

// create our window
let window = createWindow "Window2.xaml"

let mesh =
    // grab the 3D view port
    let viewport = window.FindName("ViewPort") :?> Viewport3D
    // find all the meshes and get the first one
    let meshes = findMeshes viewport
    let mesh = Seq.head meshes
    // add plane to the mesh
    addPlaneToMesh mesh 20 20
    mesh

let changePositions () =
    let dispatcherTimer = new DispatcherTimer()
    dispatcherTimer.Tick.Add
        (fun e ->
            let t = (float DateTime.Now.Millisecond) / 2000.0
            let newPositions =
                mesh.Positions
                |> Seq.map
                    (fun position ->
                        let z = movingWaves t position.X position.Y
                        new Point3D(position.X, position.Y, z))
            mesh.Positions <- new Point3DCollection(newPositions))
    dispatcherTimer.Interval <- new TimeSpan(0,0,0,0,100)
    dispatcherTimer.Start()

let main() =
    let app = new Application()
    changePositions()
```

```
    // show the window
    app.Run(window) |> ignore

[<STAThread>]
do main()
```

Executing the code in Listing 8-8 produces the window shown in Figure 8-8. It doesn't show off the animated results, but you should try out the application and see the animated effects for yourself.

Figure 8-8. *A 3D scene created using XAML and F#*

You should also play with this sample in fsi. You can subtly alter the sample to run inside fsi, and then dynamically alter the function you apply to the plane. You must alter the original script in several small ways.

Begin by setting the reference to the .dll files in an fsi style:

```
#I @"C:\Program Files\Reference Assemblies\Microsoft\Framework\v3.0" ;;
#r @"PresentationCore.dll" ;;
#r @"PresentationFramework.dll" ;;
#r @"WindowsBase.dll" ;;
```

Next, you must alter the changePositions function to use a mutable function:

```
// mutable function that is used within changePositions function
let mutable f  = (fun (t : float) (x : float) (y : float) -> 0.0)

// function for changing the plane over time
let changePositions () =
    let dispatcherTimer = new DispatcherTimer()
    dispatcherTimer.Tick.Add
        (fun e ->
            let t = (float DateTime.Now.Millisecond) / 2000.0
            let newPositions =
                mesh.Positions
                |> Seq.map
                    (fun position ->
                        let z = f t position.X position.Y
                        new Point3D(position.X, position.Y, z))
            mesh.Positions <- new Point3DCollection(newPositions))
    dispatcherTimer.Interval <- new TimeSpan(0,0,0,0,100)
    dispatcherTimer.Start()
```

Finally, you show the window using its .Show() method rather than the Application class's Run method; be careful that you set its Topmost property to true so that it is easy to interact with the window and see the results:

```
// show the window, set it the top, and activate the function that will
// set it moving
window.Show()
window.Topmost <- true
changePositions ()
```

Finally, you need to define some other functions to map across the plane. This can be any function that takes three floating-point numbers (the first representing the time and the next two representing the X and Y coordinates, respectively) and returns a third floating-point that represents the Z coordinate. I'm particularly fond of using sine and cosine functions here because these generate interesting wave patterns. The following code includes some examples of what you might use, but please feel free to invent your own:

```
let cosXY _ x y =
    Math.Cos(x * Math.PI) * Math.Cos(y * Math.PI)

let movingCosXY (t : float) x y =
    Math.Cos((x + t) * Math.PI) * Math.Cos((y - t) * Math.PI)
```

You can then easily apply these functions to the plane by updating the mutable function:

```
f <- movingCosXY
```

Using this technique produces the image you see in Figure 8-9.

Figure 8-9. *Controlling a 3D XAML scene interactively using F# interactive*

The WPF framework contains lots of types and controls that will take any programmer some time to learn. Fortunately, you can find many resources available on the Internet to help you do this. One good resource is the NetFx3 WPF site (http://wpf.netfx3.com); another is the WPF section of MSDN (http://msdn2.microsoft.com/en-us/netframework/aa663326.aspx).

Introducing GTK#

GTK# is a .NET wrapper around the popular cross-platform GUI library, GTK+. If you want to build a local application and want it to run on platforms other than Windows, GTK is probably the logical choice. GTK# works in a similar way to both WinForms and WFP; in GTK#, you base your windows on the Gtk.Window and use *widgets* (the equivalent of controls) based on the Gtk.Widget class.

GTK# is distributed with Mono Project distribution, so the easiest way to get access to it is to install Mono (http://www.go-mono.com/mono-downloads/download.html). The classes that make up GTK# are spread across four .dlls: atk-sharp.dll, gdk-sharp.dll, glib-sharp.dll, and gtk-sharp.dll. You need to add references to these .dlls to make the example in this section work.

Before creating any GTK# widgets, you must call the Application.Init() to initialize the GTK environment. After the controls are visible, you need to call the Application.Run() method to start the event loop; if you do not call this method, the window and widgets will not react user clicks and other inputs. When the user closes all the windows, you need to close the event loop by calling Application.Quit(). In the GTK# example (see Listing 8-9), you we have only one window, so you quit the GTK environment when this window closes:

```
// close the event loop when the window closes
win.Destroyed.Add(fun _ -> Application.Quit())
```

You use a widget called an HBox or a VBox to lay out a GTK# application. Unlike the Window class, these widgets can contain more than one widget, stacking the widgets contained in them either horizontally or vertically. In Listing 8-9, you can see that you create a VBox, which means that the widgets contained within it are laid out horizontally:

```
// create a new vbox and add the sub controls
let vbox = new VBox()
vbox.Add(label)
vbox.Add(button)
```

You can see the complete example in Listing 8-9; executing the code in these listings produces the image shown in Figure 8-10.

Listing 8-9. *A Simple Example of a GTK# Application*

```
open Gtk

let main() =
    // initalize the GTK environment
    Application.Init()
```

```
    // create the window
    let win = new Window("GTK# and F# Application")
    // set the windows size
    win.Resize(400, 400)

    // create a label
    let label = new Label()

    // create a button and subscribe to
    // its clicked event
    let button = new Button(Label = "Press Me!")
    button.Clicked.Add(fun _ ->
        label.Text <- "Hello World.")

    // create a new vbox and add the sub controls
    let vbox = new VBox()
    vbox.Add(label)
    vbox.Add(button)

    // add the vbox to the window
    win.Add(vbox)

    // show the window
    win.ShowAll()

    // close the event loop when the window closes
    win.Destroyed.Add(fun _ -> Application.Quit())

    // start the event loop
    Application.Run()

do main()
```

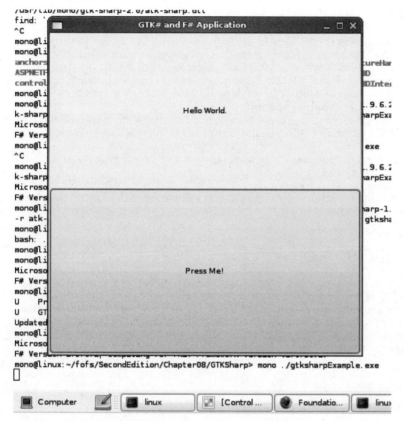

Figure 8-10. *The GTK# application running under linux*

Introducing ASP.NET

ASP.NET is a technology intended to simplify creating dynamic web pages. The simplest way to do this is to implement an interface called IHttpHandler. This interface allows the implementer to describe how an HTTP request should be responded to; the next section of the chapter will explain how this works.

Merely implementing the IHttpHandler interface doesn't allow you to take full advantage of the ASP.NET feature set. ASP.NET allows users to create web forms, which are composed of controls that know how to render themselves into HTML. The advantage of this is that the programmer has a nice object model to manipulate, rather than having to code HTML tags. It also allows a programmer to separate the layout of controls into an .aspx file. An .aspx file basically contains all the static HTML you don't want to worry about in your F# code, plus a few placeholders for the dynamic controls. This approach is great for programming in F# because it allows you to separate the code that represents the layout of a form, which can look a little long in F#, from the code that controls its behavior. ASP.NET also lets you store configuration values in an XML-based web.config file.

Working with ASP.NET presents an additional challenge; you must configure the web server that will host the ASP.NET application. Your configuration will vary, depending on your development environment.

Visual Studio has come with a built-in web server since Visual Studio 2005. Creating a new web site is a simple matter of selecting File~TRANew~TRAWeb Site and then choosing the location for the web site. This site will run only pages written in C# or Visual Basic .NET, so you need to add an F# project to the solution and then manually alter the solution file so that it lives inside the web site directory. This is easier than it sounds. All you need to do is copy the .fsproj file to the web site directory, open the .sln file in Notepad, and alter the path to the .fsproj file. After this, you need to configure the project file to output a library and write this to a bin subdirectory. This might seem like a lot of effort, but once you do this, you can press F5 to make your project compile and run.

If you do not have Visual Studio, then your next best choice is host the site in IIS. In some ways, this is easier than hosting your site in Visual Studio; however, IIS doesn't let you just execute your code once you finish writing it. To host your code in IIS, you need to create an IIS virtual directory with a subdirectory called bin. You then need to copy your .aspx pages and your web.config file to the virtual directory.

ASP.NET has always been part of the .NET framework, so you don't need to install any additional features to make these examples work; however, you do need to add a reference to the System.Web.dll to make all of the examples in this section work.

Creating an IHttpHandler

Creating an IHttpHandler is the simplest way to take advantage of ASP.NET 2.0. This simple interface has only two members. The first member is a read-only Boolean property called IsReusable that you use to indicate whether the runtime can reuse the instance of the object. It is generally best to set this to false.

The second member of the interface is the ProcessRequest method, which is called when a web request is received. It takes one parameter of HttpContent type; you can use this type to retrieve information about the request being made through its Request property, as well as to respond to the request via its Response property. The following, simple example of an IHttpHandler responds to a request with the string "<h1>Hello World</h1>":

```
namespace Strangelights.HttpHandlers
open System.Web


// a http handler class
type SimpleHandler() =
    interface IHttpHandler with
        // tell the ASP.NET runtime if the handler can be reused
        member x.IsReusable = false
        // The method that will be called when processing a
        // HTTP request
        member x.ProcessRequest(c : HttpContext) =
            c.Response.Write("<h1>Hello World</h1>")
```

Next, you must configure the URL where the IHttpHandler is available. You do this by adding an entry to the web.config file. If don't already have a web.config file in the project, you can add one by right-clicking the web project and choosing Add New Item. The handlers are added to the httpHandlers section, and you need to configure four properties for each handler: path, which is the URL of the page; verb, which configures which HTTP verbs the handler will respond to; type, which is the name of the type that you will use to handle the request; and validate, which tells the runtime whether it should check the availability of the type when the application loads:

```
<configuration>
    <system.web>
        <httpHandlers>
            <add path="hello.aspx"
                verb="*"
                type="Strangelights.HttpHandlers.SimpleHandler"
                validate="true"/>
        </httpHandlers>
    </system.web>
</configuration>
```

Executing `SimpleHandler` produces the web page shown in Figure 8-11.

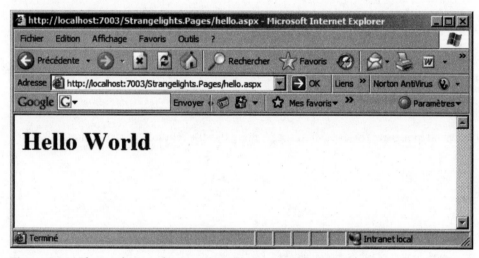

Figure 8-11. *The resulting web page when the* `SimpleHandler` *is executed*

This technique is unsatisfactory for creating web pages because it requires that you mix HTML tags t into your F# code. It does have some advantages, though. You can use this technique to put together documents other than HTML documents; for example, you can use it to dynamically create images on the server. The following example shows an `IHttpHandler` that generates a JPEG image of a pie shape. The amount of pie shown is determined by the angle value that that is passed in on the query string. Making this example work requires that you add a reference to `System.Drawing.dll`:

```
namespace Strangelights.HttpHandlers

open System.Drawing
open System.Drawing.Imaging
open System.Web
```

```
// a class that will render a picture for a http request
type PictureHandler() =
    interface IHttpHandler with
        // tell the ASP.NET runtime if the handler can be reused
        member x.IsReusable = false
        // The method that will be called when processing a
        // HTTP request and render a picture
        member x.ProcessRequest(c : HttpContext) =
            // create a new bitmap
            let bitmap = new Bitmap(200, 200)
            // create a graphics object for the bitmap
            let graphics = Graphics.FromImage(bitmap)
            // a brush to provide the color
            let brush = new SolidBrush(Color.Red)
            // get the angle to draw
            let x = int(c.Request.QueryString.Get("angle"))
            // draw the pie to bitmap
            graphics.FillPie(brush, 10, 10, 180, 180, 0, x)
            // save the bitmap to the output stream
            bitmap.Save(c.Response.OutputStream, ImageFormat.Gif)
```

Again, you still need to register this type in the web.config file; the required configuration looks like this:

```
<configuration>
    <system.web>
        <httpHandlers>
            <add path="pic.aspx"
                 verb="*"
                 type="Strangelights.HttpHandlers.PictureHandler"
                 validate="true"/>
        </httpHandlers>
    </system.web>
</configuration>
```

Executing this code produces the image in shown in Figure 8-12. In this case, I passed in an angle of 200.

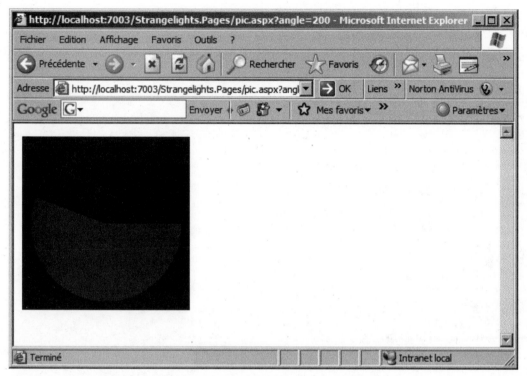

Figure 8-12. *Using an* IHttpHandler *to dynamically generate a picture*

Although this is a great technique for spicing up web sites, but you should be careful when using it. Generating images can be processor intensive, especially if the images are large or complicated. This can lead to web sites that do not scale up to the required number of concurrent users; therefore, if you do use this technique, ensure you profile your code correctly.

Working with ASP.NET Web Forms

If you want to create dynamic web pages, then you will probably have an easier time using ASP.NET forms than implementing your own IHttpHandler. The main advantage of web forms is that you do not need to deal with HTML tags in F# code; most of this is abstracted away for you. This approach confers other, smaller advantages too. For example, it means you do not have to register the page in web.config.

To create an ASP.NET web form, you generally start by creating the user interface, defined in an .aspx file. The .aspx file contains all your static HTML, plus some placeholders for the dynamic controls. An .aspx file always starts with a Page directive; you can see this at the top of the next example. The Page directive allows you to specify a class that the page will inherit from; you do this by using the Inherits attribute and giving the full name of the class. You will use an F# class to provide the dynamic functionality.

The following example includes some tags prefixed with asp: among the regular HTML tags. These are ASP.NET web controls, and they provide the dynamic functionality. A web control is a class in the .NET Framework that knows how to render itself into HTML; for example, the <asp:TextBox /> tag will

221

become an HTML <input /> tag. You can take control of these controls in your F# class and use them to respond to user input:

```
<%@ Page Inherits="Strangelights.HttpHandlers.HelloUser" %>
<html>
    <head>
        <title>F# - Hello User</title>
    </head>
    <body>
        <p>Hello User</p>
        <form id="theForm" runat="server">
        <asp:Label
            ID="OutputControl"
            Text="Enter you're name ..."
            runat="server" />
        <br />
        <asp:TextBox
            ID="InputControl"
            runat="server" />
        <br />
        <asp:LinkButton
            ID="SayHelloButton"
            Text="Say Hello ..."
            runat="server"
            OnClick="SayHelloButton_Click" />
        </form>
    </body>
</html>
```

When designing your class, you need to provide mutable fields with the same name as the controls you want to manipulate. The HTML page you created had three controls in it, but you provide only two mutable fields, because you don't want to manipulate the third control, a link button. You just want that button to call the SayHelloButton_Click function when a user clicks it. You do this by adding the function name to the OnClick attribute of the asp:LinkButton control.

When the other two controls are created, a label and a textbox, they will be stored in the mutable fields OutputControl and InputControl, respectively. It is the code contained in the .aspx page, not your class, that is responsible for creating these controls. This is why you explicitly initialize these controls to null in the constructor. All that remains in SayHelloButton_Click is to take the input from InputControl and place it into OutputControl:

```
namespace Strangelights.HttpHandlers

open System
open System.Web.UI
open System.Web.UI.WebControls
```

```
// class to handle to provide the code behind for the .aspx page
type HelloUser =
    inherit Page
    // fields that will hold the controls reference
    val mutable OutputControl: Label
    val mutable InputControl: TextBox
    // the class must have a parameterless constructor
    new() =
        { OutputControl = null
          InputControl = null }
    // method to handle the on click event
    member x.SayHelloButton_Click((sender : obj), (e : EventArgs)) =
        x.OutputControl.Text <- ("Hello ... " + x.InputControl.Text)
```

Executing the preceding example produces the web page shown in Figure 8-13.

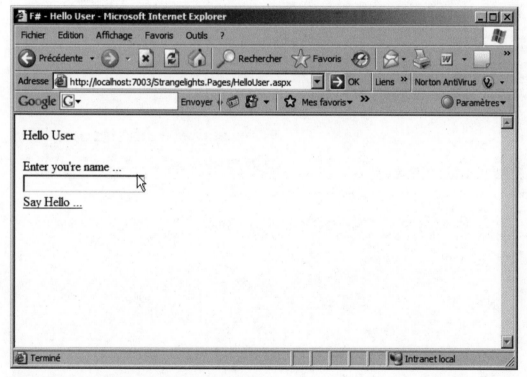

Figure 8-13. *A page created using an ASP.NET form*

This form doesn't look great, but the nice thing about defining your application in HTML is that you can quickly use images and Cascading Style Sheets (CSS) to spice up the application. Figure 8-14 shows the results of adding a little CSS magic.

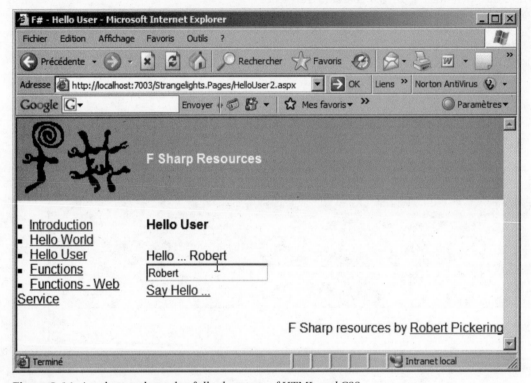

Figure 8-14. *A web page that takes full advantage of HTML and CSS*

You have taken only a brief look at all the functionality offered by ASP.NET. Table 8-5 summarizes all the namespaces available in System.Web.dll that contain ASP.NET functionality.

Table 8-5. *A Summary of the Namespaces Available in* `System.Web.dll`

Namespace	Description
`System.Web`	This namespace provides types that form the basis of ASP.NET's HTML rendering process; this is where the `IHttpHander` interface discussed in this chapter lives.
`System.Web.Mail`	This namespace provides types that you can use to send emails from ASP.NET applications.
`System.Web.HtmlControls`	This namespace provides controls that are exact copies of HTML tags.
`System.Web.WebControls`	This namespace provides controls that behave like HTML tags, but are more abstract. For example, the `TextBox` control is rendered as an `input` tag if you set its `TextMode` property to `TextBoxMode.SingleLine` and as a `textarea` if you set that property to `TextBoxMode.MultiLine`.
`System.Web.WebControls.Adapters`	This namespace provides adapters that you can use to affect the rendering of other controls. For example, you can alter their behavior or render different HTML tags for different types of browsers.
`System.Web.WebControls.WebParts`	This namespace provides *web parts*, controls that support a system where users can add, remove, and dynamically configure them within a page to give a personalized experience.

Summary

This chapter provided an overview of various options for creating user interfaces with F#. The scope of this topic is frankly enormous, and it would be impossible to cover all the options for user-interface programming in F#. For example, you can find hundreds of third-party components built on ASP.NET, WinForms, or WPF. These help raise the level of abstraction when creating user interfaces. You can also find libraries that offer complete alternative programming models, such as DirectX, which is designed for high-performance 3D graphics.

The next chapter will take a look at another important programming task—how to access data.

CHAPTER 9

■ ■ ■

Data Access

Computers are designed to process data, so it's a rare program that doesn't require some form of data access, whether it's reading a small configuration file or an enterprise application that accesses a full-scale relational database management system. In this chapter, you will learn about F#'s wide range of data access options.

In F# data access relies heavily on tools and libraries within, or built upon, the .NET BCL. This means that a lot of the data access code you write in F# will resemble code data access code in C# or VB.NET, although the F# code will often been more concise than in those other languages.

The System.Configuration Namespace

Whenever you execute any program written in any .NET language, the .NET runtime will automatically check whether a configuration file is available. This is a file with the same name as the executable, plus the extension .config that you must place in the same directory as the executable; thus, the configuration file for MyApp.exe would be MyApp.exe.config. In ASP.NET applications, these files are called web.config files because there is no executable, and they live in the web root. These files are useful for storing settings that you want to be able to change without recompiling the application—a classic example of this is a connection string to a database. You should be careful not to store values that are specific to a user in the configuration file because any changes to the file will affect all users of the application. The best place to store user-specific settings is in a relational database. You'll learn more about relational database access in this chapter's "ADO.NET" section.

The System.Configuration namespace provides an easy way to access configuration values; the simplest way of accessing configuration data is with ConfigurationManager. The next example shows how to load a simple key-value pair from a configuration file. Imagine you have the following configuration file, and you want to read "MySetting" from the file:

```
<configuration>
    <appSettings>
        <add key="MySetting" value="An important string" />
    </appSettings>
</configuration>
```

The following code loads the setting by using ConfigurationManager's static AppSettings property:

```
open System.Configuration

// read an application setting
let setting = ConfigurationManager.AppSettings.["MySetting"]

// print the setting
printfn "%s" setting
```

Executing the preceding code produces the following result:

```
An important string
```

■**Note** To compile this example, you will need to add a reference to System.Configuration.dll. The way to access these values in .NET version 1.1 was through the ConfigurationSettings type in System.dll. This type is still available in .NET 2.0, but it has been deprecated, so it is best to avoid using it.

Typically, you use these name-value pairs to store connection strings. It is customary to use a separate section specifically for this purpose, which can help you separate them from other configuration settings. The providerName property allows you to store information about which database provider the connection string should be used with. The next example shows how to load the connection string "MyConnectionString" from a configuration file:

```
<configuration>
    <connectionStrings>
        <add
            name="MyConnectionString"
            connectionString=" Data Source=server;
                Initial Catalog=pubs;
                Integrated Security=SSPI;"
            providerName="System.Data.SqlClient" />
    </connectionStrings>
</configuration>
```

The following example loads the connection string via another static property on the ConfigurationManager class, the ConnectionString property. This is a collection that gives access to a type called ConnectionStringSettings, which has a ConnectionString property that gives access to the connection string, as well as a ProviderName property that gives access to the provider name string:

```
open System.Configuration

// get the connection string
let connectionStringDetails =
    ConfigurationManager.ConnectionStrings.["MyConnectionString"]

// print the details
printfn "%s\r\n%s"
    connectionStringDetails.ConnectionString
    connectionStringDetails.ProviderName
```

Executing the preceding code gives you the following results:

```
Data Source=server;
Initial Catalog=pubs;
Integrated Security=SSPI;
System.Data.SqlClient
```

■**Caution** Notice that I added spaces and newline characters to the configuration file to improve the formatting. This meant that I also had to add them to the connection string, which you can see when output to the console. Most libraries consuming the connection string will correct for this, but some might not, so be careful when formatting your configuration file.

It's also possible to load configuration files associated with other programs, web applications, and even machine.config, which contains the default settings for .NET on a particular machine. You can query, update, and save these files. The following sample shows how to open machine.config and enumerate the various sections within it:

```
open System.Configuration

// open the machine config
let config =
    ConfigurationManager.OpenMachineConfiguration()

// print the names of all sections
for x in config.Sections do
    printfn "%s" x.SectionInformation.Name
```

When I execute the preceding code on my machine, I get the following results:

```
system.data
windows
system.webServer
mscorlib
system.data.oledb
system.data.oracleclient
system.data.sqlclient
configProtectedData
satelliteassemblies
system.data.dataset
startup
system.data.odbc
system.diagnostics
runtime
system.codedom
system.runtime.remoting
connectionStrings
assemblyBinding
appSettings
system.windows.forms
```

This section has shown you how to work with configuration files, a particular kind of XML file. A later section, "The System.Xml Namespace," will show you how to use the System.Xml namespace to work with any kind of XML file. In the next section, you'll take a general look at accessing files using the System.IO namespace.

The System.IO Namespace

The main purpose of the System.IO namespace is to provide types that give easy access to the files and directories of the operating system's file store, although it also provides ways of writing to memory and network streams.

The namespace offers two main ways to deal with files and directories. You can use FileInfo and DirectoryInfo objects to get or alter information about a file or directory. You can also find File and Directory classes that offer the same functionality, but which are exposed as static members that require the filename to be passed to each method. Generally, you use the File and Directory classes if you want a single piece of information about a file system object, and you use the FileInfo and DirectoryInfo classes if you need lots of information about a single file system object. The two techniques are complementary; for example, you might use the Directory type to get information about all the files in a directory, and then use the FileInfo object to find out the name and other information about the file. Here's an example of how to do this:

```
open System.IO

// list all the files in the root of C: drive
let files = Directory.GetFiles(@"c:\")
```

```
// write out various information about the file
for filepath in files do
    let file = new FileInfo(filepath)
    printfn "%s\t%d\t%O"
        file.Name
        file.Length
        file.CreationTime
```

When I execute the preceding code on my machine, I get the following results:

```
.rnd      1024      07/03/2009 14:02:23
autoexec.bat    24        02/11/2006 11:23:09
bootmgr 333203   21/01/2007 09:36:26
BOOTSECT.BAK    8192      21/01/2007 09:36:28
config.sys      10        02/11/2006 07:25:08
hiberfil.sys    2143363072        06/09/2008 06:49:56
ImageUploader4.ocx        2663944 13/11/2007 17:42:08
IO.SYS  0        22/12/2007 14:44:31
MSDOS.SYS       0         22/12/2007 14:44:31
pagefile.sys    2459238400        18/12/2007 07:21:04
trace.ini       11        22/12/2007 14:41:28
```

The namespace also provides an extremely convenient way to work with the contents of files. Files in F# are open and are represented as streams, which gives you a way to read or write bytes, characters, or strings from a file. Opening a file and reading text from it could not be simpler—just call the File.ReadAllLines method, and you return an array that contains all the lines in a file. The following example demonstrates how to read a comma-separated file that contains three columns of data:

```
open System.IO
//test.csv:
//Apples,12,25
//Oranges,12,25
//Bananas,12,25

// open a test file and print the contents
let readFile() =
    let lines = File.ReadAllLines("test.csv")
    let printLine (line: string) =
        let items = line.Split([|','|])
        printfn "%O %O %O"
            items.[0]
            items.[1]
            items.[2]
    Seq.iter printLine lines

do readFile()
```

When you execute the preceding code with the text file in the comments, you get the following results:

Apples	12	25
Oranges	12	25
Bananas	12	25

■**Note** The `File.ReadAllLines` method assumes your file has a UTF-8 encoding. If your file does not use this text encoding, you can use another overload of the method that allows you to pass in the appropriate encoding object. For example, if your file uses the encoding Windows-1252 for Western languages, you should open it using this line of code: `File.ReadAllLines("accents.txt")`, `Encoding.GetEncoding(1252)`).

Using Sequences with System.IO

One interesting aspect of F# is its ability to generate lazy sequences (you learned about this originally in Chapter 3). You can use these when working with large files to avoid the overhead of allocating all the memory for the file up front. This can potentially allow you to work with files that would otherwise be too large to fit into memory on a 32-bit system.

Generating a sequence is straightforward. You open the file as a text-file stream using the `File.OpenText` method. This method provides a stream reader that allows you to iterate over the file's contents using a while loop:

```
// open a file path and create a lazy stream from it
let allLinesSeq path =
    let stream = File.OpenText(path)
    seq { while not stream.EndOfStream do
            yield stream.ReadLine() }
```

Let's look at a quick test that demonstrates how this improves memory performance by measuring the memory consumed using performance counters. Performance counters are the standard way to measure and tune a program's performance in Windows. Windows includes a tool called *Performance Monitor* (`perfmon.exe`) that allows you to view performance counter values, or you can access their values in code using a class in the .NET framework, as you'll learn how to do in this test.

■**Note** You can also create your own custom performance counters in .NET; I've written a blog post that describes how to do this. You can check it out at `http://strangelights.com/blog/archive/2008/05/08/1615.aspx`.

Begin by measuring the memory performance of the File.ReadAllLines method, as demonstrated in the previous section. To do this, you use PerformanceCounter class to create an instance of the Process, Private Bytes counter. It's important that you create the counter before the test because creating it afterwards could cause a garbage collection that would destroy your test results:

```
open System.IO
open System.Diagnostics

// print out the contents of the file
let printFile () =
    let lines = File.ReadAllLines("FieldingTomJones.txt")
    Seq.iter (printfn "%s") lines

let main() =
    // get the "Private Bytes" performance counter
    let proc = Process.GetCurrentProcess()
    let counter = new PerformanceCounter("Process",
                                         "Private Bytes",
                                         proc.ProcessName)
    // run the test
    printFile()
    // print the result
    printfn "All  - Private bytes: %f" (counter.NextValue())

do main()
```

Next, you measure the performance of lazy loading a file using your F# sequence code. You use exactly the same method to try and ensure the test is as fair as possible:

```
open System.IO
open System.Diagnostics

// open a file path and create a lazy stream from it
let allLinesSeq path =
    let stream = File.OpenText(path)
    seq { while not stream.EndOfStream do
            yield stream.ReadLine() }

// print out the contents of the file
let printFile () =
    let lines = allLinesSeq "FieldingTomJones.txt"
    Seq.iter (printfn "%s") lines
```

```
let main() =
    // get the "Private Bytes" performance counter
    let proc = Process.GetCurrentProcess()
    let counter = new PerformanceCounter("Process",
                                         "Private Bytes",
                                         proc.ProcessName)
    // run the test
    printFile()
    // print the result
    printfn "Lazy - Private bytes: %f" (counter.NextValue())

do main()
```

You can see the results of a test I ran using a file that is around 1.9 MB here:

```
Lazy - Private bytes: 14651390.000000
All  - Private bytes: 20787200.000000
```

The version where you use File.ReadAllLines takes about 6 MB more space than the reversion in F#'s sequence. In fact, the sequence version hardly uses any additional memory because an empty .NET program takes around 14 MB of memory.

So it's fine (and very convenient) for you to use File.ReadAllLines when you know the contents of the file will be reasonably small or that memory performance is not an issue. However, using F#'s sequences to lazy load a file line-by-line will give great memory performance in situations where you need it.

■**Note** Measuring memory consumption is a complex topic, but often just measuring the Process, Private Byte counter is enough to give you a good indication of your current memory consumption. The following article has a nice discussion of how to take a relevant measurement: http://www.itwriting.com/dotnetmem.php.

The System.Xml Namespace

XML has become a popular data format for a number of reasons, probably because it gives most people a convenient format to represent their data and because the resulting files tend to be reasonably human readable. Programmers tend to like that you can have files be unstructured, which means your data don't follow a set pattern; or you can have the files be structured, which means you can have the data conform to a contract defined by an *XSD schema)*. Programmers also like the convenience of being able to query the data using *XPath*, which means that writing custom parsers for new data formats is rarely necessary, and files can quickly be converted between different XML formats using the powerful *XSLT language* to transform data.

The System.Xml namespace contains classes for working with XML files using all the different technologies I have described and more besides this. You'll look at the most common way to work with XML files—the .NET implementation of the W3C recommendation for the XML Document Object Model (DOM), which is generally represented by the class XmlDocument. The first example in this section reads information from the following short XML file, fruits.xml:

```
<fruits>
  <apples>2</apples>
  <oranges>3</oranges>
  <bananas>1</bananas>
</fruits>
```

The following code loads fruits.xml, binds it to the identifier fruitsDoc, then uses a loop to display the data:

```
open System.Xml

// create an xml dom object
let fruitsDoc =
    let temp = new XmlDocument()
    temp.Load("fruits.xml")
    temp

// select a list of nodes from the xml dom
let fruits = fruitsDoc.SelectNodes("/fruits/*")

// print out the name and text from each node
for x in fruits do
    printfn "%s = %s " x.Name x.InnerText
```

Executing the preceding code produces the following results:

```
apples = 2
oranges = 3
bananas = 1
```

The next example looks at how to build up an XML document and then write it to disk. Assume you have a set of data, bound to the identifier animals, and you'd like to write it as XML to the file animals.xml. You start by creating a new XmlDocument object, and then you build the document by creating the root node via a call to the XmlDocument instance member CreateElement method and appending to the document object using its AppendChild method. You build up the rest of the document by enumerating over the animals list and creating and appending nodes:

```
open System.Xml

// create an xml dom object
let fruitsDoc =
    let temp = new XmlDocument()
    temp.Load("fruits.xml")
    temp

// select a list of nodes from the xml dom
let fruits = fruitsDoc.SelectNodes("/fruits/*")

// print out the name and text from each node
for x in fruits do
    printfn "%s = %s " x.Name x.InnerText
```

Running this code creates a file, animals.xml, that contains the following XML document:

```
<animals>
  <ants>6</ants>
  <spiders>8</spiders>
  <cats>4</cats>
</animals>
```

The System.Xml namespace is large, and it includes many interesting classes to help you work with XML data. Table 9-1 describes some of the most useful classes.

Table 9-1. *Summary of Useful Classes from the* System.XML *Namespace*

Class	Description
System.Xml.XmlDocument	This class is the Microsoft .NET implementation of the W3C's XML DOM.
System.Xml.XmlNode	This class can't be created directly, but it's often used; it is the result of the XmlDocument's SelectSingle node method.
System.Xml.XmlNodeList	This class is a collection of nodes; it's the result of the XmlDocument's SelectNode method.
System.Xml.XmlTextReader	This provides forward-only, read-only access to an XML document. It isn't as easy to use as the XmlDocument class, but neither does it require the whole document to be loaded into memory. When working with big documents, you can often use this class to provide better performance than the XmlDocument.

Class	Description
`System.Xml.XmlTextWriter`	This class provides a forward-only way to write to an XML document. If you must start your XML document from scratch, this is often the easiest way to create it.
`System.Xml.Schema.XmlSchema`	This class provides a way of loading an XML schema into memory and then allows the user to validate XML documents with it.
`System.Xml.Serialization.XmlSerializer`	This class allows a user to serialize .NET objects directly to and from XML. However, unlike the `BinarySerializer` available elsewhere in the framework, this class serializes only public fields.
`System.Xml.XPath.XPathDocument`	This class is the most efficient way to work with XPath expressions. Note that this class is only the wrapper for the XML document; the programmer must use `XPathExpression` and `XPathNavigator` to do the work.
`System.Xml.XPath.XPathExpression`	This class represents an XPath expression to be used with an `XPathDocument`; it can be compiled to make it more efficient when used repeatedly.
`System.Xml.XPath.XPathNavigator`	Once an `XPathExpression` has been executed against the `XPathDocument`, this class can be used to navigate the results; the advantage of this class is that it pulls only one node at a time into memory, making it efficient in terms of memory.
`System.Xml.Xsl.XslTransform`	This class can be used to transform XML using XSLT style sheets.

ADO.NET

Relational database management systems (RDBMSs) are the most pervasive form of data storage. ADO.NET—and its `System.Data` and associated namespaces—makes it easy to access relational data. In this section, you'll look at various ways you can use F# with ADO.NET.

■**Note** All database providers use a connection string to specify the database to connect to. You can find a nice summary of the connection strings you need to know at `http://www.connectionstrings.com`.

All examples in this section use the AdventureWorks sample database and SQL Server 2005 Express Edition; you can download both for free at `http://www.microsoft.com`. It should be easy to port these samples to other relational databases. To use this database with SQL Server 2005 Express Edition, you can use the following connection settings (or an adaptation of them appropriate to your system):

```
<connectionStrings>
  <add
    name="MyConnection"
    connectionString="
        Database=AdventureWorks;
        Server=.\SQLExpress;
        Integrated Security=SSPI;
        AttachDbFilename=
C:\Program Files\Microsoft SQL Server\MSSQL.1\MSSQL\Data\AdventureWorks_Data.mdf"
    providerName="System.Data.SqlClient" />
</connectionStrings>
```

I'll discuss options for accessing other relational databases in the section, "ADO.NET Extensions." The following example shows a simple way of accessing a database:

```
open System.Configuration
open System.Data
open System.Data.SqlClient

// get the connection string
let connectionString =
    let connectionSetting =
        ConfigurationManager.ConnectionStrings.["MyConnection"]
    connectionSetting.ConnectionString

let main() =
    // create a connection
    use connection = new SqlConnection(connectionString)

    // create a command
    let command =
        connection.CreateCommand(CommandText = "select * from Person.Contact",
                                 CommandType = CommandType.Text)

    // open the connection
    connection.Open()

    // open a reader to read data from the DB
    use reader = command.ExecuteReader()

    // fetch the ordinals
    let title = reader.GetOrdinal("Title")
    let firstName = reader.GetOrdinal("FirstName")
    let lastName = reader.GetOrdinal("LastName")
```

```
    // function to read strings from the data reader
    let getString (r: #IDataReader) x =
        if r.IsDBNull(x) then ""
        else r.GetString(x)

    // read all the items
    while reader.Read() do
        printfn "%s %s %s"
            (getString reader title )
            (getString reader firstName)
            (getString reader lastName)

main()
```

Executing the preceding code produces the following results:

```
Mr. Gustavo Achong
Ms. Catherine Abel
Ms. Kim Abercrombie
Sr. Humberto Acevedo
Sra. Pilar Ackerman
Ms. Frances Adams
Ms. Margaret Smith
Ms. Carla Adams
Mr. Jay Adams
Mr. Ronald Adina
Mr. Samuel Agcaoili
Mr. James Aguilar
Mr. Robert Ahlering
Mr. François Ferrier
Ms. Kim Akers
...
```

In the previous example, you begin by finding the connection string you will use; after this, you create the connection:

```
use connection = new SqlConnection(connectionString)
```

Notice how you use the use keyword instead of let to ensure it is closed after you finish what you're doing. The use keyword ensures that the connection's Dispose method is called when it goes out of scope. You use the connection to create a SqlCommand class, and you use its CommandText property to specify which command you want to execute:

```
let command =
    connection.CreateCommand(CommandText = "select * from Person.Contact",
                             CommandType = CommandType.Text)
```

Next, you execute the command to create a `SqlDataReader` class; you use this class to read from the database:

```
use reader = command.ExecuteReader()
```

This too is bound with the use keyword, instead of let, to ensure it is closed correctly.

You probably wouldn't write data access code in F# if you had to write this amount of code for every query. One way to simplify things is to create a library function to execute commands for you. Doing this allows you to parameterize which command to run and which connection to use.

The following example shows you how to write such a function. You implement the execCommand function using `Seq.generate`, which provides a way of generating an `IEnumerable` sequence collection. The generate function takes three arguments. The first function opens a connection to the database; you call it each time you enumerate the resulting collection. This function is called the opener, and you could also use it to open a connection to a file. The second function generates the items in the collection, called the generator. This code creates a `Dictionary` object for a row of data. The third function is designed to be used to close the database connection or file you are reading from:

```
open System.Configuration
open System.Collections.Generic
open System.Data
open System.Data.SqlClient
open System.Data.Common
open System

/// create and open an SqlConnection object using the connection string found
/// in the configuration file for the given connection name
let openSQLConnection(connName:string) =
    let connSetting = ConfigurationManager.ConnectionStrings.[connName]
    let conn = new SqlConnection(connSetting.ConnectionString)
    conn.Open()
    conn

/// create and execute a read command for a connection using
/// the connection string found in the configuration file
/// for the given connection name
let openConnectionReader connName cmdString =
    let conn = openSQLConnection(connName)
    let cmd = conn.CreateCommand(CommandText=cmdString,
                                 CommandType = CommandType.Text)
    let reader = cmd.ExecuteReader(CommandBehavior.CloseConnection)
    reader
```

```
/// read a row from the data reader
let readOneRow (reader: #DbDataReader) =
    if reader.Read() then
        let dict = new Dictionary<string, obj>()
        for x in [ 0 .. (reader.FieldCount - 1) ] do
            dict.Add(reader.GetName(x), reader.[x])
        Some(dict)
    else
        None

/// execute a command using the Seq.generate
let execCommand (connName: string) (cmdString: string) =
    Seq.generate
        // This function gets called to open a connection and create a reader
        (fun () -> openConnectionReader connName cmdString)
        // This function gets called to read a single item in
        // the enumerable for a reader/connection pair
        (fun reader -> readOneRow(reader))
        (fun reader -> reader.Dispose())

/// open the contacts table
let contactsTable =
    execCommand
        "MyConnection"
        "select * from Person.Contact"

/// print out the data retrieved from the database
for row in contactsTable do
    for col in row.Keys do
        printfn "%s = %O" col (row.Item(col))
```

After you define a function such as execCommand, it becomes easy to access a database. You call execCommand, passing it the chosen connection and command, and then enumerate the results, as in the following example:

```
let contactsTable =
    execCommand
        "MyConnection"
        "select * from Person.Contact"

for row in contactsTable do
    for col in row.Keys do
        printfn "%s = %O" col (row.Item(col))
```

Executing the preceding code produces the following results:

```
...
ContactID = 18
NameStyle = False
Title = Ms.
FirstName = Anna
MiddleName = A.
LastName = Albright
Suffix =
EmailAddress = anna0@adventure-works.com
EmailPromotion = 1
Phone = 197-555-0143
PasswordHash = 6Hwr3vf9bo8CYMDbLuUt78TXCr182Vf8Zf0+uil0ANw=
PasswordSalt = SPfSr+w=
AdditionalContactInfo =
rowguid = b6e43a72-8f5f-4525-b4c0-ee84d764e86f
ModifiedDate = 01/07/2002 00:00:00
...
```

Here's an important caveat you should keep in mind when dealing with relational databases. You need to ensure that the connection is closed in a timely manner. Closing the connection quickly makes the connection available to other database users, which improves concurrent access. Let's look at how the previous sample creates connections and how they are "cleaned up" automatically. In the previous example, you call the opener function openConnectionReader every time the collection is enumerated using Seq.iter. The code uses an IEnumerator object to iterate the data, which in turn uses the generator function to generate individual results. Each call to Seq.iter creates one SqlDataReader and one SqlDataReader object. You must close these at the end of the iteration or if the iteration terminates abruptly for some reason. Fortunately, the Seq.generate function allows you to give it a close function to clean up resources on both complete and partial iterations. The close function will be called when the client has finished enumerating the collection. You should use the function to call the IDisposable. Dispose methods on the on the SqlDataReader which will cause it to close. You must also close the corresponding SqlConnection object, which you do by linking the closing of the database connection to the closing of the SqlDataReader:

```
command.ExecuteReader(CommandBehavior.CloseConnection)
```

To avoid keeping the connection open for too long, you should avoid complicated or time-consuming operations while iterating the resulting IEnumerable collection. And you should especially avoid any user interaction with the collection, for the same reason. For example, the following example, which rewrites the previous example so the user can move on to the next record by pressing Enter, would be bad for database performance:

```
for row in contactsTable do
    for col in row.Keys do
        printfn "%s = %O" col (row.Item(col))
    printfn "Press <enter> to see next record"
    read_line() |> ignore
```

If you want to use the collection more than once or let the user interact with it, you should generally convert it to a list or an array, as in the following example:

```
let contactsTable =
    execCommand
        "select * from Person.Contact"
        "MyConnection"

let contactsList = Seq.tolist contactsTable
```

Yes, connections will be closed when the cursors are garbage collected, but this process usually takes too long, especially if a system is under stress. For example, if the code you are writing will run in a server application that will handle lots of concurrent users, then not closing connections will cause errors because the server will run out of database connections.

Data Binding

Data binding is the process of mapping a value or set of values to a user interface control. The data does not need to be from a relational database, but it is generally from some system external to the program. The process of accessing this data and transforming it into a state where it can be bound is more complicated than the binding itself, which is straightforward. This is why I cover the topic in this chapter, rather than in Chapter 8. The next example shows how to bind data from a database table to a combo box:

```
open System
open System.Collections.Generic
open System.Configuration
open System.Data
open System.Data.SqlClient
open System.Windows.Forms

// creates a connections then executes the given command on it
let opener commandString =
    // read the connection string
    let connectionSetting =
        ConfigurationManager.ConnectionStrings.["MyConnection"]

    // create the connection and open it
    let conn = new SqlConnection(connectionSetting.ConnectionString)
    conn.Open()

    // excute the command, ensuring the read will close the connection
    let cmd = conn.CreateCommand(CommandType = CommandType.Text,
                                 CommandText = commandString)
    cmd.ExecuteReader(CommandBehavior.CloseConnection)
```

```fsharp
// read each row from the data reader into a dictionary
let generator (reader: IDataReader) =
    if reader.Read() then
        let dict = new Dictionary<string, obj>()
        for x in [ 0 .. (reader.FieldCount - 1) ] do
            dict.Add(reader.GetName(x), reader.Item(x))
        Some(dict)
    else
        None

// executes a database command returning a sequence containing the results
let execCommand commandString =
    Seq.generate
        (fun () -> opener commandString)
        (fun r -> generator r)
        (fun r -> r.Dispose())

// get the contents of the contacts table
let contactsTable =
    execCommand
        "select top 10 * from Person.Contact"

// create a list of first and last names
let contacts =
    [| for row in contactsTable ->
        Printf.sprintf "%O %O"
            (row.["FirstName"])
            (row.["LastName"]) |]

// create form containing a ComboBox with results list
let form =
    let temp = new Form()
    let combo = new ComboBox(Top=8, Left=8, DataSource=contacts)
    temp.Controls.Add(combo)
    temp

// show the form
Application.Run(form)
```

You can see the form that results from running the preceding code in Figure 9-1.

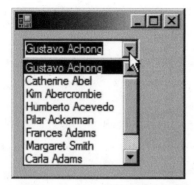

Figure 9-1. *A data-bound combo box*

Let's break the previous example down a bit. You begin by executing the query:

```
let contactsTable =
    execCommand
        "select top 10 * from Person.Contact"
```

Next, you need to turn the resulting IEnumerable collection into something suitable that you can bind to the combo box; you do this by first grabbing the important members, mapping them into a string collection, and finally, by converting the string collection to an array. Then you must bind the collection to the control that will display it; you do this by setting the control's DataSource property, which is the last named argument:

```
let combo = new ComboBox(Top=8, Left=8, DataSource=contacts)
```

The examples in this chapter cover only the ComboBox class, but most Windows and web controls can be data bound in a similar way. These include the ListBox and CheckListBox classes. Next, you'll look at binding data to a more complicated control, the DataGridView class.

Data Binding and the DataGridView Control

Unlike the controls you saw in the previous section, the DataGridView control can display more than one column; however, you must format the data in such a way that the data grid knows which columns to display. You can achieve this in two ways. First, you can bind the DataGridView to a DataTable. Second, you can bind the grid to a list of objects that have properties; the various properties will become the grid's columns.

Binding to a DataSet is the simpler solution, as in the next example:

```
open System
open System.Collections.Generic
open System.Configuration
open System.Data
open System.Data.SqlClient
open System.Windows.Forms
```

```
// creates a connections then executes the given command on it
let createDataSet commandString =
    // read the connection string
    let connectionSetting =
        ConfigurationManager.ConnectionStrings.["MyConnection"]

    // create a data adapter to fill the dataset
    let adapter = new SqlDataAdapter(commandString, connectionSetting.ConnectionString)

    // create a new data set and fill it
    let ds = new DataSet()
    adapter.Fill(ds) |> ignore
    ds

// create the data set that will be bound to the form
let dataSet = createDataSet "select top 10 * from Person.Contact"

// create a form containing a data bound data grid view
let form =
    let temp = new Form()
    let grid = new DataGridView(Dock = DockStyle.Fill)
    temp.Controls.Add(grid)
    grid.DataSource <- dataSet.Tables.[0]
    temp

// show the form
Application.Run(form)
```

You can see the results of running the preceding code in Figure 9-2.

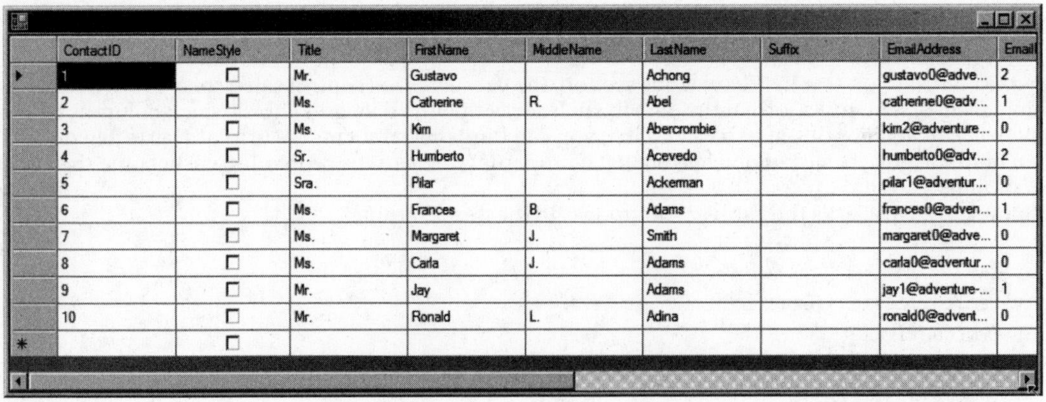

	ContactID	NameStyle	Title	FirstName	MiddleName	LastName	Suffix	EmailAddress	Email
►	1	☐	Mr.	Gustavo		Achong		gustavo0@adve...	2
	2	☐	Ms.	Catherine	R.	Abel		catherine0@adv...	1
	3	☐	Ms.	Kim		Abercrombie		kim2@adventure...	0
	4	☐	Sr.	Humberto		Acevedo		humberto0@adv...	2
	5	☐	Sra.	Pilar		Ackerman		pilar1@adventur...	0
	6	☐	Ms.	Frances	B.	Adams		frances0@adven...	1
	7	☐	Ms.	Margaret	J.	Smith		margaret0@adve...	0
	8	☐	Ms.	Carla	J.	Adams		carla0@adventur...	0
	9	☐	Mr.	Jay		Adams		jay1@adventure-...	1
	10	☐	Mr.	Ronald	L.	Adina		ronald0@advent...	0
*		☐							

Figure 9-2. *A data-bound data grid*

An alternative to using a DataSet is to use an F# record type; to do this, you typically create a generic function that uses reflection to create and populate your strongly typed collection. The next example shows what a generic function might look like. You wrap it in a module so you can use it in other code more easily, and then use this module to execute a query against the database:

```fsharp
module Strangelights.DataTools
open System
open System.Collections.Generic
open System.Configuration
open System.Data
open System.Data.SqlClient
open Microsoft.FSharp.Reflection

// a command that returns dynamically created stongly typed collection
let execCommand<'a> commandString : seq<'a> =
    // the opener that executes the command
    let opener() =
        // read the connection string
        let connectionSetting =
            ConfigurationManager.ConnectionStrings.["MyConnection"]

        // create the connection and open it
        let conn = new SqlConnection(connectionSetting.ConnectionString)
        conn.Open()

        // excute the command, ensuring the read will close the connection
        let cmd = conn.CreateCommand(CommandType = CommandType.Text,
                                     CommandText = commandString)
        cmd.ExecuteReader(CommandBehavior.CloseConnection)

    // the generator, that generates an strongly typed object for each row
    let generator (reader : IDataReader) =
        if reader.Read() then
            // get the type object and its properties
            let t = typeof<'a>

            // get the values for the row from the reader
            let values = Array.create reader.FieldCount (new obj())
            reader.GetValues(values) |> ignore
            let convertVals x = match box x with | :? DBNull -> null | _ -> x
            let values = Array.map convertVals values
```

```
        // create the record and return it
        Some (FSharpValue.MakeRecord(t, values) :?> 'a)
    else
        None


// generate the sequence
Seq.generate
    opener
    generator
    (fun r -> r.Dispose())
```

The first line of the sample uses a technique that you have not met before. Here, you explicitly declare your function's type parameter:

```
let execCommand<'a> commandString : seq<'a>
```

You do this so you can explicitly give the generic argument, 'a. The type parameter is then used to create a type object that you then reflect over:

```
let t = typeof<'a>
```

The function is designed to work with an F# record type, the fields of which exactly match the fields that result from the query. If this precondition is not met, then the code fails; however, such preconditions are typical in applications that use reflection in this way.

Your previously defined function execCommand is generic, and you can use it with any query and matching record type. The following example shows how to apply it:

```
open System
open System.Windows.Forms
open Strangelights.DataTools

// a type that mirrors the type of row being created
type Contact =
    { ContactID: Nullable<int>;
      NameStyle: Nullable<bool>;
      Title: string;
      FirstName: string;
      MiddleName: string;
      LastName: string;
      Suffix: string;
      EmailAddress: string;
      EmailPromotion: Nullable<int>;
      Phone: string;
```

```
        PasswordHash: string;
        PasswordSalt: string;
        AdditionalContactInfo: string;
        rowguid: Nullable<Guid>;
        ModifiedDate: Nullable<DateTime> }

// a form containing a data bound data grid
let form =
    let temp = new Form()
    let grid = new DataGridView(Dock = DockStyle.Fill)
    temp.Controls.Add(grid)
    let contacts =
        execCommand<Contact> "select top 10 * from Person.Contact"
    let contactsArray = contacts |> Seq.to_array
    grid.DataSource <- contactsArray
    temp

// show the form
Application.Run(form)
```

The most important line follows:

```
let contacts =
    execCommand<Contact> "select top 10 * from Person.Contact"
```

Here you have explicitly declared the type parameter for the generic function execCommand. The results from this example are the same as the previous example and are shown in Figure 9-2.

■**Note** It has become common to use object-relational mappers, such as NHibernate, to perform this kind of task. These tools provide a high degree of flexibility, but they tend to rely on features that are idiomatic to C#. You can make them work with F#, but the experience is not great. This is why I chose not to include any information on them in this book. Efforts are underway, by myself and others, to rectify this problem; meanwhile, I recommend keeping an eye on my blog for more information: http://strangelights.com/blog.

ADO.NET Extensions

ADO.NET has been successful at providing a set of bases classes and interfaces that others have used to provide access to their relational database of choice. The result: You can access most relational databases from F# with little effort. You have already seen most of these classes (or at least classes that implement the functionality they are intended to provide); Table 9-2 summarizes the key classes.

Table 9-2. *The Key Classes in ADO.NET*

Class	Description
System.Data.Common.DbConnection	This class represents a connection to a particular instance of a relational database; you use classes derived from this class to specify which database you want the query to be executed against.
System.Data.Common.DbCommand	Classes derived from this base class can be used to configure what query you want to execute against the database, whether it's an actual SQL query or a stored procedure.
System.Data.Common.DbParameter	This class represents the parameters of a query; typically, parameterized queries promote reuse in the relational database, so they execute more efficiently.
System.Data.Common.DbDataReader	Classes derived from this class allow you to access the results of a query in a linear manner; you use this class for fast access to your results.
System.Data.Common.DbDataAdapter	This class is used to fill a DataSet class with data from a relational database.
System.Data.DataSet	This class provides an in-memory representation of a database that can contain tables and relationships between them; unlike the other class in this table, this class is concrete, and you can use it directly.

With the exception of System.Data.DataSet, the classes in Table 9-2 are abstract classes, so you must use concrete implementations of them. For example, this example shows you how to create an instance of System.Data.SqlClient.SqlConnection, which is an implementation of System.Data.Common.DbConnection. Doing this gives you access to a SQL Server database:

```
Use connection = new SqlConnection(connectionString)
```

If you want to access an Oracle database, you replace the SqlConnection class with the OracleConnection class. Table 9-3 summarizes some of the most popular libraries and namespaces that implement these classes; note that this table is incomplete because the range of providers is quite large.

Table 9-3. *Database Providers for .NET*

Namespace	DLL	Description
System.Data.Odbc	System.Data.dll	This namespace allows you to connect to any database that provides drivers that support the Open Database Connectivity standard. Most databases provide drivers that support this standard, but typically you should avoid using them in favor of a more specific driver, which will probably be more efficient.
System.Data.OleDb	System.Data.dll	OleDb is a COM-based standard for database drivers; again, a huge number of relational databases provide drivers that support this standard, but where possible, you should use something more specific. This namespace is often used to connect to Access databases or Excel spreadsheets, which do not have .NET drivers of their own.
System.Data.SqlClient	System.Data.dll	This is the native .NET Microsoft SQL Server driver. It will work with all supported versions of SQL Server, and it is the *de facto* choice when working with SQL Server. The examples in this book use this namespace.
System.Data.OracleClient	System.Data.OracleClient.dll	This is the native .NET provider for the Oracle database created by Microsoft; it is distributed with the .NET Framework.
Oracle.DataAccess.Client	Oracle.DataAccess.Client.dll	The Oracle data provider for .NET (ODP.NET) is a database provider for .NET developed by Oracle; it is available from www.oracle.com/technology/software/tech/windows/odpnet.
IBM.Data.DB2	IBM.Data.DB2.dll	This is the native .NET provider developed by IBM; it is provided with the distribution of the database.
MySql.Data.MySqlClient	MySql.Data.dll	This is the open source native .NET provider created by the MySQL team. You can download it from dev.mysql.com/downloads/connector/net.
FirebirdSql.Data.FirebirdClient	FirebirdSql.Data.FirebirdClient.dll	This is the native provider for the open source database, Firebird; you can download it from www.firebirdsql.org/index.php?op=files&id=netprovider.

Connecting to an RDBMS with other .NET providers works as you would expect. The next example shows you how to connect to the Firebird employee sample database. To run this sample, you will need to install the Firebird database engine and the Firebird .NET provider components from http://www.firebirdsql.org. You will also need to run the Firebird database service on your local machine:

```
open System.Configuration
open System.Collections.Generic
open System.Data
open FirebirdSql.Data.FirebirdClient
open System.Data.Common
open System

// firebird connection string
let connectionString =
    @"Database=C:\Program Files\Firebird\" +
    @"Firebird_2_0\examples\empbuild\EMPLOYEE.FDB;" +
    @"User=SYSDBA;" + "Password=masterkey;" +
    @"Dialect=3;" + "Server=localhost";

// open firebird connection
let openFBConnection() =
    let connection = new FbConnection (connectionString)
    connection.Open();
    connection

// create a reader to read all the information
let openConnectionReader cmdString =
    let conn = openFBConnection()
    let cmd = conn.CreateCommand(CommandText = cmdString,
                                 CommandType = CommandType.Text)
    let reader = cmd.ExecuteReader(CommandBehavior.CloseConnection)
    reader

// read a row from the database and convert into a dictionary
let readOneRow (reader: #DbDataReader) =
    if reader.Read() then
        let dict = new Dictionary<string, obj>()
        for x = 0 to (reader.FieldCount - 1) do
            dict.Add(reader.GetName(x), reader.Item(x))
        Some(dict)
    else
        None

// execute a database command creating a sequence of the results
let execCommand cmdString =
    Seq.generate
        // This function gets called to open a conn and create a reader
        (fun () -> openConnectionReader cmdString)
```

```
            // This function gets called to read a single item in
            // the enumerable for a reader/conn pair
            (fun reader -> readOneRow(reader))
            (fun reader -> reader.Dispose())

// select all from the Employee's table
let employeeTable =
    execCommand
        "select * from Employee"

// print out the Employee's information
for row in employeeTable do
    for col in row.Keys do
        printfn "%s = %O " col (row.Item(col))
```

Executing the preceding example produces the following results:

```
...
EMP_NO = 145

FIRST_NAME = Mark

LAST_NAME = Guckenheimer

PHONE_EXT = 221


HIRE_DATE = 02/05/1994 00:00:00

DEPT_NO = 622

JOB_CODE = Eng

JOB_GRADE = 5

JOB_COUNTRY = USA

SALARY = 32000

FULL_NAME = Guckenheimer, Mark
```

Note that you need to make extremely few changes to convert the SQL Server AdventureWorks contact table example to one that you can execute against the Firebird employee example database.

Introducing LINQ

Language-Integrated Query (LINQ) is the next generation of .NET data access technology. It borrows heavily from functional programming, so it fits nicely with F#.

At its heart, LINQ is a set of libraries for manipulating collections that implement the IEnumerable<T> interface; in this respect, it is a lot like F#'s Seq module, which you learned about in Chapter 7. The idea is that you can use this library to query any in-memory collection, whether the data comes from a database, an XML file, or objects returned from another API.

Although the concepts implemented in the LINQ library will be familiar to you by now, they follow a slightly different naming convention, based on SQL. For instance, the equivalent of Seq.map is called Sequence.Select, and the equivalent Seq.filter is called Sequence.Where. The next example shows how to use this library. The first step is to import the methods exposed by the LINQ library into a more usable form:

```
module Strangelights.LinqImports
open System
open System.Linq
open System.Reflection

// define easier access to LINQ methods
let select f s = Enumerable.Select(s, new Func<_,_>(f))
let where f s = Enumerable.Where(s, new Func<_,_>(f))
let groupBy f s = Enumerable.GroupBy(s, new Func<_,_>(f))
let orderBy f s = Enumerable.OrderBy(s, new Func<_,_>(f))
let count s = Enumerable.Count(s)
```

Once you import these functions, you can apply them easily, typically by using the pipe-forward operator. The following example demonstrates how to do this. It uses the LINQ library to query the string class and group the overloads of its nonstatic methods together:

```
open System
open Strangelights.LinqImports

// query string methods using functions
let namesByFunction =
    (typeof<string>).GetMethods()
    |> where (fun m -> not m.IsStatic)
    |> groupBy (fun m -> m.Name)
    |> select (fun m -> m.Key, count m)
    |> orderBy (fun (_, m) -> m)

// print out the data we've retrieved from about the string class
namesByFunction
|> Seq.iter (fun (name, count) -> printfn "%s - %i" name count)
```

Executing the preceding code produces the following results:

```
ToLowerInvariant - 1
TrimEnd - 1
GetHashCode - 1
TrimStart - 1
GetEnumerator - 1
GetType - 1
GetTypeCode - 1
ToUpperInvariant - 1
Clone - 1
CopyTo - 1
get_Length - 1
Insert - 1
get_Chars - 1
PadLeft - 2
CompareTo - 2
PadRight - 2
ToUpper - 2
ToLower - 2
ToString - 2
Trim - 2
Remove - 2
ToCharArray - 2
Substring - 2
IsNormalized - 2
Normalize - 2
Replace - 2
IndexOfAny - 3
EndsWith - 3
Equals - 3
StartsWith - 3
LastIndexOfAny - 3
Split - 6
LastIndexOf - 9
IndexOf - 9
```

Using LINQ to XML

The goal of LINQ to XML is to provide an XML object model that works well with LINQ's functional style of programming. Table 9-4 summarizes the important classes within this namespace.

Table 9-4. *A Summary of the Classes Provided by LINQ to XML*

Class Name	Parent Class	Description
XNode		This class provides the basic functionality that applies to all nodes in an XML document.
XContainer	XNode	This class provides the functionality for XML nodes that can contain other nodes.
XDocument	XContainer	This class represents the XML document as a whole.
XElement	XContainer	This class represents an element in the XML document; that is, it represents a regular XML node that can be a tag (such as`<myTag />`) or can contain other tags or an attribute, such as `myAttribute="myVal"`.
XDocumentType	XNode	This class represents a document type tag.
XProcessInstruction	XNode	This class represents a processing instruction, which is a tag of the form `<? name instruction ?>`.
XText	XNode	This class represents text contained within the XML document.
XName		This class represents the name of a tag or an attribute.

You can see this object model in action by revising the example from the previous section to output XML instead of plain text. LINQ to XML makes this easy to do; begin by modifying the select statement to return an XElement instead of a tuple:

```
|> select (fun m -> new XElement(XName.Get(m.Key), count m))
```

This gives you an array of XElements that you can then use to initialize another XElement, which provides the root of the document. At that point, it is a simple matter of calling the root XElement's ToString method, which will provide the XML in the form of a string:

```
open System
open System.Linq
open System.Reflection
open System.Xml.Linq
```

```
// define easier access to LINQ methods
let select f s = Enumerable.Select(s, new Func<_,_>(f))
let where f s = Enumerable.Where(s, new Func<_,_>(f))
let groupBy f s = Enumerable.GroupBy(s, new Func<_,_>(f))
let orderBy f s = Enumerable.OrderBy(s, new Func<_,_>(f))
let count s = Enumerable.Count(s)

// query string methods using functions
let namesByFunction =
    (typeof<string>).GetMethods()
    |> where (fun m -> not m.IsStatic)
    |> groupBy (fun m -> m.Name)
    |> select (fun m -> new XElement(XName.Get(m.Key), count m))
    |> orderBy (fun e -> int e.Value)

// create an xml document with the overloads data
let overloadsXml =
    new XElement(XName.Get("MethodOverloads"), namesByFunction)

// print the xml string
printfn "%s" (overloadsXml.ToString())
```

Compiling and executing this code produces the following results:

```
<MethodOverloads>
  <Contains>1</Contains>
  <ToLowerInvariant>1</ToLowerInvariant>
  <TrimEnd>1</TrimEnd>
  <GetHashCode>1</GetHashCode>
  <TrimStart>1</TrimStart>
  <GetEnumerator>1</GetEnumerator>
  <GetType>1</GetType>
  <GetTypeCode>1</GetTypeCode>
  <ToUpperInvariant>1</ToUpperInvariant>
  <Clone>1</Clone>
  <CopyTo>1</CopyTo>
  <get_Length>1</get_Length>
  <Insert>1</Insert>
  <get_Chars>1</get_Chars>
  <PadLeft>2</PadLeft>
  <CompareTo>2</CompareTo>
  <PadRight>2</PadRight>
  <ToUpper>2</ToUpper>
```

```
    <ToLower>2</ToLower>
    <ToString>2</ToString>
    <Trim>2</Trim>
    <Remove>2</Remove>
    <ToCharArray>2</ToCharArray>
    <Substring>2</Substring>
    <IsNormalized>2</IsNormalized>
    <Normalize>2</Normalize>
    <Replace>2</Replace>
    <IndexOfAny>3</IndexOfAny>
    <EndsWith>3</EndsWith>
    <Equals>3</Equals>
    <StartsWith>3</StartsWith>
    <LastIndexOfAny>3</LastIndexOfAny>
    <Split>6</Split>
    <LastIndexOf>9</LastIndexOf>
    <IndexOf>9</IndexOf>
</MethodOverloads>
```

Summary

This chapter looked at the options for data access in F#. It has shown you how the combination of F# with .NET libraries is powerful yet straightforward, no matter what your data source is. The next chapter will walk you through the emerging topic of how to parallelize applications.

CHAPTER 10

■ ■ ■

Parallel Programming

Recently parallel programming has moved from being a relatively obscure topic, practiced only by specialist developers, to a more mainstream endeavor. This is due to the increasing prevalence of multicore processors. At the time of writing, it is almost impossible buy a PC with a single core processor—the standard is dual core—and quad core processors are beginning to arrive in the shops. It is fully expect that this trend will continue in the years to come.

To a certain extent, this interest in parallel programming has driven the renewed interest in functional programming. Functional programming is certainly not a silver bullet for all parallel programming problems, but it can help you design your software so it executes in parallel. In this chapter, you will learn about some of the simpler techniques to help your software execute in parallel, as well as how to take advantage of several processors.

It's often helpful to break down parallel programming into several smaller subtopics, all of which you'll learn about this chapter:

- *Threads, Memory, Locking, and Blocking*: You'll learn about basic techniques for creating and controlling threads in .NET programming. You'll also take a quick look at how you can share resources (such as memory) between threads, as well as how you can control access to these shared resources.

- *Reactive programming*: It's often important to the user experience that programs remain reactive to input. To do this, it's important that you avoid doing too much processing on the thread responsible for reacting to user input. This is particularly relevant to GUI programming, but it can also apply to a server that needs to stay responsive to incoming requests.

- *Data parallelism*: This term refers to executing one piece of code concurrently on several processors with varying input data. This is a good way to parallelize the processing of large data structures such as collections. It's often possible to apply a transformation to several items in a collection in parallel, which will generally speed the overall execution time. The classic example of this is the parallel map, which provides one of the simplest ways to parallelize a functional program.

- *Asynchronous programming*: Some tasks, particularly I/O, need to happen asynchronously to make program execution efficient. It is important that threads are not blocked for long periods while IO takes place.

- *Message passing*: This technique is more formally referred to as the actor model. You use it to coordinate tasks that execute in parallel. This is the most advanced parallel-programming topic covered in this chapter.

Parallel programming is a large topic, so this chapter won't be exhaustive, but it will provide some straightforward ways to help you get started with parallel programming in F#.

Threads, Memory, Locking, and Blocking

If you are serious about parallel programming, it's worth investing time to understand threads and memory. In this section, you'll take a look at explicitly creating threads and how to control their access to shared resources, such as memory. My advice is to avoid explicitly creating and managing threads like this; however, when using the other parallel programming techniques, it's useful to understand the underlying threading concepts.

When a program is executed, the operating system creates a *process* to execute it. The process represents the resources that are allocated to the program, most notably the memory allocated to it. A process has one or more *threads* that are responsible for executing the program's instructions and share the process memory. In .NET, a program starts with one thread to execute the programs code. To create an extra thread in F#, you use the System.Threading.Thread class. The Thread class's constructor takes a delegate that represents the function the thread will start executing. Once a Thread class has been constructed, it does not start executing automatically, you must call its Start method. The following example demonstrates how to create and start a new thread:

```
open System.Threading

let main() =
    // create a new thread passing it a lambda function
    let thread = new Thread(fun () ->
        // print a message on the newly created thread
        printfn "Created thread: %i" Thread.CurrentThread.ManagedThreadId)
    // start the new thread
    thread.Start()
    // print an message on the original thread
    printfn "Orginal thread: %i" Thread.CurrentThread.ManagedThreadId
    // wait of the created thread to exit
    thread.Join()

do main()
```

Compiling and executing the preceding program will output results similar to this:

```
Orginal thread: 1
Created thread: 3
```

You should look at a couple important things in this example. First, notice that the original thread prints its message before the second thread does. This is because calling a thread's Start method does not immediately start the thread; rather, it schedules a new thread for execution and the operating system chooses when to start it. Normally, the delay will be short, but as the original thread will continue to execute, it's probable that the original thread will execute a few instructions before the new thread starts executing. Second, notice how you use the thread's Join function to wait for it to exit. If you did not do this, it is highly probable that the original thread would finish executing before the second thread had a chance to start. While the original thread is waiting for the create thread to do its work, you say that it is *blocked*. Threads can become blocked for a number of reasons. For example, they might be waiting on a *lock*, or might be waiting for I/O to complete. When a thread becomes blocked, the operating system switches to the next runnable thread; this is called a *context switch*. You'll learn about locking in the next section; in this section, you'll look at blocking I/O operations in asynchronous programming.

Any resource that can be updated by two different threads at the same time is at risk of being corrupted. This is because a thread can context switch at any time, leaving operations that should have been atomic half done. To avoid corruption, you need to use locks. A lock, sometimes referred to as a *monitor*, is a section of code where only one thread can pass through it at a time. In F#, we use the lock function to create and control locking. You do this by locking on an object; the idea is that, as soon as the lock is taken, any thread attempting to enter the section of code will be blocked until the lock is released by the thread that holds it. Code protected in this way is sometimes called a critical section. You achieve this calling System.Threading.Monitor.Enter at the start of the code that you want to protect and System.Threading.Monitor.Exit at the end of that code. You must guarantee that Monitor.Exit is called, or this could lead to threads being locked forever. The lock function is a nice way to ensure that Monitor.Exit is always called if Monitor.Enter has been called. This function takes two parameters: the first is the object you want to lock on, while the second is a function that contains the code you want to protect. This function should take unit as its parameter, and it can return any value.

The following example demonstrates the subtle issues involved in locking. The code to accomplish the lock needs to be quite long, and this example has been deliberately written to exaggerate the problem of context switching. The idea behind this code is this: if two threads run at the same time, both try to write the console. The aim of the sample is to write the string "One ... Two ... Three ... " to the console atomically; that is, one thread should be able to finish writing its message before the next one starts. The example has a function, called makeUnsafeThread, that creates a thread that won't be able to write to the console atomically and a second thread, makeSafeThread, that writes to the console atomically by using a lock:

```
open System
open System.Threading

// function to print to the console character by character
// this increases the chance of there being a context switch
// between threads.
let printSlowly (s : string) =
    s.ToCharArray()
    |> Array.iter (printf "%c")
    printfn ""

// create a thread that prints to the console in an unsafe way
let makeUnsafeThread() =
    new Thread(fun () ->
    for x in 1 .. 100 do
        printSlowly "One ... Two ... Three ... ")

// the object that will be used as a lock
let lockObj = new Object()
```

```fsharp
// create a thread that prints to the console in a safe way
let makeSafeThread() =
    new Thread(fun () ->
        for x in 1 .. 100 do
            // use lock to ensure operation is atomic
            lock lockObj (fun () ->
                printSlowly "One ... Two ... Three ... "))

// helper function to run the test to
let runTest (f: unit -> Thread) message =
    printfn "%s" message
    let t1 = f() in
    let t2 = f() in
    t1.Start()
    t2.Start()
    t1.Join()
    t2.Join()

// runs the demonstrations
let main() =
    runTest
        makeUnsafeThread
        "Running test without locking ..."
    runTest
        makeSafeThread
        "Running test with locking ..."

do main()
```

The part of the example that uses the lock is repeated next to highlight the important points. You should note a couple of important factors. First, you use the declaration of the lockObj to create the critical section. Second, you embed your use of the lock function in the makeSafeThread function. The most important thing to notice is how, when printing the functions you want to be atomic, you place them inside the function you want to pass to lock:

```fsharp
// the object that will be used as a lock
let lockObj = new Object()

// create a thread that prints to the console in a safe way
let makeSafeThread() =
    new Thread(fun () ->
        for x in 1 .. 100 do
            // use lock to ensure operation is atomic
            lock lockObj (fun () ->
                printSlowly "One ... Two ... Three ... "))
```

The results of the first part of the test will vary each time it runs because it depends on when a thread context switches. It might also vary based on the number of processors, because multiple threads can run at the same time if a machine has two or more processors, so the messages will be more tightly packed together. On a single-processor machine, the output will be less tightly packed together because printing a message will go wrong only when a content switch takes place. The results of the first part of the sample, run on a dual-processor machine, look like this:

```
Running test without locking ...
...
One ... Two ... Three ...
One One ... Two ... Three ...
One ... Two ... Three ...
...
```

The lock means that the results of the second half of the example will not vary at all, so they will always look like this:

```
Running test with locking ...
One ... Two ... Three ...
One ... Two ... Three ...
One ... Two ... Three ...
...
```

Locking is an important aspect of concurrency. You should lock any resource that you write to and share between threads. A resource is often a variable, but it can also be a file or even the console, as shown in this example. Although locks can provide a solution to concurrency, they also can also create problems of their own because they can create a deadlock. A deadlock occurs when two or more different threads lock resources that the other thread needs and neither can advance. The simplest solution to concurrency is often to avoid sharing a resource that different threads can write to. In the rest of this chapter, you'll look at solutions for creating parallel programs that do not rely on explicitly creating locks.

■**Note** This book provides an extremely brief introduction to threading. You will need to learn much more about threading if you want to become good at parallel programming. A good place to start is the MSDN section on managed threads: http://msdn.microsoft.com/en-us/library/hyz69czz.aspx. You might also find this tutorial useful: http://www.albahari.com/threading/.

Reactive Programming

Reactive programming refers to the practice of ensuring you're your programs react to events or input. In this section, you'll concentrate on reactive programming in terms of GUI programming; GUIs should always be reactive. However, other styles of programming also need to take reactive programming into account. For example, programs running on servers often need to stay reactive to input, even as they process other, longer running tasks. You must also apply some of the techniques discussed here to server programming, as you'll see when you implement a chat server in Chapter 11.

Most GUI libraries use an event loop to handle drawing the GUI and the interactions with the user. This means that one thread takes care of drawing the GUI and raising all the events on it. You refer to this thread as the GUI thread. Another consideration: You should update GUI objects only with the GUI thread; you want to avoid creating situations where other threads can corrupt the state of GUI objects. This means that computations or IO operations that take a significant amount of time should not take place on the GUI thread. If the GUI thread is involved with a long-running computation, it cannot process interactions from the user, nor can it draw the GUI. This is the number one cause of unresponsive GUIs.

You can see this in action in the following example that creates a GUI that could easily become unreactive because it tries to do too much computation on the GUI thread. This example also illustrates how to ensure your GUI remains reactive by making a few simple changes. You will look primarily at a useful abstraction called the `BackgroundWorker` class, which you find in the `System.ComponentModel` namespace. This useful class allows you to run some work, raising a notification event when this work is complete. This is especially useful for GUI programming because the completed notification is raised on the GUI thread. This helps you enforce the rule that GUI objects should only be altered from the thread that created them.

Specifically, the example creates a GUI for calculating the Fibonacci numbers using the simple Fibonacci calculation algorithm you saw in Chapter 7:

```
module Strangelights.Extensions
let fibs =
    (1I,1I) |> Seq.unfold
        (fun (n0, n1) ->
            Some(n0, (n1, n0 + n1)))

let fib n = Seq.nth n fibs
```

Creating a simple GUI for this calculation is straightforward; you can do this using the WinForms GUI toolkit you saw in Chapter 8:

```
open Strangelights.Extensions
open System
open System.Windows.Forms

let form =
    let form = new Form()
    // input text box
    let input = new TextBox()
    // button to launch processing
    let button = new Button(Left = input.Right + 10, Text = "Go")
    // label to display the result
    let output = new Label(Top = input.Bottom + 10, Width = form.Width,
                           Height = form.Height - input.Bottom + 10,
                           Anchor = (AnchorStyles.Top ||| AnchorStyles.Left |||
                                     AnchorStyles.Right ||| AnchorStyles.Bottom))
```

```
// do all the work when the button is clicked
button.Click.Add(fun _ ->
    output.Text <- Printf.sprintf "%A" (fib (Int32.Parse(input.Text))))
// add the controls
let dc c = c :> Control
form.Controls.AddRange([|dc input; dc button; dc output |])
// return the form
form
```

```
// show the form
do Application.Run(form)
```

Executing this example creates the GUI you see in Figure 10-1.

Figure 10-1. *A GUI for the Fibonacci numbers*

This GUI lets you display the results of your calculation in a reasonable way; unfortunately, your GUI becomes unreactive as soon as the calculation starts to take a long time. The code is responsible for the unresponsiveness:

```
// do all the work when the button is clicked
button.Click.Add(fun _ ->
    output.Text <- Printf.sprintf "%A" (fib (Int32.Parse(input.Text))))
```

This code means that you do all the calculation on the same thread that raised click event: the GUI thread. This means that it is the GUI thread that is responsible for making the calculations, and it cannot process other events while it performs the calculation.

It's fairly easy to fix this using the background worker:

```
open Strangelights.Extensions
open System
open System.ComponentModel
open System.Windows.Forms

let form =
    let form = new Form()
    // input text box
    let input = new TextBox()
    // button to launch processing
    let button = new Button(Left = input.Right + 10, Text = "Go")
    // label to display the result
    let output = new Label(Top = input.Bottom + 10, Width = form.Width,
                           Height = form.Height - input.Bottom + 10,
                           Anchor = (AnchorStyles.Top ||| AnchorStyles.Left |||
                                     AnchorStyles.Right ||| AnchorStyles.Bottom))

    // create and run a new background worker
    let runWorker() =
        let background = new BackgroundWorker()
        // parse the input to an int
        let input = Int32.Parse(input.Text)
        // add the "work" event handler
        background.DoWork.Add(fun ea ->
            ea.Result <- fib input)
        // add the work completed event handler
        background.RunWorkerCompleted.Add(fun ea ->
            output.Text <- Printf.sprintf "%A" ea.Result)
        // start the worker off
        background.RunWorkerAsync()

    // hook up creating and running the worker to the button
    button.Click.Add(fun _ -> runWorker())
    // add the controls
    let dc c = c :> Control
    form.Controls.AddRange([|dc input; dc button; dc output |])
    // return the form
    form

// show the form
do Application.Run(form)
```

Using the background worker imposes few changes on the code. You do need to split the code does between the DoWork and the RunWorkerCompleted events, and this means you need to write slightly more code, but this will never require more than a few extra lines. Let's step though the required code changes; begin by creating a new instance of the background worker class:

```
let background = new BackgroundWorker()
```

You place the code that you need to happen in the background on a different thread—in the DoWork event. You also need to be careful that you extract any data you need from controls outside of the DoWork event. Because this code happens on a different thread, letting that code interact with the GUI objects would break the rule that they should only be manipulated by the GUI thread. You can see the code you use to read the integer and wire up the DoWork event here:

```
// parse the input to an int
let input = Int32.Parse(input.Text)
// add the "work" event handler
background.DoWork.Add(fun ea ->
    ea.Result <- fib input)
```

In the preceding example, you extract the input integer from the text box and parse it just before adding the event handler to the DoWork event. Next, the lambda function you added to the DoWork event captures the resulting integer. You should place the result that interests you in the DoWork event's Result property of the event argument. You can then recover the value in this property can then be recovered in the RunWorkerCompleted event. It two has a result property that you can see in the following code:

```
// add the work completed event handler
background.RunWorkerCompleted.Add(fun ea ->
    output.Text <- Printf.sprintf "%A" ea.Result)
```

You can be certain that the RunWorkerCompleted event runs on the GUI thread, so it is fine to interact with GUI objects. You've wired up the events, but you have a couple tasks remaining. First, you need to start the background worker:

```
// start the worker off
background.RunWorkerAsync()
```

Second, you need to add all this code to the button's Click event. You've wrapped the preceding code in a function called runWorker(), so it's a simple matter of calling this code in the event handler:

```
// hook up creating and running the worker to the button
button.Click.Add(fun _ -> runWorker())
```

Notice how this means you create a new background worker each time the button is clicked. This happens because a background worker cannot be reused once it's in use.

Now the GUI remains reactive no matter how many times someone clicks the Go button. This does leads to some other problems; for example, it's fairly easy to set off two calculations that will take some time to complete. If this happens, the results of both are placed in the same result label, so the user might have no idea which one finished first and is being displayed at the time she sees it. Your GUI remains reactive, but it's not well adapted to this multithreaded style of programming. One option might be to disable all the controls while the calculation takes place. This might be appropriate for a few case, but it's not a great option overall because it means the user can take little advantage of your reactive GUI. A better option is to create a system capable of displaying multiple results, along with their initial parameters. Ensuring that the user knows what a given result means. This example uses a data grid view to display the results:

```
open Strangelights.Extensions
open System
open System.ComponentModel
open System.Windows.Forms
open System.Numerics

// define a type to hold the results
type Result =
    { Input: int;
      Fibonacci: BigInteger; }

let form =
    let form = new Form()
    // input text box
    let input = new TextBox()
    // button to launch processing
    let button = new Button(Left = input.Right + 10, Text = "Go")
    // list to hold the results
    let results = new BindingList<Result>()
    // data grid view to display multiple results
    let output = new DataGridView(Top = input.Bottom + 10, Width = form.Width,
                                  Height = form.Height - input.Bottom + 10,
                                  Anchor = (AnchorStyles.Top ||| AnchorStyles.Left |||
                                               AnchorStyles.Right ||| AnchorStyles.Bottom),
                                  DataSource = results)

    // create and run a new background worker
    let runWorker() =
        let background = new BackgroundWorker()
        // parse the input to an int
        let input = Int32.Parse(input.Text)
        // add the "work" event handler
        background.DoWork.Add(fun ea ->
            ea.Result <- (input, fib input))
        // add the work completed event handler
        background.RunWorkerCompleted.Add(fun ea ->
            let input, result = ea.Result :?> (int * BigInteger)
            results.Add({ Input = input; Fibonacci = result; }))
        // start the worker off
        background.RunWorkerAsync()
```

```
    // hook up creating and running the worker to the button
    button.Click.Add(fun _ -> runWorker())
    // add the controls
    let dc c = c :> Control
    form.Controls.AddRange([|dc input; dc button; dc output |])
    // return the form
    form

// show the form
do Application.Run(form)
```

You can see this new GUI in Figure 10-2.

Figure 10-2. *A GUI that is better adapted to multi-threaded programming*

Data Parallelism

Data parallelism relies on executing a single function in parallel with varying data inputs. This breaks work into discrete units, so it can be processed in parallel, on separate threads, ensuring that work can be partitioned between the available processors.

Typically this means processing a collection of data in parallel. This method takes advantage of the fact that the items in the collection provide a natural way to partition the work. In the simplest case, a parallel map function, you apply a transformation to each item in the collection, and the results form a new collection. This simple case generally works because each item in the collection can typically be processed independently and in any order. It's also possible to use this technique to handle more complex scenarios, such as summing all the items in a list; however, it can also prove tricky for some complex cases, and the processing order can take on added significance.

Data parallelism typically relies on libraries and frameworks to provide parallel processing. Although they use multiple threads or processes to provide the parallelism, parallelism doesn't typically require the user to create or control these threads explicitly; instead, it's the job of the library or framework to do this. Work units can be distributed between different physical machines that form a computing grid; for the sake of simplicity and because multicore systems are becoming more common and powerful, this chapter will concentrate on systems where work is distributed between multiple processors of a single physical machine. Microsoft is working on providing new parallel programming facilities in the .NET framework, which will be available in version of the .NET framework 4.0. A few other libraries exist that implement data and task parallelism on the .NET platform, but this chapter will concentrate on what's available in .NET 4.0.

You have two main ways to achieve data parallelism in .NET 4.0: you can use the System.Threading. Parallel class available in mscorlib.dll, or you can use the System.Linq.ParallelEnumerable class available in System.Core.dll. The System.Threading.Parallel class is perfectly usable from F#, but the System.Linq.ParallelEnumerable class is probably the preferred way for F# programmers to achieve data parallelism because this library is written much more in a functional style.

Let's start with a quick example that illustrates how to use the System.Threading.Parallel class's parallel For, and then discuss why you probably don't want to use it. Assume that you want to write out the integers from 0 to 99 in parallel, as in this program:

```
open System.Threading
```

```
Parallel.For(0, 100, (printfn "%i"))
```

When executed on my dual-core machine, the preceding code produces the following output:

```
0
13

8
9
6
7
14
10
...
```

The numbers from the loop appear in a non deterministic order. This is because they were executed in parallel, and the threads assigned to execute each function are scheduled at random. The problem with using this kind of function in F# is that typically it will rely on a side effect at some point. It's easy to create functions with side effects in F#, but it can be undesirable when dealing with concurrency because it introduces problems. Even in this simple example, you face a risk that the numbers won't print atomically, but instead become mixed up as they print out. For example, you might see output like this:

```
...
6
174
10
...
```

Here two numbers form a three digit number that didn't exist in the collection.

Bearing that in mind, the System.Threading.Parallel class can still be useful on some occasions. Imagine you need to send out a large number of emails, and you want to send these emails concurrently.

You might choose to parallelize this with a parallel `ForEach` from the `Parallel` class because sending an email is I/O and therefore a side effect:

```
open System.Threading

let emails = [ "robert@strangelights.com"; "jon@doe.com";
               "jane@doe.com"; "venus@cats.com" ]

Parallel.ForEach(emails, (fun addr ->
    // code to create and send email goes here
    ()))
```

Even in this simple example, you need to ensure that you can call any function called inside `Parallel.For` from multiple threads.

The `System.Linq.ParallelEnumerable` class is much more promising for easily parallelizing F# programs. Essentially, it is a parallel implementation of the functions available in F#'s Seq module. Because there are plenty of name changes between Seq module and `ParallelEnumerable` class, it's common to create a thin wrapper of `ParallelEnumerable` to make it feel more like the Seq module, as shown in this code:

```
namespace Strangelights.Extensions
open System
open System.Linq

// Import a small number of functions from ParallelLinq
module PSeq =
    // helper function to convert an ordinary seq (IEnumerable) into a IParallelEnumerable
    let asParallel list: IParallelEnumerable<_> = ParallelQuery.AsParallel(list)
    // the parallel map function we going to test
    let map f list = ParallelEnumerable.Select(asParallel list, new Func<_, _>(f))

    // other parallel functions you may consider using
    let reduce f list = ParallelEnumerable.Aggregate(asParallel list, new Func<_, _, _>(f))
    let fold f acc list = ParallelEnumerable.Aggregate(asParallel list, acc,↩
new Func<_, _, _>(f))
```

You can use the finished version of this code to replace calls to functions from the Seq module with their equivalent calls from the PSeq wrapper module and expect your program to go faster in *most cases*—you will find some circumstances where it might be slower. For example, this code might execute more slowly for short lists where a relatively small amount of work is required for each item. You can see this at work in a micro benchmark for a parallel map function by comparing your parallel map function to normal map function. To do this, you vary both the size of the input list and the amount of work performed for each item in the input list.

■**Note** Micro benchmarking is a useful tool for helping you to understand the performance consequences of a small section of code. Vance Morrison has a nice MSDN article on how to run micro benchmarks on the .NET platform at http://msdn.microsoft.com/en-us/magazine/cc500596.aspx.

The following example shows how you might do this:

```
open System.Diagnostics
open Strangelights.Extensions

// the number of samples to collect
let samples = 5
// the number of times to repeat each test within a sample
let runs = 100

// this function provides the "work", by enumerating over a
// collection of a given size
let addSlowly x =
    Seq.fold (fun acc _ -> acc + 1) 0 (seq { 1 .. x })

// tests the sequentual map function by performing a map on a
// a list with the given number of items and performing the given
// number of opertions for each item.
// the map is then iterated, to force it to perform the work.
let testMap items ops =
    Seq.map (fun _ -> addSlowly ops) (seq { 1 .. items })
    |> Seq.iter (fun _ -> ())

// test the parallel map function, works as above
let testPMap items ops =
    PSeq.map (fun _ -> addSlowly ops) (seq { 1 .. items })
    |> Seq.iter (fun _ -> ())

// a test harness function, takes a function and passes it the give
let harness f items ops =
    // run once to ensure everything is JITed
    f items ops
    // collect a list of results
    let res =
        [ for _ in 1 .. samples do
                let clock = new Stopwatch()
                clock.Start()
                for _ in 1 .. runs do
```

```
                f items ops
            clock.Stop()
            yield clock.ElapsedMilliseconds ]
    // calculate the average
    let avg = float (Seq.reduce (+) res) / (float samples)
    // output the results
    printf "Items %i, Ops %i," items ops
    Seq.iter (printf "%i,") res
    printfn "%f" avg

// the parameters to use
let itemsList = [ 10; 100; 200; 400; 800; 1000 ]
let opsList = [ 1; 10; 100; 200; 400; 800; 1000 ]

// test the sequential function
for items in itemsList do
    for ops in opsList do
        harness testMap items ops

// test the parallel function
for items in itemsList do
    for ops in opsList do
        harness testPMap items ops
```

Before you examine the results of the tests, it's probably worth looking at the micro benchmarking code in a bit more detail because it can help you understand the results better. Perhaps the most important function is harness, which has the job of running the test code. You need to keep a couple things in mind when setting up the test. First, you always run each test 100 times when measuring a test result. You do this because some of the tests on small list can run exceptionally fast, so running them only once might make it hard to measure how long they take. Running the test repeatedly helps you avoid this problem. Second, you can always create a list of five results, then take the average time of this list. This is because other background processes on the computer can affect some tests Running the test several times and taking an average time helps you avoid this. You could also take this technique further and compute the standard deviation, which would highlight any tests were significantly longer or shorter than others.

The other interesting function is testMap, which has the job of providing the work for the map function to do. You want to vary two things: the number of items each input list has and the amount of processing that each item in the list will take. The testMap function achieves this through two parameters: items and ops. The items parameter is the number of items in a list that the map function must process, and the ops parameter is the number of operations on each item that must be performed. It's also worth noting that, because your Seq.map and PSeq.map function are both lazy, you need to force them by iterating over the resulting list. Iterating over the list will cause the lazy sequence to be created and evaluated. If you did not do this, you could expect to see a small and constant time result. It would show only the time it takes to create an object that is *capable* of generating the list, but not the *generation* of the list itself. You force the generation of the list by iterating over it using the Seq.iter function.

Now you're ready to look at the results themselves (see Table 10-1).

Table 10-1. *The results of the sequence micro benchmark*

Items	10		100		200		400		800	
Ops	*Serial*	*Parallel*	*Serial*	*Parallel*	*Serial*	*Parallel*	*Serial*	*Parallel*	*Serial*	*Parallel*
1	1.6	30.6	12	36.2	23.2	42.6	45	88.8	93.2	100
10	2	30.8	33.2	50.8	61.8	74.4	125.4	122.6	251.6	201
100	23.8	39.2	213.4	198.8	421.6	307	822.8	589.6	1660	1024.6
200	40.4	57.8	407.8	299.8	798.8	577.8	1634	1071.2	3262.4	1954.6
400	78.8	94	841	601.8	1676.8	1135.4	3237.4	2228.4	6424.2	3669.2
800	157.2	147.2	1591.4	1095	3174.6	2136.4	6388.4	4238.8	12747.6	7159.8
1000	196.8	181.4	1971.2	1329.6	3966.6	2630.6	7964	5279.6	16026	9111.6

It's difficult to interpret the raw numbers, but a good place to start is with some graphs of the numbers. Figures 10-3, 10-4, and 10-5 show the time it takes in milliseconds for a sequence to be processed by the Seq.map function versus the PSeq.map function. This is for a sequence of a fixed length (10 items, 100 items, and 1000 items respectively), but with varying numbers of operations on the sequence.

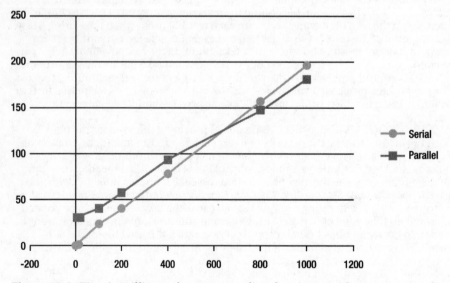

Figure 10-3. *Time in milliseconds to process a list of ten items with a varying number of operations*

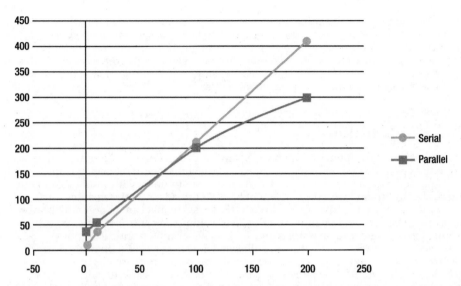

Figure 10-4. *Time in milliseconds to process a list of 100 items with a varying number of operations*

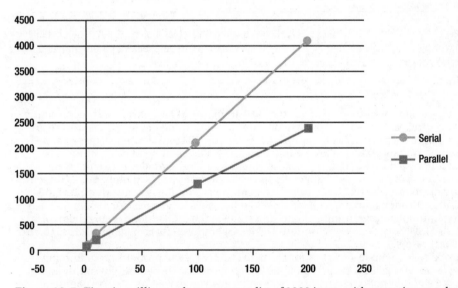

Figure 10-5. *Time in milliseconds to process a list of 1000 items with a varying number of operations*

These three diagrams illustrate nicely the results of the experiment. For a sequence with a small number of items (the ten items in Figure 10-3), you can see that the parallel function (PSeq.map) is slower than the serial function (Seq.map) when you perform a small amount of work for each item. As the amount of work you need to perform for each item increases, the parallel processing becomes slightly quicker than the serial version, but the difference is never that great. For a sequence of 100 items (see Figure 10-4), you see a similar curve, but the point where the parallel version of the function becomes quicker than the serial version occurs much earlier, and the gains that the parallel function makes over the serial version are more pronounced. Finally, for a sequence of 1000 items (see Figure 10-5), you can see that the overhead incurred by the parallel function has been completely amortized. The parallel function is linearly two times faster that the sequential version because you perform the test on a dual processor. You can conclude from this that it will be often worth using the parallel version of the map function as long as you can ensure your input list is reasonably large.

Asynchronous Programming

Asynchronous programming is slightly different than the other forms of parallel programming you've seen so far. The other topics covered allow a number of threads to execute work in parallel, taking advantage of all available processors in a system. In asynchronous programming, your want to avoid blocking threads. You're already familiar with the concept of blocked threads from this chapter's first section, "Threads, Memory, Locking and Blocking."A blocked thread is one that can do no work because it is waiting for some task to finish; commonly the task a thread is waiting for is the operating system performing IO, but sometimes it might also be waiting for a lock, so it can enter a critical section. Threads are relatively expensive resources; each thread is allocated a 1 MB stack, and there are other expenses concerning how the operating system kernel handles a large number of threads. In performance critical code, it's important to keep the number of blocked threads low. Ideally, you will only have only as many threads as you have processors, and you will have no blocked threads.

■**Note** For an overview of the kind of results that you can achieve using these techniques, see Amanda Laucher's 2009 Lang.NET talk in which she describes using F# asynchronous workflows to parallelize a C# program and achieves some impressive results: www.langnetsymposium.com/2009/speakers.aspx.

In this section, you will look at how you can use the .NET frameworks asynchronous programming model to avoid blocking threads during IO. The asynchronous programming model means using the pairs of Begin/End, such as the BeginRead/EndRead, on the Stream class. Typically you use these pairs of methods to perform some kind IO task, such as reading from a file. This method of programming has acquired a reputation for being difficult, mainly because you need to find a good way to store state between the Begin/End calls. This section will not cover the asynchronous programming model directly; instead, you'll look at how to use a feature of F# called asynchronous workflows to avoid some of the work associated with asynchronous programming model in other .NET languages. For a more detailed explanation of the asynchronous programming model and some of the difficulties in using them, please refer to Jeffrey Richter's MSDN article, "Asynchronous Device Operations" (http://msdn.microsoft.com/en-us/magazine/cc163415.aspx).

Asynchronous workflows are not exclusively for use with the .NET asynchronous programming model. In the next section, "Message Passing," you'll see how you can use these workflows with F#'s *mailboxes* to coordinate a number of different tasks. This will allow you to wait for tasks to complete without blocking threads.

The first step in understanding asynchronous workflows in F# is to understand the syntax itself. To create an asynchronous workflow, you use monadic syntax, similar to the sequence expressions you saw in Chapter 3. The basic syntax is the keyword async with the workflow expression surrounded by curly brackets: async { ... }. A simple workflow program that uses workflows looks like this:

```
open System.IO

// a function to read a text file asynchronusly
let readFile file =
    async { let! stream = File.AsyncOpenText(file)
            let! fileContents = stream.AsyncReadToEnd()
            return fileContents }

// create an instance of the workflow
let readFileWorkflow = readFile "mytextfile.txt"

// invoke the workflow and get the contents
let fileContents = Async.RunSynchronously readFileWorkflow
```

To compile this program, you need to add a reference to the FSharp.PowerPack.dll. This program shows a function readFile that creates a workflow that reads a file asynchronously, then returns its contents. Next, you create an instance of the workflow called readFileWorkflow, and finally, you execute the workflow to get the file's contents. It's important to understand that simply calling the readFile function won't actually read the file. Instead, it creates a new instance of the workflow, and you can then execute the workflow to perform the task of reading the file. The Async.RunSynchronously function is actually responsible for executing the workflow. A workflow instance is a small data structure, rather like a small program, that can be interpreted to do some work.

The most important thing to notice about this example is the let followed by an explanation mark (let!), often pronounced *let bang*. The workflows/monadic syntax allows library writers to give different meanings to let!. In the case of asynchronous workflows, it means that an asynchronous operation will take place. The workflow will stop executing while the asynchronous operation takes place. A callback will be placed in the thread pool, and it will be invoked when the operation has completed, possibly on a different thread if the thread making the original call is not free. After the async call, the original thread is free to carry on doing other work.

You've probably also noticed that the let! is used with some special methods prefixed with Async. These functions are defined as type augmentations, which are F#'s equivalent of C#'s extension methods, in FSharp.PowerPack.dll. These methods handle the calling of the Begin/End method pairs. If no Async method is available, it's fairly easy to create your own using the Async.Primitive function and the Begin/End method pairs.

The flow of your simple example would look like this:

- *Step 1*: The main program thread starts the process of opening the file stream, and a callback is placed in thread pool that can be used when this completes. This thread is now free to continue doing other work.

- *Step 2*: A thread pool thread will activate when the file stream has opened. It will start reading the contents of the file and place a callback in thread pool that can be used when this completes. Because it is a thread pool thread, it will return to the thread pool.

- *Step 3*: A thread pool thread will activate when the files has been completely read. It will return the text data that has been read from the file and return to thread pool.

- *Step 4*: Because you have usedthe Async.RunSynchronously function, the main program thread is waiting for the results of the workflow. It will receive the file contents.

You will have probably spotted that there is a flaw in this simple example. You do not block the main program thread waiting for IO, but as you wait for the asynchronous workflow to complete, you do block the main program thread until the IO has completed. To put this another way, there's little or no advantage to executing one asynchronous workflow on its own and waiting for the result. However, it's fairly simple to execute several workflows in parallel. Executing several workflows at once does have a distinct advantage because the original thread is not blocked after it starts executing the first "Async" task; this means it is free to go on and execute more asynchronous tasks.

It's fairly easy to illustrate this using a slightly modified version of the original example where, instead of reading one file, you read three of them. You will also compare this to a synchronous version of the program, which will help demonstrate the differences. First, take a look at the synchronous version:

```
open System
open System.IO
open System.Threading

let print s =
    let tid = Thread.CurrentThread.ManagedThreadId
    Console.WriteLine(sprintf "Thread %i: %s" tid s)

let readFileSync file =
    print (sprintf "Beginning file %s" file)
    let stream = File.OpenText(file)
    let fileContents = stream.ReadToEnd()
    print (sprintf "Ending file %s" file)
    fileContents


// invoke the workflow and get the contents
let filesContents =
    [| readFileSync "text1.txt";
       readFileSync "text2.txt";
       readFileSync "text3.txt"; |]
```

This program is fairly straightforward. Note that the preceding includes some debugging code to show when you begin and end processing a file. Now look at the asynchronous version:

```
open System
open System.IO
open System.Threading

let print s =
    let tid = Thread.CurrentThread.ManagedThreadId
    Console.WriteLine(sprintf "Thread %i: %s" tid s)
```

```
// a function to read a text file asynchronusly
let readFileAsync file =
    async { do print (sprintf "Beginning file %s" file)
            let! stream = File.AsyncOpenText(file)
            let! fileContents = stream.AsyncReadToEnd()
            do print (sprintf "Ending file %s" file)
            return fileContents }

let filesContents =
    Async.RunSynchronously
        (Async.Parallel [ readFileAsync "text1.txt";
                          readFileAsync "text2.txt";
                          readFileAsync "text3.txt"; ])
```

Again, this version incorporates some debugging code, so you can see how the program executes. The biggest change is that you now use the `Async.Parallel` function to compose several workflows into a single workflow. This means that when the first thread finishes processing the first asynchronous call, it will be free to carry on processing the other workflows. This is probably easiest to see when you look at the results of the two programs:

Synchronous results

```
Thread 1: Beginning file text1.txt
Thread 1: Ending    file text1.txt
Thread 1: Beginning file text2.txt
Thread 1: Ending    file text2.txt
Thread 1: Beginning file text3.txt
Thread 1: Ending    file text3.txt
```

Asynchronous results

```
Thread 3: Beginning file text1.txt
Thread 4: Beginning file text2.txt
Thread 3: Beginning file text3.txt
Thread 4: Ending    file text2.txt
Thread 4: Ending    file text1.txt
Thread 4: Ending    file text3.txt
```

The two sets of results look quite different. For synchronous results, you see that each *Beginning file* is followed by an *Ending file,* and they all occur on the same thread. In the second case, you can see that all instances of the *Beginning file* occur at once, on two different threads. This occurs because once the first thread comes to an asynchronous operation, it is free to carry on and start another operation. The ending files occur later, once the IO has completed.

Message Passing

It's often useful to think of a parallel program as a series of independent components that send and receive messages. This is often referred to as the Actor Model—you can find a more formal description of the actor model on Wikipedia at http://en.wikipedia.org/wiki/Actor_model. Although the scenarios in which you would use message passing tend to be quite complex, the ideas behind it are relatively simple, as you'll see in a handful of simple examples.

The basic idea behind message passing is that a system is composed of agents, or actors. These can both send and receive messages. When an agent receives a message, the message is placed in a queue until the agent is ready to process it. When an agent processes a message, it makes a decision about what to do with it based on its internal state and contents of the message. The agent has a number of possibilities open to it in response to an incoming message: it might send a reply to the agent that initiated the exchange, create a new message for a different agent, create a new agent, or perhaps update some internal data structure.

F# provides the generic `MailboxProcessor` class as its implementation of message passing and the actor model. When a `MailboxProcessor` is created, it has (as the name suggests) a message queue that it can use to receive messages. `MailboxProcessor` is responsible for deciding what it will do with the message once it receives it. The implementation of a `MailboxProcessor` tends to follow a few simple patterns; the next example illustrates the simplest pattern for a `MailboxProcessor`:

```
open System

let mailbox =
    MailboxProcessor.Start(fun mb ->
        let rec loop x =
            async { let! msg = mb.Receive()
                    let x = x + msg
                    printfn "Running total: %i - new value %i" x msg
                    return! loop x }
        loop 0)

mailbox.Post(1)
mailbox.Post(2)
mailbox.Post(3)

Console.ReadLine() |> ignore
```

Executing the preceding code produces the following results:

```
Running total: 1 - new value 1
Running total: 3 - new value 2
Running total: 6 - new value 3
```

In the first part of the example, you create a mailbox that receives messages of type int. When the mailbox receives a message, it adds it to a running total and then displays the running total, along with the value received. Let's take a closer look at how you achieve this. The `MailboxProcessor` has a static start method that receives a function as a parameter. The function the start method receives has an instance of the new `MailboxProcessor`, and it must return an asynchronous workflow. You should use the asynchronous workflow to read messages from the queue. You make it an asynchronous workflow because messages need to be read asynchronously; this ensures that a mailbox is not tied to a single thread, which would cause scalability issues if you were using lots of mailboxes. You need to keep checking the queue for new messages that arrive; typically, you do this by using an infinite loop to keep checking the queue. In this case, you define a recursive function called `loop`, which reads from the queue by calling the `Receive` function, processes the message, and then calls itself to start the process again. This is an infinite recursion, but there's no danger of the stack overflowing because the function is *tail recursive*. The `loop` function takes a single parameter; you use this to store the mailbox's state—an integer that represents the running total in this case.

It's also worth noting that `Console.ReadLine()` at the end of this example is important. This is because the message queue is processed in a separate thread. Once we finish posting messages to mailbox using the `Post` method, the main thread has no more work to do, so it exits, causing the process to exit. In this case, the process will probably exit before the mailbox has had chance to process the messages in its queue. Calling `Console.ReadLine()` provides a simple way to block the main thread until the user has had chance to see the results of the mailbox processing the messages.

One final detail about this example: The mailbox's `Post` member function is safe to call from any thread because of the mailbox's work queue that ensures each message is processed in turn in an atomic way. The current example does not take advantage of this, but you will see this used in the next two examples.

This particular asynchronous workflow isn't that useful; however, it does represent the simplest usage pattern of workflow: receive a message, update some internal state, and then react to the message. In this case, reacting to the message means writing to the console, which probably is too simplistic to be of much use. However, you can find more realistic scenarios for this usage pattern. A good example of this would be using a mailbox to gather up a number of values, then marshal to the GUI thread so the values can be viewed. You'll learn more about this technique in the next pair of examples.

Begin by looking at the problem you're trying to solve in a bit more detail. If you have a simulation that generates data, you might want to be able to see this data in real time, as it is generated. When working with GUIs, you face two related constraints that make this quite challenging. First, the GUI must run on its own thread, and this thread must not be occupied for a long time, or the GUI will become unresponsive. This makes it impossible to execute a long running simulation on the GUI thread. Second, you can only access GUI objects from the thread that created them: the GUI thread. If your simulation is running on anther thread, then it cannot write directly to the GUI. Fortunately, GUI objects provide an `Invoke` method that allows you to invoke a function on the GUI thread and safely update the GUI with the generated data. Calling the invoke function too often can have a negative impact on performance because marshalling data to the GUI thread is fairly expensive. If your simulation outputs a small amount of data frequently, it's often a good idea to batch up the results, so you can print them to the screen 12 to 20 times a second to get a smooth animation effect. You'll begin by learning how to use mailboxes to solve a specific instance of this problem; next, you'll see a second example where you tidy this up into a more generic example.

F#'s mailboxes can help here by providing an elegant way to buffer the data before you print it to the screen. The basics of the algorithm are fairly simple. The thread running the simulation posts messages to the mailbox; when the mailbox has received enough messages, it notifies the GUI of the new updates to be drawn. This programming style also provides a neat way of separating the logic for generating the data from the logic presenting the data in the UI. Let's have a look at the whole code example, then step through and examine the how it all works. You'll need to add references to `System.Drawing.dll` and `System.Windows.Forms.dll`:

```
open System
open System.Threading
open System.Windows.Forms
open System.Drawing.Imaging
open System.Drawing
```

```fsharp
// the width & height for the simulation
let width, height = 500, 600

// the bitmap that will hold the output data
let bitmap = new Bitmap(width, height, PixelFormat.Format24bppRgb)

// a form to display the bitmap
let form = new Form(Width = width, Height = height,
                    BackgroundImage = bitmap)

// the function which recieves that points to be plotted
// and marshals to the GUI thread to plot them
let printPoints points =
    form.Invoke(new Action(fun () ->
        List.iter bitmap.SetPixel points
        form.Invalidate()))
    |> ignore

// the mailbox that will be used to collect the data
let mailbox =
    MailboxProcessor.Start(fun mb ->
        // main loop to read from the message queue
        // the parameter "points" holds the working data
        let rec loop points =
            async { // read a message
                    let! msg = mb.Receive()
                    // if we have over 100 messages write
                    // message to the GUI
                    if List.length points > 100 then
                        printPoints points
                        return! loop []
                    // otherwise append message and loop
                    return! loop (msg :: points) }
        loop [])

// start a worker thread running our fake simulation
let startWorkerThread() =
    // function that loops infinitely generating random
    // "simulation" data
    let fakeSimulation() =
        let rand = new Random()
        let colors = [| Color.Red; Color.Green; Color.Blue |]
        while true do
            // post the random data to the mailbox
            // then sleep to simulate work being done
```

```
            mailbox.Post(rand.Next(width),
                rand.Next(height),
                colors.[rand.Next(colors.Length)])
            Thread.Sleep(rand.Next(100))
    // start the thread as a background thread, so it won't stop
    // the program exiting
    let thread = new Thread(fakeSimulation, IsBackground = true)
    thread.Start()


// start 6 instances of our simulation
for _ in 0 .. 5 do startWorkerThread()


// run the form
Application.Run form
```

This example has three key parts: how the simulation posts data to the mailbox, how the mailbox buffers points to be sent to the GUI, and how the GUI receives the points. Let's examine each of these in turn. Posting data to the mailbox remains simple; you continue to call the Post method on the mailbox. Two important differences exist between this example and the previous one. First, you pass a different data structure; however, the post method is generic, so you remain strongly typed. Second, you call the Post method from six different threads. The message queue enables this to work just fine, so everything just works. You use a simple technique to buffer data, which means you can simply count the number of you messages receive. When you receive 100, you send them to the GUI:

```
            async { // read a message
                    let! msg = mb.Receive()
                    // if we have over 100 messages write
                    // message to the GUI
                    if List.length points > 100 then
                        printPoints points
                        return! loop []
                    // otherwise append message and loop
                    return! loop (msg :: points) }
```

The number 100 is fairly arbitrary; it was chosen because it seemed to work well for this particular simulation. It's also worth noting that you count the number of messages you receive at each iteration by calling the List.length function. This is suboptimal from a performance point of view because the List.length function will traverse the list each time you call it. This won't matter much in the current example because it uses a fairly small list; however, if you increase the buffer size, this approach could become a bottle neck. A better approach might be to store a separate parameter that you increment during each iteration of the function; however, this example avoids doing that for the sake of maintaining simplicity. Another alternative might be to store the time of the previous update, updating again only if the previous update was more than a twentieth of a second ago. This approach works well because it allows you to aim for the correct number of frames per second required to achieve a smooth animation effect. Again, this book's examples don't rely on this approach because adopting it would add an unnecessary element of complexity to the examples. The example includes one more technique worth mentioning, which is how you write the data to the screen:

```
let printPoints points =
    form.Invoke(new Action(fun () ->
        List.iter bitmap.SetPixel points
        form.Invalidate()))
    |> ignore
```

This is fairly straightforward. The printPoints function takes a points parameter, then invokes a delegate in the context of the form and allows you to write the points to the bitmap. Finally, you need to call the forms Invalidate function to ensure the points are displayed correctly.

The previous example provides a nice demonstration of how to use mailboxes, but the main problem with it is that the code is not reusable. It would be better if you could wrap your mailbox into a reusable component. F#'s object-oriented features provide a great way of doing this. This following example also demonstrates a couple of other important concepts, such as how you can support messages of different types within the same mailbox, as well as how you can return messages to a client of the mailbox. Again, you'll need to add references to System.Drawing.dll and System.Windows.Forms.dll:

```
open System
open System.Threading
open System.ComponentModel
open System.Windows.Forms
open System.Drawing.Imaging
open System.Drawing

// type that defines the messages types our updater can handle
type Updates<'a> =
    | AddValue of 'a
    | GetValues of AsyncReplyChannel<list<'a>>
    | Stop

// a generic collecter that recieves a number of post items and
// once a configurable limit is reached fires the update even
type Collector<'a>(?updatesCount) =
    // the number of updates to cound to before firing the update even
    let updatesCount = match updatesCount with Some x -> x | None -> 100

    // Capture the synchronization context of the thread that creates this object. This
    // allows us to send messages back to the GUI thread painlessly.
    let context = AsyncOperationManager.SynchronizationContext
    let runInGuiContext f =
        context.Post(new SendOrPostCallback(fun _ -> f()), null)

    // This events are fired in the synchronization context of the GUI (i.e. the thread
    // that created this object)
    let event = new Event<list<'a>>()
```

```
let mailboxWorkflow (inbox: MailboxProcessor<_>) =
    // main loop to read from the message queue
    // the parameter "curr" holds the working data
    // the parameter "master" holds all values received
    let rec loop curr master =
        async { // read a message
                let! msg = inbox.Receive()
                match msg with
                | AddValue x ->
                    let curr, master = x :: curr, x :: master
                    // if we have over 100 messages write
                    // message to the GUI
                    if List.length curr > updatesCount then
                        do runInGuiContext(fun () -> event.Trigger(curr))
                        return! loop [] master
                    return! loop curr master
                | GetValues channel ->
                    // send all data received back
                    channel.Reply master
                    return! loop curr master
                | Stop -> () } // stop by not calling "loop"
    loop [] []

// the mailbox that will be used to collect the data
let mailbox = new MailboxProcessor<Updates<'a>>(mailboxWorkflow)

// the API of the collector

// add a value to the queue
member w.AddValue (x) = mailbox.Post(AddValue(x))
// get all the values the mailbox stores
member w.GetValues() = mailbox.PostAndReply(fun x -> GetValues x)
// publish the updates event
[<CLIEvent>]
member w.Updates = event.Publish
// start the collector
member w.Start() = mailbox.Start()
// stop the collector
member w.Stop() = mailbox.Post(Stop)

// create a new instance of the collector
let collector = new Collector<int*int*Color>()

// the width & height for the simulation
let width, height = 500, 600
```

```fsharp
// a form to display the updates
let form =
    // the bitmap that will hold the output data
    let bitmap = new Bitmap(width, height, PixelFormat.Format24bppRgb)
    let form = new Form(Width = width, Height = height, BackgroundImage = bitmap)
    // handle the collectors updates even and use it to post
    collector.Updates.Add(fun points ->
        List.iter bitmap.SetPixel points
        form.Invalidate())
    // start the collector when the form loads
    form.Load.Add(fun _ -> collector.Start())
    // when the form closes get all the values that were processed
    form.Closed.Add(fun _ ->
        let vals = collector.GetValues()
        MessageBox.Show(sprintf "Values processed: %i" (List.length vals))
        |> ignore
        collector.Stop())
    form

// start a worker thread running our fake simulation
let startWorkerThread() =
    // function that loops infinitely generating random
    // "simulation" data
    let fakeSimulation() =
        let rand = new Random()
        let colors = [| Color.Red; Color.Green; Color.Blue |]
        while true do
            // post the random data to the collector
            // then sleep to simulate work being done
            collector.AddValue(rand.Next(width),
                rand.Next(height),
                colors.[rand.Next(colors.Length)])
            Thread.Sleep(rand.Next(100))
    // start the thread as a background thread, so it won't stop
    // the program exiting
    let thread = new Thread(fakeSimulation, IsBackground = true)
    thread.Start()

// start 6 instances of our simulation
for _ in 0 .. 5 do startWorkerThread()

// run the form
Application.Run form
```

The output of this example is exactly the same as that of the previous example, and the code base follows largely the same pattern; however you can see a couple several important differences in the two examples. Perhaps the most noticeable one is that mailbox is now wrapped in an object that provides a strongly typed interface. The class you have created is called a Collector<'a>; its interface looks like this:

```
type Collector<'a> =
  class
    new : ?updatesCount:int -> Collector<'a>
    member AddValue : x:'a -> unit
    member GetValues : unit -> 'a list
    member Start : unit -> unit
    member Stop : unit -> unit
    member Updates : IEvent<'a list>
  end
```

The class is generic in terms of the type of values that it collects. It has an AddValue method to post a value to the internal mailbox and a GetValues method to get all the messages that have been passed to the mailbox so far. The collector must now be explicitly started and stopped by its Start and Stop methods. Finally, the collector has an Update event that is raised when enough messages have been collected. The number of messages collected is configurable by an optional integer that you can pass to the class constructor. The fact you use an event is an important design detail. Using an event to notify clients that updates exist means that your Collector<'a> needs no knowledge of the clients it uses, which greatly improves its reusability.

You now use a union type to represent your messages; this gives you the flexibility to have different types of messages. Clients of the Collector<'a> don't deal with it directly, but instead use the member methods it provides. The member methods have the job of creating the different types of messages. In addition to providing a value to the message queue, you can also send a message to retrieve all the current messages, as well as a message to stop the mailbox from reading new messages:

```
type Updates<'a> =
    | AddValue of 'a
    | GetValues of AsyncReplyChannel<list<'a>>
    | Stop
```

Next, you implement these different types of messages by pattern matching over the received messages:

```
let! msg = inbox.Receive()
match msg with
| AddValue x ->
    let curr, master = x :: curr, x :: master
    // if we have over 100 messages write
    // message to the GUI
    if List.length curr > updatesCount then
        do runInGuiCtxt(fun () -> fireUpdates(curr))
        return! loop [] master
    return! loop curr master
| GetValues channel ->
```

```
                          // send all data received back
                          channel.Reply master
                          return! loop curr master
              | Stop -> ()
```

The AddValue union case is basically what you did in the previous example, except that this time you add the values to both the curr and master lists. The curr list stores the current values you will pass to the GUI on the next update, while the mast list provides a list of all the values that you've received. The master list enables you to accommodate any client that requests all the values.

For the union case GetValues, it's worth spending some time looking at how a client can return values. You start this process by calling the mailbox's PostAndReply method rather than its Post method; you can see this at work in the GetValues member method implementation:

```
// get all the values the mailbox stores
member w.GetValues() = mailbox.PostAndReply(fun x -> GetValues x)
```

The PostAndReply method accepts a function that is passed a AsyncReplyChannel< 'a> type. You can use this AsyncReplyChannel< 'a> type to send a message back to the call via its Reply member. This is what you see in the GetValues case of your union. Users of this method should be careful because it blocks until the message is returned, which means the message won't be processed until it reaches the front of the queue. This can take a long time if you have a long queue. Users tend to prefer the AsyncPostAndReply approach because it enables you to avoid blocking a thread while waiting for the reply; however, this example doesn't do this for the sake of keeping the example simple.

The Stop union case is the simplest way to stop reading messages from the queue; all you need to do is avoid calling the loop method recursively. That's not an issue in this case, but you still need to return a value, which you do this by returning the unit type, which is represented by empty parentheses (). The only subtlety you need to be careful of here is that calling the Stop method will not stop the mailbox immediately; it will stop the mailbox only when the stop message reaches the front of the queue.

You've seen how our Collector<'a> type handles messages; now let's look at how the Collector<'a> raises the Update event, so that it runs on the GUI thread. You create the Update event using new Event, just as you create any other event in F#. You use the function runInGuiContext to make this event run in the context of the GUI:

```
let context = AsyncOperationManager.SynchronizationContext
let runInGuiContext f =
    context.Post(new SendOrPostCallback(fun _ -> f()), null)
```

First, you store the SynchronizationContext of the thread that created the object. You do this by using a static property on the AsyncOperationManager available in the System.ComponentModel namespace. The SynchronizationContext enables you to marshal to the thread that created it using its Post member method. The only thing you need to be careful about is that the thread that creates the collector object becomes the GUI thread; however, typically you'll use the main program thread to do both things, so you this won't be a problem. This technique where you capture the synchronization context is also used in the BackgroundWorker class from the "Reactive Programming" section of this chapter.

The definition of the form is now somewhat simpler because you no longer need to provide a function for the mailbox to call. You simply handle the Updates event instead:

```
// handle the collectors updates even and use it to post
collector.Updates.Add(fun points ->
    List.iter bitmap.SetPixel points
    form.Invalidate())
```

You can also now take advantages of the form's Closed event to stop the mailbox processor and obtain a list of all the messages processed when a user closes the form:

```
// when the form closes get all the values that were processed
form.Closed.Add(fun _ ->
    let vals = collector.GetValues()
    MessageBox.Show(sprintf "Values processed: %i" (List.length vals))
    |> ignore
    collector.Stop())
```

You haven't changed the behavior of your example, but these additions greatly improved the design of the code by decoupling the code for the mailbox from the GUI code, which improves the reusability of the Collector<'a> class tremendously.

Summary

In this chapter, you've covered quite a lot of ground. You've also seen five different concurrency techniques, all of which have their place in certain kinds of applications.

In the next chapter, you'll see how some of these techniques, especially asynchronous workflows, can be used to make programming *Distributed Applications* easier.

CHAPTER 11

■ ■ ■

Distributed Applications

Applications that use networks, called distributed applications, become more important every day. Fortunately, the .NET BCL and other libraries offer many constructs that make communicating over a network easy, which in turn makes creating distributed applications in F# is straightforward.

Networking Overview

Several types of distributed applications exist; they're generally classified into either *client-server* applications, in which clients make requests to a central server; or peer-to-peer applications, in which computers exchange data among themselves. In this chapter, you'll focus on building client-server applications because these are currently more common. Whichever type of distributed application you want to build, the way computers exchange data is controlled by a protocol. A protocol is a standard that defines the rules for communication over a network.

Building a network-enabled application is generally considered one of the most challenging tasks a programmer can undertake, with good reason. When building a network application, you must consider three important requirements:

Scalability: The application must remain responsive when used by many users concurrently; typically this means you must perform extensive testing and profiling of your server code to ensure that it performs when a high load is placed on it.

Fault tolerance: Networks are inherently unreliable, and you shouldn't write code that assumes that the network will always be there. If you do, your applications will be frustrating to end users. Every application should go to great lengths to ensure communication failures are handled smoothly, which means giving the user appropriate feedback, displaying error messages, and perhaps offering diagnostic or retry facilities. Do not let your application crash because of a network failure. You should also consider data consistency (that is, can you be sure that all updates necessary to keep data consistent reached the target computer?). Using transactions and a relational database as a data store can help with this. Depending on the type of application, you might also want to consider building an offline mode where the user can access locally stored data, and network requests are queued up until the network comes back online. A good example of this kind of facility is the offline mode that most email clients offer.

Security: Security should be a concern for every application you write, but it becomes a hugely important issue in network programming. This is because, when you expose your application to a network, you open it up to attack from any other user of the network; therefore, if you expose your application to the Internet, you might be opening it up to thousands or even millions of potential attackers. Typically you need to think about whether data traveling across the network needs to be secured, whether signed to guarantee it has not been tampered with or encrypted to guarantee only the appropriate people can read it. You also need to ensure that the people connecting to your application are who they say they are, and that they are authorized to do what they are requesting to do.

Fortunately, modern programmers don't have to tackle these problems on their own; network protocols can help you tackle these problems. For example, if it is important that no one else on the network can read the data you are sending, you should not attempt to encrypt the data yourself. Instead, you should use a network protocol that offers this facility. These protocols are exposed through components from libraries that implement them for you. The type of protocol, and the library used, is dictated by the requirements of your applications. Some protocols offer encryption and authentication, and others don't. Some are suitable for client-server applications, and others are suitable for peer-to-peer applications. You'll look at the following components and libraries, along with the protocols they implement, in this chapter:

TCP/IP sockets: Provide a great deal of control over what passes over a network for either client-server or peer-to-peer applications

HTTP/HTTPS requests: Support requests from web pages to servers, typically only for client-server applications

Web services: Expose applications so other applications can request services, typically used only for client-server applications

Windows Communication Foundation (WCF): Extends web services to support many features required by modern programmers including, but not limited to, security, transactions, and support for either client-server or peer-to-peer applications

These protocols are built on top of each other, where TCP/IP is the lowest level API, and WCF is the highest level API. Web services exist independently of WCF, but since WCF also implements the web services protocol, you can think of web services as being a subset of WCF. Figure 11-1 shows a diagram that gives an overview of how they fit together.

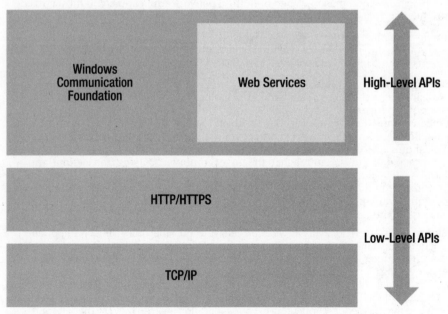

Figure 11-1. *An overview of .NET network programming APIs*

Despite the inherent challenge of distributed programming, it is generally worth the effort because it enables you to access interesting data and share the results of your programs with others. By the end of this chapter, you will be able to build chat client/server, read RSS feeds, access data stored in Google spread sheets, find all of your friends of friends on Twitter, and create an expose web and WCF services.

A simple way of providing a user interface over a network is to develop a web application. Web applications are not covered here, but you can refer to the ASP.NET sections in Chapter 8.

Using TCP/IP Sockets

TCP/IP sockets provide a low level of control over what crosses over a network. A TCP/IP socket is a logical connection between two computers through which either computer can send or receive data at any time. This connection remains open until it is explicitly closed by either of the computers involved. This provides a high degree of flexibility, but it raises various issues that you'll examine in this chapter. Unless you need a high degree of control, you're better off using the more abstract network protocols you'll look at later in this chapter.

The classes you need to work with TCP/IP sockets are contained in the namespace System.Net, as summarized in Table 11-1.

Table 11-1. *Classes Required for Working with TCP/IP Sockets*

Class	Description
System.Net.Sockets.TcpListener	This class is used by the server to listen for incoming requests.
System.Net.Sockets.TcpClient	This class is used by both the client and the server to control how data is sent over a network.
System.Net.Sockets.NetworkStream	This class can be used to both send and receive data over a network. It sends bytes over a network, so it is typically wrapped in another stream type to send text.
System.IO.StreamReader	This class can be used to wrap the NetworkStream class to read text from it. The StreamReader provides the methods ReadLine and ReadToEnd, which both return a string of the data contained in the stream. Various different text encodings can be used by supplying an instance of the System.Text.Encoding class when the StreamWriter is created.
System.IO.StreamWriter	This class can be used to wrap the NetworkStream class to write text to it. The StreamWriter provides the methods Write and WriteLine, which both take a string of the data to be written to the stream. Different text encodings can be used by supplying an instance of the System.Text.Encoding class when the StreamWriter is created.

In this chapter's first example, you'll build a chat application, consisting of a chat server (see Listing 11-1) and a client (see Listing 11-2). It is the chat server's job to wait and listen for clients that connect. Once a client connects, it must ask the client to provide a username, and then it must constantly listen for incoming messages from all clients. Once it receives an incoming message, it must push that message out to all clients. It is the job of the client to connect to the server and provide an interface to allow the user to read the messages received and to write messages to send to the other users. The TCP/IP connection works well for this type of application because the connection is always available, and this allows the server to push any incoming messages directly to the client without polling from the client.

Listing 11-1. *A Chat Server*

```
open System
open System.IO
open System.Net
open System.Net.Sockets
open System.Text
open System.Threading
open System.Collections.Generic

// Enhance the TcpListener class so it can handle async connections
type System.Net.Sockets.TcpListener with
    member x.AsyncAcceptTcpClient() =
        Async.FromBeginEnd(x.BeginAcceptTcpClient, x.EndAcceptTcpClient)

// Type that defines protocol for interacting with the ClientTable
type ClientTableCommands =
    | Add of (string * StreamWriter)
    | Remove of string
    | SendMessage of string
    | ClientExists of (string * AsyncReplyChannel<bool>)

// A class that will store a list of names of connected clients along with
// streams that allow the client to be written too
type ClientTable() =
    // create the mail box
    let mailbox = MailboxProcessor.Start(fun inbox ->
        // main loop that will read messages and update the
        // client name/stream writer map
        let rec loop (nameMap: Map<string, StreamWriter>) =
            async { let! msg = inbox.Receive()
                    match msg with
                    | Add (name, sw) ->
                        return! loop (Map.add name sw nameMap)
                    | Remove name ->
                        return! loop (Map.remove name nameMap)
                    | ClientExists (name, rc) ->
                        rc.Reply (nameMap.ContainsKey name)
                        return! loop nameMap
```

```
            | SendMessage msg ->
                for (_, sw) in Map.toSeq nameMap do
                    try
                        sw.WriteLine msg
                        sw.Flush()
                    with _ -> ()
                return! loop nameMap }
    // start the main loop with an empty map
    loop Map.empty)
/// add a new client
member x.Add(name, sw) = mailbox.Post(Add(name, sw))
/// remove an existing connection
member x.Remove(name) = mailbox.Post(Remove name)
/// handles the process of sending a message to all clients
member x.SendMessage(msg) = mailbox.Post(SendMessage msg)
/// checks if a client name is taken
member x.ClientExists(name) = mailbox.PostAndReply(fun rc -> ClientExists(name, rc))


/// perform async read on a network stream passing a continuation
/// function to handle the result
let rec asyncReadTextAndCont (stream: NetworkStream) cont  =
    // unfortunatly we need to specific a number of bytes to read
    // this leads to any messages longer than 512 being broken into
    // different messages
    async { let buffer = Array.create 512 0uy
            let! read = stream.AsyncRead(buffer, 0, 512)
            let allText = Encoding.UTF8.GetString(buffer, 0, read)
            return cont stream allText  }

// class that will handle client connections
type Server() =

    // client table to hold all incoming client details
    let clients = new ClientTable()

    // handles each client
    let handleClient (connection: TcpClient) =
        // get the stream used to read and write from the client
        let stream = connection.GetStream()
        // create a stream write to more easily write to the client
        let sw = new StreamWriter(stream)

        // handles reading the name then starts the main loop that handles
        // conversations
        let rec requestAndReadName (stream: NetworkStream) (name: string) =
```

```
        // read the name
        let name = name.Replace(Environment.NewLine, "")
        // main loop that handles conversations
        let rec mainLoop (stream: NetworkStream) (msg: string) =
            try
                // send received message to all clients
                let msg = Printf.sprintf "%s: %s" name msg
                clients.SendMessage msg
            with _ ->
                // any error reading a message causes client to disconnect
                clients.Remove name
                sw.Close()
            Async.Start (asyncReadTextAndCont stream mainLoop)
        if clients.ClientExists(name) then
            // if name exists print error and relaunch request
            sw.WriteLine("ERROR - Name in use already!")
            sw.Flush()
            Async.Start (asyncReadTextAndCont stream requestAndReadName)
        else
            // name is good lanch the main loop
            clients.Add(name, sw)
            Async.Start (asyncReadTextAndCont stream mainLoop)
    // welcome the new client by printing "What is you name?"
    sw.WriteLine("What is your name? ");
    sw.Flush()
    // start the main loop that handles reading from the client
    Async.Start (asyncReadTextAndCont stream requestAndReadName)


// create a tcp listener to handle incoming requests
let listener = new TcpListener(IPAddress.Loopback, 4242)

// main loop that handles all new connections
let rec handleConnections() =
    // start the listerner
    listener.Start()
    if listener.Pending() then
        // if there are pending connections, handle them
        async { let! connection = listener.AsyncAcceptTcpClient()
                printfn "New Connection"
                // use a thread pool thread to handle the new request
                ThreadPool.QueueUserWorkItem(fun _ ->
                        handleClient connection) |> ignore
                // loop
                return! handleConnections() }
    else
```

```
        // no pending connections, just loop
        Thread.Sleep(1)
        async { return! handleConnections() }

    /// allow tot
    member server.Start() = Async.RunSynchronously (handleConnections())

// start the server class
(new Server()).Start()
```

Let's work our way through Listing 11-1, starting at the top and working down. The first step is to define a class to help you manage the clients connected to the server: the ClientTable class. This class serves as a good example of how to use a MailboxProcessor to share data safely between several threads. You used a very similar technique to this in the "Message Passing" section of chapter 10. As you will recall, the MailboxProcessor queues messages from its clients, and you receive these messages by calling the Receive method on the MailboxProcessor class:

```
let! msg = inbox.Receive()
```

You always receive messages asynchronously, so that you do not block a thread while waiting for a message. You post messages to the class using its posted method:

```
mailbox.Post(Add(name, sw))
```

You use a union type to define the messages that you can send and receive. In this case, you define four operations, which are Add, Remove, SendMessage, and ClientExists:

```
type ClientTableCommands =
    | Add of (string * StreamWriter)
    | Remove of string
    | SendMessage of string
    | ClientExists of (string * AsyncReplyChannel<bool>)
```

These operations are implemented by pattern matching over the received message within the asynchronous workflow that receives the message. Typically, you use an infinite recursive loop to read messages continuously. In this example, the function is called loop. The loop has a parameter of F#'s immutable Map class, which provides the mapping between the client name, a string, and the connection to the client, which is represented by a StreamWriter:

```
    let rec loop (nameMap: Map<string, StreamWriter>) =
        ...
```

This provides an elegant way to share state between the operations. The operations update the map, and then pass the new instance on to the next iteration. The operations Add and Remove are straightforward to implement; a new updated version of the map is created and passed forward to the next iteration of the loop. This example shows only the Add operation because the Remove operation is so similar:

```
| Add (name, sw) ->
      return! loop (Map.add name sw nameMap)
```

The ClientExists operations are a little more interesting because you must return a result. For this, you use an AsyncReplyChannel, which is contained in the ClientExists union case:

```
| ClientExists (name, rc) ->
      rc.Reply (nameMap.ContainsKey name)
      return! loop nameMap
```

The reply channel is loaded into the union case when the message is passed to the MailboxProcessor class using its PostAndReply method, rather than the Post method you saw earlier:

```
mailbox.PostAndReply(fun rc -> ClientExists(name, rc))
```

Perhaps the most interesting operation is the SendMessage operation. Here you need to enumerate all of the clients and send a message to them. You perform this operation within the MailboxProcessor class because this class implements a queuing system, so you can be sure that only one message will be sent to each client at once. This approach ensures that message text does not become mixed with other messages and that messages do not arrive out of order:

```
| SendMessage msg ->
      for (_, sw) in Map.to_seq nameMap do
          try
              sw.WriteLine msg
              sw.Flush()
          with _ -> ()
```

Next you're going to look at the most difficult part of the code: how to read from the connected clients efficiently. To read messages efficiently, you need to read them asynchronously to ensure that precious server threads are not blocked while waiting from clients that might send messages relatively infrequently. F# has made writing asynchronous code easier with its asynchronous workflows. However, F# asynchronous workflows work best when you have lots of operations to perform concurrently. In this situation, you want to perform one asynchronous operation repeatedly. This is possible, but it's a little tricky because you have to use continuation style passing. You define a function, asyncReadTextAndCont, which reads from a network stream asynchronously and passes the resulting string and the original network stream to a continuation function that it receives. The continuation function is called cont in this case:

```
/// perform async read on a network stream passing a continuation
/// function to handle the result
let rec asyncReadTextAndCont (stream: NetworkStream) cont  =
    async { let buffer = Array.create 512 0uy
            let! read = stream.AsyncRead(buffer, 0, 512)
            let allText = acc + Encoding.UTF8.GetString(buffer, 0, read)
            return cont stream allText }
```

So the important thing to note about this function is that, when the read takes places, the physical thread will return from the function and probably return to the thread pool. However, you don't need to worry about the physical thread too much because it will restart when the async I/O completes the operation, and the result will be passed to your cont function.

You then use this function to perform all your reading from the client, For example, your main recursive loop looks like this:

```
let rec mainLoop (stream: NetworkStream) (msg: string) =
    try
        // send received message to all clients
        let msg = Printf.sprintf "%s: %s" name msg
        clients.SendMessage msg
    with _ ->
        // any error reading a message causes client to disconnect
        clients.Remove name
        sw.Close()
    Async.Start (asyncReadTextAndCont stream mainLoop)
```

You perform the operation of sending the message with the string msg you receive. Then you loop recursively using the asyncReadTextAndCont function, passing it the mainLoop function as a parameter. You use the Async.Start function to send a message to launch the asynchronous workflow in a *fire-and-forget* mode, which means it will not block and wait for the workflow to complete.

Next, you create an instance of the TcpListener class. This is the class that does the work of listening to the incoming connections. You normally initialize this with the IP address and the port number the server will listen on. When you start the listener, you tell it to listen on the IPAddress. Normally, the listener would listen for all traffic on any of the IP addresses associated with the computer's network adapters; however, this is just a demonstration application, so you tell the TcpListener class to listen to IPAddress.Loopback, which means it will pick up requests only from the local computer. You use the port number to tell whether the network traffic is for your application and not another. The TcpListener class permits only one listener to listen to a port at once. The number you choose is somewhat arbitrary, but you should choose a number greater than 1023, because the port numbers from 0 to 1023 are reserved for specific applications. You can use the TcpListener instance in the final function you define, handleConnections, to create a listener on port 4242:

```
let server = new TcpListener(IPAddress.Loopback, 4242)
```

This function is an infinite loop that listens for new clients connecting and creates a new thread to handle them. Once you have a connection, the following code enables you to retrieve an instance of the connection and start the work of handling it on a new thread pool thread:

```
let! connection = listener.AsyncAcceptTcpClient()
printfn "New Connection"
// use a thread pool thread to handle the new request
ThreadPool.QueueUserWorkItem(fun _ -> handleClient connection) |> ignore
```

Now that you understand how the server works, let's take a look at the client, which is in many ways a good deal simpler than the server. Listing 11-2 shows the full code for the client; note that you will need to add a reference to Systems.Windows.Forms.dll to make it compile. The listing is followed by a discussion of how the code works.

Listing 11-2. *A Chat Client*

```
open System
open System.ComponentModel
open System.IO
open System.Net.Sockets
open System.Threading
open System.Windows.Forms



let form =
    // create the form
    let form = new Form(Text = "F# Talk Client")

    // text box to show the messages received
    let output =
        new TextBox(Dock = DockStyle.Fill,
                    ReadOnly = true,
                    Multiline = true)
    form.Controls.Add(output)

    // text box to allow the user to send messages
    let input = new TextBox(Dock = DockStyle.Bottom, Multiline = true)
    form.Controls.Add(input)

    // create a new tcp client to handle the network connections
    let tc = new TcpClient()
    tc.Connect("localhost", 4242)

    // loop that handles reading from the tcp client
    let load() =
        let run() =
            let sr = new StreamReader(tc.GetStream())
            while(true) do
                let text = sr.ReadLine()
                if text <> null && text <> "" then
                    // we need to invoke back to the "gui thread"
                    // to be able to safely interact with the controls
                    form.Invoke(new MethodInvoker(fun () ->
                        output.AppendText(text + Environment.NewLine)
                        output.SelectionStart <- output.Text.Length))
                    |> ignore
```

```
        // create a new thread to run this loop
        let t = new Thread(new ThreadStart(run))
        t.Start()

    // start the loop that handles reading from the tcp client
    // when the form has loaded
    form.Load.Add(fun _ -> load())

    let sw = new StreamWriter(tc.GetStream())

    // handles the key up event - if the user has entered a line
    // of text then send the message to the server
    let keyUp () =
        if(input.Lines.Length > 1) then
            let text = input.Text
            if (text <> null && text <> "") then
                try
                    sw.WriteLine(text)
                    sw.Flush()
                with err ->
                    MessageBox.Show(sprintf "Server error\n\n%O" err)
                    |> ignore
                input.Text <- ""

    // wire up the key up event handler
    input.KeyUp.Add(fun _ -> keyUp ())

    // when the form closes it's necessary to explicitly exit the app
    // as there are other threads running in the back ground
    form.Closing.Add(fun _ ->
        Application.Exit()
        Environment.Exit(0))

    // return the form to the top level
    form

// show the form and start the apps event loop
[<STAThread>]
do Application.Run(form)
```

Executing the preceding code produces the client-server application shown in Figure 11-2.

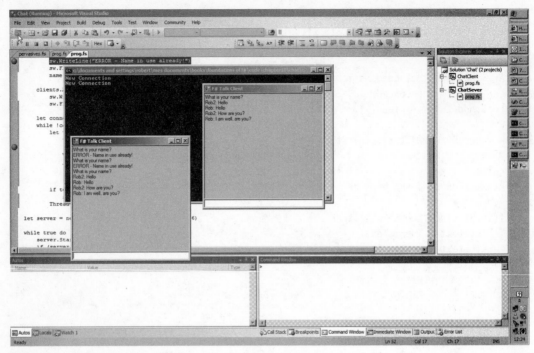

Figure 11-2. *The chat client-server application*

Now you'll look at how the client in Listing 11-2 works. The first portion of code in the client is taken up with initializing various aspects of the form; this is not of interest to you at the moment, although you can look up the details of how WinForms applications work in Chapter 8. The first part of Listing 11-2 that is relevant to TCP/IP sockets programming occurs when you connect to the server. You do this by creating a new instance of the TcpClient class and calling its Connect method:

```
let tc = new TcpClient()
tc.Connect("localhost", 4242)
```

In this example, you specify localhost, which is the local computer, and port 4242, which is the same port on which the server is listening. In a more realistic example, you'd probably give the DNS name of the server or allow the user to give the DNS name, but localhost is good because it allows you to run the sample on one computer easily.

The function that drives reading data from the server is the load function. You attach this to the form's Load event; to ensure this executes after the form is loaded and initialized properly, you need to interact with the form's controls:

```
temp.Load.Add(fun _ -> load())
```

To ensure that you read all the data coming from the server in a timely manner, you create a new thread to read all incoming requests. To do this, you define the function run, which you then use to start a new thread:

```
let t = new Thread(new ThreadStart(run))
t.Start()
```

Within the definition of run, you begin by creating a StreamReader to read text from the connection. Next, you loop infinitely, so the thread does not exit and continuously reads from the connection. When you find data, you must use the form's Invoke method to update the form; you need to do this because you cannot update the form from a thread other than the one on which it was created:

```
temp.Invoke(new MethodInvoker(fun () ->
    output.AppendText(text + Environment.NewLine)
    output.SelectionStart <- output.Text.Length))
```

The other part of the client that is functionally important is that it lets you write messages to the server. You do this in the keyUp function, which is attached to the input text box's KeyUp event. The code fires every time a key is pressed in the text box:

```
input.KeyUp.Add(fun _ -> keyUp ())
```

The implementation of the keyUp function is fairly straightforward: if you find that there is more than one line—which means the Enter key has been pressed—you send any available text across the wire and clear the text box.

Now that you know how to implement both the client and server, it's time to take a look at a few general points about the application. In both Listings 11-1 and 11-2, you called Flush() after each network operation. Otherwise, the information won't be sent across the network until the stream cache fills up, which leads to one user having to type many messages before they appear on the other user's screen.

This approach has several problems, particularly on the server side. Allocating a thread for each incoming client ensures a good response to each client; as the number of client connections grows, so too does the amount of context switching needed for the threads, and the overall performance of the server will decrease. Also, each client requires its own thread, so the maximum number of clients is limited by the maximum number of threads a process can contain. Although you can solve these problems, it's often easier to use one of the more abstract protocols discussed in the next section.

Using HTTP

The Web uses Hypertext Transfer Protocol (HTTP) to communicate, typically with web browsers, but you might want to make web requests from a script or a program for several reasons. For example, you might use this to aggregate site content through RSS or Atom feeds.

To make an HTTP request, you use the static method Create from the System.Net.WebRequest class. This creates a WebRequest object that represents a request to the uniform resource locator (URL, an address used to address a resource on a network uniquely) that was passed to the Create method. You then use the GetResponse method to get the server's response to your request, which is represented by the System.Net.WebResponse class.

The following example (Listing 11-3) illustrates how to call an RSS on the BBC's web site. The core of the example is the function getUrlAsXml, which does the work of retrieving the data from the URL and loading the data into an XmlDocument. The rest of the example illustrates the kind of post-processing you might want to do on the data; in this case, it displays the title of each item on the console, allowing users to choose which item to display.

Listing 11-3. *Using HTTP*

```
open System
open System.Diagnostics
open System.Net
open System.Xml

/// makes a http request to the given url
let getUrlAsXml (url: string) =
    let request = WebRequest.Create(url)
    let response = request.GetResponse()
    let stream = response.GetResponseStream()
    let xml = new XmlDocument()
    xml.Load(stream)
    xml

/// the url we interested in
let url = "http://newsrss.bbc.co.uk/rss/newsonline_uk_edition/sci/tech/rss.xml"

/// main application function
let main() =
    // read the rss fead
    let xml = getUrlAsXml url

    // write out the tiles of all the news items
    let nodes = xml.SelectNodes("/rss/channel/item/title")
    for i in 0 .. (nodes.Count - 1) do
        printf "%i. %s\r\n" (i + 1) (nodes.[i].InnerText)

    // read the number the user wants from the console
    let item = int(Console.ReadLine())

    // find the new url
    let newUrl =
        let xpath = sprintf "/rss/channel/item[%i]/link" item
        let node = xml.SelectSingleNode(xpath)
        node.InnerText

    // start the url using the shell, this automaticall opens
    // the default browser
    let procStart = new ProcessStartInfo(UseShellExecute = true,
                                         FileName = newUrl)
    let proc = new Process(StartInfo = procStart)
    proc.Start() |> ignore

do main()
```

The results of this example at the time of writing were as follows (your results will vary):

```
1. Five-step check for nano safety
2. Neanderthal DNA secrets unlocked
3. Stem cells 'treat muscle disease'
4. World Cup site threat to swallows
5. Clues to pandemic bird flu found
6. Mice star as Olympic food tasters
7. Climate bill sets carbon target
8. Physics promises wireless power
9. Heart 'can carry out own repairs'
10. Average European 'is overweight'
11. Contact lost with Mars spacecraft
12. Air guitar T-shirt rocks for real
13. Chocolate 'cuts blood clot risk'
14. Case for trawl ban 'overwhelming'
15. UN chief issues climate warning
16. Japanese begin annual whale hunt
17. Roman ship thrills archaeologists
18. Study hopeful for world's forests
```

Using HTTP with Google Spreadsheets

Because of its simplicity and its platform independence exposing data by HTTP and XML is one of the most popular ways to expose data publicly across the Internet. You can access a surprising amount of data using only HTTP and some XML processing. A useful application of this is accessing Google Spreadsheets that have been published by their owners. You can see how to access Google Spreadsheets in Listing 11-4.

■**Note** The spreadsheet you'll access comes from the Guardian Data Store, which publishes many UK and world statics via Google Spreadsheets. You can find this extremely useful resource at: http://www.guardian.co.uk/data-store.

Listing 11-4. *Using HTTP to Access Google Spreadsheets*

```
open System
open System.IO
open System.Net
open System.Xml
open System.Xml.XPath
```

```
// some namespace information for the XML
let namespaces =
    [ "at", "http://www.w3.org/2005/Atom";
      "openSearch", "http://a9.com/-/spec/opensearchrss/1.0/";
      "gsx", "http://schemas.google.com/spreadsheets/2006/extended" ]

// read the XML and process it into a matrix of strings
let queryGoogleSpreadSheet (xdoc: XmlDocument) xpath columnNames =
    let nav = xdoc.CreateNavigator()
    let mngr = new XmlNamespaceManager(new NameTable())
    do List.iter (fun (prefix, url) -> mngr.AddNamespace(prefix, url)) namespaces
    let xpath = nav.Compile(xpath)
    do xpath.SetContext(mngr)
    let iter = nav.Select(xpath)
    seq { for x in iter ->
            let x  = x :?> XPathNavigator
            let getValue nodename =
                let node = x.SelectSingleNode(nodename, mngr)
                node.Value
            Seq.map getValue columnNames }

// read the spreadsheet from its web address
let getGoogleSpreadSheet (url: string) columnNames =
    let req = WebRequest.Create(url)
    use resp = req.GetResponse()
    use stream = resp.GetResponseStream()
    let xdoc = new XmlDocument()
    xdoc.Load(stream)
    queryGoogleSpreadSheet xdoc "/at:feed/at:entry" columnNames

// a location to hold the information we're interested in
type Location =
    { Country: string;
      NameValuesList: seq<string * option<float>> }

// creates a location from the row names
let createLocation names row  =
    let country = Seq.head row
    let row = Seq.skip 1 row
    let tryParse s =
        let success,res = Double.TryParse s
        if success then Some res else None
    let values = Seq.map tryParse row
    { Country = country;
      NameValuesList = Seq.zip names values }
```

```
// get the data and process it into records
let getDataAndProcess url colNames =
    // get the names of the columns we want
    let cols = Seq.map fst colNames
    // get the data
    let data = getGoogleSpreadSheet url cols

    // get the readable names of the columns
    let names = Seq.skip 1 (Seq.map snd colNames)
    // create strongly typed records from the data
    Seq.map (createLocation names) data

// function to create a spreadsheets URL from it's key
let makeUrl = Printf.sprintf "http://spreadsheets.google.com/feeds/
list/%s/od6/public/values"

let main() =
    // the key of the spreadsheet we're interested in
    let sheatKey = "phNtm3LmDZEP61UU2eSN1YA"
    // list of column names we're interested in
    let cols =
        [ "gsx:location", "";
          "gsx:hospitalbedsper10000population",
            "Hospital beds per 1000";
          "gsx:nursingandmidwiferypersonneldensityper10000population",
            "Nursing and Midwifery Personnel per 1000" ];
    // get the data
    let data = getDataAndProcess (makeUrl sheatKey) cols
    // print the data
    Seq.iter (printfn "%A") data

do main()
```

When you compile execute the results of the preceding code, you get the following results:

```
...
{Country = "Sweden";
 NameValuesList =
  seq
    [("Hospital beds per 1000", null);
     ("Nursing and Midwifery Personnel per 1000", Some 109.0)];}
```

```
{Country = "Switzerland";
 NameValuesList =
  seq
    [("Hospital beds per 1000", Some 57.0);
     ("Nursing and Midwifery Personnel per 1000", Some 110.0)];}
...
```

The important thing to notice about this example is that the method you use to retrieve the data changes little; at the core of the example, you find the same few lines of code for making the HTTP request and retrieving an XML document from it:

```
let req = WebRequest.Create(url)
use resp = req.GetResponse()
use stream = resp.GetResponseStream()
let xdoc = new XmlDocument()
xdoc.Load(stream)
```

Most of the rest of the example treats the XML data that's returned.

Using HTTP Posts

You've seen a couple of different things you can retrieve using the HTTP protocol; next, you'll learn how to use HTTP to make updates. To allow clients to send data, the HTTP protocol supports the POST verb, which allows the client to send data as part of the HTTP request body.

Your next step is to update your status in the popular social networking tool *twitter*, which you can find at http://twitter.com (see Listing 11-5).

Listing 11-5. *Using a HTTP POST to Update a twitter Status*

```
open System
open System.Net
open System.Text


let postTweet username password tweet =
    // create a token to authenticate
    let (token: string) = username + ":" + password
    let user = Convert.ToBase64String(Encoding.UTF8.GetBytes(token))
    // determine what we want to upload as a status
    let bytes = Encoding.ASCII.GetBytes("status=" + tweet)
    // connect with the update page
    let request =
        WebRequest.Create("http://twitter.com/statuses/update.xml",
                          Method = "POST",
                          ContentLength = Convert.ToInt64(bytes.Length),
                          ContentType = "application/x-www-form-urlencoded")
                          :?> HttpWebRequest
```

```
request.ServicePoint.Expect100Continue <- false

// set the authorisation levels
request.Headers.Add("Authorization", "Basic " + user)

// set up the stream
use reqStream = request.GetRequestStream()
reqStream.Write(bytes, 0, bytes.Length)
reqStream.Close()
```

```
postTweet "you" "xxx" "Test tweet from F# interactive"
```

Posting data via HTTP is not too different from retrieving data. The main difference is that, when you create the WebRequest, you have to configure a couple of properties differently, such as when setting the Method, ContentLength, and ContentType properties. You want only the actual user to be able to update his status, so you need to add authentication token to the HTTP headers:

```
// set the authorisation levels
request.Headers.Add("Authorization", "Basic " + user)
```

Finally, you need to write the data to the request stream. This is very straightforward; it's just a matter of writing to the data stream:

```
use reqStream = request.GetRequestStream()
reqStream.Write(bytes, 0, bytes.Length)
reqStream.Close()
```

Perhaps the most interesting aspect of this listing is that you can use it in F# interactive. If you are a twitter fan, you can update your twitter status without having to leave your programming environment.

Using HTTP Asynchronously

So far you've concentrated on retrieving a single document via HTTP or making one update at time. In these cases, it doesn't make much sense to use the asynchronous programming model. However, you'll often want to make many HTTP requests at once, so that you can retrieve and aggregate data from multiple data sources. In these situations, using the F#'s asynchronous workflows that you first encountered in Chapter 10's Asynchronous Programming section can seriously improve your application's performance. In fact, you can probably expect to see a bigger performance pay off than when working with the local disk, as you did in Chapter 10, because network I/O is generally slower that the local disk. This is because the asynchronous programming model allows us to wait on I/O without blocking a thread, which means the thread can carry on and do other work. Essentially this allows you to wait on multiple I/O completions in parallel. As you parallelize waiting time, you can expect the biggest speed increase from high latency services.

Imagine you want to retrieve a list of all your friends, then retrieve a list of all of their friends from the popular social network, twitter. Perhaps you want to do some analysis of this network, and try to find other people that you might know among the friends of your friends. Listing 11-6 shows you how to do this.

Listing 11-6. *Using HTTP Asynchronously*

```
open System
open System.IO
open System.Net
open System.Text
open System.Xml
open System.Xml.XPath
open System.Globalization
open Microsoft.FSharp.Control.WebExtensions

// a record to hold details about a tweeter
type Tweeter =
    { Id: int;
      Name: string;
      ScreenName: string;
      PictureUrl: string; }

// turn the xml stream into a strongly typed list of tweeters
let treatTweeter name (stream: Stream) =
    printfn "Processing: %s" name
    let xdoc = new XPathDocument(stream)
    let nav = xdoc.CreateNavigator()
    let xpath = nav.Compile("users/user")
    let iter = nav.Select(xpath)
    let items =
        [ for x in iter ->
            let x  = x :?> XPathNavigator
            let getValue (nodename: string) =
                let node = x.SelectSingleNode(nodename)
                node.Value
            { Id = Int32.Parse(getValue "id");
              Name = getValue "name";
              ScreenName = getValue "screen_name";
              PictureUrl = getValue "profile_image_url"; } ]
    name, items

// function to make the urls of
let friendsUrl = Printf.sprintf "http://twitter.com/statuses/friends/%s.xml"

// asynchronously get the friends of the tweeter
let getTweetters name =
  async { do printfn "Starting request for: %s" name
          let req = WebRequest.Create(friendsUrl name)
          use! resp = req.AsyncGetResponse()
          use stream = resp.GetResponseStream()
          return treatTweeter name stream }
```

```
// from a single twitter username get all the friends of friends of that user
let getAllFriendsOfFriends name =
    // run the first user synchronously
    let name, friends = Async.RunSynchronously (getTweetters name)
    // only take the first 99 users since we're only allowed 100
    // requests an hour from the twitter servers
    let length = min 99 (Seq.length friends)
    // get the screen name of all the twitter friends
    let friendsScreenName =
        Seq.take length (Seq.map (fun { ScreenName = sn } -> sn) friends)
    // create asynchronous workflows to get friends of friends
    let friendsOfFriendsWorkflows =
        Seq.map (fun sn -> getTweetters sn) friendsScreenName
    // run this in parallel
    let fof = Async.RunSynchronously (Async.Parallel friendsOfFriendsWorkflows)
    // return the friend list and the friend of friend list
    friendsScreenName, fof
```

As you can see, the asynchronous part is not too different from its synchronous counterpart. The code needs to be wrapped in the async { ... } workflow, and you need to use an explanation mark (!) when you make the asynchronous call; however, the code is unchanged apart from that:

```
let getTweetters name =
  async { let req = WebRequest.Create(friendsUrl name)
          use! resp = req.AsyncGetResponse()
          use stream = resp.GetResponseStream()
          return treatTweeter name stream }
```

When you get the original list of friends, you need to execute a single workflow. Because you need to wait for the result of this workflow, you're effectively executing this synchronously. You use the Async.Run function to execute a workflow and wait for the result:

```
let name, friends = Async.Run (getTweetters name)
```

The other important bit is how you make the calls in parallel. This is simple: once you obtain the original list of friends, you can create a list of asynchronous workflows that are ready to be executed:

```
// create asynchronous workflows to get friends of friends
let friendsOfFriendsWorkflows =
    Seq.map (fun sn -> getTweetters sn) friendsScreenName
```

Once you have this list, you can use Async.Parallel to execute the workflows in parallel and then Async.Run to get the result:

```
// run this in parallel
let fof = Async.Run (Async.Parallel friendsOfFriendsWorkflows)
```

Executing all these requests in parallel gives a performance boost because the server can handle many of the requests in parallel, which will reduce the time you need to wait for a response.

Creating Web Services

Web services are based on standards (typically SOAP) that allow applications to exchange data using HTTP. Web services consist of web methods; that is, methods that have been exposed for execution over a network. You can think of this as somewhat similar to F# functions because a web method has a name, can have parameters, and returns a result. The parameters and results are described in metadata that the web services also exposes, so clients know how to call it.

Creating web services in F# is straightforward. In fact, when creating a web service, the main problem is probably exposing code through a web server. Web servers receive requests for files in the form of a URL; you must tell the web server which .NET class this request will map to. Typically you use an .asmx file to run a specific F# class that will respond to the web service request if the web server gets a request for the .asmx file. The exact way of doing this varies depending on your development environment and the web server that you host your services on.

Visual Studio comes with a built-in web server, so creating a new web site is a simple matter of selecting File ➤ New ➤ Web Site and then choosing the location for the web site. This site will run only those pages written in C# or Visual Basic .NET, so you need to add an F# project to the solution and then manually alter the solution file so that it lives inside the web site's directory. This is easier than it sounds. You just need to copy the .fsproj file to the website directory, open the .sln file in Notepad, and alter the path to the .fsproj file. To help you do this, Figure 11-3 shows the .sln file before and after the edit, with the original on the left-hand side.

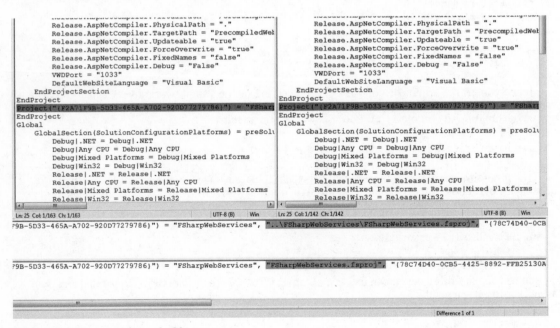

Figure 11-3. *How to edit a .sln file*

After you do this, you need to configure the project file to output a library and write this to a bin subdirectory. This might seem like a lot of effort, but afterward you will be able to press F5 to make your project will compile and run.

If you don't have Visual Studio, then the next best thing to do is to host the site in Internet Information Services (IIS), Microsoft's own web server for Windows. In some ways, this is easier than hosting your site in Visual Studio, but this approach doesn't provide the convenience of letting you execute your code once it is complete. To host your code in IIS, you need to create an IIS virtual directory with a subdirectory called bin. You then need to copy your .asmx pages and your web.config file to the virtual directory.

The service itself is straightforward. You should make this service a class that derives from System.Web.Service.WebService and has a parameterless constructor. You should also mark it with the System.Web.Service.WebServiceAttribute. If you intend to expose your web service publicly, you must set the attribute's Namespace. The default is http://tempuri.org; even if you don't intend to expose your service publicly, setting this attribute will lead to more manageable web services. You can make the members of the class web methods by marking them with System.Web.Service.WebServiceAttribute. This too has a number of useful properties; it's particularly worth setting the Description property, so clients of your service know what they're getting.

Listing 11-7 shows the definition of a simple web service. You create a type Service with one member, Addition, that must have its parameters in the tuple style.

Listing 11-7. *Creating a Simple Web Service*

```
namespace Strangelights.WebServices

open System.Web.Services

[<WebService(Namespace =
    "http://strangelights.com/FSharp/Foundations/WebServices")>]
type Service =
    inherit WebService
    new() = {}
    [<WebMethod(Description = "Perfoms integer addition")>]
    member x.Addition ((x : int), (y : int)) = x + y
```

To enable the web server to find the web service, you need to create an .asmx file. An example .asmx file follows; the most important thing is to set the Class attribute to the name of the class that is your service. When the server receives a request for this file, it invokes the appropriate service:

```
<%@ WebService Class="Strangelights.WebServices.Service" %>
```

If you run the service locally, you can test the service by opening it in a browser. In a browser, you see the interface shown in Figure 11-4, which allows you to give values for the web service's parameters and then invoke the service.

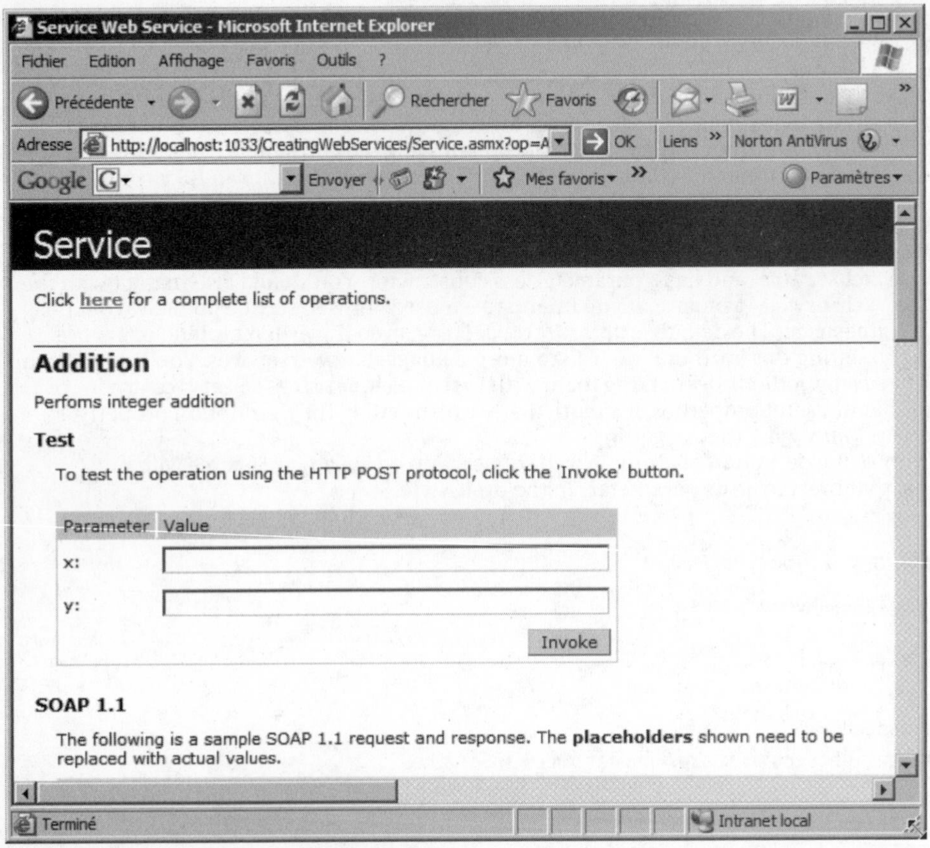

Figure 11-4. *Invoking a local web service*

Invoking this service with the arguments 46 and 28 produces the following XML:

```
<?xml version="1.0" encoding="utf-8" ?>

<int xmlns="http://strangelights.com/FSharp/Foundations/WebServices">74</int>
```

It is generally not efficient to send small amounts of data across the network because you must send a certain amount of metadata with each request. In general, it is better to build applications that are not "chatty"; that is, applications should make one big request, rather than repeatedly make a lot of small ones.

A web service will attempt to serialize any .NET object that is returned from one for its methods to XML; however, the results can be a little unpredictable, and the resulting XML data might not contain all the fields you expect it to, which can make it difficult to work with from other programming languages. To avoid this, it's best to use XSD schemas to define the objects that you want to pass across the web service. An XSD schema is a type of XML document that describes the structure of an XML document, stating things such as which fields are mandatory and the order in which the fields should appear. These schemes then become part of the web service definition, and anyone using the web service will be able to understand what field she can expect from the web service. This is preferable to defining a web service that has a single field containing binary or hexadecimal data because the user of the web service has a much better chance of understanding what the results mean.

Although it's possible to define your own XML schemas, Visual Studio has several graphical modes and a text-based mode for creating them; it's also possible to build on the work of others in this field—many predefined schemas are available for download on the Web. For instance, the example you'll look at next uses RNAML, a schema you can find at http://www-lbit.iro.umontreal.ca/rnaml/; it is one attempt to provide a schema for people who want to exchange information on RNA (ribonucleic acid, a substance studied by molecular biologist) in XML. Once you download the schema from the site, you can turn this into a .NET representation of the schema using the command-line tool, xsd.exe. This tool produces C# classes that represent the XML data; typically, each tag in the XML becomes a class in .NET. You can then compile this C# file into a .NET assembly and use it from F# like any other .NET library. The complete command line you would use looks like this: xsd rnaml.xsd /classes. You need to rename the downloaded schema file from rnaml.xml to rnaml.xsd for the tool to work correctly.

The following example shows you how to create a web service that returns the structure of a yeast RNA molecule. This is an abridged version of the sequence sample available from the RNAML web site (http://www-lbit.iro.umontreal.ca/rnaml/). As before, you need an .asmx file to link the file requested to the .NET type that will handle the request:

```
<%@ WebService Class="Strangelights.WebServices.DnaWebService" %>
```

Listing 11-8 shows the web service; you will notice how the basic components of the service are the same as your simple web service. You have a class definition as before, marked with the WebService attribute. The code that does the work is the method definition GetYeastMolecule; here you create and populate various objects that are defined in the library you created from the rnaml.xsd file, such as a molecule object and a sequence object.

Listing 11-8. *Creating a Web Service Returning the Definition of an RNA Molecule*

```
namespace Strangelights.WebServices

open System.Web.Services

// the web service class
[<WebService(Namespace =
    "http://strangelights.com/FSharp/Foundations/DnaWebService")>]
type DnaWebService() =
    inherit WebService()

    // the web method
    [<WebMethod(Description = "Gets a representation of a yeast molecule")>]
    member x.GetYeastMolecule () =
        // the code that populates the yeast xml structure
        let tax = new taxonomy(domain = "Eukaryota", kingdom = "Fungi",
                               phylum = "Ascomycota", ``class`` = "Saccharomycetes",
                               order = "Saccharomycetales",
                               family = "Saccharomycetaceae",
                               genus = "Saccharomyces",
                               species = "Saccharomyces cerevisiae")
```

```
        let id = new identity(name = "Saccharomyces cerevisiae tRNA-Phe",
                              taxonomy = tax)
        let yeast = new molecule(id = "Yeast-tRNA-Phe", identity = id)
        let numRange1 = new numberingrange(start = "1", Item = "10")
        let numRange2 = new numberingrange(start = "11", Item = "66")
        let numSys = new numberingsystem(id="natural", usedinfile=true)
        numSys.Items <- [|box numRange1; box numRange2|]
        let seqData = new seqdata()
        seqData.Value <- "GCGGAUUUAG CUCAGUUGGG AGAGCGCCAG ACUGAAGAUC
          UGGAGGUCCU GUGUUCGAUC CACAGAAUUC GCACCA"
        let seq = new sequence(numberingsystem = [|numSys|], seqdata = seqData)
        yeast.sequence <- [|seq|]
        yeast
```

Again, the same simple, web-based testing option is available; executing the preceding code produces the following XML:

```
<?xml version="1.0" encoding="utf-8"?>
<molecule xmlns:xsi="http://www.w3.org/2001/XMLSchema-instance"
  xmlns:xsd="http://www.w3.org/2001/XMLSchema" id="Yeast-tRNA-Phe">
  <identity>
    <name>Saccharomyces cerevisiae tRNA-Phe</name>
    <taxonomy>
      <domain>Eukaryota</domain>
      <kingdom>Fungi</kingdom>
      <phylum>Ascomycota</phylum>
      <class>Saccharomycetes</class>
      <order>Saccharomycetales</order>
      <family>Saccharomycetaceae</family>
      <genus>Saccharomyces</genus>
      <species>Saccharomyces cerevisiae</species>
    </taxonomy>
  </identity>
  <sequence>
    <numbering-system id="natural" used-in-file="true">
      <numbering-range>
        <start>1</start>
        <end>10</end>
      </numbering-range>
      <numbering-range>
        <start>11</start>
        <end>66</end>
      </numbering-range>
    </numbering-system>
```

```
  <seq-data>GCGGAUUUAG CUCAGUUGGG AGAGCGCCAG ACUGAAGAUC
        UGGAGGUCCU GUGUUCGAUC CACAGAAUUC GCACCA</seq-data>
  </sequence>
</molecule>
```

This example returns a static unchanging XML document; it is not particularly realistic, but it is easy to see the potential of this sort of application. Instead of using a GetYeastMolecule method, a more realistic approach would be to provide a GetMolecule method that takes a name of a molecule, looks up the details of the molecule in a database, and returns the resulting molecule data. The advantage is that a program running on almost any platform can work with the resulting data; in this case, the example site already provides an API for working with the data in C++ and Java. You've already seed that working with this kind of data in F# is straightforward. Of course, this technology is not limited to molecular biology; you can find XML schemas becoming available for almost every field of science, engineering, math, and finance.

You can use several methods to secure web services such as these. Securing them lets you ensure that they can be accessed by only a subset of users or that the information traveling over the network is encrypted or signed. One option is to upgrade to Windows Communication Foundation (WCF), which is similar to web services but offers more flexibility in this area; you'll learn more about this topic in the next section. A second option is to configure your web server to handle these security requirements for you.

Windows Communication Foundation

It is the goal of the Windows Communication Framework (WCF) to provide a unified model for creating distributed applications. The idea is that you create a service, something similar to a web service, that contains the functionality you want to expose. You can then expose this service in a variety of different ways. For example, web services always pass XML messages, but you can configure WCF services to pass binary data or XML messages. Further, you can host WFC services in any process, rather than only on a web server. This means you can create a desktop application that listens for incoming messages without having to install a web server on the desktop.

■**Note** WCF is part of the .NET Framework 3, a group of APIs that were released at the same time as Windows Vista and come already installed on that operating system. You can also download them from www.microsoft.com and install them on Windows XP and Windows Server 2003 (http://is.gd/4URUN). The protocols that WCF uses are based on a group of specifications that extend web services and are sometimes referred to as the WS-* protocols because each protocol is generally given a name prefixed by WS-, such as WS-Security or WS-Reliability. Each of these protocols either has been standardized or is currently being put forward for standardization. To develop with WCF, you need to download the .NET Framework 3.5 SDK from http://is.gd/4US4W.

In the first example (see Listing 11-9), you'll build a simple WCF service that is hosted on a web server and looks like a simple web service. You'll refine this service to show off some of the interesting features of WCF. To create a WCF service that is hosted in a web server, you follow the same steps discussed in the "Creating Web Services" section, except that hosting in Apache on Linux is not possible because WCF relies on some features that are specific to Windows.

Listing 11-9. *Creating a Simple WCF Service*

```
namespace Strangelights.Services
open System.ServiceModel

// the service contract
[<ServiceContract
    (Namespace =
        "http://strangelights.com/FSharp/Foundations/WCFServices")>]
type IGreetingService =
    [<OperationContract>]
    abstract Greet : name:string -> string

// the service implementation
type GreetingService() =
    interface IGreetingService with
        member x.Greet(name)  = "Hello: " + name
```

You define this service in two parts: an interface that describes the service contract and an implementation of that contract. You define all WCF services this way. This interface is named IGreetingService and exposes one function, Greet. To make it a valid WCF contract, you mark the interface with System.ServiceModel.ServiceContractAttribute, which should contain a namespace for the service. Use OperationContractAttribute to mark each function within the interface that you want the service to expose. Each parameter must have a name. It's possible to create interfaces in F# where the parameters don't have names, but those are defined by their types. You can compile an interface with parameterless functions that acts as a WCF contract, but you'll receive an error when you invoke the service because the parameter names are used (via reflection) in the WCF framework to create the data that you send across the wire. The class GreetingService provides the implementation of the contract. You offer a greeting by appending "hello: " to whatever name is passed.

To integrate the service with the web server, you need to create a .svc file, which plays a similar role to the web service's .asmx file. This tells the web server what type it should use to handle the service request. You can see an example of an .svc in the service that follows. Note that you see the complete file in this example—such files are typically only one line long. The most important attribute in the .svc file is the Service attribute that tells the web server which type it should use:

```
<% @ServiceHost Debug="true" Service="Strangelights.Services.GreetingService" %>
```

Finally, you must configure the service. Because WCF offers a choice of protocols, you use the configuration file to tell it which one to use. The configuration file in Listing 11-10 shows a configuration file that you might use to configure your service. The service element defines two endpoints; these are the protocols that a client can use to talk to this service. One of the endpoints is a standard web service HTTP binding, and the other is a metadata exchange binding; this allows the service to expose metadata about itself that will tell any potential client how it should talk to the service. This is the endpoint you'll use when you create the client proxy.

Listing 11-10. *The Configuration File for a WCF Service*

```xml
<configuration xmlns="http://schemas.microsoft.com/.NetConfiguration/v2.0">
  <system.serviceModel>
    <services>
      <service
        name="Strangelights.Services.GreetingService"
        behaviorConfiguration="MyServiceTypeBehaviors">

        <endpoint
          contract="Strangelights.Services.IGreetingService"
          binding="wsHttpBinding"/>

        <endpoint
          contract="Strangelights.Services.IGreetingService"
          binding="mexHttpBinding" address="mex"/>
      </service>
    </services>
    <behaviors>
      <serviceBehaviors>
        <behavior name="MyServiceTypeBehaviors" >
          <serviceDebug includeExceptionDetailInFaults="true" />
          <serviceMetadata httpGetEnabled="true" />
        </behavior>
      </serviceBehaviors>
    </behaviors>
  </system.serviceModel>

  <system.web>
    <compilation debug="true"/>
  </system.web>

</configuration>
```

To create a client for the service, you use the utility SvcUtil.exe, which has a similar purpose to the utility wsdl.exe that I discussed in the "Creating Web Services" section. To use SvcUtil.exe to create a proxy for your service, you need to use the following command line, taking care to adapt the URL appropriately:

```
svcutil.exe http://localhost:1033/WCFService/Service.svc?wsdl
```

This generates a C# proxy file that you can compile into a .NET assembly that you can use from F#. It also generates a .config file, which you can use to configure any client application.

Using the proxy is straightforward. Once you add a reference to the proxy .dll file—simply create an instance of the proxy and call its Greet method with the appropriate arguments. Listing 11-11 shows an example of a proxy; because it is important to call the proxy's Dispose method, you wrap it in the using function.

Listing 11-11. *Invoking the WCF Service*

```
open System

let main() =
    use client = new GreetingServiceClient()
    while true do
        printfn "%s" (client.Greet("Rob"))
        Console.ReadLine() |> ignore
    use client = new GreetingServiceClient()
    printfn "%s" (client.Greet("Rob"))
    Console.ReadLine() |> ignore

do main()
```

Listing 11-12 is an example of a generated configuration file that has had certain things removed from it to make the sample run more smoothly. The security settings have been removed because these can cause the example to fail if it is run on a computer disconnected from its domain controller (a common case for programmers on the move!). Also, one of the two generated endpoints has been removed, so there is no need to specify an endpoint in the code.

Listing 11-12. *The Configuration File for Invoking the WCF Service*

```
<configuration>
    <system.serviceModel>
        <bindings>
            <wsHttpBinding>
                <binding name="WSHttpBinding_IGreetingService"
                    closeTimeout="00:01:00" openTimeout="00:01:00"
                    receiveTimeout="00:10:00" sendTimeout="00:01:00"
                    bypassProxyOnLocal="false" transactionFlow="false"
                    hostNameComparisonMode="StrongWildcard"
                    maxBufferPoolSize="524288"
                    maxReceivedMessageSize="65536" messageEncoding="Text"
                    textEncoding="utf-8" useDefaultWebProxy="true"
                    allowCookies="false">
                    <readerQuotas maxDepth="32"
                        maxStringContentLength="8192"
                        maxArrayLength="16384"
                        maxBytesPerRead="4096"
                        maxNameTableCharCount="16384" />
                    <reliableSession ordered="true"
                        inactivityTimeout="00:10:00"
                        enabled="false" />
                </binding>
            </wsHttpBinding>
        </bindings>
```

```
        <client>
            <endpoint address="http://localhost:8080/service"
                binding="wsHttpBinding"
                bindingConfiguration="WSHttpBinding_IGreetingService"
                contract="IGreetingService"
                name="WSHttpBinding_IGreetingService">
            </endpoint>
        </client>
    </system.serviceModel>
</configuration>
```

Executing the code in Listing 11-11 produces the following result:

```
Hello: Rob
```

Hosting WCF Services

To me, the most exciting aspect of WCF is the ability to host a service in any program without the need for a web server. One possibility this opens up: You can create services where the implementation can be changed dynamically because you host the services in fsi.exe. You need to make some modifications to the previous sample to get it running in fsi.exe, but these modifications are surprisingly straightforward.

Listing 11-13 shows a modified version of Listing 11-8 that can run in fsi.exe.

Listing 11-13. *A Service Designed to be Hosted in F# Interactive*

```
#I @"C:\Program Files\Reference Assemblies\Microsoft\Framework\v3.0";;
#r "System.ServiceModel.dll";;
open System
open System.ServiceModel
open System.Runtime.Serialization

// a range of greetings that could be used
let mutable f = (fun x -> "Hello: " + x)
f <- (fun x -> "Bonjour: " + x)
f <- (fun x -> "Goedendag: " + x)

// the service contract
[<ServiceContract
    (Namespace =
        "http://strangelights.com/FSharp/Foundations/WCFServices")>]
type IGreetingService =
    [<OperationContract>]
    abstract Greet : name:string -> string
```

```
// the service implementation
type GreetingService() =
    interface IGreetingService with
        member x.Greet( name ) = f name

// create a service host
let myServiceHost =
    let baseAddress = new Uri("http://localhost:8080/service")

    let temp = new ServiceHost(typeof<GreetingService>, [|baseAddress|])

    let binding =
        let temp =
            new WSHttpBinding(Name = "binding1",
                                HostNameComparisonMode =
                                  HostNameComparisonMode.StrongWildcard,
                                TransactionFlow = false)
        temp.Security.Mode <- SecurityMode.Message
        temp.ReliableSession.Enabled <- false
        temp

    temp.AddServiceEndpoint(typeof<IGreetingService>, binding, baseAddress)
    |> ignore
    temp

// open the service host
myServiceHost.Open()
```

Notice that in Listing 11-13 the IGreetingService and GreetingService types are basically unchanged from Listing 11-9, except that you modify the GreetingService type to use a mutable function, so you can manipulate what it does at runtime. You then need to create a service host to do what the web server and web.config did in the previous example. You can see the web.config file in Listing 11-10 and the service itself in Listing 11-8. Note that myServiceHost contains a baseAddress, which the service will listen for a request on; and a binding, which controls which protocols are used. Finally, you call the myServiceHost's Open method to set the service listening.

Next you make an alteration to the client to call the service repeatedly, so you can see the service results change overtime (see Listing 11-14).

Listing 11-14. *A Client to Access the Service Hosted in F# Interactive*

```
let client = new GreetingServiceClient()
    while true do
        printfn "%s" (client.Greet("Rob"))
        Console.ReadLine() |> ignore
```

You also need to alter the client's `.config` file to point to the correct address:

```
<endpoint address="http://localhost:8080/service"
```

Doing these things lets you change the service dynamically (see Figure 11-5).

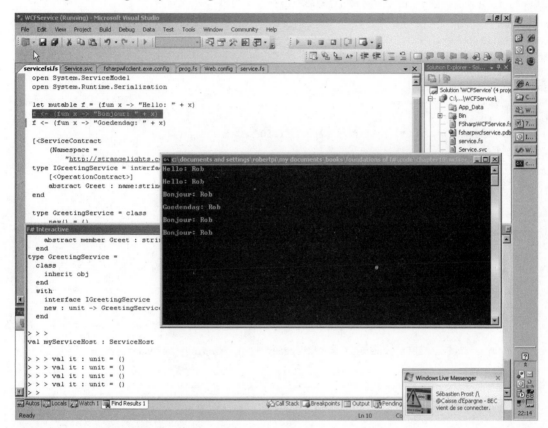

Figure 11-5. *Invoking a dynamic WCF service*

Another interesting reason to host services in a program: This approach enables you to create desktop applications that can listen for updates from some kind of central server. Traditionally, developers have used these kinds of applications to poll a central server; however, you should be aware that this can lead to a large amount of unnecessary network traffic if the polling is too frequent.

Listing 11-15 demonstrates how to do this. It shows a blank form that hosts a service that will listen to updates from a client; in this case, the update will be a background image to display. The service defines one function, ReceiveImage, which receives the binary data that makes up an image. The implementation of the service raises an event, newImgEvent, every time an image is received; this enables you to update the form every time a new image is received. Hooking the form up to the event is straightforward:

```
newImgEvent.Add(fun img -> form.BackgroundImage <- img)
```

You need to call the event's Add method and pass it a function that updates the form. Notice that the code required to host the service (that is, the code that defines myServiceHost) is unchanged from the previous example.

Listing 11-15. *A Windows Form with a Service Built In*

```
open System
open System.IO
open System.Drawing
open System.ServiceModel
open System.Windows.Forms

let myServiceHost =
    let baseAddress = new Uri("http://localhost:8080/service")

    let temp = new ServiceHost((type Service.ImageService), [|baseAddress|])

    let binding =
        let temp = new WSHttpBinding()
        temp.Name <- "binding1"
        temp.HostNameComparisonMode <-
            HostNameComparisonMode.StrongWildcard
        temp.Security.Mode <- SecurityMode.Message
        temp.ReliableSession.Enabled <- false
        temp.TransactionFlow <- false
        temp

    temp.AddServiceEndpoint((type Service.IImageService), binding, baseAddress)
    |> ignore
    temp

myServiceHost.Open()

let form = new Form()

Service.newImgEvent.Add(fun img -> form.BackgroundImage <- img)

[<STAThread>]
do Application.Run(form)
```

To create the client, you must first create a proxy, using the same technique that you used in Listing 11-11. You run the utility SvcUtil.exe by passing it the URL of the service; this creates a proxy in C# that you can compile into a .NET assembly and used from F#. In this case, you name the proxy ImageServiceClient. The definition of the client in Listing 11-16 might look a little complicated, but a lot of the code just lays out the form's controls or opens the image files. The interesting code comes right at the end, where you add a function to the Send button's click event. This code reads an image from disk and loads it into a byte array. This byte array is then passed to the proxy's ReceiveImage method.

Listing 11-16. *A Client That Sends Images to Its Server*

```
open System
open System.IO
open System.Windows.Forms

// create a form for sending images
let form =
    // create the form itself
    let temp = new Form(Width=272, Height=64)
    // text box for path to the image
    let imagePath = new TextBox(Top=8, Left=8, Width=128)
    // browse button to allow the user to search for files
    let browse = new Button(Top=8, Width=32, Left=8+imagePath.Right,
                            Text = "...")
    browse.Click.Add(fun _ ->
        let dialog = new OpenFileDialog()
        if dialog.ShowDialog() = DialogResult.OK then
            imagePath.Text <- dialog.FileName)

    // send button to send the image to the server
    let send = new Button(Top=8, Left=8+browse.Right, Text = "Send")
    send.Click.Add(fun _ ->
        // open and send the file
        let buffer = File.ReadAllBytes(imagePath.Text)
        let service = new ImageServiceClient()
        service.ReceiveImage(buffer))

    // add the controls and return the form
    temp.Controls.Add(imagePath)
    temp.Controls.Add(browse)
    temp.Controls.Add(send)
    temp

// show the form
[<STAThread>]
do Application.Run(form)
```

Figure 11-6 shows the example being executed; the user is about to select an image to send to the client.

Figure 11-6. *A WCF service hosted in a Windows form*

This is not quite the whole story for a desktop application that listens for updates. The client that sends out updates needs to know the services and desktop applications to which it should send updates. You can let the client know this by hard-coding the address of the service in the service. In the real world, you'd need to implement a service in the other direction as well. This service would tell the central client that a service is listening for updates; it would also alert the central client when a service stops. Then the central client would need to loop through all services that are listening for updates and push the data out to each one of them.

Summary

This chapter covered the main options for creating distributed applications in F#. You learned how combining F# with .NET libraries can help you concentrate on the key technical challenges of creating distributed applications. You also learned how you can use the features of F# to control the complexity of these applications. In the next chapter, you will look at language-oriented programming, a technique that has been tried and trusted by functional programmers for years, and one that can make a programmer's life significantly simpler.

CHAPTER 12

■ ■ ■

Language-Oriented Programming

In this chapter, you will begin by taking a look at what I mean by *language-oriented programming*, a term that has been used by many people to mean different things. I'll also briefly discuss its advantages and disadvantages. Next, you'll look at several different approaches to language-oriented programming in F#. These techniques include using F# literals to create *little languages* and using F# quotations. You'll spend the bulk of this chapter looking at examples where you create a language, then create an interpreter to execute that language. Finally, you'll take a more detailed look at how languages are executed, including a performance comparison of interpreted or compiled execution techniques.

What Is Language-Oriented Programming?

People use the term *language-oriented programming* to describe many different programming techniques, but the techniques they refer to tend to share a common theme. It's quite common for programmers to have to implement a predefined language; often this is because you need to extract structured data from information stored or received as string or XML data that conforms to this predefined language. The techniques introduced in this chapter will help you do this more reliably. Related to this is the idea of little languages, or *domain-specific languages* (DSLs); you might want to create a DSL when the best way to solve a problem is to create a custom language to describe the problem and then use this language to solve that problem. Functional programming has always had a strong relationship with language-oriented programming because functional programming languages generally have features that are well suited to creating parsers and compilers.

Data Structures as Little Languages

Taking advantage of language-oriented development doesn't necessarily mean writing your own parser or compiler. That said, you will learn how to create parsers in the next chapter; you can them combine such parsers with the techniques in this chapter to start building a simple compiler. You can accomplish a lot by creating data structures that describe *what* you want to do and then creating functions or modules that define *how* the structure should be interpreted.

You can create data structures that represent a program in just about any language, but F# lends itself well to this approach. F#'s literal lists and arrays are easy to define and require no bulky type annotations. Its union types allow you to create structures that express related concepts, but do not necessarily contain the same types of data. You can take advantage of this to build tree-like structures, which prove useful when creating languages. Finally, you can treat functions as values, so you can easily embed functions within data structures. This means F# expressions can become part of your language, usually as an action in response to some particular condition of the language.

Let's start by taking a look at a DSL predefined in the FSharp.PowerPack.dll. The Arg module allows users to build a command-line argument parser quickly. It does this by using F#'s union and list types to create a little language that is then interpreted by a number of functions provided in the Arg module.

The Arg module exposes a tuple type called argspec that consists of two strings and a union type called spec. The first string in the tuple specifies the name of the command-line argument. The second item in the tuple is the union-type spec, which specifies what the command-line argument is; for example, it specifies whether it is followed by a string value or just a flag? It also specifies what should be done if and when the command-line token is found. The final string in the tuple is a text description of what the flag does. This will be printed to the console in the case of a mistake in the command-line arguments. It also serves as a useful note to the programmer.

The Arg module exposes two functions for parsing arguments: parse, which parses the command passed in on the command line; and parse_argv, which requires that you pass the arguments directly to it. You should pass both functions a list of type argspec describing the command-line arguments expected, a function that will be passed all the command-line arguments not prefixed with -, and finally, a string to describe the usage.

The module also exposes a third function usage, which you can pass a list of type argspec and use to write out the usage directly.

The following example demonstrates how to build an argument parser in this manner. You store the parameters collected from the command line in identifiers for later use; in this case, you will write them to the console:

```
let myFlag = ref true
let myString = ref ""
let myInt = ref 0
let myFloat = ref 0.0
let (myStringList : string list ref) = ref []

let argList =
    [ "-set", Arg.Set myFlag, "Sets the value myFlag";
      "-clear", Arg.Clear myFlag, "Clears the value myFlag";
      "-str_val", Arg.String(fun x -> myString := x), "Sets the value myString";
      "-int_val", Arg.Int(fun x -> myInt := x), "Sets the value myInt";
      "-float_val", Arg.Float(fun x -> myFloat := x), "Sets the value myFloat"; ]

if System.Environment.GetCommandLineArgs().Length <> 1 then
    Arg.parse
        argList
        (fun x -> myStringList := x :: !myStringList)
        "Arg module demo"
else
    Arg.usage
        argList
        "Arg module demo"
    exit 1
```

```
printfn "myFlag: %b" !myFlag
printfn "myString: %s" !myString
printfn "myInt: %i" !myInt
printfn "myFloat: %f" !myFloat
printfn "myStringList: %A" !myStringList
```

When you run the preceding code with no command-line arguments or faulty command-line arguments, the program will output these results:

```
Arg module demo
        -set: Sets the value my_flag
        -clear: Clears the value my_flag
        -str_val <string>: Sets the value my_string
        -int_val <int>: Sets the value my_int
        -float_val <float>: Sets the value my_float
        --help: display this list of options
        -help: display this list of options
```

The preceding example will output the following when you run it with the command line, args.exe -clear -str_val "hello world" -int_val 10 -float_val 3.14 "file1" "file2" "file3"::

```
myFlag: false
myString: hello world
myInt: 10
myFloat: 3.140000
myStringList: ["file3"; "file2"; "file1"]
```

I am particularly fond of this kind of DSL because I think it makes it clear what arguments the program is expecting and what processing should take place if that argument is received. The fact that the help text is also stored in the structure serves a double purpose; it allows the function processing command-line arguments to print out a help automatically if anything goes wrong, and it also reminds you what the argument is in case you forget. I also like this method of creating a command-line interpreter because I have written several command-line interpreters in imperative languages, and it is not a satisfying experience—you end up having to write lots of code to detail how your command line should be broken up. If you write that code in .NET, then you usually spend way too much time calling the string type's IndexOf and Substring methods.

A Data Structure–Based Language Implementation

Creating any DSL should start with defining what problem you need to solve; in this case, you need to define a DSL library (sometimes called a *combinators library*) for drawing 2D images. This is something of an obvious choice. This example demonstrates how you can build up complicated structures out a number of simple primitives. An image on a computer screen is essentially just a collection of lines and polygons, although the image displayed might be extremely intricate. This example is presented in four modules: the first, Listing 12-1, provides the primitives for creating a picture; the second, Listing 12-2, shows you how to implement an interpreter for the picture; and Listings 12-3 and 12-4 provide examples that illustrate how to use the libraries. You'll need to use listings 12-1 and 12-2 together with either

Listing 12-3 or 12-4 to see any results. You begin by walking through the main points of the design process and conclude by looking at the full listing.

■**Note** This example was largely inspired by working with the guys at A6 Systems (http://a6systems.com/), who have a similar but more complex library for rendering 3D animated scenes. They use this library for a wide range of industrial purposes.

You start by designing a set of types that that will describe your picture; these types form the primitives of your image:

```
// represents the basic shapes that will make up the scene
type Shape =
    | Line of Position * Position
    | Polygon of List<Position>
    | CompersiteShape of List<Shape>
```

This type is recursive, and the CompersiteShape union case contains a list of shapes that it will use to form a tree-like structure. In compiler development, this tree-like structure is referred to as the *Abstract Syntax Tree* (AST). You'll see another example of using an AST to represent a program at the end of the chapter.

So far, you have created your picture using three basic elements: lines, polygons and shapes. The fact that your type is made up of just three simple elements is an important design decision; making your primitives simple makes implementing the engine that will render the image much simpler. The fact that your primitives are so simple means you don't expect your user to spend time interacting with them directly; instead you'll provide a set of higher-level wrapper functions that return values of type shape. These are your *combinators*. The CompersiteShape case in your union is an important example of this; it allows you to build up more complicated shapes out of simpler elements. You expose this through the compose function:

```
// allows us to compose a list of elements into a
// single shape
let compose shapes = CompersiteShape shapes
```

You use this function to implement a number of higher-level functions; for example, the lines function, which takes a list of positions and returns a shape that is a path through those positions, takes advantage of the compose function to combine a number of individual lines into a single line:

```
// a line composed of two or more points
let lines posList =
    // grab first value in the list
    let initVal =
        match posList with
        | first :: _ -> first
        | _ -> failwith "must give more than one point"
```

```
// creates a new link in the line
let createList (prevVal, acc) item =
    let newVal = Line(prevVal, item)
    item, newVal :: acc
// folds over the list accumlating all points into a
// list of line shapes
let _, lines = List.fold createList (initVal, []) posList
// compose the list of lines into a single shape
compose lines
```

Next, you use this lines function in the implementation of several high-level shapes, such as the square function:

```
let square filled (top, right) size =
    let pos1, pos2 = (top, right), (top, right + size)
    let pos3, pos4 = (top + size, right + size), (top + size, right)
    if filled then
        polygon [ pos1; pos2; pos3; pos4; pos1 ]
    else
        lines [ pos1; pos2; pos3; pos4; pos1 ]
```

The square function uses the lines function to plot the outline of a square with the calculated points. You can see the full module in Listing 12-1, although a more realistic implementation would probably contain more basic shapes for the users of the library to choose from. You will need to add references to System.Drawing.dll and System.Windows.Forms.dll to make the example compile.

Listing 12-1. *A Combinator Library for Creating Images*

```
namespace Strangelights.GraphicDSL
open System.Drawing

// represents a point within the scene
type Position = int * int

// represents the basic shapes that will make up the scene
type Shape =
    | Line of Position * Position
    | Polygon of List<Position>
    | CompersiteShape of List<Shape>

// allows us to give a color to a shape
type Element = Shape * Color

module Combinators =
    // allows us to compose a list of elements into a
    // single shape
```

```
let compose shapes = CompersiteShape shapes

// a simple line made from two points
let line pos1 pos2 = Line (pos1, pos2)

// a line composed of two or more points
let lines posList =
    // grab first value in the list
    let initVal =
        match posList with
        | first :: _ -> first
        | _ -> failwith "must give more than one point"
    // creates a new link in the line
    let createList (prevVal, acc) item =
        let newVal = Line(prevVal, item)
        item, newVal :: acc
    // folds over the list accumlating all points into a
    // list of line shapes
    let _, lines = List.fold createList (initVal, []) posList
    // compose the list of lines into a single shape
    compose lines

// a polygon defined by a set of points
let polygon posList = Polygon posList

// a triangle that can be either hollow or filled
let triangle filled pos1 pos2 pos3 =
    if filled then
        polygon [ pos1; pos2; pos3; pos1 ]
    else
        lines [ pos1; pos2; pos3; pos1 ]

// a square that can either be hollow or filled
let square filled (top, right) size =
    let pos1, pos2 = (top, right), (top, right + size)
    let pos3, pos4 = (top + size, right + size), (top + size, right)
    if filled then
        polygon [ pos1; pos2; pos3; pos4; pos1 ]
    else
        lines [ pos1; pos2; pos3; pos4; pos1 ]
```

You now have the basic elements of your language; next you need to implement an interpreter to display the image. The interpreter described in this chapter is a WinForm. The advantage to this approach is that you might also implement an interpreter in WPF, Silverlight, or GTK#, which means that it is quite portable between GUI libraries and platforms. Implementing the interpreter is straightforward. You just need to implement each of your union cases. In the case of Line and Polygon, you draw these shapes using the GDI+ objects that WinForms are based on. Fortunately, GDI+ makes it straightforward to draw a line or polygon. The third CompositeShape case is also straightforward; you simply call your drawing function recursively. You can see the full source code for this in Listing 12-2. You will need to add references to System.Drawing.dll and System.Windows.Forms.dll to make it compile.

Listing 12-2. *An Interpreter to Render Images from Your Combinator Library*

```
namespace Strangelights.GraphicDSL

open System.Drawing
open System.Drawing.Drawing2D
open System.Windows.Forms

// a form that can be used to display the scene
type EvalForm(items: List<Element>) as x =
    inherit Form()
    // handle the paint event to draw the scene
    do x.Paint.Add(fun ea ->
        let rec drawShape (shape, (color: Color)) =
            match shape with
            | Line ((x1, y1), (x2, y2)) ->
                // draw a line
                let pen = new Pen(color)
                ea.Graphics.DrawLine(pen, x1, y1, x2, y2)
            | Polygon points ->
                // draw a polygon
                let points =
                    points
                    |> List.map (fun (x,y) -> new Point(x, y))
                    |> Array.ofList
                let brush = new SolidBrush(color)
                ea.Graphics.FillPolygon(brush, points)
            | CompersiteShape shapes ->
                // recursively draw the other contained elements
                List.iter (fun shape -> drawShape(shape, color)) shapes
        // draw all the items we have been passed
        items |> List.iter drawShape)
```

Putting together a simple image composed of two squares and a triangle now becomes straightforward. You simply call the appropriate functions from your combinator library and then combine them with a color to make a full description of the scene. Listing 12-3 shows how to do this; you can see the resulting image in Figure 12-1.

Listing 12-3. *A Simple Example of Using Your Combinator Library*

```
open System.Drawing
open System.Windows.Forms
open Strangelights.GraphicDSL

// two test squares
let square1 = Combinators.square true (100, 50) 50
let square2 = Combinators.square false (50, 100) 50

// a test triangle
let triangle1 =
    Combinators.triangle false
        (150, 200) (150, 150) (250, 200)

// compose the basic elements into a picture
let scence = Combinators.compose [square1; square2; triangle1]

// create the display form
let form = new EvalForm([scence, Color.Red])

// show the form
Application.Run form
```

The simple example given in Listing 12-3 probably doesn't represent how you would create images using the combinator library. You'll take look at a more realistic scenario in Listing 12-4. The best approach to using the combinator library would probably be to carry on programming in the style you wrote the original combinator library in; that is, you would build up simple elements that you can reuse in your image. Next, you'll look at how to create a scene composed of seven stars. The obvious place to start is with the creation of the star; you can see how to create the star function defined in Listing 12-4. This function creates triangles that are mirror images and combines them with a slight offset to form a six-sided star. This example might give you some idea of how to build up more complex shapes out of simpler ones. Once you have the definition of your star, you simply need a list of positions that tell where to print the stars. You can see this list of points in Listing 12-4. Once you have these two elements, you can combine them using the List.map function and the compose function to create your scene. Next, you can display your scene the same way you did in the previous listing.

Listing 12-4. *Creating a More Complex Image Using Your Combinator Library*

```
open System.Drawing
open System.Windows.Forms
open Strangelights.GraphicDSL
```

```
// define a function that can draw a 6 sided star
let star (x, y) size =
    let offset = size / 2
    // calculate the first triangle
    let t1 =
        Combinators.triangle false
            (x, y - size - offset)
            (x - size, y + size - offset)
            (x + size, y + size - offset)
    // calculate another inverted triangle
    let t2 =
        Combinators.triangle false
            (x, y + size + offset)
            (x + size, y - size + offset)
            (x - size, y - size + offset)
    // compose the triangles
    Combinators.compose [ t1; t2 ]

// the points where stars should be plotted
let points = [ (10, 20); (200, 10);
               (30, 160); (100, 150); (190, 150);
               (20, 300); (200, 300);  ]

// compose the stars into a single scene
let scence =
    Combinators.compose
        (List.map (fun pos -> star pos 5) points)

// show the scene in red on the EvalForm
let form = new EvalForm([scence, Color.Red],
                        Width = 260, Height = 350)

// show the form
Application.Run form
```

Figure 12-1 shows the resulting image.

You've now seen two approaches for creating combinator libraries (libraries that create little languages though data structures). At this point, you're probably beginning to see how you can break a problem down into an abstract description of the problem based on a small set of primitives, possibly with aid of other libraries that you build on these primitives.

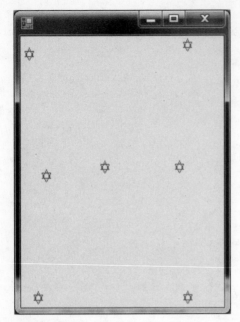

Figure 12-1. *A scene rendered by your combinator library*

■**Note** If you're looking for a more in-depth view of a combinator library, take a look at the paper by Simon Peyton Jones, Jean-Marc Eber, and Julian Seward called "Composing contracts: an adventure in financial engineering.". The paper gives an in depth, yet understandable, study of a combinator library for describing derivatives contracts. The examples in the paper are in Haskell rather than F#, but you could translate them to F# with some effort. You can read this paper at `http://research.microsoft.com/en-us/um/people/simonpj/papers/financial-contracts/contracts-icfp.htm`.

Metaprogramming with Quotations

In Chapter 6, you used quotations; these are quoted sections of F# code where the quote operator instructs the compiler to generate data structures representing the code, rather than IL representing the code. This means you have a data structure that represents the code that was coded, rather than code you can execute, and you're free to do what you want with it. You can either interpret it, performing the actions you require as you go along, or you can compile it into another language. Or you can simply ignore it if you want. You could, for example, take a section of quoted code and compile it for another runtime, such as the Java virtual machine (JVM). Or, as in the LINQ example in Chapter 9, you could turn it into SQL and execute it against a database.

   In the next example, you'll write an interpreter for integer-based arithmetic expressions in F#. This might be useful for learning how stack-based calculations work. Here, your language is already designed for you; it is the syntax available in F#. You'll work exclusively with arithmetic expressions of the form, `<@ (2 * (2 - 1)) / 2 @>`. This means you need to generate an error whenever you come across syntax that is neither an integer nor an operation. Quotations are based on discriminating union type. When working with quotations, you have to query the expression that you receive using F#'s pattern matching and active patterns. For example, here you query an expression using an active pattern and a when guard to see whether it is an integer; if it is, you push it onto the stack:

```
| Value (x,ty) when ty = typeof<int>      ->
                                let i = x :?> int
                                printfn "Push %i" i
                                operandsStack.Push(x :?> int)
```

If it isn't an integer, you could go on to check whether it is of several other types. There also several parameterized active patterns that you might find useful. For example, SpecificCall accepts a quotation that is a function expression and allows you to query whether the quotation being matched over is a call to that function. You use this to determine whether a call to an operator is made; for example, this example checks whether a call to the plus operator is made:

```
| SpecificCall <@ (+) @> (_,_, [l;r])  -> interpretInner l
                                          interpretInner r
                                          preformOp (+) "Add"
```

You can see the full listing in Listing 12-5.

Listing 12-5. *Stack-Based Evaluation of F# Quoted Arithmetic Expressions*

```
open System.Collections.Generic
open Microsoft.FSharp.Quotations
open Microsoft.FSharp.Quotations.Patterns
open Microsoft.FSharp.Quotations.DerivedPatterns

let interpret exp =
    let operandsStack = new Stack<int>()
    let preformOp f name =
        let x, y = operandsStack.Pop(), operandsStack.Pop()
        printfn "%s %i, %i" name x y
        let result = f x y
        operandsStack.Push(result)
    let rec interpretInner exp =
        match exp with
        | SpecificCall <@ (*) @> (_,_, [l;r])  -> interpretInner l
                                                  interpretInner r
                                                  preformOp (*) "Mult"
        | SpecificCall <@ (+) @> (_,_, [l;r])  -> interpretInner l
                                                  interpretInner r
                                                  preformOp (+) "Add"
        | SpecificCall <@ (-) @> (_,_, [l;r])  -> interpretInner l
                                                  interpretInner r
                                                  preformOp (-) "Sub"
```

```
        | SpecificCall <@ (/) @> (_,_, [l;r])  -> interpretInner l
                                                  interpretInner r
                                                  preformOp (/) "Div"
        | Value (x,ty) when ty = typeof<int>     ->
                                                  let i = x :?> int
                                                  printfn "Push: %i" i
                                                  operandsStack.Push(x :?> int)

        | _ -> failwith "not a valid op"
    interpretInner exp
    printfn "Result: %i" (operandsStack.Pop())

interpret <@ (2 * (2 - 1)) / 2 @>
```

Running this code produces the following results:

```
Push: 2
Push: 2
Push: 1
Sub 1, 2
Multi 1, 2
Push: 2
Div 2, 2
Result: 1
```

You are always working with F# syntax when you use quotations, which is both an advantage and a disadvantage. The advantage is that you can produce powerful libraries based on this technique that integrate well with F# code, but without having to create a parser. The disadvantage is that it is difficult to produce tools suitable for end users based on this technique; however, libraries that consume or transform F# quotations can still be used from other .NET languages because the F# libraries include functions and samples to convert between F# quotations and other common metaprogramming formats, such as LINQ quotations. For some interesting uses of quotations as little languages, you can see the F# DSL in "Microsoft Solver Foundation" at http://code.msdn.microsoft.com/solverfoundation. You can also see my discussion of it on my blog at http://strangelights.com/blog/archive/2008/09/21/1628.aspx.

This concludes your examination of DSLs; the rest of the chapter will dig a bit deeper into the implementation of an interpreter or compiler for your language.

Implementing a Compiler and an Interpreter for an Arithmetic-Language

So far, you've focused more on the design of the languages themselves, the *frontend*, rather than the implementation of the compiler or interpreter for the language, the *backend*. In this section, you'll focus on the implementation of a backend for a simple arithmetic-language defined by an AST. The AST syntax tree shown in the first section is based on a union type.

You will return to this example in the next chapter, "Parsing Text," to build a front end for this language. At this point, you have effectively built a small compiler, but that is not the focus of this chapter—right now the focus is exclusively on the backend.

You have two distinct modes of acting on the results of the parser: compiling the results and interpreting them. Compiling refers to changing the AST into some other format that is faster or easier for a machine to execute. Originally, this nearly always meant native code; these days, it's more likely to refer to something a little more abstract, such as IL, F#, or even C#. Interpreting the results means acting on the results straightaway, without any transformation of the AST. You'll look briefly at both of these topics in the sections "Interpreting the AST" and "Compiling the AST"; then you'll compare the two approaches to get some idea of when to use each in the section, "Compilation vs. Interpretation."

The Abstract Syntax Tree

An AST is a representation of the construct that makes up the program; it's intended to be easy for the programmer to use. One reason F# is good for this kind of development is its union type. This type is great for representing languages because you can use it to represent items that are related yet do not share the same structure. The following example shows how to use an AST:

```
type Ast =
    | Ident of string
    | Val of System.Double
    | Multi of Ast * Ast
    | Div of Ast * Ast
    | Plus of Ast * Ast
    | Minus of Ast * Ast
```

The tree consists of only one type because it is quite simple. A complicated tree would contain many more types, but it would still follow this basic pattern. Here you can see that the tree, which is of the type Expr, will consist of either identifiers (the Ident type); the names of the identifiers represented by a string; or values (the Val type), which will be values represented by a System.Double. The type Expr consists of four more types (Multi, Div, Plus, and Minus) that represent the arithmetic operations. They use recursion, so they are composed of other expressions.

Interpreting the AST

Once you create your AST, you have two choices: you can either interpret it or compile it. Interpreting it simply means walking the tree and performing actions as you go. Compiling it means changing it into some other form that is easier, or more typically faster, for the machine to execute. This section will examine how to interpret the results; the next section will look at the options for compiling them; finally, you will look at when you should use interpretation and when you should use compilation.

The following example shows a short interpreter for your program. The main work of interpreting the AST is done by the function interpret, which walks the tree, performing the necessary actions as it goes. The logic is quite simple. If you find a literal value or an identifier, you return the appropriate value:

```
| Ident (s) -> variableDict.[s]
| Val (v) -> v
```

If you find an operand, you recursively evaluate the expressions it contains to obtain its values and then perform the operation:

```
| Multi (e1, e2) -> (interpretInner e1) * (interpretInner e2)
```

You can see the complete interpreter in Listing 12-6.

Listing 12-6. *Interpreting an AST Generated from Command-Line Input*

```
open System
open System.Collections.Generic
open Strangelights.Expression

// requesting a value for variable from the user
let getVariableValues e =
    let rec getVariableValuesInner input (variables : Map<string, float>) =
        match input with
        | Ident (s) ->
            match variables.TryFind(s) with
            | Some _ -> variables
            | None ->
                printf "%s: " s
                let v = float(Console.ReadLine())
                variables.Add(s,v)
        | Multi (e1, e2) ->
            variables
            |> getVariableValuesInner e1
            |> getVariableValuesInner e2
        | Div (e1, e2) ->
            variables
            |> getVariableValuesInner e1
            |> getVariableValuesInner e2
        | Plus (e1, e2) ->
            variables
            |> getVariableValuesInner e1
            |> getVariableValuesInner e2
        | Minus (e1, e2) ->
            variables
            |> getVariableValuesInner e1
            |> getVariableValuesInner e2
        | _ -> variables
    getVariableValuesInner e (Map.empty)
```

```
// function to handle the interpretation
let interpret input (variableDict : Map<string,float>) =
    let rec interpretInner input =
        match input with
        | Ident (s) -> variableDict.[s]
        | Val (v) -> v
        | Multi (e1, e2) -> (interpretInner e1) * (interpretInner e2)
        | Div (e1, e2) -> (interpretInner e1) / (interpretInner e2)
        | Plus (e1, e2) -> (interpretInner e1) + (interpretInner e2)
        | Minus (e1, e2) -> (interpretInner e1) - (interpretInner e2)
    interpretInner input

// the expression to be interpreted
let e = Multi(Val 2., Plus(Val 2., Ident "a"))

// collect the arguments from the user
let args = getVariableValues e

// interpret the expression
let v = interpret e args

// print the results
printf "result: %f" v
```

Compiling and executing the preceding example produces the following results:

```
[a]: 12
result: 28.000000
```

Compiling the AST

To many developers, compilation means generating native code, so it has a reputation for being difficult. But it doesn't have to mean generating native code. For a DSL, you typically generate another, more general-purpose programming language. The .NET Framework provides several features for compiling an AST into a program.

Your choice of technology depends on several factors. For example, if you want to target your language at developers, it might be enough to generate a text file containing F#, some other language, or a compiled assembly that can then used within an application. However, if you want to target end users, you will almost certainly have to compile and then execute it on the fly. Table 12-1 summarizes the various options available.

Table 12-1. *.NET Code-Generation Technologies*

Technology	Description
Microsoft.CSharp. CSharpCodeProvider	This class supports compilation of a C# file that has been created on the fly, either by using simple string concatenation or by using the System.CodeDom namespace. Once the code has been compiled into an assembly, it can be loaded dynamically into memory and executed via reflection. This operation is relatively expensive because it requires writing to the disk and using reflection to execute methods.
System.CodeDom	This is a set of classes aimed at abstracting between operations available in different languages. The idea is to describe your operations using the classes available in this namespace, and then use a provider to compile them into the language of your choice. .NET ships with a provider for both C# and Visual Basic.
FSharp.Compiler.CodeDom.dll	This is the CodeDom provider that ships with F#. It can be used to compile F# on the fly in a similar way to the C# CodeDom provider.
System.Reflection.Emit	This namespace allows you to build up assemblies using IL. IL offers more features than either F#, C#, or System.CodeDom, so it provides more flexibility; however, it is lower level so it also requires more patience and will probably take more time to get right.
Mono.Cecil	This is a library extensively used in the Mono framework for both parsing assemblies and dynamically creating them.

You use the System.Reflection.Emit.DynamicMethod class, not because you need the flexibility of IL, but because IL includes built-in instructions for floating-point arithmetic, which makes it well-suited for implementing a little language. The DynamicMethod also provides a fast and easy way to let you call into the resulting program.

The method createDynamicMethod compiles the AST by walking the AST and generating code. It begins by creating an instance of the DynamicMethod class to hold the IL you define to represent the method:

```
let temp = new DynamicMethod("", (type float), paramsTypes, meth.Module)
```

Next, createDynamicMethod starts walking the tree. When you encounter an identifier, you emit some code to load an argument of your dynamic method:

```
| Ident name ->
    il.Emit(OpCodes.Ldarg, paramNames.IndexOf(name))
```

When you encounter a literal, you emit the IL code to load the literal value:

```
| Val x -> il.Emit(OpCodes.Ldc_R8, x)
```

When you encounter an operation, you must recursively evaluate both expressions and then emit the instruction that represents the required operation:

```
| Multi (e1 , e2) ->
    generateIlInner e1
    generateIlInner e2
    il.Emit(OpCodes.Mul)
```

Note how the operation is emitted last, after both expressions have been recursively evaluated. You do it this way because IL is stack-based, so data from the other operations must be pushed onto the stack before you evaluate the operator.

You can see the complete compiler in Listing 12-7.

Listing 12-7. *Compiling an AST Generated from Command-Line Input*

```
open System
open System.Collections.Generic
open System.Reflection
open System.Reflection.Emit
open Strangelights.Expression

// get a list of all the parameter names
let rec getParamList e =
    let rec getParamListInner e names =
        match e with
        | Ident name ->
            if not (List.exists (fun s -> s = name) names) then
                name :: names
            else
                names
        | Multi (e1 , e2) ->
            names
            |> getParamListInner e1
            |> getParamListInner e2
        | Div (e1 , e2) ->
            names
            |> getParamListInner e1
            |> getParamListInner e2
        | Plus (e1 , e2) ->
            names
            |> getParamListInner e1
            |> getParamListInner e2
```

```
        | Minus (e1 , e2) ->
            names
            |> getParamListInner e1
            |> getParamListInner e2
        | _ -> names
    getParamListInner e []

// create the dyncamic method
let createDynamicMethod e (paramNames: string list) =
    let generateIl e (il : ILGenerator) =
        let rec generateIlInner e  =
            match e with
            | Ident name ->
                let index = List.findIndex (fun s -> s = name) paramNames
                il.Emit(OpCodes.Ldarg, index)
            | Val x -> il.Emit(OpCodes.Ldc_R8, x)
            | Multi (e1 , e2) ->
                generateIlInner e1
                generateIlInner e2
                il.Emit(OpCodes.Mul)
            | Div (e1 , e2) ->
                generateIlInner e1
                generateIlInner e2
                il.Emit(OpCodes.Div)
            | Plus (e1 , e2) ->
                generateIlInner e1
                generateIlInner e2
                il.Emit(OpCodes.Add)
            | Minus (e1 , e2) ->
                generateIlInner e1
                generateIlInner e2
                il.Emit(OpCodes.Sub)
        generateIlInner e
        il.Emit(OpCodes.Ret)

    let paramsTypes = Array.create paramNames.Length (typeof<float>)
    let meth = MethodInfo.GetCurrentMethod()
    let temp = new DynamicMethod("", (typeof<float>), paramsTypes, meth.Module)
    let il = temp.GetILGenerator()
    generateIl e il
    temp
```

```
// function to read the arguments from the command line
let collectArgs (paramNames : string list) =
    paramNames
    |> Seq.map
        (fun n ->
            printf "%s: " n
            box (float(Console.ReadLine())))
    |> Array.ofSeq

// the expression to be interpreted
let e = Multi(Val 2., Plus(Val 2., Ident "a"))

// get a list of all the parameters from the expression
let paramNames = getParamList e

// compile the tree to a dynamic method
let dm = createDynamicMethod e paramNames

// print collect arguments from the user
let args = collectArgs paramNames

// execute and print out the final result
printfn "result: %O" (dm.Invoke(null, args))
```

Compiling the code in Listing 12-7 produces the following results:

```
a: 14
result: 32
```

Compilation vs. Interpretation

You might be wondering when should you use compilation and when should you use interpretation. The final result is basically the same, so the answer generally comes down to the raw speed of the final generated code, though memory usage and start-up times can also play a role in the decision. If you need your code to execute more quickly, then compilation will generally give you better results, with some activities.

The test harness in Listing 12-8 enables you to execute the interpret function results of createDynamicMethod repeatedly and time how long this takes. It also tests an important variation on dynamic methods; that is where you also generate a new .NET delegate value to act as the handle by which you invoke the generated code. As you can see, it turns out that this is by far the fastest technique. Remember, you're timing how long it takes to evaluate the AST either directly or in a compiled form; you're not measuring the parse time or compilation time.

Listing 12-8. *A Test Harness for Comparing Performance*

```
open System
open System.Diagnostics
open Strangelights.Expression

// expression to process
let e = Multi(Val 2., Plus(Val 2., Val 2.))

// collect the inputs
printf "Interpret/Compile/Compile Through Delegate [i/c/cd]: "
let interpertFlag = Console.ReadLine()
printf "reps: "
let reps = int(Console.ReadLine())

type Df0 = delegate of unit -> float
type Df1 = delegate of float -> float
type Df2 = delegate of float * float -> float
type Df3 = delegate of float * float * float -> float
type Df4 = delegate of float * float * float * float -> float

// run the tests
match interpertFlag with
| "i" ->
    let args = Interpret.getVariableValues e
    let clock = new Stopwatch()
    clock.Start()
    for i = 1 to reps do
        Interpret.interpret e args |> ignore
    clock.Stop()
    printf "%i" clock.ElapsedTicks
| "c" ->
    let paramNames = Compile.getParamList e
    let dm = Compile.createDynamicMethod e paramNames
    let args = Compile.collectArgs paramNames
    let clock = new Stopwatch()
    clock.Start()
    for i = 1 to reps do
        dm.Invoke(null, args) |> ignore
    clock.Stop()
    printf "%i" clock.ElapsedTicks
```

```
| "cd" ->
    let paramNames = Compile.getParamList e
    let dm = Compile.createDynamicMethod e paramNames
    let args = Compile.collectArgs paramNames
    let args = args |> Array.map (fun f -> f :?> float)
    let d =
        match args.Length with
        | 0 -> dm.CreateDelegate(typeof<Df0>)
        | 1 -> dm.CreateDelegate(typeof<Df1>)
        | 2 -> dm.CreateDelegate(typeof<Df2>)
        | 3 -> dm.CreateDelegate(typeof<Df3>)
        | 4 -> dm.CreateDelegate(typeof<Df4>)
        | _ -> failwith "too many parameters"
    let clock = new Stopwatch()
    clock.Start()
    for i = 1 to reps do
        match d with
        | :? Df0 as d -> d.Invoke() |> ignore
        | :? Df1 as d -> d.Invoke(args.[0]) |> ignore
        | :? Df2 as d -> d.Invoke(args.[0], args.[1]) |> ignore
        | :? Df3 as d -> d.Invoke(args.[0], args.[1], args.[2]) |> ignore
        | :? Df4 as d -> d.Invoke(args.[0], args.[1], args.[2], args.[4]) |> ignore
        | _ -> failwith "too many parameters"
    clock.Stop()
    printf "%i" clock.ElapsedTicks
| _ -> failwith "not an option"
```

Table 12-2 summarizes the results of executing this program against this expression: Multi(Val 2., Plus(Val 2., Val 2.)).

Table 12-2. *Summary of Processing the Expression Multi(Val 2., Plus(Val 2., Val 2.)) for Various Numbers of Repetitions (times in milliseconds)*

Repetitions	1	10	100	1,000	10,000	100,000	1,000,000
Interpreted	6,890	6,979	6,932	7,608	14,835	84,823	799,788
Compiled via delegate	8,65	856	854	1,007	2,369	15,871	151,602
Compiled	1,112	1,409	2,463	16,895	151,135	1,500,437	14,869,692

Table 12-2 and Figure 12-2 indicate that *Compiled* and *Compiled via delegate* are much faster over a small number of repetitions. But notice that over 1, 10, and 100 repetitions, the amount of time required grows negligibly. This is because over these small numbers of repetitions, the time taken for each repetition is insignificant. It is only the time that the JIT compiler takes to compile the IL code into native code that is significant. This is why the *Compiled* and *Compiled via delegate* times are so close. They both have a similar amount of code to JIT compile. The *Interpreted* time takes longer because you must JIT compile more code; specifically, the interpreter. But JIT is a one-off cost because you need to JIT each method only once; therefore, as the number of repetitions goes up, this one-off cost is paid for, and you begin to see a truer picture of the relative performance cost.

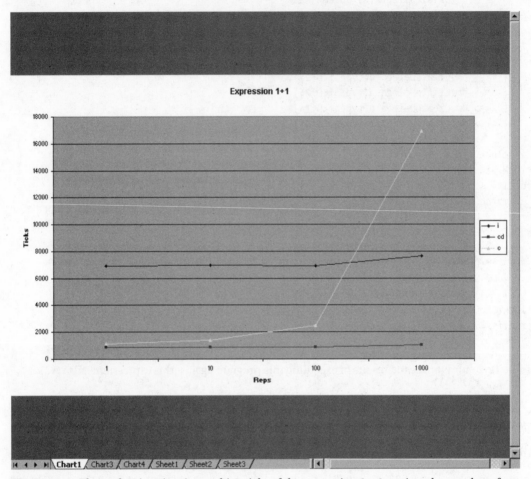

Figure 12-2. *The evaluation time in machine ticks of the expression 1 + 1 against the number of evaluations of the express*

You can see clearly from Figure 11-2 that, as the number of repetitions goes up, the cost of *Compiled* goes up steeply. This is because accessing the compiled DynamicMethod through its Invoke method is expensive, and you incur this cost on every repetition. This means that the time taken for a *Compiled* method increases at the same rate as the number of repetitions. However, the problem lies not with compilation, but with how you invoke the compiled code. It turns out that calling a DynamicMethod through a delegate rather than the Invoke member on the dynamic delegate allows you to pay only once for the cost of binding to the method, so executing a DynamicMethod this way is much more efficient if you intend to evaluate the expression multiple times. Based on these results, compilation with invocation via a delegate provides the best option in terms of speed.

This analysis shows the importance of measurement: don't assume that compilation has given you the expected performance gains until you actually see the benefits on realistic data sets and have used all the available techniques to ensure no unnecessary overhead is lurking in your code. However, many other factors can affect your performance in the real world. For example, if your expressions change often, your interpreter will need to be JIT compiled only once, but each compiled expression will need to be to JIT compiled, which means you'll need to run your compiled code many times if you want to see any performance gains. Given that interpreted code is usually easier to implement and that compiled code provides significant performance gains only in certain situations, interpreted code is often your best choice.

When dealing with situations that require code to perform as quickly as possible, it's generally best to try a few different approaches and then profile your application to see which approach gives the best results. You can find more information about performance profiling in Chapter 12.

Summary

In this chapter, you looked at the main features and techniques for language-oriented programming in F#. You have seen various techniques; some use data structures as little languages or work with quotations, which involve working with the existing F# syntax to change or extend it. Others, such as implementing a parser, enable you to work with just about any language that is text-based, whether this language is of your own design (or perhaps more commonly) a preexisting language. All these techniques can lead to big productivity gains if you use them correctly.

The next chapter will look at how to parse text using F#. This will allow you to create languages that are not embedded within F#, yet will allow you to work with the main text-based formats that are defined.

CHAPTER 13

■ ■ ■

Parsing Text

Structured text formats that are readable by both humans and machines have been popular almost since the beginning of computing. Programming languages are a good example of this, but there are many others. Parsing text is related to the previous chapter, language orient programming, because if you want to implement a language that is not embedded in F# then creating a parser for that format would be the first step. However, there are many reasons that you may want to parse an existing text format, so I did not want to limit this chapter to parsing languages.

Simple text formats such as comma separated values (CSV) are generally quite straightforward to parse, although even CVS can have its challenges, like handling escape characters correctly. As languages become more complicated, parsing them becomes more challenging. Even apparently simple languages like HTML can present some challenges when parsing. To a certain extent this has driven the popularity of XML, because parsers as prepackaged software components remove a lot of the work of parsing XML. Due to some of the limitations of XML other text formats that do require parsers to be written are still popular. The renewed interest in domain specific languages has led to a renewed interest in parsing text, so new DSLs that are external to programming languages can be created.

Fortunately, F# comes with several different tools for parsing text. In this chapter, you'll examine two of them:

- using fslex.exe & fsyacc.exe

- using the open source library FParsec

As these two examples relate to parsing languages, I'll start off with an example of how you might parse a simple CSV format.

Parsing CSV Format

In this section, I'll consider two simple approaches to parsing the CSV format. The CSV, *comma separated values*, format is a way of storing tabular data in a text format. A comma is used to delimit the values stored in each column. It is one of the oldest text formats, and it was in use well before the PC era yet has no standard specification. The only real complexity in the CSV format is when you need to handle escape characters, and that is when you could have string value which contains a comma. In this case, you need to consider how to encode the comma so it doesn't create a new column. However, we'll not consider this because you'd have to use a parser tool like fslex.exe/fsyacc.exe or FParsec.

A useful CSV parser, to return you the file data in a tabular format, can be written in just a few lines of F#:

```
open System.IO

let parseFile filename =
    let lines = File.ReadAllLines filename
    seq { for line in lines -> line.Split(',') }
```

This example uses the .NET BCL libraries to open a file and then uses F# sequence expressions and the String.Split method to create a sequence of arrays that contain the values in the columns. While this nice and simple approach works quite well, it has a couple of disadvantages. First, it doesn't validate that each row contains the same number of columns and secondly the results are always typed as strings, so the client of this code needs to handle values transformation.

To tackle these two problems, you can create a CSV parser class that uses F#'s reflection to dynamically create strongly typed tuples. The basic idea is you give the class a type parameter, which must be tuple, and the class uses reflection to determine what the elements are of that tuple and how they should be parsed. This information is then used to parse each row of the given file. Finally, we implement the IEnumerable<'a> interface, to allow client code to simply enumerate the list of tuples that are produced. The use of reflection means that the implementation of the class is not trivial:

```
open System
open System.IO
open System.Collections
open System.Reflection
open Microsoft.FSharp.Reflection

// a class to read CSV values from a file
type CsvReader<'a>(filename) =
    // fail if the gernic type is no a tuple
    do if not (FSharpType.IsTuple(typeof<'a>)) then
        failwith "Type parameter must be a tuple"
    // get the elements of the tuple
    let elements = FSharpType.GetTupleElements(typeof<'a>)
    // create functions to parse a element of type t
    let getParseFunc t =
        match t with
        | _ when t = typeof<string> ->
            // for string types return a function that down
            // casts to an object
            fun x -> x :> obj
        | _   ->
```

```
            // for all other types test to see if they have a
            // Parse static method and use that
            let parse = t.GetMethod("Parse",
                                    BindingFlags.Static |||
                                    BindingFlags.Public,
                                    null,
                                    [| typeof<string> |],
                                    null)
        fun (s: string) ->
              parse.Invoke(null, [| box s |])
// create a list of parse functions from the tuple's elements
let funcs = Seq.map getParseFunc elements
// read all lines from the file
let lines = File.ReadAllLines filename
// create a function parse each row
let parseRow row =
    let items =
        Seq.zip (List.ofArray row) funcs
        |> Seq.map (fun (ele, parser) -> parser ele)
    FSharpValue.MakeTuple(Array.ofSeq items, typeof<'a>)
// parse each row cast value to the type of the given tuple
let items =
    lines
    |> Seq.map (fun x -> (parseRow (x.Split(',')))) :?> 'a)
    |> Seq.toList
// implement the generic IEnumerable<'a> interface
interface seq<'a> with
    member x.GetEnumerator() =
        let seq = Seq.ofList items
        seq.GetEnumerator()
// implement the non-generic IEnumerable interface
interface IEnumerable with
    member x.GetEnumerator() =
        let seq = Seq.ofList items
        seq.GetEnumerator() :> IEnumerator
```

However, once you have done the work of implementing this class, using it to work with data in CVS files in a strongly typed way then becomes easy.

```
let values = new CsvReader<int*int*int>("numbers.csv")

for x, y, z in values do
    assert (x + y = z)
    printfn "%i + %i = %i" x y z
```

Language Definition for the Other Examples

In the remainder of the chapter, you'll look at two extended examples of how to parse a simple arithmetic language. The first implementation will use fslex.exe and fsyacc.exe. The second will use an open source parsing library FParsec. The language will be very similar to the one shown in the previous chapter. The language will have exactly the same specification, a language with four operations, except instead of using combinators the language will have its own textual format using *, +, /, - to represent the operations. An EBNF, *Extended Backus–Naur Form*, definition of the language is shown in the following code:

```
digit        = "1" | "2" | "3" | "4" | "5" | "6" | "7" | "8" | "9" | "0" ;
numpart      = digit , { digit } ;
number       = [ "-" ] , numpart , [ "." , numpart ] ;
operator     = "+" | "-" | "*" | "/" ;
character    =   "A" | "B" | "C" | "D" | "E" | "F" | "G"
               | "H" | "I" | "J" | "K" | "L" | "M" | "N"
               | "O" | "P" | "Q" | "R" | "S" | "T" | "U"
               | "V" | "W" | "X" | "Y" | "Z"
               | "a" | "b" | "c" | "d" | "e" | "f" | "g"
               | "h" | "i" | "j" | "k" | "l" | "m" | "n"
               | "o" | "p" | "q" | "r" | "s" | "t" | "u"
               | "v" | "w" | "x" | "y" | "z" | "_" ;
ident        = character , { character } ;
ident or num = ident | number ;
expression   = ident or num ;
               | [ "(" ] , ident or num , operator , ident or num , [ ")" ] ;
```

Some examples of expressions in the language are as follows:

```
1 + 2
5.87 + (8.465 / 3.243)
```

Using fslex.exe and fsyacc.exe

In this section, you will look at how to use fslex.exe and fsyacc.exe, two tools that are available with F# and were created by the F# to create the parser for the F# language.

■**Note** fslex.exe and fsyacc.exe are based on the ocamllex.exe and ocamlyacc.exe tools available with the O'Caml distribution.

As discussed in the previous chapter, creating a language can be broken down into two steps: parsing the user input and then acting on the input. These are called the frontend and the backend. This chapter will focus exclusively on the frontend, but it's worth reminding ourselves what the AST from the previous chapter looked like.

```
module Strangelights.ExpressionParser.Ast

type Expr =
    | Ident of string
    | Val of System.Double
    | Multi of Expr * Expr
    | Div of Expr * Expr
    | Plus of Expr * Expr
    | Minus of Expr * Expr
```

Tokenizing the Text: Fslex

Tokenizing the text (sometimes called *lexical analysis* or *lexing*) basically means breaking up the text into manageable lumps, or tokens. To do this, you use the tool fslex.exe, which is itself a DSL for creating *lexers* (sometimes called *scanners*), programs, or modules for tokenizing text. The program fslex.exe is a command-line application that takes a text file representing the lexer and turns into an F# file that implements the lexer.

An fslex.exe file has the extension .fsl. The file can have an optional header, which is placed between braces ({}) and is pure F# code, generally used to open modules or possibly to define helper functions. The rest is used to define the regular expressions that make up the lexer. You can bind a regular expression to an identifier using the let keyword, like this

```
let digit = ['0'-'9']
```

or you can define a regular expression as part of a rule. A *rule* is a collection of regular expressions that are in competition to match sections of the text. A rule is defined with the keyword rule and followed by a name for the rule and then an equal sign and the keyword parse. Next are the definitions of the regular expressions, which should be followed by an action, which is an F# expression surrounded by braces. Each rule is separated by a vertical bar (|). Each rule will become a function that is capable of matching against a stream of text. If a match is found, then the rule fires and the F# expression is executed. If several regular expressions match the rule, then the longest match is used. The value returned by the function is the value returned by the action. This means that each action must be of the same type. If no match is found, then an exception is raised.

Although the actions can be any valid F# expressions, it's normal to return the token declarations that you will make in the fsyacc file. See the next section, "Generating a Parser: Fsyacc," for more information about this. If you want to use the lexer on its own, you will place whatever logic you want to happen here, such as writing the token to the console or storing the token found in a list.

The following example shows a file that is capable of tokenizing your little language. You usually do one of two things in the actions. If you're interested in the match, you return a token that has been defined in the parser file. These are the identifiers in block capitals like RPAREN or MULTI. If you're not interested, you call token with the special lexbuf value function to start the parsing again. The lexbuf value is automatically placed in your parser definition and represents the text stream being processed. It is of type Microsoft.FSharp.Text.Lexing.LexBuffer. Also notice how in places where you're actually interested in the value found rather than just the fact a value was found that you use a function called curLexeme to get the string representing the match from the lexbuf.

```
{
module Strangelights.ExpressionParser.Lexer

open System
open System.Text
open Strangelights.ExpressionParser.Parser
open Microsoft.FSharp.Text.Lexing

let curLexeme (lb: LexBuffer<byte>) =
    Encoding.ASCII.GetString(lb.Lexeme, 0, lb.Lexeme.Length)
}


let digit = ['0'-'9']
let whitespace = [' ' '\t' ]
let newline = ('\n' | '\r' '\n')

rule token = parse
| whitespace     { token lexbuf }
| newline { token lexbuf }
| "("                 { LPAREN }
| ")"                 { RPAREN }
| "*"                 { MULTI }
| "/"                 { DIV }
| "+"                 { PLUS }
| "-"                 { MINUS }
| ['a'-'z' 'A'-'Z' '_']+ { ID( curLexeme(lexbuf)) }
| ['-']?digit+('.'digit+)?(['e''E']digit+)?
                      { FLOAT (Double.Parse(curLexeme(lexbuf))) }
| eof                 { EOF }
```

A lexer can contain several rules. Any further rules are separated from each other by the keyword and, a name for the rule, then an equal sign, and the keyword parse. After this are the definitions of the regular expressions that make up this rule. This is often useful if you want to implement comments in your language. Comments often produce false positives in lexers, since they can contain any text. To deal with this, when a start-comment token is detected, it is customary to switch to another rule that looks only for an end-comment token and ignores all other input.

The following example shows a simple parser that either finds strings that are like F# identifiers or discards C#-style multiline comments. Notice how when you find the start of a comment, you call the comment function to hop into the comment rule, and to find the end of it, you return unit to hop out of it.

```
{
open Microsoft.FSharp.Text.Lexing
}
```

```
rule token = parse
| "/*"            { comment lexbuf; token lexbuf }
| ['_''a'-'z''A'-'Z']['_''a'-'z''A'-'Z''0'-'9']*
                  { lexeme lexbuf }
and comment = parse
| "*/" | eof     { () }
| _               { comment lexbuf }
```

Generating a Parser: Fsyacc

A *scanner* is a program or module that breaks a text stream into pieces. You can think of a parser as the thing that reorganizes the text into something more meaningful. The aim of the parser is usually to produce an AST, and this is done by defining rules that determine the order in which the tokens should appear. The tool fsyacc.exe can generate parsers that are look-ahead left-to-right parsers, more commonly called LALR(1). This is an algorithm for parsing grammars. Not all grammars can be parsed by this algorithm, but grammars that can't are quite rare.

■**Note** The YACC part of the name fsyacc.exe is an acronym for Yet Another Compiler Compiler.

The tool fsyacc.exe works with text files with the extension .fsy. These files have three distinct parts. First is the header, which is a section of pure F# code surrounded by percentage signs and braces (%{ for opening and %} for closing). This section is typically used to open your AST module and to define short helper functions for creating the AST. Next are the declarations, defining the terminals of your language. A terminal is something concrete in your grammar such as an identifier name or a symbol. Typically these are found by the lexer. Declarations have several different forms that are summarized in Table 13-1. The third section contains the rules that make up the grammar and are described in the next paragraph.

Table 13-1. *Declarations of Terminals in an* fsyacc.exe *File*

Declaration	Description
%token	This declares the given symbol as the token in the language.
%token< *type* >	This declares the given symbol as a token, like %token, but with arguments of the given type. This is useful for things such as identifiers and literals when you need to store information about them.
%start	This declares the rule at which the parser should start parsing.
%type< *type* >	This declares the type of a particular rule; it is mandatory for the start rule but optional for all other rules.

Table 13-1. *Continued*

Declaration	Description
%left	This declares a token as left-associative, which can help resolve ambiguity in the grammar.
%right	This declares a token as right-associative, which can help resolve ambiguity in the grammar.
%nonassoc	This declares a token as nonassociative, which can help resolve ambiguity in the grammar.

The declarations are separated from the rules by two percentage signs, which make up the last section of the file. Rules are the nonterminals of the grammar. A nonterminal defines something that can be made up of several terminals. So, each rule must have a name, which is followed by a colon and then the definition of all the items that make up the rule, which are separated by vertical bar. The items that make up rule are either the names of tokens you have defined or the names of rules; this must always be followed by an action that is F# code surrounded by braces. The following code is a snippet of a rule:

```
Expression: ID { Ident($1) }
    | FLOAT {  Val($1)  }
```

Expession is the rule name and ID and FLOAT are two rules made up of just terminals. The sections { Ident($1) } and { Ident($1) } are the rule actions. Within these actions, you can grab the data associated with the terminal or nonterminal using a dollar sign and then the number representing the position of the item in which you are interested. The result of the action will itself become associated with the rule. All the actions of a rule must be of the same type, since a rule will be implemented as an F# function with the actions making up the items that it returns. Any comments within the rules should use the C-style comment markers, /* */.

The following example shows a simple parser definition for your language. Note how all the actions associated with rules are simple, just creating instances of types from the AST, and that all the languages terminals are in block capitals. When compiling this example with the fsyacc.exe tool, it's important to specify a module name using the --module switch. In this case you should specify Strangelights.ExpressionParser.Parser as the module name.

```
/* This example shows how to write a parser file which creates */
/* nodes that carry F# values. */

%{

open Strangelights.ExpressionParser.Ast

%}

%start Expression
%token <string> ID
```

```
%token <System.Double> FLOAT
%token LPAREN RPAREN EOF MULTI DIV PLUS MINUS
%type < Strangelights.ExpressionParser.Ast.Expr > Expression

%left MULTI
%left DIV
%left PLUS
%left MINUS

%%

Expression: ID { Ident($1) }
    | FLOAT {  Val($1)  }
    | LPAREN Expression RPAREN {  $2  }
    | Expression MULTI Expression {  Multi($1, $3)  }
    | Expression DIV Expression {  Div($1, $3)  }
    | Expression PLUS Expression {  Plus($1, $3)  }
    | Expression MINUS Expression {  Minus($1, $3)  }
```

Let's take a closer look at the items that make up your rule. The simplest rule item you have consists of one terminal, ID, in this case an identifier:

```
ID { Ident($1) }
```

In the rule item's action, the string that represents the identifier is used to create an instance of the Ident constructor from the AST. A slightly more complex rule is one that involves both terminals and nonterminals:

```
| Expression MULTI Expression {  Multi($1, $3)  }
```

This rule item recognizes the case where you have a valid expression followed by a multiplication sign and then a valid expression. These expressions are then loaded into the constructor Multi from your AST. These expressions could be terminals in your language, such as an identifier or a literal, or they might be an expression composed of several terminals, such as a multiplication operation.

The hardest thing about creating a grammar is making sure it is not ambiguous. A grammar is ambiguous when two or more rules could be matched by the same input. Fortunately, fsyacc.exe can spot this automatically and warns you when this has occurred. It is only a warning because the parser can still function, it just has some rules that will not be matched so is probably incorrect in some way.

Using the Parser

Using the parser is very straightforward. You can use a lexer on its own, but a parser generated with fsyacc.exe always requires a lexer to work. You'll look at how to use your lexer on its own and combined with a parser in this section.

■**Caution** Remember, .fsl and .fsy files cannot be used directly by the F# compiler. You need to compile them using fslex.exe and fsyacc.exe and then use the generated .fs files. Typically you'll use a pre-build event, which is available in the project properties dialog in visual studio to do this.

To use your lexer, you first need to create a LexBuffer that represents the text to be processed. The LexBuffer class has a number of static methods that allow you to create an instance of it from different text sources. These include FromBinaryReader, FromBytes, FromChars, and FromTextReader. Typically to create a LexBuffer class from a string you use the Encoding class to encode it to a byte array then call the FromBytes static method.

The following example shows your lexer in action. You've compiled the lexer into a module, Lex, and you use the token function to find the first, and in this case the only, token in the string.

```
open System.Text
open Microsoft.FSharp.Text.Lexing
let lexbuf = LexBuffer<byte>.FromBytes(Encoding.ASCII.GetBytes("1"))
let token = Lex.token lexbuf
printfn "%A" token
```

The result of this example is as follows:

FLOAT 1.0

Just grabbing the first token from the buffer is rarely of much value, so if you use the lexer in stand-alone mode, it is much more common to create a loop that repeatedly grabs all tokens from the buffer. The next example demonstrates how to do this, printing the tokens found as you go.

```
open System.Text
open Microsoft.FSharp.Text.Lexing
let lexbuf2 =
    LexBuffer<byte>.FromBytes(Encoding.ASCII.GetBytes("(1 * 1) + 2"))
while not lexbuf2.IsPastEndOfStream do
    let token = Lexer.token lexbuf2
    printfn "%A" token
```

The results of this example are as follows:

```
LPAREN
FLOAT 1.0
MULTI
FLOAT 1.0
RPAREN
PLUS
FLOAT 2.0
EOF
```

It is much more common for a lexer to be used in conjunction with a parser module. The functions generated by the parser expect their first parameter to be a function that takes a LexBuffer and transforms it into a token (LexBuffer<'a,'cty> -> Pars.token in this case). Fortunately, this is the signature that your lexer's token function has. The next example shows how you would implement this:

```
open System.Text
open Microsoft.FSharp.Text.Lexing
open Strangelights.ExpressionParser
let lexbuf3 =
    LexBuffer<byte>.FromBytes(Encoding.ASCII.GetBytes("(1 * 1) + 2"))
let e = Parser.Expression Lexer.token lexbuf3
printfn "%A" token
```

The result of this example is as follows:

```
Plus (Multi (Val 1.0,Val 1.0),Val 2.0)
```

And, that's it! Once you have your AST, you have a nice abstract form of your grammar, so now it is up to you to create a program that acts on this tree. At this point, you'd want to hop back to the previous chapter and look at how you might transform the AST by either interpreting it or compiling it.

FParsec Library

FParsec is an open source combinator library for parsing text. It's available from http://www.quanttec.com/fparsec/. It's been implemented by Stephan Tolksdorf and is based on the popular Haskell parsing library Parsec http://www.haskell.org/haskellwiki/Parsec. It is an example of a combinator library, using similar ideas to the ones discussed in the previous chapter, parse are build up by combining a number of basic parsers defined in FParsec libraries via functions and operators also defined in the FParsec libraries.

If you are used to reading BNF grammars and using regular expressions then you'll probably find using fslex.exe and fsyacc.exe a little more intuitive than using FParsec. Despite this, FParsec is still fairly easy to use once you get your head round a few key concepts. The big advantage it has is that it is just library and no code generation or external tools are required. This means parser definitions tend to be shorter and leaves less awkward configuration for the development environment. Also, FParsec has been designed with performance in mind and generally produces parsers that are very fast and produce good error messages.

To demonstrate the use of FParsec we're going to look at implementing the same arithmetic language we implemented with fslex and fsyacc. But first, you will start by looking at a few simple examples.

FParsec comes with a number of predefined parsers, so the simplest usage is to just use these. The following example shows the use of the pfloat parser, which parses a float and returns a string.

```
open FParsec

let pi = CharParsers.run CharParsers.pfloat "3.1416"

printfn "Result: %A" pi
```

The result of this example when compiled and run is as follows:

```
Result: Success: 3.1416
```

Even in this simple, three line example there's a few important things to note. We've already mentioned the parser, pfloat, this one of many predefined parsers that can be used as building blocks. Table 13-2 summarizes the important ones. The function run runs the parser on a string. There are a number of other functions to allow you to run a parser on just about any other input type. Table 13-3 lists all of these functions along with the type of input they should be run on. Finally, notice that the result is printed out as "Success: 3.1416". This is because not just the floating point number is returned. The result is actually a discriminating union which indicates success or failure of the parsing and also contains information about the position of the parser as well as the result of the parser, in this case a floating point number. You'll look at the result in more detail in the next example.

Table 13-2. *Useful Predefined Parsers*

Function	Description
upper	Matches a single uppercase letter
lower	Matches a single lower case letter
digit	Matches a single digit from 0 to 9
hex	Matches a single hexadecimal digit, from 0 to F, including both upper and lowercase letters
spaces	Matches zero or more whitespace character, that is space, tab, and new line
spaces1	Matches one or more whitespace, that is space, tab, and new line
pfloat	Matches a floating point number
pint32	Matches a 32 bit integer

It's worth noting that "letter" as used in Table 13-2 refers to the UTF-16 notion of letter and includes many accented and non-latin characters.

Table 13-3. *Functions for Executing Parsers on Various Text Types*

Function	Description
run	The simplest way to run a parser on a string
runParser	Runs the parser on text contained in a FParsec.CharStream class, a class used internally by FParsec to represent the text being parsed
runParserOnString	Runs the parser on a string
runParserOnSubstring	Runs the parser on part of a string specified by a start and end index
runParserOnStream	Runs the parser on a System.IO.Stream
runParserOnSubstream	Runs the parser on part of a FParsec.CharStream specified by a start and end position
runParserOnFile	Runs the parser on a file

When parsing it's generally important to know whether the operation succeeded or failed. FParsec use the ParserResult discriminating union to do that. This type gives access to the result if parsing was successful and error information if it was not. In both cases, information about the position of the parser is also returned. The next example shows how to use the ParserResult type.

```
open FParsec

let parseAndPrint input =
    let result = CharParsers.run CharParsers.pfloat input
    match result with
    | CharParsers.Success (result, _, _) ->
        printfn "result: %A" result
    | CharParsers.Failure (_, errorDetails, _) ->
        printfn "Error details: %A" errorDetails

parseAndPrint "3.1416"
parseAndPrint "    3.1416"
parseAndPrint "Not a number"
```

The result of this example when compiled and run is as follows:

```
result: 3.1416, pos: (Ln: 1, Col: 7)
Message: Error in Ln: 1 Col: 1
    3.1416
^
Expecting: floating-point number
 Error details: Error in Ln: 1 Col: 1
Expecting: floating-point number

Message: Error in Ln: 1 Col: 1
Not a number
^
Expecting: floating-point number
 Error details: Error in Ln: 1 Col: 1
Expecting: floating-point number
```

We can see from the output of this example that the first time the `parseAndPrint` function is called the parser successfully parsers the input, but the other two times it fails. While you would not expect a floating point parser to be able to parse the input "Not a number" you'd probably like it to be able to parse "   3.1416", which is simply a number prefixed with whitespace. The parser `pfloat` does not handle whitespace, but you can create a parser that does by combining `pfloat` with the spaces parser.

```
open FParsec
open FParsec.Primitives

let wsfloat = CharParsers.spaces >>. CharParsers.pfloat

let pi = CharParsers.run wsfloat "    3.1416"

printfn "Result: %A" pi
```

The result of this example when compiled and run is as follows:

```
Result: Success: 3.1416
```

In this example, you used the operator `>>.`, one of FParsec's custom operators, to combine the two parsers. This operator means combining the two parsers and only returning the result of the second. In this context combine looks for text matching first parser followed by text that matches the second parser. A similar operator `.>>` is also defined. This combines two parsers, keeping only the input from the first parser. It useful to think of the dot in these operators as representing which parsers result will be returned. The operator `.>>` is useful if, for example, the whitespace you're trying to ignore is postfixed rather than prefixed.

While being able to combine parsers and ignore the results of one is useful in some contexts it's often important to be able to combine the results of the parser as well as the parsers themselves. The operator >>= allows you to do this. On the left-hand side of the >>= operator accepts a parser, just like the >>. and .>> operators, but the right-hand side accepts a function which is passed the results of the first parsers and must return a parser. The following example illustrates a common usage pattern of this operator.

```
open FParsec
open FParsec.Primitives

let simpleAdd = CharParsers.pfloat >>= fun x ->
                CharParsers.spaces >>= fun () ->
                CharParsers.pfloat >>= fun y ->
                preturn (x + y)

let pi2 = CharParsers.run simpleAdd "3.1416 3.1416"

printfn "Result: %A" pi2
```

The result of this example when compiled and run is as follows:

```
Result: Success: 6.2832
```

Here we combine two pfloat parsers separated by a spaces parser. The result of each parse is passed to the next parser via the parameter to a lambda function. In this case, you call them x and y. I'd like to be able to add x and y, or perform some other operation, and return the result, but the result of the lambda function must be of type Parser. In this case, x and y are both of type float. To avoid this typing problem, you can use the preturn function, which you use in the previous example. This function takes any value and creates a parser that will return that value. So you can add your two floating point numbers and use preturn to create a parser that will always return that value.

In addition to being able to combine the results of two parsers it's often useful to be able to apply some transformation to the results of parser. In FParsec you use the |>> operator to do this, which has a similar behavior to F#'s native |> operator. The following example illustrates this.

```
open FParsec
open FParsec.Primitives

let addTwo = CharParsers.pfloat |>> (fun x -> x + 2.0)

let pi2 = CharParsers.run addTwo "3.1416"

printfn "Result: %A" pi2
```

The result of this example when compiled and run is as follows:

```
Result: Success: 5.1416
```

Here we use the |>> operator to simply add two to the result of our parser. This is not a particularly realistic example, but there many uses for this operator. I find it useful to transform the results of a parser into a case from a discriminating union.

So far you've looked at combing parsers sequentially and combining or transforming their results. Another common task is being able to combine parsers to make a choice between two input types. In the following example, you create a parser that can handle parsing either floating point numbers or chains of letters. To do this, you use the <|> operator. This operator combines two parsers to create a new parser which will accept an input that matches either the first parser or the second. The way it works is a little subtle; it returns the results of the first parser to consume input. If the first parse succeeds or fails and it consumes input then the results of the first parse is returned. If it does not consume input then the second parser will be executed and its result will be returned. This means that the order that the parsers appear in is important.

```
open FParsec
open FParsec.Primitives

type AstFragment =
    | Val of float
    | Ident of string

let number = CharParsers.pfloat |>> (fun x -> Val x)

let id =
    CharParsers.many1Satisfy CharParsers.isLetter
    |>> (fun x -> Ident x)

let stringOrFloat = id <|> number

let num = CharParsers.run stringOrFloat "3.1416"
let ident = CharParsers.run stringOrFloat "anIdent"


printfn "Result 'num': %A Result 'ident': %A" num ident
```

The result of this example when compiled and run is as follows:

```
Result 'num': Success: Val 3.1416 Result 'ident': Success: Ident "anIdent"
```

The other interesting point to note about this example is you use the function many1Satisfy. This is a function that allows us to create a parser from a predicate function, which it accepts as a parameter. The FPrasec library contains a number of other similar functions that are summarized in Table 13-4. The input text is fed to the predicate function and if it returns true for one or more charters then the parser created by many1Satisfy is successful. The predicate function takes a character and must return a Boolean, which represents whether the character is one that the parser accepts. In this case, you use the predefined predicate function isLetter which will return true for any character that is a letter. This is a powerful and convenient way to create parsers. Our examples show CharParsers.many1SatisfyL CharParsers.isLetter "identifier", which matches a continuous chain of more than one letter, but can easily imagine other combinations like CharParsers.many1SatisfyL CharParsers.isLower "lower case identifier", which will match any chain of continuous lowercase letters. In both cases, the string provide is a label that will be used to generate error messages.

Table 13-4. *Functions for Creating Parsers from Predicates*

Function	Description
manySatisfy	Creates a parser that will be successful if zero or more characters make the predicate function return true. The input is returned as a string.
skipManySatisfy	Creates a parser that will be successful if zero or more characters make the predicate function return true. The input is ignored.
many1Satisfy	Creates a parser that will be successful if one or more characters make the predicate function return true. The input is returned as a string.
skipMany1Satisfy	Creates a parser that will be successful if zero or more characters make the predicate function return true. The input is ignored.
manyMinMaxSatisfy	Allows you to specify the minimum and maximum number of characters that the predicate function must match for the parser to be successful. The input is returned as a string.

Note that all these functions have a version post fixed with a capital L, for label, which allows the user to provide a label that will be used in error message generation.

You now have most of the elements you need to implement your little algebraic language. Again, you keep the same AST definition as before.

```
module Strangelights.ExpressionParser.Ast

type Expr =
    | Ident of string
    | Val of System.Double
    | Multi of Expr * Expr
    | Div of Expr * Expr
    | Plus of Expr * Expr
    | Minus of Expr * Expr
```

The actual algebraic language definition looks like the following:

```
open Strangelights.ExpressionParser.Ast
open FParsec
open FParsec.Primitives
open FParsec.OperatorPrecedenceParser
```

```
// skips any whitespace
let ws = CharParsers.spaces

// skips a character possibly postfixed with whitespace
let ch c = CharParsers.skipChar c >>. ws

// parses a floating point number ignoring any postfixed whitespace
let number = CharParsers.pfloat .>> ws |>> (fun x -> Val x)

// parses an identifier made up of letters
let id =
    CharParsers.many1Satisfy CharParsers.isLetter
    |>> (fun x -> Ident x)
    .>> ws

// create an new operator precedence parser
let opp = new OperatorPrecedenceParser<_,_>()

// name the expression parser within operator precendence parser
// so it can be used more easily later on
let expr = opp.ExpressionParser

// create a parser to parse everything between the operators
let terms =
    Primitives.choice
        [ id; number; ch '(' >>. expr .>> ch ')']
opp.TermParser <- terms

// add the operators themselves
opp.AddOperator(InfixOp("+", ws, 1, Assoc.Left, fun x y -> Plus(x, y)))
opp.AddOperator(InfixOp("-", ws, 1, Assoc.Left, fun x y -> Minus(x, y)))
opp.AddOperator(InfixOp("*", ws, 2, Assoc.Left, fun x y -> Multi(x, y)))
opp.AddOperator(InfixOp("/", ws, 2, Assoc.Left, fun x y -> Div(x, y)))

// the complete expression that can be prefixed with whitespace
// and post fixed with an enf of file character
let completeExpression = ws >>. expr .>> CharParsers.eof

// define a function for parsing a string
let parse s = CharParsers.run completeExpression s

// run some tests and print the results
printfn "%A" (parse "1.0 + 2.0 + toto")
printfn "%A" (parse "toto + 1.0 * 2.0")
```

```
// will give an error
printfn "%A" (parse "1.0 +")
```

The results of this example when compiled and run are as follows:

```
Success: Plus (Plus (Val 1.0,Val 2.0),Ident "toto")
Success: Plus (Ident "toto",Multi (Val 1.0,Val 2.0))
Success: Plus (Ident "toto",Plus (Val 1.0,Val 2.0))
Failure:
Error in Ln: 1 Col: 6
1.0 +
     ^(end of input)
Expecting: '(' or floating-point number
```

Note how the second parse tree differs from the first simply because multiplication has a higher precedence than addition. Also note how the library generates an understandable error message for the last input which is not correctly formed.

The major new feature introduced by this example is the use of the `OperatorPrecedenceParser` class. This provides a convenient way to parse expressions involving (infix/prefix/postfix/ternary) operators based on the precedence and associativity of the operators. You use the member function `AddOperator` to add the operators you are interested in along with flags representing their associatively and precedence settings. You then set a property `TermParser`, which is a parse which will parse the tokens in between the operators. The `OperatorPrecedenceParser` class has a property `ExpressionParser` which provides the parser finished operator parser, and can be used in the same way as the other parsers you've met in this section.

Summary

In this chapter, you've looked at two robust mechanisms for parsing text, a task that can seem trivial at first glance but can provide some interesting challenges. The combination of the tools `fslex.exe` and `fsyacc.exe` provide a useful technique for writing parsers for those that are already familiar with regular expressions and BNF grammars. However, the fact that they rely on external tools that use code generation and custom syntax can make things a little tricky in some situations. This is where the combinator parser library, FParsec, we have looked at is a real win. This allows a user to create parser using nothing other than the built in F# syntax. Another good feature of FParsec is that the quality of the error messages it produces are considerably better than those generated by `fslex.exe` and `fsyacc.exe`.

■ ■ ■

CHAPTER 14

Compatibility and Advanced Interoperation

In this chapter, you will look at everything you need to make F# interoperate well with other languages, not just within the .NET Framework but also using unmanaged code from F# and using F# from unmanaged code.

■**Caution** Throughout this book, I have made every effort to make sure the only language you need to understand is F#. However, in this chapter, it will help if you know a little C# (version 2.0), C++, or .NET Common IL, although I've kept the code in these languages to the minimum necessary.

Calling F# Libraries from C#

You can create two kinds of libraries in F#: libraries that are just designed to be used from F# only and libraries that are designed to be used from any .NET language. This is because F# utilizes the .NET type system in a rich and powerful way, so some types can look a little unusual to other .NET languages. However, these types will always look like they should when viewed from F#.

Although you could use any library written in F# from any .NET language, you need to follow a few rules if you want to make the library as friendly as possible. Here is how I would summarize these rules:

- Always use a signature .fsi file or the private and internal to hide implementation details and document the API expected by clients.

- Avoid public functions that return tuples.

- If you want to expose a function that takes another function as a value, expose the value as a delegate.

- Do not use union types in the API, but if you absolutely must use these types, add members to make them easier to use.

- Avoid returning F# lists, and use the array, System.Collections.Generic.IEnumerable or better yet Collection or ReadOnlyCollection from the System.Collections.ObjectModel namespace instead.

- When possible, place type definitions in a namespace, and place only value definitions within a module.

- Be careful with the signatures you define on classes and interfaces; a small change in the syntax can make a big difference.

I will illustrate these points with examples in the following sections.

Returning Tuples

First, I'll talk about why you should avoid tuples. If you return a tuple from your function, you will force the user to reference FSharp.Core.dll. Also, the code needed to use the tuple just doesn't look that great from C#. Consider the following example where you define the function hourAndMinute that returns the hour and minute from a DateTime structure:

```
#light
module Strangelights.DemoModule
open System

// returns the hour and minute from the give date as a tuple
let hourAndMinute (time: DateTime) = time.Hour, time.Minute

// returns the hour from the given date
let hour (time: DateTime) = time.Hour
// returns the minutes from the given date
let minute (time: DateTime) = time.Minute
```

To call this from C#, you will need to follow the next example. If you are a Visual Studio user you'll need to create a C# project alongside your F# solution. To do this choose File ➤ Add ➤ New Project …, then choose a C# console project, as shown in Figure 14-1.

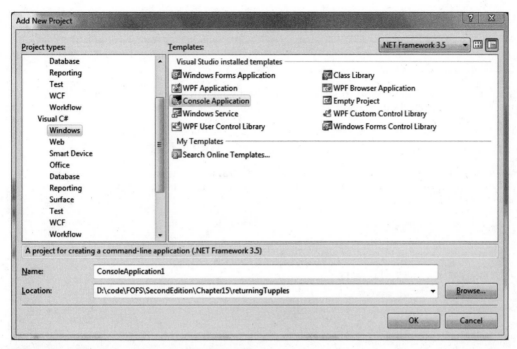

Figure 14-1. *How to create a new C# project file*

Next, you'll need to add a project reference from the C# project to the F# project. Then add the following C# class to the newly created project.

```csharp
// !!! C# Source !!!
using System;
using Strangelights;
using Microsoft.FSharp.Core;

static class PrintClass {
        internal static void HourMinute() {
                // call the "hourAndMinute" function and collect the
                // tuple that's returned
                Tuple<int, int> t = DemoModule.hourAndMinute(DateTime.Now);
                // print the tuple's contents
                Console.WriteLine("Hour {0} Minute {1}", t.Item1, t.Item2);
        }
}
```

The results of this example, when compiled and executed, are as follows:

```
Hour 16 Minute 1
```

Although the C# in the previous example isn't too ugly, it would be better if the function had been split in two, one to return the hour and one to return the minute.

Exposing Functions That Take Functions As Parameters

If you want to expose functions that take other functions as parameters, the best way to do this is using delegates. Consider the following example that defines one function that exposes a function and one that exposes this as a delegate:

```
module Strangelights.DemoModule
open System

/// a function that provides filtering
let filterStringList f ra =
    ra |> Seq.filter f

// another function that provides filtering
let filterStringListDelegate (pred: Predicate<string>) ra =
        let f x = pred.Invoke(x)
        new ResizeArray<string>(ra |> Seq.filter f)
```

Although the `filterStringList` is considerably shorter than `filterStringListDelegate`, the users of your library will appreciate the extra effort you've put in to expose the function as a delegate. When you look at using the functions from C#, it's pretty clear why. The following example demonstrates calling `filterStringList`. To call your function, you need to create a delegate and then use the `FuncConvert` class to convert it into a `FastFunc`, which is the type F# uses to represent function values. As well as being pretty annoying for the user of your library, this also requires a dependency on `FSharp.Core.dll` that the user probably didn't want.

```
// !!! C# Source !!!
using System;
using System.Collections.Generic;
using Strangelights;
using Microsoft.FSharp.Core;
```

```
class MapOneClass {
    public static void MapOne() {
        // define a list of names
        List<string> names = new List<string>(
            new string[] { "Stefany", "Oussama",
"Sebastien", "Frederik" });

        // define a predicate delegate/function
        Converter<string, bool> pred =
            delegate(string s) { return s.StartsWith("S"); };

        // convert to a FastFunc
        FastFunc<string, bool> ff =
            FuncConvert.ToFastFunc<string, bool>(pred);

        // call the F# demo function
        IEnumerable<string> results =
            DemoModule.filterStringList(ff, names);

        // write the results to the console
        foreach (var name in results) {
            Console.WriteLine(name);
        }
    }
}
```

The results of this example, when compiled and executed, are as follows:

```
Stefany
Sebastien
```

Now, compare and contrast this to calling the `filterStringListDelegate` function, shown in the following example. Because you used a delegate, you can use the C# anonymous delegate feature and embed the delegate directly into the function call, reducing the amount of work the library user has to do and removing the compile-time dependency on `FSharp.Core.dll`.

```
// !!! C# Source !!!
using System;
using System.Collections.Generic;
using Strangelights;
```

```
class MapTwoClass {
        public static void MapTwo() {
                // define a list of names
                List<string> names = new List<string>(
                        new string[] { "Aurelie", "Fabrice",
            "Ibrahima", "Lionel" });

                // call the F# demo function passing in an
                // anonymous delegate
                List<string> results =
                        DemoModule.filterStringListDelegate(
                                delegate(string s) { return s.StartsWith("A"); }, names);

                // write the results to the console
                foreach (var s in results) {
                        Console.WriteLine(s);
                }
        }
}
```

The results of this example, when compiled and executed, are as follows:

```
Aurelie
```

Using Union Types

You can use union types from C#, but because C# has no real concept of a union type, they do not look very pretty when used in C# code. In this section, you will examine how you can use them in C# and how you as a library designer can decide whether your library will expose them (though personally I recommend avoiding exposing them in cross-language scenarios).

For the first example, you will define the simple union type Quantity, which consists of two constructors, one containing an integer and the other a floating-point number. You also provide the function getRandomQuantity() to initialize a new instance of Quantity.

```
module Strangelights.DemoModule
open System

// type that can represent a discrete or continuous quantity
type Quantity =
| Discrete of int
| Continuous of float
```

```
// initalize random number generator
let rand = new Random()
// create a random quantity
let getRandomQuantity() =
    match rand.Next(1) with
    | 0 -> Quantity.Discrete (rand.Next())
    | _ ->
        Quantity.Continuous
            (rand.NextDouble() * float (rand.Next()))
```

Although you provide getRandomQuantity() to create a new version of the Quantity type, the type itself provides static methods for creating new instances of the different constructors that make up the type. These static methods are available on all union types that are exposed by the assembly by default; you do not have to do anything special to get the compiler to create them. The following example shows how to use these methods from C#:

```
using System;
using Strangelights;

static class GetQuantityZeroClass {
        public static void GetQuantityZero() {
                // initialize both a Discrete and Continuous quantity
                DemoModule.Quantity d = DemoModule.Quantity.Discrete(12);
                DemoModule.Quantity c = DemoModule.Quantity.Continuous(12.0);
        }
}
```

Now you know how to create union types from C#, so the next most important task is being able to determine the constructor to which a particular Quantity value belongs. You can do this in three ways. I cover the first two in the next two code examples, and I cover the third at the end of this section.

The first option is that you can switch on the value's Tag property. This property is just an integer, but the compiled version of the union type provides constants, always prefixed with tag_, to help you decode the meaning of the integer. If you want to use the Tag property to find out what kind of Quantity you have, you would usually write a switch statement, as shown in the following example:

```
// !!! C# Source !!!
using System;
using Strangelights;

static class GetQuantityOneClass {
        public static void GetQuantityOne() {
                // get a random quantity
                DemoModule.Quantity q = DemoModule.getRandomQuantity();
```

```
                // use the .Tag property to switch over the quatity
                switch (q.Tag) {
                        case DemoModule.Quantity.tag_Discrete:
                                Console.WriteLine("Discrete value: {0}", q.Discrete1);
                                break;
                        case DemoModule.Quantity.tag_Continuous:
                                Console.WriteLine("Continuous value: {0}", q.Continuous1);
                                break;
                }
        }
}
```

The results of this example, when compiled and executed, are as follows:

```
Discrete value: 65676
```

If you prefer, the compiled form of the union type also offers a series of methods, all prefixed with Is. This allows you to check whether a value belongs to a particular constructor within the union type. For example, on the Quantity union type, two methods, IsDiscrete() and IsContinuous(), allow you to check whether the Quantity is Discrete or Continuous. The following example demonstrates how to use them:

```
// !!! C# Source !!!
using System;
using Strangelights;

static class GetQuantityTwoClass {
        public static void GetQuantityTwo() {
                // get a random quantity
                DemoModule.Quantity q = DemoModule.getRandomQuantity();
                // use if ... else chain to display value
                if (q.IsDiscrete()) {
                        Console.WriteLine("Discrete value: {0}", q.Discrete1);
                }
                else if (q.IsContinuous()) {
                        Console.WriteLine("Continuous value: {0}", q.Continuous1);
                }
        }
}
```

The results of this example, when compiled and executed, are as follows:

```
Discrete value: 2058
```

Neither option is particularly pleasing because the code required to perform the pattern matching is quite bulky. There is also a risk that the user could get it wrong and write something like the following example where they check whether a value is `Discrete` and then mistakenly use the `Continuous1` property. This would lead to a `NullReferenceException` being thrown.

```
DemoModule.EasyQuantity q = DemoModule.getRandomQuantity();
if (q.IsDiscrete()) {
    Console.WriteLine("Discrete value: {0}", q.Continuous1);
}
```

To give your libraries' users some protection against this, it is a good idea to add members to union types that perform the pattern matching for them. The following example revises the `Quantity` type to produce `EasyQuantity`, adding two members to transform the type into an integer or a floating-point number:

```
module Strangelights.ImprovedModule
open System

// type that can represent a discrete or continuous quantity
// with members to improve interoperability
type EasyQuantity =
| Discrete of int
| Continuous of float
    // convert quantity to a float
    member x.ToFloat() =
        match x with
        | Discrete x -> float x
        | Continuous x -> x
    // convert quantity to a integer
    member x.ToInt() =
        match x with
        | Discrete x -> x
        | Continuous x -> int x

// initalize random number generator
let rand = new Random()

// create a random quantity
let getRandomEasyQuantity() =
    match rand.Next(1) with
    | 0 -> EasyQuantity.Discrete (rand.Next())
    | _ ->
        EasyQuantity.Continuous
            (rand.NextDouble() * float (rand.Next()))
```

This will allow the user of the library to transform the value into either an integer or a floating-point without having to worry about pattern matching, as shown in the following example:

```
// !!! C# Source !!!
using System;
using Strangelights;

class GetQuantityThreeClass {
        public static void GetQuantityThree() {
                // get a random quantity
                ImprovedModule.EasyQuantity q = ImprovedModule.getRandomEasyQuantity();
                // convert quantity to a float and show it
                Console.WriteLine("Value as a float: {0}", q.ToFloat());
        }
}
```

Using F# Lists

It is entirely possibly to use F# lists from C#, but I recommend avoiding this since a little work on your part will make things seem more natural for C# programmers. For example, it is simple to convert a list to an array using the List.toArray function, to a System.Collections.Generic.List using the new ResizeArray<_>() constructor, or to a System.Collections.Generic.IEnumerable using the List.toSeq function. These types are generally a bit easier for C# programmers to work with, especially System.Array and System.Collections.Generic.List, because these provide a lot more member methods. You can do the conversion directly before the list is returned to the calling client, making it entirely feasible to use the F# list type inside your F# code. MSDN recommends using the yet Collection or ReadOnlyCollection from the System.Collections.ObjectModel namespace to expose collections. Both of these classes have a constructor that accepts an IEnumerable, and so can be constructed from an F# list.

If you need to return an F# list directly, you can do so, as shown in the following example:

```
module Strangelights.DemoModule

// gets a preconstructed list
let getList() =
    [1; 2; 3]
```

To use this list in C#, you typically use a foreach loop:

```
using System;
using Strangelights;
using Microsoft.FSharp.Core;
using Microsoft.FSharp.Collections;
```

```
class Program {
      static void Main(string[] args) {
            // get the list of integers
            List<int> ints = DemoModule.getList();

            // foreach over the list printing it
            foreach (int i in ints) {
                  Console.WriteLine(i);
            }
      }
}
```

The results of this example, when compiled and executed, are as follows:

```
1
2
3
```

Defining Types in a Namespace

If you are defining types that will be used from other .NET languages, then you should place them inside a namespace rather than inside a module. This is because modules are compiled into what C# and other .NET languages consider to be a class, and any types defined within the module become inner classes of that type. Although this does not present a huge problem to C# users, the C# client code does look cleaner if a namespace is used rather than a module. This is because in C# you can open namespaces only using the using statement, so if a type is inside a module, it must always be prefixed with the module name when used from C#.

Let's take a look at an example of doing this. The following example defines TheClass, which is defined inside a namespace. You also want to provide some functions that go with this class. These can't be placed directly inside a namespace because values cannot be defined inside a namespace. In this case, you define a module with a related name, such as TheModule, to hold the function values.

```
namespace Strangelights
open System.Collections.Generic

// this is a counter class
type TheClass(i) =
    let mutable theField = i
    member x.TheField
        with get() = theField
    // increments the counter
    member x.Increment() =
        theField <- theField + 1
```

```
    // decrements the count
    member x.Decrement() =
        theField <- theField - 1

// this is a module for working with the TheClass
module TheModule = begin
    // increments a list of TheClass
    let incList (theClasses: List<TheClass>) =
        theClasses |> Seq.iter (fun c -> c.Increment())
    // decrements a list of TheClass
    let decList (theClasses: List<TheClass>) =
        theClasses |> Seq.iter (fun c -> c.Decrement())
end
```

Using the TheClass class in C# is now straightforward because you do not have to provide a prefix, and you can also get access to the related functions in TheModule easily:

```
// !!! C# Source !!!
using System;
using System.Collections.Generic;
using Strangelights;

class Program {
        static void UseTheClass() {
                // create a list of classes
                List<TheClass> theClasses = new List<TheClass>() {
                        new TheClass(5),
                        new TheClass(6),
                        new TheClass(7)};

                // increment the list
                TheModule.incList(theClasses);

                // write out each value in the list
                foreach (TheClass c in theClasses) {
                        Console.WriteLine(c.TheField);
                }
        }
        static void Main(string[] args) {
                UseTheClass();
        }
}
```

Defining Classes and Interfaces

In F# there are two ways you can define parameters for functions and members of classes: the "curried" style where members can be partially applied and the "tuple" style where all members must be given at once. When defining classes, your C# clients will find it easier to use your classes if you use the tuple style.

Consider the following example in which you define a class in F#. Here one member has been defined in the curried style, called CurriedStyle, and the other has been defined in the tuple style, called TupleStyle.

```
namespace Strangelights

type DemoClass(z: int) =
    // method in the curried style
    member this.CurriedStyle x y = x + y + z
    // method in the tuple style
    member this.TupleStyle (x, y) = x + y + z
```

When viewed from C#, the member CurriedStyle has the following signature:

```
public FastFunc<int, int> CurriedStyle(int x)
```

whereas the TupleStyle will have the following signature:

```
public int TupleStyle(int x, int y);
```

If you want to use both methods from C#, you would end up with code that looks like the following:

```
// !!! C# Source !!!
using System;
using Strangelights;
using Microsoft.FSharp.Core;

class Program {
    static void UseDemoClass() {
        DemoClass c = new DemoClass(3);
        FastFunc<int, int> ff = c.CurriedStyle(4);
        int result = ff.Invoke(5);
        Console.WriteLine("Curried Style Result {0}", result);
        result = c.TupleStyle(4, 5);
        Console.WriteLine("Tuple Style Result {0}", result);
    }
    static void Main(string[] args) {
        UseDemoClass();
    }
}
```

It is clear from this sample that users of your library will be much happier if you use the tuple style for the public members of your classes.

Specifying abstract members in interfaces and classes is slightly more complicated because you have a few more options. The following example demonstrates this:

```
namespace Strangelights

type IDemoInterface =
    // method in the curried style
    abstract CurriedStyle: int -> int -> int
    // method in the tupled style
    abstract TupleStyle: (int * int) -> int
    // method in the C# style
    abstract CSharpStyle: int * int -> int
    // method in the C# style with named arguments
    abstract CSharpNamedStyle: x : int * y : int -> int
```

Note that the only difference between OneArgStyle and MultiArgStyle is that the latter is not surrounded by parentheses. This small difference in the F# definition has a big effect on the signature as seen from C#. With the former, you see the following signature:

```
int OneArgStyle(Tuple<int, int>);
```

whereas the latter is seen as the following signature:

```
int MultiArgStyle(int, int);
```

The latter is a good bit friendlier for the C# user. However, you can take it a bit further and add names to each of your parameters. This won't change the signature the C# user will use when implementing the method, but it will change the names they see when using Visual Studio tools to implement the interface. Furthermore, some other .NET languages treat argument names as significant. This may sound like a small difference, but it will make implementing your interface a lot easier, because the implementer will have a much better idea of what the parameters of the method actually mean.

The following example shows the C# for implementing the interface IDemoInterface defined in the previous example. It makes it clear that C# users will be happier with interfaces containing methods specified using either MultiArgStyle or NamedArgStyle.

```
// !!! C# Source !!!
using System;
using Strangelights;
using Microsoft.FSharp.Core;

// shows how to implement an interface
// that has been created in F#
class DemoImplementation : IDemoInterface {
```

```
        // curried style implementation
        public FastFunc<int, int> CurriedStyle(int x) {
                // create a delegate to return
                Converter<int, int> d =
                        delegate(int y) { return x + y; };
                // convert delegate to a FastFunc
                return FuncConvert.ToFastFunc(d);
        }

        // tuple style implementation
        public int TupleStyle(Tuple<int, int> t) {
                return t.Item1 + t.Item2;
        }

        // C# style implementation
        public int CSharpStyle(int x, int y) {
                return x + y;
        }

        // C# style implementation, named arguments
        // make no difference here
        public int CSharpNamedStyle(int x, int y) {
                return x + y;
        }
}
```

Calling Using COM Objects

Most programmers who work with the Windows platform will be familiar with the Component Object Model (COM). To a certain extent the .NET Framework was meant to replace COM, but the system remains popular and is likely to be with us for some time. Many of the APIs in Windows are exposed as COM objects, and although more and more now have managed equivalents within the .NET Framework, there are still some without managed equivalents. Also, there are still some vendors that sell software that exposes its APIs via COM.

The .NET Framework was designed to interoperate well with COM, and calling COM components is generally quite straightforward. Calling COM components is always done through a managed wrapper that takes care of calling the unmanaged code for you. You can produce these wrappers using a tool called TlbImp.exe, the Type Library Importer, that ships with the .NET SDK.

■**Note** You can find more information about the TlbImp.exe tool at the following site: http://msdn2.microsoft.com/en-us/library/tt0cf3sx(VS.80).aspx.

However, despite the existence of TlbImp.exe, if you find yourself in a situation where you need to use a COM component, first check whether the vendor provides a managed wrapper for it, called *Primary Interop Assemblies*. For more information on Primary Interop Assemblies, see the next section "Using COM Style APIs."

However, sometimes it is necessary to use TlbImp.exe directly. Fortunately, this is very straightforward. Normally all that is necessary is to pass TlbImp.exe the location of the .dll that contains the COM component, and the managed wrapper will be placed in the current directory. If you want to create a managed wrapper for the Microsoft Speech API, you would use the following command line:

```
tlbimp "C:\Program Files\Common Files\Microsoft Shared\Speech\sapi.dll"
```

■**Note** There are two command-line switches that I find useful with TlbImp.exe. These are /out:, which controls the name and location of the resulting manage wrapper, and /keyfile:, which can provide a key to sign the output assembly.

The resulting .dll is a .NET assembly and can be used just like any .NET assembly, by referencing it via the fsc.exe command-line switch -r. A useful side effect of this is if the API is not well documented, you can use an assembly browser, such as Reflector discussed in Chapter 12, to find out more about the structure of the API.

After that, the worst thing I can say about using managed wrappers is you might find the structure of these assemblies a little unusual since the COM model dictates structure and therefore they do not share the same naming conversions as most .NET assemblies. You will notice that all classes in the assembly are postfixed with the word Class and each one is provided with a separate interface: this is just a requirement of COM objects. The following example shows the wrapper for the Microsoft Speech API that you created in the previous example being used:

```
open SpeechLib

let main() =
    // create an new instance of a com class
    // (these almost always end with "Class")
    let voice = new SpVoiceClass()
    // call a method Speak, ignoring the result
    voice.Speak("Hello world", SpeechVoiceSpeakFlags.SVSFDefault) |> ignore

do main()
```

Using COM Style APIs

Rather than using COM libraries directly, creating your own wrappers, it's more likely you'll have to use COM style API's. This is because many vendors now distribute their applications with *Primary Interop Assemblies*. These are pre-created COM wrappers, so generally you won't need to bother creating wrappers with TlbImp.exe yourself.

■**Note** More information about Primary Interop Assemblies can be found on MSDN: http://msdn.microsoft.com/ en-us/library/aax7sdch.aspx.

Although Primary Interop Assemblies are just ordinary .NET assemblies, there are typically a few quirks you have to watch out for, which the following outlines:

- Some arrays and collections often start at one rather than zero.

- There are often methods that are composed of large numbers of optional arguments. Fortunately, F# supports optional and named arguments to make interacting with these more natural and easier to understand.

- Many properties and methods have a return type of object. The resulting object needs to be cast to its true type.

- COM classes contain unmanaged resources that need to be disposed of. However, these classes do not implement the standard .NET IDisposable interface, meaning they cannot be used in an F# use binding. Fortunately, you can use F# object expressions to easily implement IDisposable.

A key difference from C# when interacting with COM in F# is you must always create instances of objects not interfaces. This may sound strange, but in COM libraries each object typically has an interface and a class that implements it. In C# if you try and create an instance of a COM interface using the new keyword in C#, the compiler will automatically redirect the call to appropriate class, but this is not the case in F#.

Interacting with Microsoft Office is probably the most common reason for interacting with COM style libraries. Here is a listing that reads information from an excel spreadsheet.

```
open System
open Microsoft.Office.Interop.Excel

let main() =
    // initalize an excel application
    let app = new ApplicationClass()

    // load a excel work book
    let workBook = app.Workbooks.Open(@"Book1.xls", ReadOnly = true)
```

```
    // ensure work book is closed corectly
    use bookCloser = { new IDisposable with
                           member x.Dispose() = workBook.Close() }

    // open the first worksheet
    let worksheet = workBook.Worksheets.[1] :?> _Worksheet

    // get the A1 ceel and all surround cells
    let a1Cell = worksheet.Range("A1")
    let allCells = a1Cell.CurrentRegion
    // load all cells into a list of lists
    let matrix =
        [ for row in allCells.Rows ->
             let row = row :?> Range
             [ for cell in row.Columns ->
                  let cell = cell :?> Range
                  cell.Value2 ] ]

    // close the workbook
    workBook.Close()

    // print the matrix
    printfn "%A" matrix

do main()
```

Notice how this sample deals with some of the quirks I mentioned earlier. You implement IDisposable and bind it to bookCloser to ensure the work book is closed, even in the case of an error. The Open method actually has 15 arguments, though you only use two: .Open(@"Book1.xls", ReadOnly = true). The first worksheet is an index one: workBook.Worksheets.[1]. Finally, each row must be upcast in order to use it: let row = row :?> Range.

Using P/Invoke

P/Invoke, or *platform invoke* to give its full name, is used to call unmanaged flat APIs implemented in DLLs and is called using the C or C++ calling conventions. The most famous example of this is the Win32 API, a vast library that exposes all the functionality built into Windows.

To call a flat unmanaged API, you must first define the function you want to call; you can do this in two parts. First, you use the DllImport attribute from the System.Runtime.InteropServices namespace, which allows you to define which .dll contains the function you want to import, along with some other optional attributes. Then, you use the keyword, extern, followed by the signature of the function to be called in the C style, meaning you give the return type, the F# type, the name of the function, and finally the types and names of the parameters surrounded by parentheses. The resulting function can then be called as if it were an external .NET method.

The following example shows how to import the Windows function MessageBeep and then call it:

```
open System.Runtime.InteropServices

// declare a function found in an external dll
[<DllImport("User32.dll")>]
extern bool MessageBeep(uint32 beepType)

// call this method ignoring the result
MessageBeep(0ul) |> ignore
```

■**Note** The trickiest part of using P/Invoke can often be working out what signature to use to call the function. The web site http://pinvoke.net contains a list of signatures for common APIs in C# and VB .NET, which are similar to the required signature in F#. The site is a wiki, so feel free to add the F# signatures as you find them.

The following code shows how to use P/Invoke when the target function expects a pointer. You need to note several points about setting up the pointer. When defining the function, you need to put an asterisk (*) after the type name to show that you are passing a pointer. You need to define a mutable identifier before the function call to represent the area of memory that is pointed to. This may not be global, in the top level, but it must be part of a function definition. This is why you define the function main, so the identifier status can be part of the definition of this. Finally, you must use the address of operator (&&) to ensure the pointer is passed to the function rather than the value itself.

■**Tip** This compiled code will always result in a warning because of the use of the address of operator (&&). This can be suppressed by using the compiler flag --nowarn 51 or the command #nowarn 51.

```
open System.Runtime.InteropServices

// declare a function found in an external dll
[<DllImport("Advapi32.dll")>]
extern bool FileEncryptionStatus(string filename, uint32* status)

let main() =
    // declare a mutable idenifier to be passed to the function
    let mutable status = 0ul
    // call the function, using the address of operator with the
    // second parameter
    FileEncryptionStatus(@"C:\test.txt", && status) |> ignore
```

```
    // print the status to check it has be altered
    printfn "%d" status

main()
```

The results of this example, when compiled and executed (assuming you have a file at the root of your C: drive called test.txt that is encrypted), are as follows:

```
1ul
```

■**Note** P/Invoke also works on Mono while in F# the syntax is exactly the same. The tricky bit is ensuring the library your invoking is available on all the platforms you're targeting and following the different naming conventions of libraries on all the different platforms. For a more detailed explanation see the article available at: http://www.mono-project.com/Interop_with_Native_Libraries.

The DllImport attribute has some useful functions that can be set to control how the unmanaged function is called. I summarize them in Table 14-1.

Table 14-1. *Useful Attributes on the* DllImport *Attribute*

Attribute Name	Description
CharSet	This defines the character set to be used when marshaling string data. It can be CharSet.Auto, CharSet.Ansi, or CharSet.Unicode.
EntryPoint	This allows you to set the name of the function to be called. If no name is given, then it defaults to the name of the function as defined after the extern keyword.
SetLastError	This is a Boolean value that allows you to specify whether any error that occurs should be marshaled and therefore available by calling the Marshell.GetLastWin32Error() method.

■**Note** As with COM components, the number of flat unmanaged APIs that have no .NET equivalent is decreasing all the time. Always check whether a managed equivalent of the function you are calling is available, which will generally save you lots of time.

Using Inline IL

Inline IL allows you to define your function's body directly in intermediate language (IL), the language into which F# is compiled. This was mainly added to the language to implement certain low operators and functions such as addition and box and not. It is rare that you will need to use this feature because the F# library FSharp.Core.dll already expose all of the functionality built into IL that you are likely to need. However, for those rare occasions where you need to do something that you can't do in F# but you can in IL, it's nice to know you have the option of inline IL.

Using inline IL is simple. You just place the IL instructions you would like between parentheses with pound signs, as in (# #). The IL instructions are placed inside a string and use the standard notation that can be compiled with ilasm.exe. This must be a correctly formed IL, or you will get a compiler error. You can then pass parameters to your IL instruction. They are pushed onto the IL evaluation stack. You must also use the standard colon notation to tell the compiler what the return type will be. This is placed inside the parentheses. You will also need to be explicit about the types of the parameters since the compiler has no way of inferring their types.

You'll now look at an example of using inline IL. Imagine for whatever reason that you do not want to use the add and subtract operators defined in the F# base library fslib.dll, because you may want to replace them with your own functions. You define two functions, add and sub, whose bodies are defined using IL:

```
// declare add function using the IL add instruction
let add (x:int) (y:int) = (# "add" x y : int #)
// declare sub function using the IL sub instruction
let sub (x:int) (y:int) = (# "sub" x y : int #)

// test these functions
let x = add 1 1
let y = sub 4 2

// print the results
printfn "x: %i y: %i" x y
```

The results of this example, when compiled and executed, are as follows:

```
x: 2 y: 2
```

The programmer should be careful when using this technique because it is trivial to write a program that does not make any sense, and the compiler is unable to warn you about this. Consider the following program where you revise your previous example to replace the "add" instruction with a "ret" instruction, which means "return a value" and makes no sense in this context. This example will compile without error or warning; on execution, you will get an error.

```
// create a faulty add function
let add (x:int) (y:int) = (# "ret" x y : int #)

// attempt to use fault function
let x = add 1 1
```

The results of this example, when compiled and executed, are as follows:

```
Unhandled Exception: System.InvalidProgramException: Common Language Runtime
detected an invalid program.
   at Error.add(Int32 x, Int32 y)
```

■**Note** There is a tool distributed with .NET SDK that can help you detect these kinds of errors. The tool is called peverify.exe, and you can find more information about peverfiy.exe at http://msdn2.microsoft.com/en-us/library/62bwd2yd(vs.80).aspx.

Using F# from Native Code via COM

Although it is more likely that you will want to call native code from F# code, there may be some circumstances that you would want to call F# library functions from native code. For example, suppose you have a large application written in C++, and perhaps you are happy for the user interface to remain in C++ but want to migrate some logic that performs complicated mathematical calculations to F# for easier maintenance. In this case, you would want to call F# from native code. The easiest way to do this is to use the tools provided with .NET to create a COM wrapper for your F# assembly. You can then use the COM runtime to call the F# functions from C++.

To expose functions though COM, you need to develop them in a certain way. First, you must define an interface that will specify the contract for your functions, the members of the interface must be written using named arguments (see the section on "Calling F# Libraries from C#" earlier in the chapter), and the interface itself must be marked with the System.Runtime.InteropServices.Guid attribute. Then you must provide a class that implements the interface. This too must be marked the System.Runtime.InteropServices.Guid attribute and also the System.Runtime.InteropServices.ClassInterface, and you should always pass the ClassInterfaceType.None enumeration member to the ClassInterface attribute constructor to say that no interface should be automatically generated.

Let's look at an example of doing this. Suppose you want to expose two functions to your unmanaged client called Add and Sub. Create an interface IMath in the namespace Strangelights, and then create a class Math to implement this interface. You then need to ensure that both the class and the interface are marked with the appropriate attributes. The resulting code is as follows:

```
namespace Strangelights
open System
open System.Runtime.InteropServices
```

```
// define an interface (since all COM classes must
// have a seperate interface)
// mark it with a freshly generated Guid
[<Guid("6180B9DF-2BA7-4a9f-8B67-AD43D4EE0563")>]
type IMath =
    abstract Add : x: int * y: int -> int
    abstract Sub : x: int * y: int -> int


// implement the interface, the class must:
// - have an empty constuctor
// - be marked with its own guid
// - be marked with the ClassInterface attribute
[<Guid("B040B134-734B-4a57-8B46-9090B41F0D62");
ClassInterface(ClassInterfaceType.None)>]
type Math() =
    interface IMath with
        member this.Add(x, y) = x + y
        member this.Sub(x, y) = x - y
```

The functions Add and Sub are of course simple, so there is no problem implementing them directly in the body of the Math class. If you need to break them down into other helper functions outside of the class, then this would not have been a problem. It is fine to implement your class members any way you see fit. You simply need to provide the interface and the class so the COM runtime has an entry point into your code.

Now comes arguably the most complicated part of the process, registering the assembly so the COM runtime can find it. To do this, you need to use a tool called RegAsm.exe. Suppose you compiled the previous sample code into a .NET .dll called ComLibrary.dll, then you would need to call RegAsm.exe twice using the following command lines:

```
regasm comlibrary.dll /tlb:comlibrary.tlb
regasm comlibrary.dll
```

The first time is to create a type library file, a .tlb file, which you can use in your C++ project to develop against. The second registers the assembly itself so the COM runtime can find it. You will also need to perform these two steps on any machine to which you deploy your assembly.

The C++ to call the Add function is as follows. The development environment and how you set up C++ compiler will also play a large part in getting this code to compile. In this case, I created a Visual Studio project, choosing a console application template and activated ATL. Notice the following about this source code:

- The #import command tells the compiler to import your type library. You may need to use the full path to its location. The compiler will also automatically generate a header file, in this case comlibrary.tlh, located in the debug or release directory. This is useful because it lets you know the functions and identifiers that are available as a result of your type library.

- You then need to initialize the COM runtime. You do this by calling the CoInitialize function.

- You then need to declare a pointer to the IMath interface you created. You do this via the code comlibrary::IMathPtr pDotNetCOMPtr;. Note how the namespace comes from the library name rather than the .NET namespace.

- Next, you need to create an instance of your Math class. You achieve this by calling the CreateInstance, method passing it the GUID of the Math class. Fortunately, there is a constant defined for this purpose.

- If this was successful, you can call the Add function. Note how the result of the function is actually an HRESULT, a value that will tell you whether the call was successful. The actual result of the function is passed out via an out parameter.

```cpp
// !!! C++ Source !!!
#include "stdafx.h"
// import the meta data about out .NET/COM library
#import "..\ComLibrary\ComLibrary.tlb" named_guids raw_interfaces_only


// the applications main entry point
int _tmain(int argc, _TCHAR* argv[])
{
        // initialize the COM runtime
        CoInitialize(NULL);
        // a pointer to our COM class
    comlibrary::IMathPtr pDotNetCOMPtr;

        // create a new instance of the Math class
        HRESULT hRes = pDotNetCOMPtr.CreateInstance(comlibrary::CLSID_Math);
        // check it was created okay
        if (hRes == S_OK)
        {
                // define a local to hold the result
        long res = 0L;
                // call the Add function
                hRes = pDotNetCOMPtr->Add(1, 2, &res);
                // check Add was called okay
            if (hRes == S_OK)
            {
                    // print the result
            printf("The result was: %ld", res);
        }

                // release the pointer to the math COM class
        pDotNetCOMPtr.Release();
        }

        // uninitialise the COM runtime
        CoUninitialize ();
}
```

The results of this example, when compiled and executed, are as follows:

```
The result was: 3
```

When you execute the resulting executable, you must ensure that ComLibrary.dll is in the same directory as the executable, or the COM runtime will not be able to find it. If you intend that the library be used by several clients, then I strongly recommend that you sign the assembly and place it in the GAC. This will allow all clients to be able to find it without having to keep a copy in the directory with them.

Hosting the CLR

An alternative option to using COM to integrate for integrating F# code into existing C/C++ applications is to custom host the CLR. The CLR is just a C++ application and there are some .lib files available that allow you to link to it in a standard C++ application. The code required to host the CLR is slightly more complex than the code required to load a COM library, but the complexity of registering COM libraries is removed. You can also get very fine grain control over the behavior of the CLR using these techniques, although you'll probably find the default behavior is fine for most situations. This technique is not suitable for high performance fine grain calls between C++ and F# since you have less control over the signatures used and the CLR method invocation is done using the reflection, meaning the module and method are found using string comparison which can be quite slow. However, if you are calling quite significant portions of F# code will probably find the cost of invocation is amortized quickly.

Let's have a look at the code required to invoke an F# method using custom hosting of the CLR. The code is based on a Visual Studio C++ console project. You need to notice the following about this source code:

- The #include <mscoree.h> tells the C++ compiler to import the header files that contains the functions and interfaces for loading the CLR.

- You then need to load and initialize the CLR. You do this by calling CorBindToRuntimeEx followed by the Start method on the resulting object.

- You can call the method ExecuteInDefaultAppDomain to invoke a method in a CLR assembly.

The full C++ listing is as follows:

```cpp
// !!! C++ Source !!!
#include "stdafx.h"
// the head file that exposes the C++ methods and interfaces
#include <mscoree.h>

// the applications main entry point
int _tmain(int argc, _TCHAR* argv[])
{
    // pointer to the CLR host object
    ICLRRuntimeHost *pClrHost = NULL;
```

```
    // invoke the method that loads the CLR
    HRESULT hrCorBind = CorBindToRuntimeEx(
        NULL,   // CLR version - NULL load the latest available
        L"wks", // GC Type ("wks" = workstation or "svr" = Server)
        0,
        CLSID_CLRRuntimeHost,
        IID_ICLRRuntimeHost,
        (PVOID*)&pClrHost);

    // Start the CLR.
    HRESULT hrStart = pClrHost->Start();

        // Define the assembly, type, function to load,
        // as well as the parameter and variable for the return value
    LPCWSTR pwzAssemblyPath = L"fslib.dll";
    LPCWSTR pwzTypeName = L"Strangelights.TestModule";
    LPCWSTR pwzMethodName = L"print";
    LPCWSTR pwzMethodArgs = L"Hello world!";
    DWORD retVal;

    // Load an assembly and execute a method in it.
    HRESULT hrExecute = pClrHost->ExecuteInDefaultAppDomain(
        pwzAssemblyPath, pwzTypeName,
        pwzMethodName, pwzMethodArgs,
        &retVal);

        // print the result
    printf("retVal: %i", retVal);
}
```

In addition to this code, you need to link to mscoree.lib, which is available in Windows Platform SDK. The only "special" thing you need to know on the F# side of things is that the function invoked must have the signature string -> int. Here is very simple example of an F# function that will work with the C++ listing:

```
module Strangelights.TestModule

// function will be invoked
let print s =
    printfn "%s" s
    0
```

The results of this example, when compiled and executed, are as follows:

```
Hello world!
retVal: 0
```

■Note For more information on custom CLR hosting see Alessandro Catorcini and Piotr Puszkiewicz's excellent MSDN article: `http://msdn.microsoft.com/en-us/magazine/cc163567.aspx`.

Summary

In this chapter, you saw some advanced techniques in F# for compatibility and interoperation. Although these techniques are definitely some of the most difficult to master, they also add a huge degree of flexibility to your F# programming.

Index

X

Y, Z

You Need the Companion eBook

Your purchase of this book entitles you to buy the companion PDF-version eBook for only $10. Take the weightless companion with you anywhere.

We believe this Apress title will prove so indispensable that you'll want to carry it with you everywhere, which is why we are offering the companion eBook (in PDF format) for $10 to customers who purchase this book now. Convenient and fully searchable, the PDF version of any content-rich, page-heavy Apress book makes a valuable addition to your programming library. You can easily find and copy code—or perform examples by quickly toggling between instructions and the application. Even simultaneously tackling a donut, diet soda, and complex code becomes simplified with hands-free eBooks!

Once you purchase your book, getting the $10 companion eBook is simple:

❶ Visit **www.apress.com/promo/tendollars/**.

❷ Complete a basic registration form to receive a randomly generated question about this title.

❸ Answer the question correctly in 60 seconds, and you will receive a promotional code to redeem for the $10.00 eBook.

THE EXPERT'S VOICE™